COLLECTED WORKS OF ERASMUS

VOLUME 17

THE CORRESPONDENCE OF
ERASMUS

LETTERS 2357 TO 2471

August 1530–March 1531

translated by Charles Fantazzi

annotated by James M. Estes

University of Toronto Press

Toronto / Buffalo / London

The research and publication costs of the
Collected Works of Erasmus are supported by
University of Toronto Press.

© University of Toronto Press 2016
Toronto / Buffalo / London
www.utppublishing.com
Printed in the U.S.A.

ISBN 978-1-4426-4878-4

Printed on acid-free, 100% post-consumer recycled paper
with vegetable-based inks.

Library and Archives Canada Cataloguing in Publication

Erasmus, Desiderius, –1536
[Works. English]
Collected works of Erasmus.

Includes bibliographical references and indexes.
Contents: v. 17. The correspondence of Erasmus,
letters 2357 to 2471, August 1530–March 1531.
ISBN 978-1-4426-4878-4 (v. 17)

I. Title.

PA8500 1974   199'.492   C74006326x

University of Toronto Press acknowledges the financial assistance
to its publishing program of the Canada Council for the Arts
and the Ontario Arts Council, an agency of the Government of Ontario.

 Canada Council   Conseil des Arts
for the Arts   du Canada

Collected Works of Erasmus

The aim of the Collected Works of Erasmus
is to make available an accurate, readable English text
of Erasmus' correspondence and his
other principal writings. The edition is planned
and directed by an Editorial Board, an Executive Committee,
and an Advisory Committee.

Contents

Illustrations

Preface

This volume comprises the correspondence of Erasmus for the period 1 August 1530–31 March 1531. Much of the content of the volume falls into the category of 'old business,' which is to say that the letters continue or revive discussions or controversies that had begun months or years earlier.

The first letter in the volume, from Philippus Melanchthon, continues the series (begun in CWE 16) of those to or from persons attending the imperial diet at Augsburg. Emperor Charles v, absent from the Empire since the spring of 1521, had summoned the imperial estates to Augsburg so that he, assuming the role of benevolent judge, could preside over a negotiated settlement of the religious division in the Empire and secure financial support for the struggle against the Turks, who were expected to return to the attack following their withdrawal from the siege of Vienna in October 1529. The emperor himself arrived in Augsburg on 15 June 1530, and the formal sessions of the diet commenced on the twentieth. On 25 June the Augsburg Confession (*Confessio Augustana*), a surprisingly unpolemical summary of the Lutheran faith, was read in the presence of the emperor at a special session of the diet.[1] On 3 August, the Catholic rebuttal of the Augsburg Confession (*Confutatio pontificia*), the first draft of which had been toned down at the insistence of the emperor, was in its turn read to him, and he announced that it was to be the basis for confessional reunion. The refusal of the Lutherans to accept the *Confutatio* should, in theory, have been the end of the attempt at a settlement, but since no one, least of all the emperor himself, was at this stage prepared – politically or militarily – to settle the dispute by force, the emperor stood aside while a group of princes and their theologians spent several weeks in search of a negotiated settlement that would preserve peace in the Empire and assure unity against the Turks. The collapse of these talks

* * * * *

1 See CWE 16 xiii–xiv.

on 16 September led on the twenty-second to the issuance by the emperor of a draft of the recess of the diet. It harshly condemned the Protestants, declaring their confession refuted and giving them until 15 April 1531 to return to the Catholic fold. There followed several weeks of vain attempts to get the Protestants to accept the draft recess and vote aid against the Turks. The final version of the recess, proclaimed on 19 November 1530, was even harsher in tone, reiterating the deadline of 15 April 1531 and clearly implying that force would be used against the Protestants if they persisted in their defiance of imperial authority. Not surprisingly, the Protestant estates left the diet without voting aid against the Turks and took immediate steps towards the formation of a defensive military alliance.[2]

Erasmus followed these events as best he could from Freiburg. Among those attending the diet were many friends, admirers, and patrons who had hoped that he would attend in person and do his bit for religious peace. There were even rumours that the emperor had summoned him to appear. But no such summons had been issued, and Erasmus had good reasons for staying away. Apart from not wanting to get directly involved in a situation in which any suggestion of compromise would get him denounced as a 'Lutheran,' he was, for most of the duration of the diet, convalescing from what had clearly been the most serious illness he had ever suffered.[3] Nor were the rumours correct which said that Erasmus had written to the emperor, urging him to refrain from violent measures against the religious dissidents. Erasmus did, however, write to Cardinal Campeggi, the papal legate, as well as to the bishop of Augsburg and other friends, urging that differences over articles of faith not be settled by war.[4] But he worried that the pope and his legate were on the side of repression and feared that the emperor would do as they advised.[5] The outcome of the diet left him almost bereft of hope that religious war could be avoided in Germany. That war would in due course come, but not as quickly as Erasmus feared. The emperor would first have to spend another sixteen years dealing with more pressing challenges, namely his wars with the king of France and the Turks, before he was prepared to settle scores with the German Protestants. In the interim, in the 1530s and '40s,

* * * * *

2 Cf Epp 2384 n4, 2403 nn10–11.
3 For the beginning of the diet and Erasmus' illness, see CWE 16 xiv–xv.
4 See Epp 2357:7–9, 2358:5–9. The letter to Campeggi is Ep 2366. At the instigation of persons unknown, the letter to Campeggi soon appeared in print, both in Latin and in a German epitome; see Ep 2366 introduction.
5 See Ep 2366 n7.

German Protestantism would expand too widely and take root too deeply to be eradicated by the political and military means at the emperor's disposal.

Reports of confessional conflict and of the drift towards war were not the only unsettling news from the diet. Erasmus also learned that old antagonists were agitating against him there. The first disturbing report was that Johann Eck, the most vociferous and uncompromising heresy hunter among the Catholic theologians of Germany, had brought with him to Augsburg a list of 404 heretical propositions that he was prepared to refute. Most of the propositions were attributed by name to Luther and other reformers, but four of them were attributed only to 'someone,' in whom Erasmus instantly recognized himself.[6] Although Erasmus had always disliked and distrusted Eck, he had nevertheless ignored him and avoided direct controversy with him since 1523. But Eck's inclusion of him among the heretics, as well as reports of hostile comments by him heard in Augsburg, elicited Erasmus' indignant protest. In reply, Eck further angered Erasmus by charging that he had been far too slow in launching an attack on 'the enemies of the faith' (the attack presumably being *De libero arbitrio* of 1524). At the same time, however, he expressed his satisfaction with Erasmus' newly published apology against the Strasbourg reformers, the *Epistola ad fratres Inferioris Germaniae* (see below). Keenly aware, moreover, of the high favour that Erasmus enjoyed with Emperor Charles, King Ferdinand, Duke George of Saxony, a long list of German bishops, and conservative Catholic theologians like Johannes Fabri and Johannes Cochlaeus, Eck prudently avoided pushing this renewed antagonism with Erasmus into the realm of open controversy.[7]

Erasmus suspected that Eck's expression of hostility had been encouraged by the despised troublemaker Heinrich Eppendorf,[8] with whom he had been engaged in a rancorous feud since 1523. Erasmus had mercilessly lampooned Eppendorf in his *Colloquies* and harshly criticized him in letters to his prince, Duke George of Saxony. Deeming himself to have been defamed, Eppendorf now appeared in Augsburg, attempted to plead his case before Duke George, and renewed old threats to take legal action against Erasmus.[9] In so doing, he made an overwhelmingly negative impression on Erasmus' friends.[10] Thus provoked, Erasmus published the *Admonitio adversus*

* * * * *

6 See Ep 2365 n5.
7 See Epp 2387, 2406.
8 See Ep 2406:25–6.
9 See Ep 2384 n15.
10 See Epp 2384:76–84, 2392:1–11, 2437:25–8, 2438:8–24.

mendacium (October 1530), an expanded version of Ep 1992, in which he recounted the entire history of the feud as he saw it. Eppendorf responded with his *Iusta querela* (February 1531). The good news in this was that Duke George entrusted to his counsellor Julius Pflug, a recent and welcome addition to Erasmus' list of friends and correspondents,[11] the task of dealing with Eppendorf's complaints. Thanks to Pflug's skilful diplomacy, the exchange of pamphlets already noted would constitute the final episode in the long and essentially pointless quarrel.[12]

Eck's charge that Erasmus had been too slow in attacking Luther and his followers was a small matter compared to the long-standing accusation of Erasmus' French and Italian critics that he actually was a Lutheran, or at least that he was the source and inspiration of the Lutheran heresy.[13] The most formidable and persistent advocate of that view, Noël Béda, syndic of the Paris faculty of theology, had since February 1529 been maintaining a deceptive silence, which lulled Erasmus into believing that trouble from that quarter was behind him.[14] In the meantime, however, Alberto Pio, prince of Carpi, an Italian critic who had settled in Paris in 1528, had stepped into the breach. His first attack on Erasmus, in January 1529, was followed by Erasmus' rejoinder in March.[15] By January 1530 Erasmus knew that Pio was preparing a new work cataloguing all the passages in which he allegedly agreed with Luther. Erasmus believed, moreover, that Pio was doing so at the instigation of his old ally in anti-Erasmian agitation Girolamo Aleandro.[16] The work, *Tres et viginti libri in locos lucubrationum Erasmi*, was finally published in March 1531, three weeks after Pio's death. Unable to restrain himself just because his adversary was dead, Erasmus heaped ridicule on Pio in letters to friends and enemies alike[17] and dashed off a vituperative reply to the *Tres et viginti libri*, the *Apologia adversus rhapsodias Alberti Pii* (Basel: Froben, June 1531). Meanwhile, Erasmus had not forgotten his detractors among the

* * * * *

11 Ep 2395
12 See Epp 2450–1.
13 See Ep 2414 n1.
14 See Epp 2371:5–6, 2375:84–5. The controversy would resume one last time in 1531 with the long-delayed publication of the faculty of theology's formal condemnation of Erasmus' *Colloquies, Paraphrases,* and other works, to which Erasmus would respond in 1532 with *Declarationes ad censuras Lutetiae.*
15 See Epp 2080, 2118:19–33.
16 See Epp 2371 n22, 2414 n3.
17 See Epp 2441:61–79, 2443:324–49, 2466:93–115.

Franciscans, particularly Luis de Carvajal and Frans Titelmans,[18] but he was done with writing against them.

He was not, however, done with his one-time friends and admirers among the 'false Evangelicals' of Southwest Germany, particularly Martin Bucer and his colleagues in Strasbourg. The members of this group had long annoyed and embarrassed Erasmus by claiming that they were merely carrying to their logical conclusion the things that they had learned from him. Tension turned into open conflict when, in 1529, Gerard Geldenhouwer, a former friend who had joined the reformers at Strasbourg, cited Erasmus approvingly in a series of pamphlets arguing that princes had no right to put heretics to death. Enraged at what seemed to him a dishonest attempt to associate him with a movement of which he thoroughly disapproved, Erasmus' published his *Epistola contra pseudevangelicos* (December 1529). In it he took aim not only at Geldenhouwer but also at the entire body of pastors in Strasbourg and their allies elsewhere in South Germany and Switzerland, accusing them of departing from the path of the apostles, harming the church, and promoting discord and disorder. Martin Bucer responded to this attack with an *Epistola apologetica* that was published in the name of all the Strasbourg reformers in May 1530.[19] Erasmus' response, *Epistola ad fratres Inferioris Germaniae*, had apparently been completed in draft by the end of May, and by 1 August 1530 it had gone to the printers for publication in September.[20]

The publication of the *Epistola ad fratres* has significance apart from its role in an important controversy. The illness that befell Erasmus in March and from which he did not begin to recover until late June had made the summer of that year an 'almost sterile' period in which he completed and published nothing. The first fruits of the literary effort that recommenced in July and August were the *Epistola* against Bucer and the Froben edition of Chrysostom in Latin, both of them in print by September.[21] Under the circumstances it is not surprising that, by Erasmus' standards, his output for the remainder of the period covered by this volume was not particularly abundant. The *Apophthegmata* appeared in March 1531.[22] The authorized version of the *Paraphrasis in Elegantias Laurentii Vallae*, provoked by the appearance

* * * * *

18 See Epp 2371, 2417.
19 See CWE 16 xvii–xix.
20 See Ep 2377 n4.
21 See Ep 2377.
22 Ep 2431

of an unauthorized version in 1530,[23] appeared at about the same time,[24] as did the *Enarratio psalmi 33*.[25] Erasmus' contribution to two other publication projects, Simon Grynaeus' edition of Aristotle in Greek (May 1531) and his edition of the newly discovered books of Livy (spring 1531), was confined to the writing of dedicatory letters.[26]

In letters to Erasmus, two of his most distinguished admirers, Andrea Alciati and Jacopo Sadoleto, joined the ranks of those who had taken him gently to task for wasting so much time and energy writing apologies against opponents unworthy of his attention.[27] To both Erasmus responded with his standard defence, namely, that while he might overlook insults to his learning, he could not and would not ignore charges of heresy, impiety, or wilful harm to the church. 'To remain silent before these is not leniency, but impiety.'[28] It was in this spirit that, at about the same time that he wrote to Alciati, Erasmus addressed to Agostino Steuco, the future Vatican librarian, the longest letter in this volume, a long-winded, condescending, hectoring denunciation of the *Recognitio Veteris Testamenti ad Hebraicam veritatem* (1529), in which Steuco had covertly attacked Erasmus as the source of the Lutheran heresy.[29]

Erasmus had moved from Basel to Freiburg in April 1529.[30] He did not much like the place. Prices were high,[31] the plague had broken out,[32] and there was confusion about the terms under which Erasmus occupied the house that had been placed at his disposal.[33] As if that were not enough, Erasmus feared that he would not be secure there in the event that religious war should break out.[34] He longed to be elsewhere but, typically, could not make up his mind when or where he should go. He gave serious thought to moving back to Brabant but, having accepted the advice of friends that he should stay where he was pending the outcome of the Diet of Augsburg, he waited until it was

* * * * *

23 Ep 2260
24 Ep 2416
25 Ep 2428
26 Epp 2432, 2435
27 See Epp 2385:31–54, 2394:10–113.
28 Ep 2468:1–153; cf Ep 2443:42–185.
29 Ep 2465. In his reply (Ep 2513), Steuco would be equally long-winded and state his charges against Erasmus more openly.
30 See CWE 15 xi–xiii.
31 Ep 2403 n13
32 Ep 2426 n3
33 See Ep 2462 introduction.
34 See Epp 2365:23–4, 2371:26–8.

too late in the year to consider moving.[35] So he stayed put and went in search of the new house into which he would move in September 1531.

Of the 116 letters in this volume, 75 were written by Erasmus, and 41 were addressed to him. These surviving letters include more than 70 references to letters that are no longer extant. Since some of these references are to an unspecified number of letters, no exact total of letters known to have been written during the period covered by this volume can be determined, but 200 would be a cautious estimate. Of the surviving letters, 57 were published by Erasmus himself. Of these, 45 appeared in the *Epistolae floridae* of 1531. Another 5 were prefaces to works or editions by Erasmus, 3 were addenda to such publications, and 2 were prefaces to works by other scholars. The remaining letters were published by a variety of scholars in the period from 1530 to 1938. Eight of them were first published by Allen. To allow the reader to discover the sequence in which the letters became known, the introduction to each letter cites the place where it was first published and identifies the manuscript source if one exists. Allen's text and his numbering of the letters have been followed. One letter omitted by Allen, Ep 2359A, has been added.

All of Erasmus' correspondents and all of the contemporaries of Erasmus who are mentioned in the letters are referred to by the version of their name that is used in CEBR. Wherever biographical information is supplied in the notes without the citation of a source, the reader is tacitly referred to the appropriate article in CEBR and to the literature there cited. The index to this volume contains references to the persons, places, and works mentioned in the volume, following the plan for the Correspondence series in CWE. When that series of volumes is completed, the reader will also be supplied with an index of topics, as well as of classical, scriptural, and patristic references.

As with all the other volumes in this series, the basis for translation and annotation is the edition of the *Erasmi epistolae* that was founded by P.S. Allen. This is, however, the first of the volumes in the CWE Correspondence series to be based on volumes 9–11 of Allen's edition, which were completed after his death (1938) by his widow, Helen Mary Allen, and H.W. Garrod, who had been his collaborators on earlier volumes. At the time of his death Allen had, with few exceptions, collected and provisionally arranged all the letters for vols 9–11, but had written the notes for only twenty-seven of them. The remaining work of annotation had to be done by Mrs Allen and Garrod. In many cases, therefore, 'Allen' is used in the notes as shorthand for 'the

* * * * *

35 See Ep 2360 nn5–6.

Allen editors.' Where their work has needed to be corrected, updated, or expanded – more often in their case than in that of Allen himself – I was able to
rely on the advice and assistance of distinguished colleagues here in Toronto
and elsewhere. The great majority of the classical and patristic references
that were not identified by Allen were supplied by the translator, Charles
Fantazzi. Timothy J. Wengert and Mark Crane read the entire manuscript
and suggested many important corrections and other improvements to both
the translation and the notes. James K. Farge, Jonathan Reid, Erika Rummel,
James Tracy, Ulrich Kopp, Bruce Frier, and Alexander Dalzell all responded
generously to requests for help with difficult matters of history, bibliography,
or translation. The notes on coinage were contributed by Lawrin Armstrong.
Mary Baldwin once again earned her reputation as copyeditor without peer.

JME

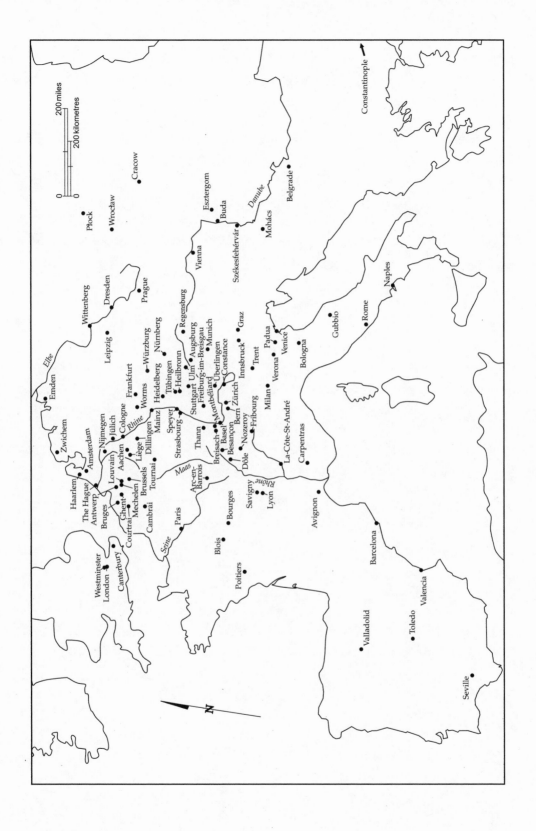

200 miles

200 kilometres

Constantinople

Cracow

Płock

Wrocław

Esztergom

Buda

Belgrade

Mohács

Danube

Vienna

Székesfehérvár

Wittenberg

Dresden

Prague

Naples

Rome

Gubbio

Leipzig

Regensburg

Würzburg

Nürnberg

Graz

Elbe

Emden

Frankfurt

Heidelberg

Tübingen

Heilbronn

Augsburg

Munich

Innsbruck

Trent

Padua

Venice

Bologna

Zwichem

Amsterdam

Nijmegen

Jülich

Cologne

Worms

Mainz

Speyer

Strasbourg

Stuttgart

Ulm

Freiburg-im-Breisgau

Überlingen

Constance

Zürich

Verona

Milan

Rhine

Aachen

Liège

Dillingen

Thann

Montbéliard

Breisach

Basel

Bern

Fribourg

La-Côte-St-André

Haarlem

Louvain

Nozeroy

Besançon

Dôle

Carpentras

The Hague

Antwerp

Ghent

Mechelen

Brussels

Tournai

Arc-en-Barrois

Maas

Rhône

Bruges

Courtrai

Cambrai

Paris

Bourges

Savigny

Lyon

Avignon

Westminster

London

Canterbury

Seine

Blois

Poitiers

Barcelona

Valencia

Valladolid

Toledo

Seville

N

THE CORRESPONDENCE OF ERASMUS

LETTERS 2357 TO 2471

2357 / From Philippus Melanchthon   Augsburg, 1 August 1530

Allen based his text of this letter (= MBW Ep 1004) on the two earliest printed sources: *Epistolae selectiores aliquot Philipp Melanthonis* ed Kaspar Peucer
(Wittenberg: Johannes Crato 1565) 36; Coelestin III 19 recto, 140 verso (corrigenda). Of the surviving sixteenth-century manuscript copies of the letter (see
MBW T 4/2 491), Allen saw only the one at Wrocław that is no longer extant; he
judged it to have been taken from the Peucer text. By the time Erasmus received
this letter, he had already written Ep 2358 to Melanchthon. Epp 2363, 2365 are
his responses to the present letter.

Melanchthon was attending the Diet of Augsburg as a member of the delegation from Electoral Saxony. Because Luther, as an imperial outlaw, could not
leave Saxon territory, Melanchthon was the principal Lutheran theologian at
the diet. Unlike Luther, Melanchthon always maintained civil relations with
Erasmus despite the deep gulf between their theological views.

PHILIPPUS MELANCHTHON TO ERASMUS OF ROTTERDAM,
GREETING

I would never have believed that such ferocity, such violence could possess
a man as I discern in Eck and some of his followers.[1] The rulers themselves
express fairly lenient and moderate opinions, but this band tries with incred-   5
ible wiles to deflect them from their views.

I hear that in a letter you are discouraging the emperor, who, as it appears to me, is inclined by an innate goodness to peace and moderation, from
taking violent measures.[2] I hope, therefore, that your letter will have great influence with him, and I beg you to persist in this service to the common good   10
as you have begun and continue to dissuade him from his purpose again
and again. You can do nothing more worthy of your wisdom and authority,

* * * * *

2357
1 Johann Eck (Ep 2387), the most vociferous German antagonist of Luther and his
   supporters, had arrived in Augsburg with a list of 404 articles denouncing the
   heresies of the reformers, any concessions to whom he vehemently opposed; cf
   Ep 2365 n5. Other Catholic hardliners present were Johannes Fabri, archbishop
   of Vienna (Ep 2374), Johannes Cochlaeus, chaplain to Duke George of Saxony
   (Ep 1928), and Conradus de Wimpina (Ep 2247 n2). Georgius Spalatinus (Ep
   501) reported that 'Dr Fabri and Eck deal with matters so shamelessly that the
   people on their own side openly denounce them as scoundrels.' See StL 21b
   3281 no 100.
2 This report was false; see Ep 2358 n3.

nothing more to ensure your glory for posterity, than calm these disturbances by your tireless efforts.

As for myself, I have presented my case simply and without great 15 clamour.[3] Although some will complain that it is too late for moderation, nevertheless I wish to show that I am not averse to a peaceful settlement if equitable terms are proposed. The present state of affairs portends an imminent alteration of our public order. Please God that those who are in power will so govern the commonwealth that the church is not laid low by a sudden 20 attack! I pray you, therefore, with all my strength, through Christ our Lord, that you do not cease to exhort the emperor not to make war on the citizens who do not refuse to accept equitable terms. Those on our side have no intention to break up the organization of the church.

I am very fond of Daniel Stiebar,[4] and although I know that you find 25 him very congenial, I nevertheless beg you for my sake to increase your feelings of good will towards him. Farewell.

At Augsburg, on the first of August in the year 1530

2358 / To Philippus Melanchthon   Freiburg, 2 August 1530

This letter (= MBW Ep 1007) was first printed in Coelestin III 19 recto–verso, 140 verso (corrigenda). Allen based his text on the manuscript in the University Library at Rostock (MS Theol 62² 2°, folio 163 recto–verso), which was made around 1550 by Johann Aurifaber, the first editor of Luther's letters. In so doing, Allen took account of collations that were supplied to him by Bruno Claussen on the basis of the text printed in Schirrmacher 187–8.

This is not an answer to Ep 2357, which had not yet reached Erasmus.

* * * * *

3 Melanchthon was the principal author of the Augsburg Confession, a notably moderate summary of Lutheran faith and practice that emphasized the things that Catholics and Lutherans have in common. The confession had been presented to the emperor and read aloud to him at a special session of the diet on 25 June; see Ep 2333 n8.
4 Stiebar (Ep 2069), who had stayed with Erasmus at Basel in 1528 and at Freiburg in 1529–30, was now back in his native Würzburg and had commenced his career in the administration of the imperial bishopric of Würzburg (Ep 2303 n3). At the moment he was a member of the Würzburg delegation at the diet in Augsburg and, it seems, carried this letter with him on a mission of unknown purpose to Freiburg. On 12 August he set out for Augsburg once again, carrying Ep 2363 with him.

A LETTER OF ERASMUS OF ROTTERDAM
TO PHILIPPUS MELANCHTHON

Greetings. I paid the Portuguese young man generously out of my own pocket.[1] There is no trace of your letter or of Stiebar.[2]

It was wrongly reported that I wrote to the emperor.[3] During the course   5
of this diet I have not written a word to him. I have written only to Cardinal Campeggi,[4] earnestly entreating that differences in articles of faith would not be settled by war. I wrote in a similar vein to the bishop of Augsburg[5] and some other friends, and you ask me not to cease doing this! Why don't you rather ask them to cease inciting the animosity of princes to war through   10
their obstinacy and their squabbles? As for myself, not only now but unceasingly I have repressed, as far as I could, the vehemence of theologians and have discouraged rulers from violence. You see what thanks they return me.

A certain drunkard named Gerard of Nijmegen, whom out of courtesy I call Vulturius Neocomus in my *Epistola*, has moved to Strasbourg.[6] He used   15
to be exaggeratedly devoted to me, but now he is a raging madman, as if I had run through with the sword his father, his mother, his grandfather, and both his grandmothers.[7] He has published four pamphlets in his own name;[8] the fifth, full of abuse and hypocrisy, appeared under the name of the Ministers of the Word of Strasbourg.[9] Nothing could be more seditious. That   20

* * * * *

2358
1 Not identified; cf Ep 2370:8.
2 The text reads 'of Stiebar's,' but it seems that it was Stiebar himself, the probable bearer of Ep 2357, not a letter from him, that had not yet arrived; see Allen's note and MBW Ep 1007 T 4/2 497 n1. Erasmus reports his arrival in Ep 2363.
3 Cf Ep 2339 n6. This false report was evidently widely circulated. On 27 July Melanchthon wrote to Luther that in a letter to the emperor Erasmus had approved the evangelical position on the marriage of priests, monastic vows, and communion in both kinds; MBW Ep 991:2. Justus Jonas and Georgius Spalatinus both reported Erasmus as having said that any reformation would have to start at the top, with the pope; WA-Br 5 512:2–4 and 7–8, StL 21b 3281 no 104.
4 Ep 2366
5 Ep 2332
6 Erasmus' *Epistola contra pseudevangelicos* (Ep 2219 n5) was addressed to Gerard Geldenhouwer of Nijmegen, whom he called Vulturius Neocomus, a parody of the Latin form of Geldenhouwer's name, Gerardus Noviomagus. 'Vulturius' was a pun on Geldenhouwer's first name, the first syllable of which sounds like the Dutch word *gier* 'vulture.' 'Neocomus' was an approximation in Latinized Greek of the Romano-Celtic 'Noviomagus' (new market).
7 Cf Ep 2353A:85–9.
8 Three of these are discussed in Ep 2219 n4. For the fourth, see Ep 2289 n2.
9 The *Epistola apologetica*, written by Martin Bucer but published in the name of all the reformers in Strasbourg; see Ep 2312 n2.

is why I have no desire from now on to try to resolve their troubles, since they themselves not only do not make any concessions but even seem to yearn for a bloody conflict. May the Lord provide a good outcome and may he preserve you safe and sound for our sake.

At Freiburg, 2 August 1530   25
Erasmus of Rotterdam

2359 / To Christoph von Stadion   Freiburg, 5 August 1530

On Christoph von Stadion, bishop of Augsburg, see Ep 2029.

This is the preface to the Froben five-volume edition of *Chrysostomi opera*, the works of the Greek Father St John Chrysostom in Latin translation. During the 1520s Erasmus had devoted much attention to Chrysostom, searching for manuscripts and publishing a variety of his works in the original Greek as well as in Latin translation (Ep 1661 n2). To his collaborator in these efforts, the French humanist Germain de Brie, he had held out the prospect of a 'splendid [Latin] edition' of Chrysostom to be published in due course by Froben (Ep 1736; cf Ep 1733 introduction). As it happened, the initiative for the publication of the edition was taken by Hieronymus Froben in the autumn of 1529 when, having completed the printing of the ten-volume edition of St Augustine (Ep 2157), he wanted a new major project to keep his presses busy. Work on the Latin Chrysostom appears to have begun immediately and continued into the late summer of 1530. Erasmus' contribution to the edition appears to have been confined largely to lending his name to it and to assisting in the search for needed translations. (In the catalogue of his works published in March 1530 he did not take credit for the edition itself but listed only the translations that he had contributed to it; Ep 2283:174–84, 231–42.) The supply of qualified translators was so meagre that reluctant use had to be made of a large number of translations by Johannes Oecolampadius (including virtually the entire content of the fifth volume – the *Psegmata* and the Homilies on Genesis), even though his efforts as a translator of Chrysostom had drawn harsh criticism from Brie and others (Epp 2016:95–102, 2052 n2, 2062:26–9, 2082:316–32 and 350–5, 2226:70–5) and there was fear that the presence of his translations would inhibit sales; see Staehelin 620–1.

In early January 1530 Erasmus reported that the new Chrysostom would be published in the autumn, in 'an equally splendid format' as the Augustine (Ep 2253:18–19), and later in the month he complained of the slowness of some of the contributing translators (Ep 2263:44–6). By the end of March the edition was so far advanced that Froben could not wait any longer for Brie's promised translation of the *Monachus* (Ep 2291) and had to fall back on an already published one by Oecolampadius. One major work, the Homilies on Romans, had to be omitted entirely because, thanks to an unfortunate breakdown of communication with prospective translators, no Latin version was available (Ep 2258 n6). Cf CWE 16 xxi.

Almost as soon as Froben's five volumes had been published, Erasmus wrote to Germain de Brie (Ep 2379) to secure his assistance with the preparation of a supplementary volume that was to include, among other things, the Homilies on Romans. Brie's translation of the first eight of the thirty-two homilies was published by Froben in March 1533, together with a separate volume of Erasmus' *Aliquot homiliae ad pietatem summopere conductibiles*. But almost immediately Erasmus and Brie lent their support and assistance to the preparation of the edition of Chrysostom in Latin (Paris: Claude Chevallon 1536) that would replace Froben's. For details on editions of Chrysostom before 1530 and on the preparation of the Chevallon edition, see Allen's introduction to this letter.

TO THE REVEREND FATHER AND MOST ILLUSTRIOUS LORD,
CHRISTOPH VON STADION, BISHOP OF AUGSBURG,
FROM DESIDERIUS ERASMUS OF ROTTERDAM, GREETING

Most illustrious prelate, we have previously published an edition of that most eloquent Doctor of the church Jerome,[1] cleansed of the corruptions   5
that had defiled the text, made whole after being scattered and dispersed, from its squalid condition now rendered elegant and splendid. With equal distinction we published that resounding trumpet of the Catholic church, Hilary.[2] We published the most impassioned defender of the Christian faith, Augustine.[3] We published Cyprian martyr,[4] who speaks with no less vigour   10
than eloquence. Now St John Chrysostom appears, that mellifluous preacher and indefatigable herald of Christ, to whom the name of the golden-mouthed was rightly given because of his most wise eloquence and most eloquent wisdom.[5] There are those who call him the greatest of all.

It is my hope that the legions of scholars will welcome him with all the   15
more enthusiasm since this incomparable bishop comes forth into the light of day under the auspices of the most esteemed of prelates. You resemble each other in many ways: in your integrity of life, love for divine writings, rectitude of judgment, unrepressed profession of truth, and uncommon zeal

* * * * *

2359
1 Ep 396
2 Ep 1334
3 Ep 2157
4 Ep 1000
5 As Chrysostom's admirers were fond of pointing out, his name means 'golden-voiced' or 'golden-mouthed.'

for the spouse of Christ. And furthermore you are so preeminent in so many 20
other virtues that among all your distinctions the renown of your family and
the splendour of the other blessings of fortune, which it is more noble to have
despised than to have possessed, are of least importance. Not even those
spiritual endowments diminish your extraordinary modesty, since you are
not unaware that they are the free gifts of God, entrusted to you so that they 25
may bear fruit.

Someone might say on occasion, 'Come, now! What's so important
about this publication if you are just giving us Chrysostom, who has been
edited so many times?' I will not defend myself with the excuse, which has
now become traditional, that everything that comes off the press with some 30
illustrious and influential name is to be commended. Nor will I mention how
much grandeur is imparted to the volumes by their large format and the
elegance and impressiveness of the type. Such things, while they represent
enormous expenditure for the printers, at the same time win no little favour
for such an outstanding Doctor of the church, and by a certain power of al- 35
lurement attract the otherwise supercilious reader. These are external matters, I admit, but I shall only concede that they are of no importance if shabby
attire, an unwashed face, and unkempt hair do not tarnish the attractions of
physical beauty and if good grooming and becoming elegance do nothing to
commend it. But, as I said, I shall not mention these matters for the moment 40
but rather speak of things that are more relevant to the subject.

In previous editions of the works of Chrysostom the translators who
have come down to us all edited the text with care, as did I, indefatigably.
Among early translators there are many who were not skilled in Greek and
Latin. Their translation has been corrected in many places by learned men 45
after a collation of the Greek manuscripts. An example of this is that passage
of Anianus,[6] who in translating commentaries on Matthew stumbled right
on the threshold,[7] translating δεύτερον πλοῦν as 'second riches,' whereas the
Greek means 'second journey' or 'sea-voyage.'[8] Likewise that passage in
Francesco Aretino right at the beginning of the commentaries on the First 50
Epistle to the Corinthians, where he had translated οἴησιν as 'opinion' instead
of 'arrogance.'[9] Let this suffice as an example, for it is not my intention to record here all the errors of the translators, which are infinite in number.

* * * * *

6 Ep 1558 n22
7 *Adagia* I v 77
8 Cf Epp 1558:234–42, 2263:66–70.
9 On Aretino, see Ep 2226 n19; on the mistake noted here, cf Ep 2263:53–8.

For the poorly translated six books *On the Dignity of the Priesthood* we have substituted the highly finished translation of Germain de Brie, whose 55 *Babylas* I have also added.[10] Finally, in addition to all the works that had been published hitherto we have added supplements of no little importance, like the commentaries on the First Epistle to the Corinthians, which Francesco Aretino had finished up to the twentieth homily. That part was sent to us by John Fisher, bishop of Rochester, incomparable glory of the church in these 60 times;[11] Simon Grynaeus, a man very well versed in the two languages, supplied what was missing.[12] Likewise the commentaries on the Second Epistle to the Corinthians, which I translated myself up to the eighth homily and would gladly have continued if the style did not lead me to suspect that this was not a genuine work of Chrysostom.[13] The remaining part was translated 65 by another person not lacking in learning.[14] We added two homilies to the commentaries on Acts besides those we had previously published,[15] but the very reason just mentioned persuaded me to abandon my intent.[16]

There are some friends in Italy who promise to send us other works of Chrysostom as well.[17] If it turns out that we obtain these – and we have 70 certain hope that this will be the case within a short time – we will not fail to share them with experts in Christian philosophy. I detect that the lukewarmness or rather the demise of Christian piety is caused by the failure to nourish the people regularly with the word of God and that those on whom this duty has devolved are either altogether silent or treat the Scriptures oth- 75 erwise than they should, either through ignorance or because they prefer to

* * * * *

10 See Epp 1733 (*De sacerdotio*), 2052 n2 (*De Babyla martyre*).
11 See Epp 2226 n19, 2263. Aretino had actually translated twenty-nine, not twenty, of the forty-four homilies on 1 Corinthians.
12 On Grynaeus see Ep 2433.
13 Cf Epp 2263 n12, 2379:43–5. The first seven of the thirty homilies were translated by Erasmus. Later scholars have not shared Erasmus' doubts about the authorship of the commentaries on 2 Corinthians or those on Acts (see n16 below).
14 Johannes Oecolampadius; see Staehelin 621.
15 Three were included in the *Chrysostomi lucubrationes* of 1527 (Epp 1801, 2263:36). In Epp 2291:9–10 Erasmus says that he has added a fourth, and the list of his works for Hector Boece gives the total as four (Ep 2283:181).
16 Ie his conviction that the work was spurious: see Epp 2263:36–40, 2291:10–11. In May 1531, Froben published, as a supplement to the five-volume edition of 1530, a sixth folio containing all fifty-five of Chrysostom's homilies on Acts, the first four in Erasmus' translation, the balance in that of Oecolampadius; see Staehelin 621.
17 Among these were Agostino Trivulzio; see Ep 2405 n1.

gain tithes rather than souls. Is there no one in our age who can imitate this man of the church, while Aquinas and Scotus have so many imitators? And yet this amiable Doctor was tossed about by so many tempests, tried by so many squalls, banished, recalled, and again confined to exile with greater 80
tumult. But from what I shall place before your eyes it will be possible for you to know more fully both the course of his life and the remarkable gifts of Chrysostom.

There you have a long and tedious hodgepodge of a preface, most distinguished prelate, but the charm of Chrysostom's words will easily dispel 85
this *longueur*, and I do not wish to detain you from it any longer. May the Lord guard and protect your reverend Eminence always.

Given at Freiburg im Breisgau, 5 August 1530

2359A / Erasmus of Rotterdam to the Reader   [Freiburg, c 5 August 1530]

> This letter to the reader was originally published on page 473 of volume 3 of
> the Froben Chrysostom of 1530 (see Ep 2359), where it serves as the preface to
> *Eruditii commentarii in evangelium Matthaei, incerto autore* (Learned Commentary
> on the Gospel of Matthew, of Uncertain Authorship). The letter was not includ-
> ed in Allen or any other edition of Erasmus' letters, but it is found in PG 56
> 601–601* as part of the introduction to the critical edition of the text. The com-
> mentary itself (PG 56 611–946) consists of a prologue and 54 homilies, which cov-
> er the text of Matthew (with major omissions) up to chapter 25 verse 31. During
> the medieval period, the work was known as *Opus imperfectum in Matthaeum*
> (Incomplete Commentary on Matthew) and, as Erasmus was the first to argue,
> it was wrongly attributed to John Chrysostom. The identity of the real author
> remains uncertain. What is known is that he wrote in Latin, though he knew
> Greek; that he was an Arian, or possibly even a Pelagian; that he stood in the
> exegetical tradition of Origen; and that the work cannot have been written much
> before the early fifth century. See Kellerman / Oden I xvii–xxiv. The day-date has
> been assigned arbitrarily so that the letter can be paired with Ep 2359.

First of all, there is no doubt that this is not a work of Chrysostom, but we have nevertheless not wished to pass over it, since up to now it has been printed under his name, and especially since it is the work of a learned and eloquent man, so proficient in divine letters that, in my opinion at least, he is not inferior to Chrysostom in this regard. I suspect that he wrote in Latin, al- 5
though he also knew Greek. His language, as far as vocabulary is concerned, is adulterated. That was the ecclesiastical style at the time, similar to that of the people and therefore popular. In other respects it is the work of an eloquent man. It would have been a crime if this work, which nevertheless

has been preserved up to now in old copies and in varied form, mutilated   10
in various ways, had perished. We have followed the latest edition, which
was the best, but collated it with older copies. It is useless to conjecture who
was the author or at what time he lived. He himself testifies that he wrote
after the church under the Christian emperors was shaken by innumerable
heresies, but, in addition to occasionally betraying a freedom in scriptural   15
commentary typical of Origen, he also included here and there opinions that
are not far removed from unapproved beliefs. I will indicate some of these to
the reader, so that he will be more cautious in reading this work.

These are not homilies, but someone or other divided up the work in
that way.[1] Homily 1: He wishes the passage 'The Holy Spirit will come upon   20
you' to be interpreted as referring to Christ, not the Paraclete, although the
passage seems corrupt to me.[2] In the same homily he unnaturally interprets
'He had marital relations with her' to mean that he did not know of her high
dignity before she gave birth but only knew of her eminence after she gave
birth.[3] In Homily 3, towards the end, he says that unbelievers are not chaff   25
by nature but by their own will,[4] as if faith existed in our will and was not
rather a gift of God, or as if we are not all born as children of wrath, without
grace.[5] But this may be excused. In Homily 4, towards the end, he openly
denies the equality of the Son and the Holy Spirit, whom he calls the servant
of the Son.[6] I think this comes from Origen. In some manuscripts someone   30
tried to emend this passage, but in vain, since the author makes the same
assertion elsewhere, as in Homily 20, where, though he acknowledges the
distinction of Persons, he openly denies their equality. A little further on he
repeats this.[7] Likewise, in Homily 48 he counts the Homoousians among the
heretics.[8] And in Homily 45 he speaks of heretics in this way: 'When you   35
hear heretics saying that the three Persons, equal in every respect, are of the
same substance and the same authority, and that all are without beginning

* * * * *

2359A
1 The division into homilies was a later addition, done for the sake of convenience.
2 PG 56 634 @ Matt 1:20 (Kellerman / Oden I 28)
3 PG 56 635 @ Matt 1:25 (Kellerman / Oden I 29)
4 PG 56 636 @ Matt 3:12 (Kellerman / Oden I 55)
5 Eph 2:3
6 PG 56 660 @ Matt 3:16 (Kellerman / Oden I 60)
7 This is in Homily 28, not 20; PG 56 777 @ Matt 11:27 (Kellerman / Oden I 205–6).
8 PG 56 903 @ Matt 24:7 (Kellerman / Oden II 376). The 'homoousians' were the
   orthodox believers in the Trinity, who accepted the Nicene Creed's definition
   of the Son as being 'of the same substance' (homoousios) with the Father, as opposed to the Arians, who said that he was 'of similar substance' (homoiousios).

and in some aspects differ from one another, do not be surprised, for they
live up to the standards of their forebears, etc.'[9] There was an attempt to
emend this passage by adding *non* twice: 'not of the same substance, not of   40
the same authority.' But this reading is self-contradictory, for how can they
be equal in all respects if they are not of the same authority? The manuscripts to which I compared it did not have the negation. Homily 22: He
seems to make the Son inferior to the Father, when the centurion says to
Christ: 'And you, although you are under the power of the Father, never-   45
theless have the power of giving orders to your angels.'[10] Someone tried to
emend this passage also in this way: 'Although you are under the power of
the Father inasmuch as you are a man.' But this addition was not present in
the oldest edition. Homily 11: He seems to deny that the real body of Christ
is in the Eucharist, but only the mystery of the body is present.[11] He speaks   50
about that same subject in Homily 19, calling the Eucharist the sacrifice of
bread and wine.[12] Homily 12: He seems to condemn every oath, threatening
even the deacon who offers the book of the Gospels to someone making an
oath.[13] Homily 18: He seems to censure marriage, speaking of the wide path
that leads to death on which men walk with their wives, and even adulter-   55
ers.[14] And yet in Homily 19 he calls marriage the second degree of chastity,[15]
whereby he seems to have understood the wide path as the wide path of
indulgence. Likewise in Homily 42 he speaks ambiguously about marital in-
tercourse.[16] Homily 19: He speaks ambiguously about baptism administered
by heretics, as if those who were wrongly taught by them receive nothing   60
more from it than they did from their teaching,[17] but this is excusable. In

* * * * *

9 PG 56 889 @ Matt 23:32 (Kellerman / Oden II 358)
10 PG 56 753 @ Matt 8:9 (Kellerman / Oden I 172). These are not the words of Christ
    in the Gospel text but rather the author's interpretive paraphrase of them.
11 PG 56 691 @ Matt 5:22 (Kellerman / Oden I 97)
12 PG 56 737 @ Matt 7:15 (Kellerman / Oden I 153)
13 PG 56 698 @ Matt 5:34–5 (Kellerman / Oden I 106)
14 PG 56 735–6 @ Matt 7:13 (Kellerman / Oden I 151–2)
15 This is not in Homily 19 but in Homily 32; PG 56 799 @ Matt 19:3 (Kellerman /
    Oden II 251).
16 PG 56 869–70 @ Matt 22:29 (Kellerman / Oden II 335–6)
17 PG 56 736 @ Matt 7:15 (Kellerman / Oden I 155). In the ancient church there was
    much controversy over the validity of sacraments administered by heretical
    or otherwise unworthy priests. Largely through the influence of St Augustine,
    it came to be accepted that the validity of the sacraments depended on the use
    of the correct form, regardless of the worthiness of the priest.

the same homily he clearly condemns digamy, agreeing with Tertullian.[18]
Homily 21: He condemns business and thinks that merchants should be expelled from the church.[19] But now the merchants expel clerics. Homily 19
has a passage that was thought to have been corrupted by the Lutherans.[20]   65
In an old manuscript that I used for collation these words were missing:
'Although it is impossible that the one thing can be found without the other.
For just as it is unheard of that fire can burn without heat, so faith cannot
exist without good works.'[21] I don't know whether it is found in any other
edition. It is possible that there are also some other passages; we have indi-   70
cated those that come to mind. Someone will say: 'Why did you mix things
into Chrysostom's works that you knew were not his?' Would that this were
the only illegitimate specimen. But just as we did not pass over anything in
Jerome and Augustine, though we were not unaware of the many divergent
opinions, so I determined to do the same thing here. We have taken note of   75
unapproved or suspect opinions, not that the book be rejected, but that it
be read with discretion, as we read Tertullian and Origen. But if we reject
all books in which there is something that is at variance with the beliefs of
our times, neither Cyprian nor Ambrose nor Chrysostom nor Augustine nor
Jerome will be read. Farewell.   80

2360 / From Johann von Vlatten   Augsburg, 9 August 1530

> This letter, which is Vlatten's answer to Ep 2346, was first published as Ep 133
> in Förstemann / Günther. The autograph was in the Burscher Collection of the
> University Library at Leipzig (Ep 1254 introduction). Vlatten (Ep 1390) was
> currently attending the diet in Augsburg as a member of the delegation from
> Jülich-Cleves.

* * * * *

---

18 This is not in Homily 19 but in Homily 32; PG 56 801 @ Matt 19:8 (Kellerman /
   Oden II 254). In contrast to bigamy, which consists of having two wives at
   once, digamy consists of having two or more wives in succession.
19 This is in Homily 38; PG 56 841 @ Matt 21:12 (Kellerman / Oden II 300).
20 An apparent reference to the following passage in Homily 19 (PG 56 741 @ Matt
   7:18 [Kellerman / Oden I 158]): 'It is better to believe well, since faith alone without works is something, even if it is dead, but a work without faith is nothing.'
   This can be read as consonant with Luther's teaching, and someone (Erasmus
   does not tell us who) apparently concluded that Lutherans had corrupted the
   text.
21 Not found in the PG text or in Kellerman / Oden

Cordial greetings in Christ. Your recent letter gave me great pleasure. I learned from it that you, a man so dear to my heart, are gradually recovering from a long illness.[1] I do not doubt but that from this meeting of such great princes, which portends for us either total peace or bloody rebellions, you expect not trivial melodramas, not fraudulent deceptions, not a tyranny worse than that of Phalaris,[2] but decisions that will lead to the tranquillity of Christendom, an increase in evangelical instruction, and the salvation of our Germany. But I fear that the whore of Babylon will pour out her potions in goodly measure to the high and mighty.[3] The heart of the prince is in the hand of the Lord; he will lead it wherever he wishes.[4] May Almighty God deign to have pity on our lot and through them, by enlightening their minds, may he may impart his peace to us as through public instruments, but I fear that there are those who will interfere with their best efforts and drag them to their destruction. The invincible Emperor Charles is of the opinion that they will not deviate from the councils, decrees of the Fathers, and ceremonies observed up to now by the church. As for the Lutheran leaders and their sworn allies, it is all too well known how much faith they put in decrees, councils, and ceremonies.

My advice to you is that you do not think of moving[5] until you have a haven suitable for your activities and free of tumult.[6] On that account I beg you once more that you let us know whether there is a place in the territory of our prince that satisfies your needs. It is clear to me from your letters that Aachen has a primitive rusticity and a foolish superstition about it,[7] that in Cologne the monks reign supreme,[8] that it is not opportune to have the cardinal of Liège as a neighbour,[9] that you are afraid of castles,[10] and that you shun princely courts.

* * * * *

2360
1 Erasmus had been gravely ill for about four months in the spring and summer (March–July) of 1530, and was still feeling the after-effects; see Ep 2320 n1. In Ep 2442:4–6 (6 March 1531) he reports that he did not regain his strength 'until the approach of winter.'
2 Cruel tyrant of Acragas (present-day Agrigento) in Sicily, who ruled from 570 to 555 BC. He is said to have roasted his victims alive so that their cries would resemble the bellowing of a bull.
3 See Rev 17:1–2, 12–14.
4 Prov 21:1
5 Cf Epp 2368:5, 2370:16–18, 2371:24–6, 2374:1–6, 2375:57–9, 2383:52–3, 2397:18–20, 2410:57–60, 2462:27–8.
6 Cf Epp 2312A:298, 2332:74–5, 2353A:77–8, 2365:25–6, 2371:2–3, 2410:95.
7 Cf Ep 2146:11–12.
8 Cf Ep 2222:19–21.
9 See Ep 2222 n14.
10 See Ep 2222:17–19 with n10.

Hermann, count of Neuenahr, is suffering from a grave illness, but I hope the Lord will give strength to his Highness and will preserve him for us as long as possible.[11] Be in good health, my good friend, to whom I am so indebted, and love me, as you do.

Augsburg, 9 August 1530. Written extempore 30

Yours, John Vlatten, etc

To the most learned Master Erasmus of Rotterdam, a friend respected and revered

2361 / To Konrad von Thüngen   Freiburg, 11 August 1530

This letter, Erasmus' reply to Ep 2314, was first published in the *Epistolae floridae*. The manuscript, an autograph rough draft, is in the Royal Library at Copenhagen (MS GKS 95 Fol, folio 214). For Konrad von Thüngen, bishop of Würzburg, see Ep 1124.

TO THE MOST REVEREND FATHER IN CHRIST AND MOST ILLUSTRIOUS PRINCE LORD KONRAD, BISHOP OF THE CHURCH OF WÜRZBURG AND DUKE OF EAST FRANCONIA, FROM ERASMUS OF ROTTERDAM, GREETING

Most distinguished prelate, no recommendation ever turned out more felici- 5 tously than the one in which in a few words I recommended to your Highness the preacher Marius and the canon of your college, Stiebar,[1] inasmuch as I understand from your letter that not only have they become dearer to you but that I too, who previously was unknown to you,[2] have won such favour with you that you have deigned to count the recommender among those most rec- 10 ommended to you. You were not merely content with thanking me in such a gracious letter, contrary to the usual custom – for it is customary that those whose recommendation has found favour give thanks to those who have rendered the favour – but you also presented me with a token and a souvenir of a most amicable spirit, since such a letter, from such a distinguished prince, 15

* * * * *

11 Count Hermann (Epp 442, 1926) was attending the diet at Augsburg in the entourage of Archbishop Hermann von Wied of Cologne. He died there on 2 October 1530.

2361
1 Ep 2303
2 Erasmus' first attempt to establish contact with Bishop Konrad (Ep 1124) does not appear to have elicited a response.

Konrad von Thüngen, prince-bishop of Würzburg
Engraving by Johann Salver (1670–1738)

written in such a courteous and amicable manner, is to me the equivalent of a gift of the highest value. And for such a magnanimous spirit an ordinary gift did not suffice, but you wished to give me a truly kingly gift,[3] keeping in mind what was more fitting for you to give rather than for Erasmus to receive.

What makes the gift more valuable is that it was given to me not because 20 I deserved it or hoped for it or even expected it but because it was a sponta- neous expression of your generosity. For that reason I declare openly that I owe you all the more gratitude. For that which is given to the well-deserving merits the name of recompense rather than good deed, and that which is ex- torted by entreaty has been bought at a great price, wrote Seneca.[4] Things long 25 promised, which have caused anguished expectation, have lost a great part of their enjoyment. But for those benefits that come before the recipient expected we owe supreme thanks. Even if they were of little value, the sentiment of the giver renders them most precious. Homer writes that the gifts of the gods are not to be rejected.[5] For my part, I gladly preserve in my home the spontaneous 30 gifts of such princes as sacred memorials, and I exhibit them as testimonies of the extraordinary honour bestowed upon me. And at times I find in them a consolation against the wickedness of certain ill-omened individuals who can neither say anything good about those deserving of credit nor be roused to do good to those from whom they have benefited. 35

What remains for me, then, most distinguished prelate, but to con- gratulate each of us in turn in lordly fashion: Marius and Steibar for having obtained the benevolence of such a great prince, and myself, whose audacity was so successful that not only did I not give offence through my temer- ity but gained the unusual privilege of being admitted into the number of 40 those whom you deem worthy of your friendship. But to you also, esteemed prelate, I pay equal homage for being so unassuming in such a high office, uncorrupted in the face of fortune's favours, and in the midst of a sea of trou- bles having nothing more at heart than the interests of the Catholic church. Tossed about as it is at the present moment by so many tempests, it obviously 45 has need of helmsmen like you, who do not hesitate to put their own private interests after the glory of Christ.

Accordingly, may your Highness be assured that Erasmus is totally at your disposal and has no other desire than to be given the opportunity to demonstrate in turn the feelings of a grateful client in whatever way pos- 50 sible. For I esteem that I am no less obliged than I am honoured by your

* * * * *

3 A gold cup bearing the insignia of Bishop Konrad; see Sieber 5, Major 41.
4 *De beneficiis* 2.1.4, 2.5.3
5 *Iliad* 3.65

kindness to me. But I do not wish to be freed of this obligation, both because I am happy to be indebted to such a prelate and because I see that I cannot discharge this debt even if I were to put at auction all my abilities and even my very life. I shall be content if I can give proof in some way that the will to 55 repay the favour is not lacking in me.

May the Lord Jesus preserve your most reverend Highness and grant you success in all your undertakings, but most especially in quelling the present tumults within the church. We must not despair. It endured greater troubles long ago in the age of St Jerome,[6] and Christ, who calms the sea with 60 a single word no matter how much it roars and threatens destruction,[7] lives even now. All we can do is call out to him with our prayers and arouse him with our good works until he awakes and bids this tempest to be still. He wishes this glory to be given to him, not to our wisdom.

Given at Freiburg im Breisgau, on the day after the feast of St Lawrence 65 1530

2362 / To Christoph von Stadion   Freiburg, 11 August 1530

> This letter was first published in the *Epistolae floridae*. On Christoph von Stadion, see Ep 2359.

ERASMUS OF ROTTERDAM TO CHRISTOPH, BISHOP OF AUGSBURG, GREETING

On the same day that I received the last letter of your Highness I had sent a messenger to you whom I had hired for precisely this purpose.[1] A certain peasant brought me your letter of 3 August,[2] saying that he had received it at 5 Augsburg from the son of a fisherman. I do not know how this came about. I fear the rest were intercepted, for the Corycaeans are ever watchful.[3]

Little by little I am regaining my strength,[4] except that the audacity of these lice all but kills me off for lack of sleep.[5] Your reprimand because I had

* * * * *

6 Cf Epp 2366:42–9, 2383:44–9.
7 Matt 8:26, Mark 4:39, Luke 8:24

2362
1 The letter is not extant; the messenger is unidentified.
2 Also not extant
3 A 'Corycaean' was a spy. See *Adagia* I ii 44: *Corycaeus auscultavit* 'A Corycaean was listening,' and cf Ep 2082 n47.
4 On Erasmus' recent illness, see Ep 2360 n1.
5 Cf Ep 2329:76–7.

written that I would not be a burdensome protégé pleased me very much.[6] 10
It testified to your unwavering friendship, which I hope I can reciprocate in
some way. The pamphlets that the great heroes of the sects are launching,[7]
far from promoting peace, actually threaten us. The three conditions you
enumerate could have been conceded, in my opinion, without any loss to
religion,[8] but I do not believe for a minute that the leaders of the sects will 15
be content with them. As for the fanatics and the captious, I know that your
Highness is beyond the reach of the reptiles' bites.[9] Yet there is nothing that
these hornets would leave untried, and if we believe fables, even a dung
beetle flying up into the sky took vengeance on an eagle.[10] I have just finished
my preface to Chrysostom.[11]   20

I suspect that what you say about Lefèvre d'Etaples is a fable unless it
happened just recently. For I received letters from Paris on the feast of the
Ascension, and no unpleasant news about him arrived here or in Basel.[12]
A few months ago they burned a certain Louis de Berquin at the stake,[13]
an excellent man by all reports – and he was not a Lutheran. I think this 25
was the source of the rumour.[14] His hatred of monks and theologians, his
free tongue, his simplicity and its companion, trust, were his undoing. Like
Enoch, Lefèvre was taken into protection by the king of France,[15] who has

* * * * *

6 See Ep 2332:67–8.
7 An apparent reference to the attacks on Erasmus by Gerard Geldenhouwer and
   Martin Bucer; see Ep 2329:86–90 with nn18–19.
8 See Ep 2353A:34–7, and cf Ep 2384:5–9 with n2.
9 An apparent reference to the Catholic hardliners who denounced Stadion as a
   Lutheran for proposing concessions to the Lutherans at Augsburg; see preceding note.
10 *Adagia* III vii 1
11 Ep 2359, addressed to Stadion
12 Ascension was 26 May 1530. None of the letters mentioned is extant. The 'fable'
   appears to have been rumours that Lefèvre had been burned at the stake; cf Ep
   2379:463–5.
13 On 16 April 1529; see Epp 2158, 2188.
14 On the connection between the cases of Berquin and Lefèvre, see Ep 2188:209–25.
15 In October 1525, Erasmus' fellow humanist Jacques Lefèvre d'Etaples, member
   of the circle of reformers in the bishopric of Meaux, had fled to Strasbourg for
   fear of the Parlement of Paris and the Paris faculty of theology. In the spring of
   1526, King Francis I summoned Lefèvre back to France and the royal court at
   Blois; see Ep 1674 n27. Erasmus here compares Lefèvre to the patriarch Enoch,
   whose faith so pleased God that he preserved him from death by taking him to
   himself. See Heb 11:5; cf Gen 5:24. Cf also CWE 44 245 (*Paraphrase on Hebrews*).

forbidden that anyone write anything either for or against him.[16] I think this
was attended to by his patron, the bishop of Lodève.[17] May the Lord prosper   30
your Highness in all things.

At Freiburg, the day after the feast of St Lawrence 1530

2363 / To Philippus Melanchthon   Freiburg, 12 August 1530

This letter (= MBW Ep 1019) is the first of two responses to Ep 2357 (the other
is Ep 2365). It was first published, with no indication of the source, in Strobel
II 471. The original manuscript is not extant. Allen judged Strobel's text to be
superior to the manuscript copies that he managed to find, but he took the
heading from a manuscript in the Bayerische Staatsbibliothek at Munich
(Clm 94 folio 15 verso). On 5 September 1530 Melanchthon wrote to Joachim
Camerarius (MBW Ep 1064) summarizing this letter, which he had received via
Daniel Stiebar.

A LETTER OF ERASMUS OF ROTTERDAM WRITTEN TO PHILIPPUS
MELANCHTHON IN AUGSBURG DURING HIS ATTENDANCE
AT THE DIET

Cordial greetings. On the same day that I sent the letter carrier whom I had
hired,[1] Stiebar came to see me after dinner, a splendid young man.[2] I see that   5
the situation is clearly moving towards war. The preachers issue such menac-
ing pamphlets, while at the same time they are not very much in agreement

* * * * *

16 In August 1526 Francis forbade the sale of Noël Béda's *Annotations* (1526)
   against Erasmus and Lefèvre; w see Epp 1722 introduction, 1875:88. But the
   book, which had the approval of the faculty of theology, had already circulated widely, and the campaign of the faculty against Lefèvre and Erasmus
   continued unabated; see Ep 1902 introduction and CWE 13 433–5 (letter of
   Francis I to the University of Paris, c 7 July 1527). By 1531 Lefèvre had taken
   refuge at the court of Margaret of Navarre in Nérac, where he remained until
   his death in 1536.
17 Guillaume (II) Briçonnet (Ep 1407 n33), who was also bishop of Meaux

   2363
 1 An unidentified special messenger who carried letters no longer extant to Cardinal Campeggi, Christoph von Stadion, and others in Augsburg. The date of
   his departure must have been shortly after 2 August (Ep 2358:1–2). By 18 August he had returned, bearing a letter from Bishop Christoph but none from the
   cardinal (Ep 2366:3–5).
 2 See Epp 2357 n4, 2358 n2.

among themselves.[3] I imagine the emperor will not leave until the preliminary discussions are over. There is a persistent rumour in circulation that the prince of the Hessians has stolen away secretly.[4] The people of Basel have issued a decree that if the canons had any possessions in their homes they should remove them within eight days.[5] What else is this but the prelude to war? As for ourselves, my dear Philippus, we can only hope for the best. In annihilating themselves in mutual slaughter the Germans are providing a spectacle not displeasing to the pope.[6]

Farewell. 12 August 1530

2364 / From Erasmus Schets   Antwerp, 13 August 1530

This letter is Schets' reply to Ep 2325. First published by Allen, the autograph is in the Öffentliche Bibliothek of the University of Basel (MS Scheti epistolae 26). Erasmus Schets (Epp 1541, 1931) was the Antwerp banker who managed Erasmus' financial affairs in England and the Netherlands.

†

Cordial greetings. The letters you sent me on the first of June I received on the twentieth of last month via Goclenius, together with some letters to be sent to England.[1] I sent these immediately and safely to Luis de Castro.[2] I

* * * * *

3 The 'preachers' (*Ecclesiastae*) in question were the reformers of Strasbourg and their allies; see Epp 2329:86–90, 2341:14–16.
4 Landgrave Philip of Hessen (Ep 2219 n12), already convinced of the need for a political alliance among the Protestants and not averse to armed resistance to the emperor and his allies, had come to the diet reluctantly and on 6 August had stolen quietly away from it.
5 There is no known documentary record of any such decree of the Basel city council, and it is not clear what incident(s) may have been behind this report; see *Melanchthons Werke in Auswahl* ed Robert Stupperich et al, 7 vols (Gütersloh 1951–75) VII 2:292–3 n2. The cathedral chapter had long since left Basel and settled in Freiburg; see Ep 2158 n15.
6 Melanchthon understood this to be an indication that the pope was inciting the emperor to make war on the German Protestants; see MBW Ep 1064 T 4/2 644:6–7 (Melanchthon to Camerarius, 5 September 1530).

2364
1 The letters are not extant. Conradus Goclenius (Epp 1209, 1994A) was professor of Latin at the Collegium Trilingue in Louvain and one of Erasmus' closest friends.
2 Schets' agent in London (Ep 1931 n3)

am awaiting his answer with the acknowledgment of the receipt of the
Canterbury pension.[3] When I receive this I will send it immediately to the   5
agents of Anton Fugger together with sixty-five florins, which Master Jan
de Hondt directed to be given to me as half of the Courtrai pension.[4] When
the archbishop gives this pension money to Luis de Castro, be assured that
it will pass from his hands to mine and then to Fugger to reach you safe and
sound.[5] The Frisian, Haio Cammingha, while he was passing this way, said   10
nothing of the debt he owes you.[6] It is a good sum of money. I shall see to it
that he will be reminded of this by his friends in Friesland and that they ask
him for the money. I have heard that he is going there to be a member of the
provincial council.[7]

You are now living near the emperor. It will be easy for you to explain   15
your tasks and your material needs to his Majesty so that he will give you
succour in your old age and refund you the part of the pension that has been
denied you up to now.[8]

Conflicting rumours reach us daily concerning the dangerous situation
at the Diet of Augsburg. The world will be in a terrible plight if war arises.   20
Things have never been in such a state of turmoil. Let us hope that since we
are dealing with matters of faith the war may be waged in a catholic manner,
that is, with the sword of the Spirit rather than by the violence of the sword,[9]
for which both sides seem to be preparing themselves. May God bring it

* * * * *

3 Ie the pensions paid to Erasmus by William Warham, archbishop of Canterbury,
   from two benefices, one at Aldington (Ep 255 introduction), and the other of
   unknown location. The combined value of the two pensions was now £35. See
   Ep 2332 n10.
4 On Jan de Hondt and Erasmus' Courtrai pension, see Ep 1993 n11. On the value
   of the pension, see Ep 2239 n2. On Anton Fugger, head of the Augsburg bank-
   ing house, see Ep 2145 introduction. On his role in the transmission to Erasmus
   of his pensions from England and the Netherlands, see the following note.
5 See Ep 2403 n4; cf Ep 2384:70–5.
6 On Cammingha's debt to Erasmus see Epp 2325 n1, 2403:35–41 and 69–71,
   2413:24–9, Allen Epp 2552:10–1, 2573:66–7, 2587:44–58, 2593:36–9.
7 The rumour was false. It was Haio Herman, not Cammingha, who in July 1528
   had been appointed to the council of Friesland. See Epp 2403:69–70, 2413:24–5.
8 Margaret of Austria, regent of the Netherlands, had made the payment of
   Erasmus' imperial pension dependent on his return to Brabant (Ep 2192:97–
   104), something that he occasionally talked about doing (see Ep 2397:18–20) but
   ultimately never did.
9 Eph 6:17: 'Take ... the sword of the Spirit, which is the word of God.'

about that the result of this meeting will be better than I fear. Farewell, my   25
beloved Erasmus, and count on me as your friend.

From Antwerp, 13 August 1530

Devotedly yours, Erasmus Schets

† To Master Erasmus of Rotterdam, outstanding man of learning, foremost friend and patron. At Freiburg   30

2365 / To Philippus Melanchthon   Freiburg, 17 August 1530

This letter (= MBW Ep 1028) is Erasmus' further reply to Ep 2357 (cf Ep 2363)
and perhaps also to an earlier letter that is no longer extant (see Ep 2353A n10).
It was first published in Strobel II 472, with no indication of the source. All the
surviving manuscripts are copies. Allen judged Strobel's text to be superior to
the extant copies, but for the heading he used the one found in a 'Frankfort MS'
that had been published by E.W. Löhn in the *Zeitschrift für historische Theologie*
Neue Folge 1 (1837) 108: 'Epistola in D. M[artinum] L[utherum] satis impia ad
P.M. (A rather disrespectful letter to Martin Luther addressed to P[hilippus]
M[elanchthon]).' From the manuscript, which is now in the British Library (MS
Add 12059), it is evident that the heading in question is a later addition in a
hand other than that of the copyist, and that it is someone's editorial comment
on the letter rather than a neutral description of it (see MBW T 4/2 563–4). We
have therefore adopted a heading similar to that found in the MBW text.

In a letter to Luther of 23 August, Georgius Spalatinus reported the arrival of
this letter and quoted extensively from it; see WA-Br 5 557–8.

ERASMUS OF ROTTERDAM TO PHILIPPUS MELANCHTHON
IN AUGSBURG

If my letters had any influence, anything else could have occurred rather
than going to war. That I vented my wrath against the Zwinglians to you was
both justified and did not pose any obstacle to your cause. I sing the same   5
song to princes: there is nothing less expedient than to resolve the matter
by the sword. There are those who manifest some hope of peace, but I am
afraid it is in vain, judging by the preludes of the drama as they appear up
to now. Would that Luther had thought about this in time! But he is a slave
of his character. Other preachers would rather go to war than settle the dis- 10
pute.[1] They promise themselves sure victory, and if things should turn out

* * * * *

2365
1 Cf Ep 2363 n3.

differently, they will take flight. If an agreement is settled upon, their reign
will be at an end.

I did not write anything either to Ferdinand or to Charles during the
course of the diet, lest I involve myself of my own will in a dangerous busi-   15
ness.[2] Many wrote to me saying, 'Would that you were here!'[3] No one ordered me, in the emperor's name, to be there.[4] And it is no secret to me that
this is done at the wish of certain people who have no great love for me. In
any event, Eck included some of my opinions among those of the heretics,
except that he says 'someone' instead of Erasmus. I had never expected this   20
from him.[5] Bucer, unpredictable as he is, together with his friend Vulturius,
a drunken and crazed idiot, has revealed his astuteness.[6] Nonetheless, no
personal wrong will ever drive me to be an instigator of war. I have long been
anxious to leave Germany, now I am compelled by necessity. Here we barely
have anything to eat or drink; what would happen in time of war? And I   25
don't see a safe haven for myself anywhere.[7] The Gospel has given birth to
this age in which we live.[8]

* * * * *

2 Cf Ep 2358:5–9.
3 See Ep 2353A n12.
4 See Ep 2339 n6.
5 Johann Eck (Ep 2387) had circulated in Augsburg a pamphlet entitled *Articulos
   404 ... partim ex scriptis pacem ecclesiae perturbantium extractos ...* (404 Articles
   ... Extracted in Part From the Writings of Those Who Disturb the Peace of
   the Church) (Ingolstadt: [Peter and Georg Apian, April] 1530), which he had
   offered to discuss in the presence of the emperor in refutation of the errors in
   question; cf Ep 2357 n1. Most of the articles were attributed by name to Luther,
   Melanchthon, Zwingli, Oecolampadius, Bucer, and others. Articles 399–402, on
   the other hand, were attributed only to *Quidam* 'Someone,' in whom Erasmus
   instantly recognized himself. The works in which the errors were found are
   (Art 399) *Apologia adversus monachos* resp 64 (LB IX 1080B–C); (Art 400) *Paraphrase
   on John* 19:11 (CWE 46 209); (Art 401) *Elenchus in censuras Bedae* nos 48 and 57
   (LB IX 498D, 499A); (Art 402) *Paraphrase on Luke* 23:28 (CWE 48 215–16). Although
   Erasmus had always disliked and distrusted Eck, he had since 1523 managed
   to ignore him and avoid controversy with him. But the inclusion of Erasmus
   among the heretics in Eck's *Articles* led to renewed antagonism between them,
   though not to an open controversy; see Epp 2387 and 2406. An English translation of Eck's articles by Robert Rosin is found in *Sources and Contexts of the Book
   of Concord* ed Robert Kolb and James Nestingen (Minneapolis 2001) 31–82.
6 For both Bucer and Vulturius (Geldenhouwer), see Ep 2358:14–20.
7 See Ep 2360 n5.
8 'Gospel' (*Evangelium*) is a sarcastic jab at the so-called Evangelicals (ie the reformers in Strasbourg and their allies in Southwest Germany), who in Erasmus'
   view had undermined the unity of Christendom in the name of 'the gospel.'

I have already written to you via Stiebar,[9] but only briefly.
Farewell. At Freiburg, 17 August 1530
I have not read this over, forgive me.   30

2366 / To Lorenzo Campeggi   Freiburg, 18 August 1530

On Lorenzo Campeggi, see Ep 961 and cf Epp 2215 n17, 2256 n7, 2328.

This letter was never published by Erasmus himself, and it is doubtful that it was ever delivered to Campeggi. No original manuscript survives. Erasmus later reported that the letter had been intercepted by an unnamed 'Evangelical,' printed without authorization at Strasbourg, and almost immediately reprinted in the same place with 'ridiculous' additions purporting to be by Erasmus himself; see Allen Ep 2615:367–71. The earlier of these unauthorized editions appears to have been *Epistola D. Eras. Rotero. nuper missa ad Legatum Apposto. Augustae agentem* (no place or date of publication), a rare little volume of four leaves, copies of which are held by the Bodleian Library at Oxford. The earliest inclusion of the letter in an edited collection was that in Coelestin (III 29 verso). Allen, judging all the surviving sixteenth-century manuscripts to be 'copies of small value,' took as the basis of his text the version of the letter published by Daniel Heinsius in his *Illustrium et clarorum virorum Epistolae selectiores* (Leiden 1617) 51–5, with some variant readings from the Bodley text and Coelestin included in the apparatus.

A German epitome of the letter was published under the title *Vrsach: warumb Erasmus von Roterodam, jnn einer schrifft an den Bepstlichen Legaten vnd Cardinal Compeium, bedenckt, das es nicht gut sein sol, das Roem. Kei. Maiestat, die Lutherische vnd andere lere, mit dem schwerd dempffe. Ynn Siebenzehen Artickel gestellet.* The copies of this pamphlet that Allen examined at the Bodleian library were undated; we have seen a digital copy of the edition published at Wittenberg in 1531 by Georg Rhau (Universitäts- und Landesbibliothek Sachsen-Anhalt at Halle).

ERASMUS OF ROTTERDAM TO CARDINAL CAMPEGGI,
CORDIAL GREETINGS
Most reverend sir, my messenger left sooner than I wished,[1] since I was anxiously awaiting a letter from your Lordship. Perhaps I will be lingering

* * * * *

9 See Ep 2363:4–5.

2366
1 On the messenger, cf Ep 2363 n1.

Title-page of the German epitome of Ep 2366: *The reason that Erasmus of Rotterdam,
in a letter to the papal legate and cardinal Campeggi, deems it inappropriate for
His Imperial Roman Majesty to suppress with the sword Lutheran and other doctrines.
Presented in seventeen articles. 1531.*

here longer than I desired. His reverend lordship the bishop of Augsburg 5
writes that he will send his personal servant here: I shall expect your letter
from him.[2]

If the emperor terrifies his adversaries by threats of war,[3] I cannot but
praise his wisdom. But if he is seriously seeking war (I would not wish to be
a bird of ill omen), my heart shudders every time I contemplate the shape 10
of things as I see them if ever we resort to arms. This evil is so widespread.
I acknowledge that the power of the emperor is supreme, but not all nations
recognize this title. The Germans do, but only on certain conditions: that they
exercise power rather than obey, for they prefer to command rather than comply.[4] Add to this that their own territories have been severely depleted by con- 15
tinual incursions and military operations, and that the flames of war have just
recently flared up in the neighbouring province of Friesland, whose leader is
now said to profess the gospel of Luther.[5] There are many territories like this
between the Easterlings and the Danes, and from there a chain of evils stretches to Switzerland.[6] If the emperor in his piety gives signs of wishing to do 20

* * * * *

2 The letter from Bishop Christoph von Stadion does not survive, nor does a letter from Campeggi.
3 Cf Ep 2330 n6.
4 'They' are the German princes, who liked to remind the emperor that he was
   elected by them and that they enjoyed 'liberties' that he could not infringe.
5 The German epitome (folio Aii recto) reads: 'Recently a new war has begun
   in East Friesland because the count of that place has accepted the Lutheran
   gospel.' The count in question was Enno II Cirksena (d 1540), who aggressive-
   ly supported the Reformation, allowing adherents of both Lutheranism and
   Zwinglianism to preach and teach. In 1530, however, he became involved in
   war with a Frisian nobleman named Balthasar who, facing defeat at the hands
   of Enno, called to his aid Karel van Egmond, the Catholic duke of Gelderland.
   The result was a treaty that permitted Enno to introduce 'the Augsburg
   Confession' (Lutheranism) but not 'sacramentarianism' (Zwinglianism). See
   Real-Encyklopädie für protestantische Theologie und Kirche 22 vols (Stuttgart and
   Hamburg 1854–68) 4 611 sv 'Friesland.'
6 The German epitome (folio Aii recto) reads: 'Denmark and the Hanse towns
   have also accepted the [Lutheran] gospel and the [chain of] those that do the
   same stretches all the way to Switzerland.' The Latin word rendered 'Hanse
   towns' in the epitome is Orientales. As Allen observed, the English word for
   citizens of the Hanse towns, which included Emden in East Friesland, was
   'Easterlings.' The 'chain of evils' refers to the evangelical territories (including Electoral Saxony and Hessen) and imperial cities (including Nürnberg and
   Strasbourg) that lie in the swathe of Germany stretching south from the North
   Sea and Baltic coasts to the Swiss border and beyond.

everything in accordance with the will of the pope,[7] there is danger that he will
not have many on his side. Take into account as well that the onslaught of the
Turks, whose might we would barely be able to overcome even if we agreed to
pool all our resources, is expected from one day to the next.[8] Moreover, we
have learned from the sack of Rome[9] and recently from what happened in   25
Vienna[10] what it means to make war against the will of the soldiers.

I do not doubt that the heart of our excellent prince is inclined towards
peace, clemency, and tranquillity, but I know not by what fate, in spite of his
feelings, one war is constantly generated from another. How long and how
pitifully France has been ravaged! How much more pitifully has Italy been   30
stricken, where a new war is increasing in violence![11] Now prospects seem to
indicate that the greater part of the world will be bathed in blood. And as the
issue of all wars is doubtful, it is to be feared that their tumult will result in
the subversion of the entire church, especially since the masses are convinced
that this whole affair is not being conducted without the connivance of the   35
pope, in great part via bishops and abbots. And I even fear that the emperor
himself will not be exempt from danger. May the gods avert this omen!

I know and I abhor the impudence of those who are in control of sects
or favour them, but in the present state of affairs we must consider what is required for the tranquillity of the whole world rather than what their shame-   40
less behavior deserves. And we must not despair to such a degree over the
state of the church. In former times, under Arcadius and Theodosius,[12] it was

* * * * *

7　Cf Epp 2308:10–12, 2371:11–12, 2375:40–2, 2376:21–2.
8　See Ep 2285.
9　The sack of Rome by the emperor's troops in May 1527
10　During and after its siege by the Turks in September–October 1529; see Ep
　　2313:20–46.
11　Although the conflict between Charles v and Francis i, fought mostly in Italy in
　　the period 1521–9, had come to a halt with the Peace of Cambrai (August 1529),
　　armed conflict continued in Italy. In accordance with the Treaty of Barcelona
　　between Charles v and Clement vii (29 June 1529), imperial forces made war
　　on the republic of Florence with the aim of restoring the rule of the pope's rela-
　　tives, the Medici family, who had been expelled from the city in May 1527; cf
　　Ep 2211 n14. The ensuing siege of Florence (24 October 1529–10 August 1530)
　　ended with the decisive defeat of the Florentine forces and the installation of
　　Alessandro de' Medici as the ruler of the city. See Pastor 10 chapter 3.
12　If the sequence of the names is intended to reflect the sequence of the reigns,
　　then the reference is to emperors Arcadius (r 383–408) and his son Theodosius
　　ii (r 408–50). But the reign of Arcadius' father, Theodosius i (376–95) was far

tossed about by tempests much greater than these. What was the state of the
world at that time! In the same polity Arians, pagans, and orthodox Christians
lived together.[13] In Africa there were Donatists and Circumcellions.[14] In many   45
places the madness of the Manichaeans was still thriving and the poison of
Marcion,[15] in addition to the incursions of the barbarians. And yet in the
midst of such discord the emperor controlled the reins of power without
bloodshed and little by little pruned back the monstrous growth of heresies.

Time alone sometimes affords the remedy for untreatable maladies. If   50
sects were allowed under certain conditions (as the Bohemians do without
acknowledging it),[16] it would be a grave evil, I admit, but more tolerable than
war – and such a war.

In the present state of affairs there is no place where I would prefer to
be than Italy, but the Fates draw me elsewhere. So let them take me where   55
they will, as long as they do not take me away from the companionship of
the dove.[17] I hear there are some persons manoeuvring at the court of the em-

* * * * *

more marked by 'tempests' in the church and campaigns against heresy than
was that of Theodosius II.

13 The word translated as 'polity' is *civitas*, which could mean 'city' (ie Rome),
but more likely means the entire area of Roman citizenship (ie the Empire).
Arians, named for their founder Arius (c 250–c 336), denied the true divinity
of Jesus, arguing that he was not eternal but created, and that he was not of
the same substance as the Father. Their views were officially condemned at the
Councils of Nicaea (325) and Constantinople (381) but survived into the sixth
century, particularly among the Franks and other Teutonic tribes that had adopted Christianity.

14 For Donatists and Circumcellions, see Ep 2157 n16.

15 For Manichaeans see Ep 2157 n5. Marcion (d c 160) was the founder of a heretical movement committed to the view that the creator God of the Old Testament
(which he rejected completely), was entirely a God of law who had nothing
to do with the God of love revealed in Jesus Christ in the New Testament (of
which he accepted only ten of the Pauline epistles and an edited version of
the Gospel of Luke). His followers were the chief threat to doctrinal orthodoxy
in the second half of the second century, and most of what is known about
Marcion's views stems from the orthodox Fathers, including Tertullian, who
wrote against him. By the end of the third century, most of the Marcionite communities had been absorbed into Manichaeism, but they persisted in small
numbers for a long time thereafter.

16 The reference is to the *modus vivendi* between Catholics and Utraquists (moderate Hussites who celebrated communion in both kinds, *sub utraque specie*) in
Bohemia; see Epp 1021:110–85, 1039:125–35, 1744:83–5.

17 Ie the church; see Ep 2037:285. On Erasmus' refusal to depart from the fellow-
ship or consensus of the church, see Epp 2082 n78, 2411:44–5, 2443:108–10.

peror who are not very well disposed towards me.[18] But I am confident that
your reverend Lordship remains true to his convictions. I pray that you may
enjoy every good fortune.   60

At Freiburg, 18 August 1530

I wrote this on the spur of the moment; the messenger was urging me
to hurry. Forgive me.

At the service of your Lordship

Erasmus of Rotterdam   65

2367 / To Charles Blount   Freiburg, 25 August 1530

This letter, Erasmus' reply to one no longer extant, was first published in the
Epistolae floridae. On Charles ·Blount (June 1516–October 1544), fifth Baron
Mountjoy, see Ep 2023 introduction.

ERASMUS OF ROTTERDAM TO CHARLES MOUNTJOY, GREETING
I can hardly express to you in words how pleased I am, Charles, most distinguished young man, to see in you the rejuvenation of my beloved Maecenas,
your father,[1] than whom I have never encountered anyone more sincere,
more kindly, more friendly. Your letter breathes such benevolence of spirit,   5
such uncommon affection that I recognize the same personality, but more
vigorous and more expansive.[2] I have no doubt that this is no less a source
of pleasure to your father than it is to me; believe me, it gives me supreme
pleasure. It is the bad fortune of many to have such children that they envy
those who are childless. But when one is blessed with an heir who resembles   10
his parent not so much in facial lineaments as in genuine spiritual blessings,
then that brings great and true pleasure.

As far as your physical appearance is concerned, I am completely uninformed save that my servant Quirinus told me that in this regard you resemble your father to an astonishing degree.[3] Your letter portrayed your gifts   15

* * * * *

18 See Ep 2371 n14.

2367
1 William Blount, the fifth baron (Ep 79). The name of Maecenas, confidant of
  Emperor Augustus and the patron of Virgil and Horace, became (and remains)
  the byword for a generous and enlightened patron of the arts.
2 The letter is not extant; see Ep 2295 n21.
3 On Erasmus' trusted famulus and messenger Quirinus Talesius, see Ep 1966.
  For his visit to England see Ep 2222 n16.

of spirit as if in a mirror. If it was composed by dint of your own efforts, which I do not doubt it was, it displays a rare and remarkable talent and gives promise of no mediocre ability.

Among the many excellent virtues with which your celebrated father is adorned, he possesses nothing more beautiful, in my opinion, than his singu-   20 lar modesty; it would be difficult to express how much charm it contributes to all his other distinctions. His modesty is accompanied by urbanity and affability. If you strive to add this as a crowning point to your other outstanding qualities, there will be nothing lacking in you of those laudable traits of your father. Modesty is the surest guardian of the other virtues. Moreover,   25 you will have a safeguard for your modesty if you reflect that whatever blessings of mind or body or material advantages have been bestowed on you proceeded from the munificence of the Divinity, to whom we must attribute in full every good fortune that comes to us in this life. It is a part of gratitude that each of us be conscious of his blessings, but not in the manner   30 of Narcissus, whose self-love was his undoing.

He makes valid account of his assets who reckons them up as loans and in contemplating his possessions recognizes how much he is indebted to divine generosity. The more he perceives that it has been lavish towards him, the more humble he should become, and the more he acknowledges   35 the generosity of the Divinity towards him, the more careful he is in preserving and rightly distributing what he has received. If he sees someone less fortunate than himself, he does not say to himself, 'How inferior this man is to me,' but 'God's generosity has conferred more upon me so that he may come to this person's aid through me.' Do not consider it an ordinary   40 blessing of the Divinity to have descended from such ancestors, to be direct heir of such an ample fortune, to be endowed with such gifts of body and mind. Compare it with the lot of others whose virtues are obstructed by humble origins, poverty of patrimony, frailty of physique, poverty of intelligence. But he who looks down on such persons does not remember that   45 whatever he has received is the gift of divine munificence. He who does not give assistance to them does not consider what use was intended for the gifts he received.

Therefore I exhort you, my very dear Charles, that you strive day after day to augment the pleasure you give to me and all of your family, vying with   50 yourself so that you may improve yourself with every passing day. I cherish deeply your extraordinary affection for me and your favourable disposition towards me although, if ever I rendered any service to your illustrious father, he repaid me most abundantly. Even if he had done less, the pleasure that I derive from your progress and your readiness to repay my friends if chance   55 should dictate that you have this opportunity after my life is at an end will be a most ample recompense. And that will increase in the measure in which you add further distinctions to your excellent beginnings.

The reason for this late response to your letter was my bad state of health, which has tormented me all through the summer.[4] If I do not answer   60
each of your points exactly it is because I had laid your letter aside so that I could respond as soon as I had the time, and I was unable to find it. I shall make up for it on another occasion. May the Lord Jesus deign to continue his generosity towards you and constantly increase it with new additions, my dear son Charles. May he also bestow his blessings on your marriage.[5]   65

At Freiburg im Breisgau, 25 August 1530

2368 / To Bonifacius Amerbach   Freiburg, 28 August 1530

> This letter (= AK Ep 1461) was first published in the *Epistolae familiares*. The auto-
> graph is in the Öffentliche Bibliothek of the University of Basel (MS AN III 15 19).
> Bonifacius' reply is Ep 2372.

Cordial greetings. Zasius has conferred immortality upon your name in publishing his book.[1] If you or our friend Simon[2] wish to give me any news,
it may be sent by this messenger. But his handwriting is such that I don't
understand what he writes any more easily than I can understand what he
says.[3] My courtier friends force me to stay here, though against my will.[4] It   5
seems that the emperor will spend a good part of the winter in Germany.
May everything turn out successfully! Farewell.

Freiburg, 28 August 1530

You will recognize the hand of your friend.

To the most illustrious doctor of laws Bonifacius Amerbach. At Basel   10

* * * * *

4 See Ep 2360 n1.
5 At about this time, Charles, just weeks past his fourteenth birthday, married his
  stepsister Anne Willoughby, daughter of Dorothy Grey, his father's fourth wife.

2368
1 On Udalricus Zasius, professor of civil law at Freiburg, see Ep 303. The book
  was *Defensio novissima contra Petrum Stellum* (Freiburg: J. Faber 1530), with an
  introductory letter (5 August 1530) addressed to Bonifacius.
2 Grynaeus (Ep 2433), currently professor of Greek at Basel
3 Grynaeus was notorious for his impossible handwriting; cf Ep 1657:14–15.
4 See Ep 2360:18–19.

2369 / From Conradus Goclenius   Louvain, 28 August 1530

This letter was first published by Allen, using the autograph in the Öffentliche
Bibliothek of the University of Basel (MS Goclenii epistolae 4). Goclenius (Epp
1209, 1994A) was professor of Latin at the Collegium Trilingue in Louvain.

Cordial greetings. People have incredible expectations here about the outcome of the diet in Germany.[1] No one doubted that you were also present,
since there were some who asserted that they had participated at the same
banquet as you in Augsburg.[2] I was relieved by this news for many reasons,
since it was a sure sign that you had recovered from your illness.[3] We were   5
given some assurance that these turbulent times in Christendom would return to a certain degree of tranquillity if those who hold the helm would
begin to set their course under the guidance of your wisdom. Moreover, the
certain hope of your return relieved our spirits, for we had no doubts that
you, now that you have been received hospitably in Germany,[4] would ac-   10
company the emperor, who, it is generally believed, will pass the winter in
these regions.[5] But from the letter Episcopius wrote to your friend Erasmius I
realize that our joy was illusory,[6] with the one exception that it confirms that
you are in slightly better health. May God grant that this will continue!

I do not know if we should wait for Jacobus, whom I recently sent to   15
you, to return.[7] I gave him no further instructions than that he should go
to see you and left the rest up to you. But if you had no reason to send him
back here, as far as I am concerned he may stay there or go elsewhere, as he
wishes. In the meanwhile nothing has happened worthy of your ears unless
you should wish to hear what I think is surely a fable. Nevertheless, since it   20

* * * * *

2369
1 Ie the imperial diet currently meeting in Augsburg
2 Erasmus had refused all requests to attend the diet, pointing out that no invitation to do so had come from the emperor, and that he was in any case too ill; see
   Ep 2339 n6.
3 See Ep 2360 n1.
4 Ie in Freiburg, after leaving Basel in 1529; see CWE 15 xi–xiii.
5 Following the conclusion of the Diet of Augsburg in November 1530, the emperor did indeed depart for the Netherlands, stopping in Cologne and Aachen
   (January 1531) long enough to witness the election and coronation of his brother Ferdinand as king of the Romans; cf Ep 2384 n7.
6 For Nicolaus Episcopius see Ep 2233A n4; for Erasmius Froben, who was
   boarding with Goclenius, see Ep 2352:281–304. The content of Episcopius' letter is unknown, but he would doubtless have known of Erasmus' disinclination
   to return to Brabant (Ep 2222 n9).
7 See Ep 2352:321–8.

is a matter that has to do especially with you, having found the opportunity
in a messenger who, as he said, is heading directly to Basel, I will write you
about it, whatever its worth. At least a fable rather than an inane letter will
be brought to you.

Last night, as soon as dusk had fallen, a certain man in leather trousers   25
came to see me. He was covered with mud and dust and in all other respects
looked like a wayfarer, and he was eager to talk to me. When I asked him
who he was and where he came from, he answered that he came from Liège,
that he was sent by Paschasius, and that he had matters of importance for
me. 'But in order not to lose any time,' he said, 'here is a memorandum from   30
Berselius,[8] in which a resumé of my business with you is fully described.' At
first I was no little surprised, hearing the name of Paschasius, with whom
after his departure from Louvain I had not had the slightest contact. I took
the piece of paper in my hand, on which was written something like the following: 'You will say to Conradus Goclenius that there is a canon here who   35
is getting rid of all the writings of our Erasmus and snatching them from
everyone's hands; he removed all the books of Erasmus from the Brothers'
home (it is the chief school of Liège),[9] and after submitting the teachers to a
close scrutiny, removed all the books of Erasmus and forbade the reading
of them to all the young students and even to the teachers. In addition he   40
has threatened the booksellers with a heavy fine besides confiscating their
merchandise, if they dare to import anything of Erasmus from then on. And
Erasmus should be made aware of this as soon as possible!'

After reading the sheet of paper I asked, 'Who is this canon, perpetrator
of such a crime?' And he said, 'Theodoricus Hezius, canon of St Lambert.'[10]   45
I answered, 'Is what is written on this sheet of paper true?' 'Absolutely true'
he said. 'I can believe neither the sheet of paper, although it seems to be an
autograph of Paschasius, nor you,' I said, 'that these things are being done

* * * * *

8 Paschasius Berselius (Ep 674), Benedictine of the abbey of Saint-Laurent at
   Liège, who had studied at Louvain in the years 1518–20 and was a confidant
   of Erard de la Marck, prince-bishop of Liège. Relations between Erasmus and
   Berselius appear to have become permanently strained as a result of the latter's
   support for the losing candidate for the professorship of Latin at the Collegium
   Trilingue in 1519; see Epp 1051 introduction, 1065 n1. Here and in lines 62, 65
   below, Goclenius uses the names 'Paschasius' and 'Berselius' interchangeably.
9 The school of the Brethren of the Common Life, founded in 1495
10 At first a friend and admirer of Erasmus, Hezius (Ep 1339) had by 1525 gone
   over to the support of the Louvain theologians in their opposition to him (Ep 1717
   n4). Erasmus appears to have written to Hezius about this incident but without
   receiving a reply; see Allen Ep 2566:174n.

by Hezius, whom I regard as a good friend of Erasmus and a man possessed
of great fairness and prudence. If anything was troubling him, I do not doubt 50
that he would make it known to Erasmus immediately. Nor do I believe that
he would forbid by his own personal authority what neither the pope nor
the emperor nor any university forbid.'[11] 'I do not know what drove him to
do this,' he said, 'but I know these things have been done and I have merely
been ordered to report them to you.' 'Therefore,' I said, 'when Berselius is 55
more fully informed of this matter, he would do well to write out a full account of it himself. He will undoubtedly earn the gratitude of Erasmus, who
remains ignorant of these things to his own great detriment.' I asked that
he do the same and said that I would see to it that a letter be carried immediately to Erasmus, which I said would be easy to arrange since so many 60
merchants were travelling to Frankfurt at that time.

And so that is how I dismissed this messenger from Paschasius. But I
am uncertain what or whom to believe except that it does not seem that such
stupidity and perfidy can be imputed to Hezius. I am expecting a letter from
Berselius, and in the meantime I will make diligent inquiry into this matter. 65
But since a messenger was opportunely available, I did not want you to remain uninformed of this tale. If anything else happens, I will make sure that
you are informed of it immediately.

Farewell. At Louvain, 28 August 1530
Devotedly yours, Conradus Goclenius 70
To Master Erasmus of Rotterdam. At Freiburg im Breisgau

2370 / To Erasmus Schets   Freiburg, 29 August 1530

This letter was first published by Allen, using the autograph in the British
Museum (MS Add 38512 folio 46). For Schets see Ep 2364.

Greetings. If I had known it was inconvenient for you, I would gladly have
waited until the fair. But I thought that it was of no importance to you when
you remitted the money. I have soaked you, the only thing left to do is to fill
the sponge again.[1] I wrote that twenty pounds sterling were owed to me last

* * * * *

11 But the University of Paris had indeed forbidden works of Erasmus; see Epp
    1902 and 2037 introductions.

2370
1 This metaphor is used frequently in the correspondence with Schets; cf Ep
   2413:15 and Allen Epp 2494:31–3, 2552:13.

Easter from my English pension.[2] Now, at the coming feast of Michaelmas,[3] 5
they will owe me fifteen pounds sterling. Thirty-five in all.[4] Have Luis collect
the money from the archbishop.[5]

An excellent Portuguese young man stayed with me.[6] I learned from
him the reason why my dedication was unsuccessful.[7] I was misinformed
about the genealogy of the king, and the allusion to monopolies was not well   10
received. Therefore they did not dare present the work to the king.[8] With that
dedication I would have won the greatest gratitude of any great prince. For a
slight little pamphlet on the Epistle to the Galatians the cardinal of Lorraine
paid out two hundred gold crowns.[9] From now on goodbye to that Jewish
race![10] The same work has been published again without a preface.[11]   15

It was almost certain that I would be with you this September, but some
people from the imperial court advise me to stay until the outcome of the
diet is known.[12] And so I remain here, although my heart cries out in protest.
Farewell.

At Freiburg, 29 August 1530   20
Yours, Erasmus of Rotterdam
To the honourable gentleman Erasmus Schets. In Antwerp

2371 / To Willibald Pirckheimer   Freiburg, 29 August 1530

This letter (= wpB Ep 1312) was first published in the *Pirckheimeri opera*. The
surviving manuscript, a copy in the hand of Melchior Goldast, the editor of the
Opera, is in the Stadtbibliothek Bremen (msa 0011/061). For Pirckheimer see

* * * * *

2 See Ep 2325:12–13.
3 29 September
4 See Ep 2332 n10.
5 Luis de Castro (Ep 1931 n3) was Schets' agent in London responsible for the
   collection and remittance of Erasmus' revenues, including those from William
   Warham, archbishop of Canterbury
6 Unidentified; cf Ep 2358:3–4.
7 See Ep 1800, the dedication to John III of Portugal of the *Chrysostomi lucubrationes* (1527).
8 See Ep 1800 introduction, and lines 20–3 with n2, 40–2 with n7.
9 See Ep 1841.
10 The Portuguese. This was a barb usually aimed at Spain; see Epp 798:24–5,
    1039:47–9.
11 In the new, more complete Latin edition of Chrysostom; see Ep 2359.
12 See Ep 2371:24–6, and cf Ep 2360 n5.

Ep 318. This is Erasmus' last letter to him; he died on 22 December 1530. Cf Ep 2493, which is Erasmus' memorial to him.

TO WILLIBALD PIRCKHEIMER

Cordial greetings. Up to now I have been pitilessly tortured by doctors and surgeons and I am still not fully recovered.[1] And yet I am making preparations to escape with no sight of any safe and tranquil haven.[2] What deters me from going to Italy is the long and dangerous journey.[3] In France it seems that I am rid of the likes of Béda,[4] but I am afraid that the flames of war will extend even there; what is more, I hardly dare to hope that Brabant will be free of warfare. War is already blazing in Friesland.[5] I suspect that in accordance with the terms of the treaty the French will invade neighbouring Switzerland if the Swiss are not willing to desist from heresy. The king has already warned them, and 'to prayers adds threats in kingly style.'[6] The emperor seems obliged to do whatever the pope prescribes;[7] this religious obedience of the best of princes causes great harm to the Florentines,[8] and I am afraid it may have the same effect in Germany. The principal actors in the

* * * * *

2371
1 See Ep 2360 n1.
2 See Ep 2360 n5.
3 Cf Ep 2366 n11.
4 Since the last exchange of pamphlets (February–March 1529) between Erasmus and his implacable French antagonist Noël Béda, syndic of the Paris faculty of theology, silence had prevailed on both sides. But the ancient quarrel would flare up one last time in 1531–2; see Ep 2213 n8.
5 See Ep 2366:16–18.
6 Ovid *Metamorphoses* 2.397. The source of this ill-founded suspicion is not clear. It is known that in 1530 Margaret of Austria, regent of the Netherlands and co-negotiator (with Louise of Savoy) of the 'Ladies Peace' of Cambrai (Ep 2207 n5), tried to bring about an alliance between Francis I and Charles V aimed at cooperation against the Turks as well as the Protestants in Switzerland and Germany. See Francis Decrue de Stoutz *Anne de Montmorency* (Paris 1885) 174–5. So Erasmus may well have heard rumours that Francis had some formal obligation to take up arms against the Swiss Protestants. Francis, however, was interested above all in the political and military support of the Swiss (and German) Protestants against the common Hapsburg foe. Consequently, far from making war on them, he had no compunction about entering into alliance with them (even while persecuting heretics at home in France).
7 See Ep 2366 n7.
8 See Ep 2366 n11.

diet are Johannes Fabri and Eck.[9] The bishop of Seville is present,[10] a severe   15
man, they say, but he did a good service to me in the tumult stirred up by the
Spanish monks.[11] There is another man of Spanish origin there, by profession
a theologian at the Sorbonne,[12] a brother of the Dominican who was the standard-bearer against me among the Spaniards.[13] There is a Franciscan present,
a preacher for the emperor, who has it in for me.[14] Eck, in a move I never   20
expected, included some of my opinions in his list of heresies, except that
he says 'someone' instead of Erasmus.[15] He says things against you, and by
name, mindful of his old hatred.[16] I have been invited to Augsburg in many
letters, but not yet in the name of the emperor.[17] I had decided to travel to
Brabant for the current fair. But Fabri and the bishop of Constance persuade   25
me not to make a move before the outcome of the diet is known.[18] But by that
time perhaps it will be too late to plan my escape, once war has broken out
and winter approaches.

A certain Gerard of Nijmegen, an exile from Brabant, who from a
close friend has become a deadly enemy, has staged a new melodrama in   30
Strasbourg; he is a scoundrel born for rebellion. He is the one with the fictitious name 'Vulturius.'[19] My little pamphlets will tell you what he is up

* * * * *

9 See Ep 2357 n1.
10 Alonso Manrique de Lara (Ep 1748)
11 Ep 1879
12 Francisco de Vitoria (Epp 1836 n9, 1909). By 'Sorbonne' Erasmus means the
   faculty of theology, not the Collège de Sorbonne.
13 Pedro de Vitoria (Ep 1902:93–7)
14 Nothing is known of a Franciscan preacher to the emperor who 'had it in' for
   Erasmus. But the Franciscan Medardus, court preacher to King Ferdinand,
   was vehemently hostile to Erasmus and made his views known at the diet; see
   Ep 2408 n3. At this stage Erasmus may have been misinformed about whose
   preacher Medardus was.
15 See Ep 2365 n5.
16 Pirckheimer (his name spelled three different ways) appears in Eck's *Articles*
   (nos 236, 245–6), accused of denying transubstantiation as well as of objecting
   to the reservation of the host and of carrying it about in procession. The 'old
   hatred' goes back to 1520, when Eck, suspecting that Pirckheimer was the author of the lampoon *Eckius dedolatus*, added his name to the bull *Exsurge domine*,
   which condemned Luther and his followers; see Ep 1182 n2.
17 See Ep 2353A:44–5.
18 Presumably in letters no longer extant written from the diet: cf Ep 2360 n5.
   On Balthasar Merklin, bishop of Constance, see Epp 1382 n8 and Ep 2123
   introduction.
19 It was Erasmus who gave him this 'fictitious' name; see Ep 2358:14–19.

to.[20] The book that appeared under the name of the Ministers of the Word at Strasbourg is said to have been written by Bucer, with Geldenhouwer's help.[21] I have never seen anything more seditious or more fabricated. Alberto   35
Pio, too, has again written a huge volume against me through some hired men, excerpting passages from the works of Erasmus that are susceptible of calumny. Aleandro is living in Venice, and it is said that he meticulously reads through all my works. He does this, I suspect, in order to supply Alberto Pio with material for calumny.[22] 'There is great accord among the   40
cowardly.'[23] Brabant has its Frans Titelmans, a talkative and boastful young man.[24] In Spain Carvajal, a member of the same club, rages like a gladiator.[25] But from now on I shall remain mute to this rabble.

I acknowledge my boorishness, my excellent Willibald, in not returning any good service to you in response to your unstinting liberality. I should   45
have sent you the works of Augustine,[26] but at that moment it did not occur to me. I have requested now that they send you Chrysostom.[27] If you have anything of his that you have translated I ask that you share it with me.[28] We have his commentaries on the Epistle to the Romans, but those to whom we commissioned the translation have hoodwinked us. We shall see to it that   50
these are added by Easter. Giambattista Egnazio has given us some hope also.[29] I wish you the best of health, you, a man most worthy of immortality.

Given at Freiburg, 29 August 1530

You will recognize Erasmus' hand.

To the most distinguished Master Willibald Pirckheimer, councillor of   55
his Majesty.

* * * * *

20 Presumably the *Epistola contra pseudevangelicos* (Ep 2219 n5) and the *Epistola ad fratres Inferioris Germaniae*, which was at this moment in process of publication; see Ep 2324 n2.
21 See Ep 2358:19–20 with n9.
22 For Pio's volume and Aleandro's alleged role in its composition, see Epp 2329:103–4, 2375:74–82, 2379:102–12, 2411:32–5, 50–1, 2414:5–20.
23 Juvenal 2.47
24 Epp 1823, 2206
25 See Ep 2110 n10. The 'same club' is the Franciscan order.
26 Ep 2157
27 Ep 2359
28 This reiterates a request made in 1525 but without result; see Ep 1558:299–300.
29 See Epp 2258 from Levinus Ammonius lines 7–10 with n6, 2448 to Egnazio line 104 with n11. On the Chrysostom edition, see Ep 2359. Erasmus' hope of producing additional translations in a supplementary volume 'within a short time' (Ep 2359:69–72), here specified as by the following April, were disappointed.

2372 / From Bonifacius Amerbach   Basel, 31 August 1530

> This letter (= AK Ep 1462) was first published as Ep 63 in Burckhardt. The sur-
> viving manuscript is a much corrected autograph rough draft in the Öffentliche
> Bibliothek of the University of Basel (MS C VIa 54 20). The original date on the
> draft, 30 August 1530, was changed to 31 August (see line 21), but the reference
> in line 15 to 'yesterday' was not correspondingly adjusted.
>   The letter replies to Ep 2368; Bonifacius' reply is Ep 2378.

Cordial greetings. I have nothing to write you at the moment, most illustrious Erasmus, unless you have time to hear about the military exploits of
Oecolampadius. Recently, by order of the city council, last year's burgomaster and the tribune[1] conscripted an army of citizens who wanted to march
out to the dedication of a church in a small town of our territory, Liestal.[2] He   5
was also present on the appointed day for fear that the troupe might not include his followers. If you had been present you would have said that he was
the general of an army, because placing himself between the burgomaster
and the tribune, he followed after the troops up and down the city on horseback. And then after supper, as the burgomaster's followers paraded to the   10
sound of drums, he marched into the square at the head of the procession;
and while the Evangelical herald[3] watched the games, which continued for
most of the night, he made a conspicuous spectacle of himself, playing the
dancer on stage wearing a toga, as the saying goes.[4]

* * * * *

2372
1 The burgomaster was Adalberg Meyer (Ep 1744 n9). It is not clear whether
  'last year's' modifies 'tribune' as well as 'burgomaster.' If it does, the tribune
  (*Oberzunftmeister*) was Marx Heidelin; if not, it was Balthasar Hiltbrand. Nothing apart from the name is known of either man.
2 Then a small town 17 km south of Basel, Liestal is now the capital of the canton Basel-Landschaft (which in 1833 was separated from canton Basel-Stadt).
  According to the chronicle of Fridolin Ryff, the date of the festivities described
  was 21 August; see *Basler Chroniken* ed Wilhelm Vischer et al I (Leipzig 1872) 113.
3 Bonifacius writes 'praeco Evangelicus.' In classical Latin, the *praeco* (crier or herald) was the official who presided over games or celebrations. In later Latin the
  term could also mean town crier, mayor (burgomaster), or preacher. Elsewhere
  in the letter Bonifacius refers to the mayor as the *consul*. Here he is having fun
  at the expense of that herald of the gospel and marshal of the parade Johannes
  Oecolampadius.
4 Ie doing something contrary to all the proprieties, 'like ... a theologian talking
  nonsense'; see *Adagia* II v 28. Ryff's chronicle (see n2 above) records only that
  Oecolampadius was present at the celebration and that he preached morning

Capito arrived yesterday, but I have not yet been able to sniff out the   15
reason.[5] The news is that he is on way to Zürich with Oecolampadius.[6] Not
knowing whether you have seen it or not, I am sending you Oecolampadius'
pamphlet *What the Greeks and the Latins Thought of the Eucharist.*[7] There is reason for you to read it, if I am not mistaken.[8] I thank you with all my heart for
the *Apologia* of Zasius.[9] Farewell, most illustrious Erasmus.   20

* * * * *

and evening on the appropriate way to celebrate a church dedication, ie not
with drinking and carousing but in the fear of God and with brotherly love.
5 Wolfgang Faber Capito (Ep 459), who had come from the diet at Augsburg,
  arrived in Basel on 29 August and departed on the thirtieth, which means that
  the references in this sentence to 'yesterday' and in n6 below to 'today' are consistent with the original date of the draft, 30 August. See BAO II 478–80 (no 769).
6 A longer version of this sentence was added as a postscript to the draft and then,
  it seems, inserted into the letter sent (cf Allen's introduction and AK Ep 1462
  n3): 'Today [ie 30 August] Capito and Oecolampadius departed on horseback
  for Zürich to see Zwingli. It is uncertain what they will do. Perhaps they will
  discuss the question of the sacrament and how they can return to favour with
  Luther.' Capito and Oecolampadius had indeed departed for Zürich for the
  purpose of joining Martin Bucer in a conference (1–4 September) with Zwingli
  and his colleague Leo Jud, as well as a delegate from Bern, to explore the possibility of reconciling the positions of the Wittenberg and the Swiss theologians
  on the contentious question of the Real Presence. As the basis for discussion
  Bucer brought with him nine articles which he hoped would, if approved at the
  conference, persuade the Wittenbergers that the Swiss theologians believed in
  a presence in the sacrament that was more than merely symbolic. In meetings
  with Melanchthon in Augsburg (22–5 August) Bucer had managed with difficulty to secure Melanchthon's approval of the articles for purposes of negotiation. But the Zürichers, who resented and distrusted Luther and Melanchthon,
  rejected the articles as too susceptible to misinterpretation. See BAO II 479 n2;
  Eells 106–8; Staehelin 612–14. Bucer and Capito would eventually achieve a
  compromise with Luther and Melanchthon, the Wittenberg Concord of May
  1536, but they would never succeed in persuading their Swiss brethren (the
  successors of the deceased Zwingli and Oecolampadius) to adhere to it.
7 *Quid de Eucharistia veteres tum Graeci, tum Latini senserint dialogus in quo epistolae
  Philippi Melanchthonis & Ioannis Oecolampadii insertae* [Basel: Johann Herwagen,
  July 1530]. This was Oecolampadius' reply to Melanchthon's *Sententiae veterum
  aliquot scriptorum de coena Domini* (Wittenberg: Josef Clug 1530). Melanchthon's
  work was included in its entirety. See Staehelin 608.
8 Probably a reference to the description of Erasmus and Melanchthon in the
  work as two fine and enlightened men who have accused Oecolampadius
  of introducing new dogma; see Staehelin 608. But Erasmus would also have
  found the learned discussion of the patristic evidence for and against the Real
  Presence intrinsically interesting; cf Ep 2175:24–9.
9 See Ep 2368 n1.

In haste, Basel 31 August 1530
Sincerely, Bonifacius Amerbach

2373 / From Karel Sucket   Bourges, 31 August 1530

The autograph of this letter, first published as Ep 87 in Enthoven, is in the
Rehdiger Collection of the University Library at Wrocław (MS Rehd 254.145).
On Sucket, who was studying law with Andrea Alciati at Bourges, see Ep 2191.

Now I have learned, most celebrated Erasmus, the true meaning of the popular saying that it is a courageous spirit that brings most aid in times of difficulty.[1] For when the rumour of uncertain source had recently been spread
abroad here that you had exchanged life for death,[2] and when the monks
were chanting their triumph in stentorian tones before the victory, as the   5
proverb has it,[3] we could do nothing, acutely concerned about you as we
were, but bolster and comfort our spirits with the hope of a more favourable fortune.[4] In the meantime our sorrow was greatly increased since you
were now given the opportunity of doing something of benefit to the commonwealth, an opportunity which the ancients depicted as being bald in the   10
back of the head to signify its uncertainty and impermanence.[5] Thus we were
more than a little afraid that, afflicted by a grave illness or discouraged by
the ill will of your adversaries, you might have allowed this opportunity to
slip by, while we vainly wished that it might be offered to you again. Finally,
as our hearts, agitated by hope and fear, were swept away in various oppos-   15
ing directions, as these emotions, one after the other, cast us down, and as
we snatched at every little rumour to see what true and false reports were
circulating, behold suddenly the utmost serenity has succeeded this tempest.
    We received a letter from Wolfgang Rem,[6] a dear fellow student at one
time, in which he indicated that you are the only man in the world to whom   20

* * * * *

2373
1 *Adagia* III iv 68
2 Erasmus had already heard similar rumours from another source; see Ep
  2379:465–7.
3 *Adagia* I vii 55
4 The sudden switch from the 'I' of line 1 to the 'we' and 'our' of the rest of the
  letter suggests that Sucket is expressing the views of the entire circle around
  Alciati at Bourges.
5 The reference is to an Aesopian fable in which Opportunity is depicted with a
  long lock of hair on his forehead but bald in back. See Phaedrus 5.8.
6 For Rem, see Ep 2419.

Pope Clement and men of the opposing faction would dare to entrust and confide the task of arbitrating a settlement in the cause of the Christian faith.[7] What greater honour could have been awarded you or what greater benefit to the whole world? For while the litigants praise you as a judge, they condemn and revoke the opinion they formerly had of you, some clamouring 25 that you were a Lutheran and others that you were a papist. As a judge must be free of both hatred and friendship, so it is proper that he should not be inclined or partial to either side. By this opinion they eliminate their own aspersions as with a sponge.

It is my understanding that a proposal has been offered to you by the 30 emperor, one far inferior to your undeniably divine talents, but honorific and truly prestigious.[8] If this is so, I rejoice that this weapon has been launched against the mad clamours of the rabble. I rejoice that Christianity, shaken by the battering rams of contrary opinions, now has a champion and restorer in you. Moreover, for those who have strayed from the path of justice I pray 35 that Christ, greatest and best, will deign through your ministrations to illumine and heal their minds. It was my wish to inform you of all these things, if you don't mind.

The person who is delivering this letter to you teaches humanities here; he is very dear to us because he has the highest opinion of you and proclaims 40 it openly.[9] You may entrust everything to him with the greatest confidence. Our friend Viglius is anxiously awaiting a letter from you. He left for Paris a few days ago.[10]

Farewell, glory of letters and refuge of the Catholic faith.

Bourges, 31 August 1530   45

Your most devoted Karel Sucket

To Master Erasmus of Rotterdam, principal restorer of true theology and of all disciplines. At Freiburg

* * * * *

7 Rem may have been reporting rumours arising out of the requests from Campeggi and Gattinara for Erasmus' views on how to settle the religious dispute in Germany; see Ep 2328 n18.
8 Nothing is known of such an offer from the emperor.
9 Tentatively identified by Allen as the 'Helvetius quidam' who was teaching Greek one hour a day; see vze Ep 11.
10 Sucket's friend and fellow student Viglius Zuichemus (Ep 2210) was still in Bourges on 21 August and (according to Allen) had returned by 6 October. The August date is documented by Ep 12 in vze. The October date is perhaps confirmed by Ep 2394:133–4, where Alciati seems to speak of Viglius as though he were present in Bourges on 7 October.

2374 / From Johannes Fabri   Augsburg, 1 September 1530

The manuscript of this letter, address sheet missing, is in the Rehdiger Collection
of the University Library at Wrocław (MS Rehd 254.62). It was first published
in Horawitz IV 7–8. Erasmus' old friend Fabri, bishop of Vienna (Ep 2097), was
currently attending the imperial diet at Augsburg; cf Ep 2357 n1.

Greetings. I am astonished, most learned Erasmus, that even now you have
such fear of tumults in Germany.[1] As far as I am concerned, you should
be convinced that if anything of this sort were to be feared, I would be
more solicitous about Erasmus than about my own affairs. For not only
would I warn you in time but would advise you where you could find   5
safety, not at your expense, but at the expense of his most revered Majesty.[2]
Therefore dismiss from your mind entirely this conception of the situation
here. Be of good hope, for everything seems to give the appearance of mutual tranquillity.[3]

The Capernaites also are now beginning to return to their senses.[4] They   10
are ashamed of their temerity and impiety; indeed they are contemplating
a rebellion from the impiety of the others. Without question they are afraid

* * * * *

2374
1 Cf Ep 2360:19–22.
2 King Ferdinand
3 At the diet hopes were at this stage still alive that the negotiations under
   way between the most moderate representatives of both sides would yield a
   settlement.
4 'Capernaites' (also 'Capharnaites'), ie inhabitants of Capernaum (Capharnaum)
   who, according to John 6:51–62, took offence at Jesus' statement about eating his
   flesh and drinking his blood (cf Ep 2387:25–7). The term is here used polemic-
   ally to designate the Evangelical theologians of Strasbourg and elsewhere, who
   denied the Real Presence in both its Catholic and Lutheran forms on the ground
   that it entailed a gross, physical eating and drinking rather than a purely spiritual one. In later sixteenth-century disputes between Lutheran and Reformed
   theologians (or even among Lutherans themselves) the term was used in the
   opposite sense: advocates of a spiritual understanding of Christ's presence in
   the Lord's Supper referred to their opponents as Capernaites because of their
   insistence on the 'real' eating and drinking of Christ's body and blood with
   the bread and wine. See *The Book of Concord: The Confessions of the Evangelical
   Lutheran Church* ed Robert Kolb and Timothy J. Wengert (Minneapolis 2000) 506
   §15, 508 §41–2.

because they have a bad conscience, and they shy away from exposing themselves more openly to the view of the eagle by committing such a crime.[5]

Farewell. Augsburg, 1 September 1530   15

Yours sincerely, Fabri

2375 / To Andrzej Krzycki   Freiburg, 1 September 1530

This letter and the two that follow, all three of them first published in the *Epistolae floridae*, were written at the suggestion of Marcin Słap Dąbrówski (Ep 2351) and carried to the Frankfurt fair by Hieronymus Froben, with whom Krzysztof Szydłowiecki (Ep 2376) had made arrangements for the forwarding of 'certain pages' of Erasmus' works; see Ep 2351:110–12. For Andrzej Krzycki, bishop of Płock, see Ep 1629.

ERASMUS OF ROTTERDAM TO ANDRZEJ KRZYCKI, BISHOP OF PŁOCK, GREETING

Revered prelate, Marcin Słap, a young man of excellent morals, faithfully delivered your Excellency's letter and your book on the mass.[1] I read through the entire book, not without great profit and enjoyment. How many things   5
are contained in such a tiny volume! It counters the beliefs of heretics, it explains to us the preaching of the Lord, it illustrates the meaning of the mass, pointing out in passing things that are done which are improper to the act of sacrifice. I was pleased that you lowered the style somewhat to the common level of simple people and preferred to play the role of a bishop rather than   10
of a rhetorician. In Brabant a certain Franciscan, in a volume published a few years ago, explained the meaning of everything the priest does at the altar.[2]

* * * * *

5 Their motive appears to have been more fear than shame. Initially the Strasbourg delegation to the diet, which arrived on 26 May, included no theologians, the city's magistrates fearing that Bucer's life was too much at risk. Once it was decided that these fears were exaggerated, Bucer and Capito were dispatched to Augsburg, the former arriving on 23 June. But for three weeks thereafter they lived in secluded quarters; see Eells 99. In Ep 2392:43–61 Johann Henckel reports an example of the reluctance of Capito and Bucer to show themselves openly in Augsburg.

2375
1 The letter is not extant. The book was *De ratione et sacrificio missae* (Cracow: M. Scharffrenbergk 1528).
2 Frans Titelmans (Epp 1823, 2206) *Tractatus de expositione mysteriorum missae* (Antwerp: Vorsterman 3 October 1528).

Here two books have appeared, one by Guitmund,[3] the other by Alger,[4] each of them defending, not without success, in my opinion, the truth of the presence of the body and blood of the Lord in the Eucharist. The same printer 15 was going to print your book as well except that he was afraid that your printers would come to Frankfurt and bring their wares.

In addition, the same Marcin also brought me a ring, the gift of your Excellency.[5] I fear that from a certain exaggerated opinion he had of me he may have said something that I had not instructed him to say. I saw in it the 20 symbol of some favourable omen, and I appreciated it all the more because it inspires me to imitate you. The gold ring contained a precious stone in the shape of a heart, of a flaming red colour. What more could one ask of a Christian man than to have a heart shining with wisdom and burning with charity? I shall strive to conform to this example to the best of my ability. It 25 is something to follow such a runner even if at a great distance, if it is not possible to overtake him.

Almost all summer long I struggled with a most distressful and unrelenting illness.[6] In the months of March and April soft breezes were blowing that were unusually agreeable, but as facts proved, most harmful. They af- 30 fected many with bad health from which they found it difficult to recover.

Andrzej Zebrzydowski has reached full maturity and I have no doubt that he is perfectly aware of what he is doing, and I hope his choice of career will have good results.[7] Not all things are suitable for all temperaments, each one arrives at wisdom in his own way. The time I spent with him was very 35 pleasant. And although thirst for glory is something of a vice in a young man, yet it gives proof of a noble character and one not at all to be despaired of.

Here, unless all signs deceive me, we will see bloody tumults. The beliefs of the heretics have been made known and the Catholic answer has been made known.[8] The emperor, who in my opinion acts always according to 40

* * * * *

3 See Ep 2284 n5.
4 See Ep 2284.
5 See Ep 2174 n9.
6 See Ep 2360 n1.
7 After an extended visit to Erasmus in the spring of 1528, followed by visits to Paris, Venice, and Padua, Zebrzydowski had now returned to Poland and the ecclesiastical career that would eventually make him bishop of Cracow; see Epp 1826, 1958 n1.
8 The Lutheran *Confessio Augustana* had been read publicly in the presence of the emperor on 25 June, the Catholic *Confutatio* on 3 August.

the pope's commands,[9] does not allow anything accepted by the church to be changed. He promises, however, to rectify the vices of the leaders of both powers, and even now cities are being urged to give back what they have taken from priests and bishops.[10] In any case it was necessary that the unbridled boldness of certain irresponsible individuals be repressed. I do not think things will turn out badly if in his religious zeal the emperor carries out faithfully all that the pope commands and if the pope, on his part, does not order anything that is not in the best interests of the universal church. The number of cardinals is increasing everywhere. I do not know if I should congratulate the church on this. The ancient church, not without good reason, tried with great zeal to avoid a multitude of cardinals. There was enough pretentiousness in the house of God and more than enough men devouring abbeys, bishoprics, and high estates, without having to add today's numerous ranks. At one time cardinal was the name of an office, now it signifies a kingdom. But it is in this way, it seems, that the pope strengthens his position, and princes have illustrious servants paid by the church.[11]

As for me, I was getting ready for a trip to Brabant, but certain friends at the court of the emperor advised me not to make a move before knowing the outcome of the diet.[12] They write that there is still hope of peace.[13] But even if the Gospel did not forbid it,[14] my health does not allow me to escape in winter. Although the emperor wishes peace more than anything else, the

* * * * *

9 See Ep 2366 n7.
10 Cf Ep 2384 n9.
11 Cf Ep 2445:31–3. It was a common complaint of church reformers that the College of Cardinals was too large, its size fed more by the income derived from the cost of an appointment to it than by the needs of the church. The fifteenth-century reform councils of Constance and Basel had wanted the total number fixed at twenty-four. At this point in his reign Clement VII had created twenty-six new cardinals, and the eventual total of new appointments would be thirty-three. That brought the total membership to forty-six, an increase of one over the forty-five at the beginning of his pontificate, and a decrease of two from the forty-eight at the time of the election of Adrian VI in 1521. See Salvador Miranda 'The Cardinals of the Holy Roman Church: Consistories for the Creation of Cardinals, Clement VII' http://www2.fiu.edu/~mirandas/consistoriesxvi.htmClementVII; John Paul Adams 'Sede Vacante 1523' http://www.csun.edu/~hcfll004/SV1523.html, and 'Sede Vacante 1534' http://www.csun.edu/~hcfll004/SV1534.html.
12 See Ep 2360 n5.
13 Cf Ep 2374:8–9.
14 Matt 24:20

evangelicals seem to have long desired war. Books fly off from every quarter to the emperor and other princes making dire threats to them if they do
not quickly cease persecuting the evangelical truth. Some have depicted the
emperor in an ignominious image with seven heads,[15] but the courts sup-   65
pressed it.

Against me they rage like madmen. Six pamphlets have been published
against me,[16] but this is only light skirmishing; I expect much more atrocious
attacks. This evil is tolerable because it has a consolation joined to it: I am attacked, but by those convicted of heresy. What is harder to digest is that the   70
group I defend contains even more hostile elements. Among the Spaniards
there is a certain Franciscan of the strict observance who rants furiously;[17]
Brabant has another one very much like him, a young man of Thrasonic vainglory.[18] Alberto Pio, once prince of Carpi, who now enjoys the favour of the
king of France, not content with the book he previously published against   75
me, has prepared a second one, three times bigger than the first. Through
some hired accomplices he has seen to it that anything that might seem con-
nected with Lutheran teachings or that could be distorted into calumny
be excerpted from all my works. He harbours under his roof, they say, a
Spaniard named Sepúlveda, whose services he makes use of to polish up his   80
style. I wonder what this man has in mind, except that I suspect that he does
this at the instigation of a mitred personage with whom he has close ties.[19]
'There is great accord among cowards,' said the satirist.[20] With the Franciscan
grackles from now on I shall be mute.[21] Perhaps I'll answer Alberto.[22] With

* * * * *

15 No such image has been identified. It may have been a depiction of Charles v
   as one of the heads of the 'beast with seven heads' described in Rev 17:7–10
   (cf Rev 13:1), a murky passage often taken to be a prophecy of the seven kings
   ('five of whom have fallen') of the seven empires (reincarnations of the Roman
   Empire), the rise and fall of which will precede the Apocalypse.
16 This is an increase from the five mentioned (and accounted for) in Ep 2329:87–90.
   Cf Epp 2382:39–40, 2383:51–2.
17 Luis de Carvajal; see Ep 2110 n10.
18 Frans Titelmans; see Ep 2206 introduction. Thraso is the boastful soldier in
   Terence's *Eunuch*.
19 Juan Ginés de Sepúlveda was a Spanish scholar resident in Rome and a protégé
   of Alberto Pio. The 'mitred personage' was Girolamo Cardinal Aleandro. For
   Erasmus' suspicion that Aleandro was behind Pio's attacks on him, see Ep 2371
   n22. On the role of Sepúlveda see Epp 2261:75–7, 2328:44–6, 2329:96–8.
20 Juvenal 2.47
21 See Ep 2275.
22 *Responsio ad epistolam Alberti Pii* (Basel: Froben 1531)

people like Cousturier and Béda a truce is on.[23] There are some theologians at 85
the court of the emperor, at whose decision public affairs are being managed,
who are not very well disposed towards me. The death of Gattinara deprived
me of a very important friend.[24]

The name of pope has generated enough hatred to the present day without having to add more to it. Now that Florence has been besieged so ruthless- 90
ly and harassed so inclemently by Clement,[25] if the rumour is not unfounded,
it is incredible how much more hatred has been added. If his aim is to be
feared rather than loved and to use violence in conducting his affairs, I fear
that fear will be a bad guarantee of lasting stability. Some portion of this hatred falls upon the emperor, who if he is at fault does not err by cruelty, but by 95
obedience. The pope extorted permission from him to besiege the Florentines,
and from him he gained authorization to be lord of Hadrian's citadel;[26] and
there can be little doubt that in their very personal encounter he extracted
many other promises.[27] But I hope that the matter is being handled better than
the general rumours describe it. For my part, I conclude that God has been 100
vehemently angered by the crimes of the people in that although we have
two brothers, Charles and Ferdinand, endowed with equal love of religion
and equal clemency, yet we are afflicted by all these calamities. First a rebellion arose in Spain because of which Ferdinand was transferred to Brabant.[28]
When our region had been exhausted by so many expeditions, an enthrone- 105

* * * * *

23 The truce with both was temporary. Pierre Cousturier (Ep 2082 n24) would
   return to the attack in 1531 and again in 1534. The final exchange with Béda
   (Ep 2082 n56) would come in 1531–2.
24 The imperial chancellor Mercurino Gattinara (Epp 1150, 1643, 2013) died in
   Innsbruck on 5 June 1530, on his way to Augsburg with the emperor to attend
   the diet.
25 See Ep 2366 n11.
26 In December 1527, after Pope Clement agreed to pay substantial sums of money
   to the emperor's forces, and after he handed over several cardinals as hostages
   to guarantee payment, the emperor restored control of the Castel Sant' Angelo
   (Hadrian's Tomb) to the pope and withdrew his troops from it; see Pastor 9
   463–6.
27 The reference here is to the negotiations between emperor and pope in Bologna
   in 1529, preceding the emperor's coronation by the pope and his departure for
   Germany; see Ep 2240 n8.
28 Ferdinand, who had been born and raised in Spain and was popular there, was
   sent to the Netherlands in May 1518, lest he become the focus of an aristocratic
   rebellion against his brother Charles, who, with his mostly Burgundian ministers, was viewed as a foreign oppressor; see Roger Bigelow Merriman *The Rise
   of the Spanish Empire in the Old World and in the New* 4 vols (New York 1918–34)

ment, processions, marriages, and the exaction of taxes, 'empire' was added, a
name bought at a great price but which yields very little.[29] Then for how many
years has France been mercilessly ravaged! How Italy has been almost completely ruined![30] Now unless God avert it, it remains for Germany to tear itself
apart in mutual slaughter. Everyone knows what Hungry and Austria have   110
suffered at the hands of the Turk;[31] what they have yet to suffer is uncertain.
Why should I now mention the mad revolts of the peasants?[32] Why the names
of countless diseases and epidemics, or more precisely, new ones that still do
not have a name?[33] Why mention the great lack or high price of things necessary for life? And yet I am inclined to believe that the first place among these   115
evils belongs to the dissensions brought about by heresy. So many evils under
the best of princes! But God will put an end to these also if we bid a lasting

* * * * *

III 17–18. Actual rebellion against the rule of Charles in Spain did not begin
   until later: in Castile (revolt of the Comuneros, 1520–2) and in Aragon (insur-
   rection of the Germanías, 1519–23).
29 The process of securing the election of Charles of Hapsburg as Holy Roman
   Emperor in 1519 was long, complicated, and very expensive. But the title of
   emperor, prestigious as it was, brought with it no reliable revenues and little
   real political power, which was mostly in the hands of the princes of the major
   imperial territories.
30 In the wars between Charles v and Francis I, fought mostly in Italy, that had
   come to a temporary halt with the Peace of Cambrai in August 1529.
31 In August 1526, four years of Turkish advance through central Europe into
   Hungary came to a conclusion at the battle of Mohács, in which the Hungarian
   army was annihilated and King Louis II, the brother-in-law of Charles v and
   Ferdinand of Austria, lost his life. Ferdinand claimed the succession to Louis
   as king of Bohemia and Hungary, but in Hungary he faced a serious rival in
   John Zápolyai. In the summer of 1527 Ferdinand invaded Hungary, defeating
   John's armies and forcing him to flee to Poland in March 1528. In despera-
   tion, Zápolyai turned to Sultan Suleiman I, who accepted him as his vassal
   and recognized him as king of Hungary. Launching an invasion of Hungary
   in May 1529, Suleiman captured Buda in early September and restored John to
   his throne. Continuing his advance westward, Suleiman laid siege to Vienna
   on 20 September, but on 15–16 October had to raise the siege and withdraw.
   Ferdinand was left in control of 'Royal Hungary,' which constituted approxi-
   mately thirty per cent of what had been the late-medieval kingdom of Hungary.
   Sporadic fighting continued in the year 1530 and was much on everyone's mind
   at the Diet of Augsburg. Cf Epp 2384 n10, 2396, 2399.
32 The great Peasants' Revolt of 1524–5
33 Cf Ep 2209:110–94, where Erasmus discourses at length on the 'English sweat,'
   which had recently spread to the continent, and the disease that was still 'without a name' (syphilis).

farewell to these vices and take refuge in his mercy. I pray that your reverend
Eminence may receive every blessing and happiness.

Given at Freiburg im Breisgau, 1 September 1530   120

2376 / To Krzysztof Szydłowiecki   Freiburg, 2 September 1530

On the circumstances and the first publication of this letter, see Ep 2375 introduction. Krzysztof Szydłowiecki (Ep 1593) was grand chancellor to King
Sigismund I of Poland and a generous patron of artists and scholars.

ERASMUS OF ROTTERDAM TO KRZYSZTOF, CHANCELLOR OF POLAND,
GREETING

Most illustrious sir, on his return here Marcin Słap of Dąbrówka[1] – a young
man so dear to me for many reasons and so devoted to me that he could not
have shown greater affection for me, nor could I have desired more friendly   5
offices from him, if he had been my son – made me feel the absence of a letter
from you less poignantly, so meticulously did he describe your unwavering
devotion towards me. From this it is clear to me that you nurture an extraordinary friendship for me, born of deep sincerity and sure judgment. For what
is feigned cannot bear the test of time, and sentiments that do not proceed   10
from sound judgment are not lasting.

I have been struggling with a most persistent illness for four full months.[2]
Intestinal spasms were followed by an abscess, and after I was almost killed
by physicians, a surgeon submitted me to even crueler torture. But thanks to
Christ I am recovering little by little and returning to my studies.   15

I am aware and mindful, excellent sir, of how much I owe to the king's
kindness and your own.[3] I am ready and willing to do whatever you ordain.
If you think that I can do something that will not be displeasing to the heart
of the king, you will do me a great service if you let it be known to me.

Here we are awaiting for a long time now what the deliberations of   20
princes will bring us.[4] The emperor, as he is a man endowed with unusual
religious sentiments, seems ready to do whatever the pope prescribes.[5] All

* * * * *

2376
1 See Ep 2351.
2 See Ep 2360 n1.
3 See Epp 1952:25–38, 2034:93–6.
4 At the Diet of Augsburg, which had been in session since 20 June and would
  continue until 19 November.
5 Cf Ep 2366 n7.

is well if the pope does not order anything but what is pleasing to Christ. I
think that, taking all into account, this will come about if only we deserve it.
May the Lord prosper all your undertakings, since you are a man born for   25
the good of all.

Given at Freiburg, 2 September 1530

2377 / To Piotr Tomicki   Freiburg, 2 September 1530

> On the circumstances and the first publication of this letter, see Ep 2375 intro-
> duction. For Piotr Tomicki, bishop of Cracow, see Ep 1919 introduction.

ERASMUS OF ROTTERDAM TO PIOTR TOMICKI, BISHOP OF CRACOW,
GREETING

Your letter cheered my spirits, reverend prelate, informing me that your reverend Eminence is alive and well and is mindful of me and, lastly, is gratified
at my eager wish to dedicate my Seneca to you.[1] But this joy was tempered   5
by Słap's report that you have not fully recovered from a long and dangerous illness.[2] However, I await more favourable news from future letters from
my friends.

During the spring months remarkably soft breezes were blowing here
but they were pernicious. They produce a feeling of languor in many, not so   10
much oppressive as persistent. In my case they nearly killed me with stomach pains. An abscess in the umbilical region followed on this long period of
excruciating pain. The treatment of doctors had bad results, but the assiduity of the surgeon made it worse. Instead of applying moderately cold compresses to break up the hardened abscess, he so scorched me with red-hot   15
compresses that my flesh seemed roasted. After four months I have scarcely
begun to come back to life and right up to this day I feel my feeble strength
increasing little by little.[3]

This summer, therefore, proved almost sterile for me save that I am
struggling against the False Evangelicals in one little book[4] and I have   20
published Chrysostom with the same careful attention that I dedicated to

* * * * *

2377
1 The letter is not extant; cf Ep 2351 n16. For the dedication of the Froben Seneca
   to Tomicki, see Ep 2091.
2 See Ep 2351:99.
3 See Ep 2360 n1.
4 On the 'False Evangelicals' see Ep 2219 n5. The 'little book' currently in preparation was the *Epistola ad fratres Inferioris Germaniae*. Apparently finished in
   draft by late May 1530, it was published in September (Ep 2324 n2).

Augustine,[5] adding to the edition many things that were never published previously, like commentaries on the two epistles to the Corinthians, and other things.[6] If it is my luck to pass a tranquil winter I shall publish something suitable for the promotion of studies.[7]   25

Marcin Słap has constantly shown such devotion towards me that if he had been born of me I could not desire more affection in a son: a natural disposition that is reserved, tranquil, patient, affectionate, faithful, modest.[8] I do not know his family background, but would that the wives of princes would always give birth to such children! Unless I am totally in error, he will one   30 day provide your Poland with a man of eminent worth. I thought I should write this so that, if the opportunity is given, your Eminence may advance his interests. And if your Eminence should ever wish any services from me I am at your command and pray that every success attend you.

Given at Freiburg im Breisgau, 2 September in the year 1530   35

2378 / To Bonifacius Amerbach   [Freiburg, September 1530]

This letter (= AK Ep 1468) was first published in the *Epistolae familiares*. The autograph is in the Öffentliche Bibliothek of the University of Basel (MS AN III 15 22). Since the letter clearly answers Ep 2372 of 31 August, Allen placed it in early September. To the new copy of Ep 2329 that was included with this letter (line 9) Alciati replied on 7 October (Ep 2394).

Cordial greetings. If your exceptional wisdom were not well known to me, I would counsel you to check the freedom of your tongue, if indeed you speak there as you write to me.[1] It is not yet clear where the situation is heading.[2] Some hope appears, not of peace, but of avoiding war. Eck has perpetrated a crime worthy of himself at Augsburg.[3] I wish you and yours the best of health.   5

* * * * *

5 See Ep 2359.
6 See Ep 2359:49–68.
7 Among the projects already under way at this point was *Apophthegmata* (Ep 2431), and the *Enarratio psalmi 33* (Ep 2428) would soon follow; both would be published in March 1531.
8 Cf Ep 2376:3–6.

2378
1 See Ep 2372:1–14.
2 Ie the situation at the Diet of Augsburg
3 See Ep 2365 n5.

My servant Quirinus substituted the name of Melchior for that of Meltinger.[4] He is certainly an intelligent fellow, but not all the time. I am waiting to see how my book will be received.[5] Once again I wish you good health.

I am sending another copy of the letter to Alciati because, as I understand it, the previous one did not reach him. Please make certain that he receives it.

You will recognize the hand of your friend.

To the most distinguished Master Bonifacius Amerbach. At Basel

2379 / To Germain de Brie   Freiburg, 5 September 1530

First published in the *Epistolae floridae*, this is Erasmus' reply to Ep 2340. Brie's response to this letter is Ep 2405.

ERASMUS OF ROTTERDAM TO GERMAIN DE BRIE, GREETING
I received your letter of 6 July, most learned Brie, on 4 September; therefore do not complain that you have received no answer until now. Another reason for my slowness in writing is that you are putting on a sort of travelling show, now the city dweller, now the countryman, now the courtier.[1]

May all the saints above protect your bishop of Verona, who looks after the commonweal from his own resources and provides such great benefits to men of learning at his own expense.[2] Would that our opulent abbots and bishops would emulate this example! I suspect it was he who once served as papal datary under Pope Clement and did me the honour of writing several letters to me, in which one could discern the distinct nobility of the man and his prudence, joined with an exceptional kindness. His name, if I am not mistaken, is Gian Matteo Giberti.[3] I have tried to prevail upon the administrators of the Aldine press, but in vain. I have often negotiated with

* * * * *

4 For Quirinus Talesius, see Ep 2367 n3; for Heinrich Meltinger, former burgomaster of Basel, see Ep 2112 n17.
5 The *Epistola ad fratres Inferioris Germaniae* (Ep 2371 n20).

2379
1 Brie, almoner to the king and secretary to the queen, owned houses in Paris and had a favourite country retreat at Gentilly. Erasmus appears to have been unsure where a letter would find him.
2 The reference is to the (never completed) Greek edition of Chrysostom organized and financed by Matteo Giberti, bishop of Verona; see Ep 2340:2–12.
3 See Ep 1443A introduction, and cf Epp 1509, 1650A.

Froben concerning the same matter, but thus far I have told a story to the 15
deaf.[4] Wherefore I rejoice all the more that God has inspired this purpose in
an excellent man and through him has granted our prayers. The Latin translation of Chrysostom issued from the Froben press some time ago now.[5] If
the Greek text must be printed again, as you indicate, I fear that will make
us suffer a much longer wait. You know that for an ardent desire any delay 20
is long.

As to your excuse that a lack of manuscripts prevented you from undertaking the translation of some portion of Chrysostom, copies would
not have been lacking, my dear Brie, if you had given some indication
that you were not averse to this task.[6] At all events, I had duplicate cop- 25
ies of the Commentary on the Epistle to the Romans, and one copy of the
Commentary on the First Epistle to the Corinthians, part of which was translated by Francesco Aretino.[7] But when I seemed to perceive that you did not
have much enthusiasm for this assignment, and when in addition I took into
consideration your congenital slowness (or perhaps as you prefer to call it, 30
your 'meticulousness'), and furthermore that the many presses of the Froben
firm were occupied with the production of a great number of volumes, I sent
the Commentary on the Epistle to the Romans to Brabant, where there are
several men equal to the task, but they are more interested in enjoying themselves than in doing a respectable job. And so those to whom we entrusted 35
the work deceived us and finally returned the Greek manuscript to us after
six months;[8] otherwise I would have taken a part of the task upon myself at
the urgent insistence of Froben.

* * * * *

4 *Adagia* I iv 87
5 See Ep 2359.
6 For the Froben edition of Chrysostom in Latin, Erasmus had been able to use
  only two translations by Brie: *De sacerdotio* and *Babylas*, both of which had been
  printed before (Ep 2359:54–6). Brie had promised a translation of *Monachus*, but
  Erasmus had been compelled to substitute for it one by Oecolampadius (see lines
  79–80 below). Earlier, in two letters that are no longer extant (see Ep 2405:99–107),
  Erasmus had asked Brie to translate Chrysostom's Homilies on Romans, and
  with one of the letters he sent the Greek text in manuscript. Brie, however, found
  both the manuscript and the available print edition unsatisfactory. An attempt to
  have the work translated by others failed (see lines 28–38 below), with the result
  that the work had to be omitted from the Latin Chrysostom (see lines 39–42 below). In 1533 Brie published with Froben the first eight of the homilies in Latin
  and Greek.
7 See Epp 2258:7–10 (Romans), 2226:75–6 (Corinthians).
8 See Epp 2258 n6, 2371:47–50.

It is commonly said that there is nothing more damaging than a false hope. At any rate this hope has brought it about that this part of Chrysostom 40 also will not appear in time for the spring fair and has put me in mind of the story of the lark.[9] I would have preferred to assume twice as much work on authentic manuscripts. Since that was not possible, I began to translate some homilies on the Second Epistle to the Corinthians, but the further I advanced the more it disgusted me to expend labour on inauthentic texts. I willingly 45 handed on the torch to another,[10] although he does not seem to have detected the very different quality of these texts, or he certainly conceals it very well. On top of that, at the invitation of the reverend Father Cuthbert Tunstall, now bishop of Durham, I took up again the Commentary on the Acts of the Apostles, to finish what was left incomplete, placing more trust in his judg- 50 ment than mine.[11] But the same dislike that I felt previously caused me to desist from the undertaking.[12] In addition, I had shown you where you could get the Greek manuscripts even if I did not send you anything. But to one who has distaste for something, any excuse for doing nothing is valid.

Even if Chrysostom is published in Greek, which for some reason I still 55 do not dare hope, there is no reason why that should make you more disinclined to translate him, since you would undertake this task not for your own sake but rather out of regard for the public interest. I think the Latin edition would sell better if the Greek were published. For you know that there are few people, especially among the theologians – and it is for them most 60 of all that this work is being prepared – who are so proficient in the Greek language that they do not prefer Latin, especially when they are in a hurry. It will be gratifying to them, therefore, to consult the Greek if they encounter some corrupt passage or one that is not faithfully translated. It is generally admitted that many of this man's works have been translated by those who 65 were not sufficiently skilled in either Greek or Latin. It would be a useful

* * * * *

9 The reference is to Aesop's fable 'The Lark and her Young Ones' (Aulus Gellius Noctes Atticae 2.29), in which young larks, knowing that the harvest is near, ask their mother when they should seek safety by leaving the farmer's field. She tells them that they are safe as long as the farmer depends on his friends to help him with the harvest, but that when he no longer trusts his friends and decides to do the work himself, they should be off.

10 'Lampadem alteri lubens tradidi.' With these words Erasmus appears to be punning with the word for torch (lampada) and the name Oecolampadius; see Ep 2359:66–7 with n14.

11 See Ep 2226:63–5.

12 See Epp 1801, 2263:36–40, 2359:66–8 with n16.

endeavour even if we sought no other advantage than practising our literary talent and style in this type of work, although in my case it is too late to exert myself in these exercises, and you perhaps would more willingly be engaged in any other subject.   70

We encountered at Basel a man of exquisite learning and equal modesty, Simon Grynaeus, to whom we delegated a part of the project.[13] He is learned in every respect, but I do not know if he is equally well trained in the sacred authors. Besides, Froben was looking not so much for learning as for reputation. The name of Germain de Brie is already an illustrious one and of   75 itself commends the book to the reader. A writer who enjoys popularity is a great attraction. Oecolampadius did not refuse to undertake the task, but with many people this name turns away the buyer, even at a good price.[14]

De monacho is of no great importance except that the printer, whose goal is profit, wanted to include as little as possible of Oecolampadius in it.[15]   80 Polidoro had translated this little work quite skilfully.[16] You cast the blame for the delay on one of my couriers, I do not know which one.[17] Were you expecting that for two pages we would send an emissary to France? How could we send one if we did not know whether you had translated it or not, or where you were? For you had indicated that you would be absent from   85 Paris for quite a long time and quite far away. And what about my having specified the way in which we could contact each other quickly if any serious matter came up? Four little crowns will always be enough to procure a messenger and I would pay half the price. The other half would be no burden to you, especially since I hear, and this gives me great pleasure, that you are   90 not suffering financially, but have ample resources, which permit you also to be generous. A letter that Budé sent to you reveals that in the organization of banquets you are a veritable Lucullus.[18] As for me, a man of slender means

* * * * *

13 See Ep 2359:61–2.
14 For fear that Oecolampadius' name would inhibit sales; see Ep 2359 introduction.
15 Erasmus had asked for Brie's translation of it, but it was so long in coming that Froben had to fall back on that by Oecolampadius; see Ep 2291:5–6.
16 Polidoro Virgilio, court historian to Henry VIII, had dedicated his translation, *De monarcho regis et monachi*, to Erasmus; see Epp 2019, 2311:1–10.
17 See Ep 2340:22–5.
18 The letter, dated 5 April 1520, is Ep 65 in *Répertoire analytique et chronologique de la correspondence de Guillaume Budé* ed Louis Delaruelle (Toulouse / Paris 1907). Lucius Licinius Lucullus (b c 115 BC) was a famous Roman general, scholar, and *bon vivant*, whose lavish entertainments gave rise to the proverbial expression 'a Lucullan feast.'

in comparison with you, I cannot get away without spending about sixty
crowns every year for messengers and couriers.[19]   95
    Concerning the cardinal chancellor,[20] I do not know yet whether I made
a correct prognosis; in any case he never gave any indication of a less than
friendly attitude towards me. He was merely rather unresponsive to Froben's
request, which I supported in a letter, but more in compliance to a friend than
of my own accord, and in such a way as to make it clear that it was not a mat-   100
ter that pertained to me.[21]
    Nor is it sufficiently clear to which foreigner each of us is referring.[22]
The one who attracted suspicion told me in Louvain that his dispute with
Budé was so bitter that it almost came to drawn daggers.[23] What sense does
it make, then, that he should be so concerned about Budé's reputation unless,   105
perhaps, wishing to return to favour with Budé, he wanted to make Budé
indebted to him by this service, or he did this with the perverse desire to set
us against each other and thus profit from the harm we would inflict upon
each other? This stratagem is not incompatible with his natural disposition.[24]
I have no doubt that this same person both arouses animosity against me in   110
Alberto Pio and provides him with ammunition.[25] They say that in Venice he
reads assiduously whatever I write.[26]

              * * * * *

19 Presumably the French écu au soleil (crown), which was valued in 1530 at 76d
   groot Flemish, so that 60 crowns were equivalent to just under two years' wages (at 253 days per year) of an Antwerp master mason/carpenter at 9.05d per
   day (CWE 12 650 Table 3, 691 Table 13).
20 Antoine du Prat, chancellor of France (Ep 2038 n15)
21 The request was for a royal privilege; see Ep 2291:22–6.
22 See Ep 2340:42–5, where the reference is to a 'foreign people,' the Italians. In
   what follows here, Erasmus specifies as 'the one who aroused suspicion' an
   individual Italian currently living in Venice and an ally of Alberto Pio. This fits
   Girolamo Aleandro (Ep 2371 n22) nicely. But there is no evidence for the further
   claim that Aleandro and Budé had ever had a bitter quarrel or that Aleandro
   had any interest in stirring up trouble between Erasmus and Budé, particularly
   over the 'trivial matters' described in lines 113–24 below.
23 This would have had to be in October 1521; see Ep 1233 n28.
24 If, as seems certain, Erasmus is referring to Aleandro, this is yet another instance of his tendency to perceive his one-time friend as the evil genius behind
   every example of hostility that could not otherwise be explained.
25 For Erasmus' long-standing conviction that Aleando and Pio were in collusion
   against him, see Ep 1987 introduction.
26 Aleandro, who had been lucky enough to be absent from Rome at the time of its
   sacking in 1527, resided at Venice in 1529–30.

But, I ask you, by what stratagems did that *Italiotes* stir up such a tempest?[27] He drew attention to some passages in my works. Which ones? The ones that criticized Budé? I never make mention of that man except in the 115 most honourable terms (and I do so frequently). But he pointed out a passage in the *Colloquies* where I have someone or other say, 'The French like what costs little'; then those passages where, on occasion, I report what Hilary and Jerome passed on concerning the character of the ancient Gauls, and other trivial matters; this was the deadliest accusation of all.[28] Which do you 120 prefer to think, my dear Germain: that these are matters of no importance, or that Budé is so lacking in loyalty and decency that he would not only undo but break off a long-standing friendship and assume a hostile attitude because of trifles of this sort? Only a heinous crime could destroy a pact entered into under the auspices of the Muses. Or shall we fall back on my nam- 125 ing of Budé and Bade on the same page?[29] It is no surprise that you rejected this argument, but it is surprising that it should occur to anyone to propose such frivolous trash. So whence came that portentous storm that stirred up more than Tyrian seas, as the saying goes?[30] What Aeolus unleashed such violent winds, which 'As if in armed array / where passage is given' rushing 130 forth, 'East wind and North and South, rich in storms, / Hovered over the sea and churned it up from the very bottom. / There followed the cries of men' etc.[31] Whence came this Typhonic whirlwind, ripping the sails, tearing apart the ropes, shattering the yardarms and the masts?[32] Whence came these immense waves, rushing one close upon the other, threatening everyone with 135 certain doom? For it must have been a tremendous storm that wrested from your hands, vigilant pilot that you are, both rudder and ropes, so that you barely arrived at your destination by an indirect route. What I particularly enjoyed in your letter, my dear Germain, was your natural tendency to

* * * * *

27 In ancient Greek *Italiotes* (Ἰταλιώτης) was the word for a Greek living in southern Italy (*Italikos* was the ordinary word for an Italian). The use of *Italiotes* here is evidently intended to be derogatory: perhaps a somewhat laboured swipe at Aleandro, an Italian who had won fame as a Greek scholar and then acquired from the pope an archdiocese (Brindisi) in southern Italy.
28 See Ep 2261:58–69.
29 See Ep 2021 introduction.
30 *Adagia* IV iv 73. 'Tyrian seas' was 'said proverbially about a situation that was very turbulent and fraught with danger' (CWE 36 110).
31 Virgil *Aeneid* 2.82–7 (freely cited). Aeolus was the god of winds.
32 Typhon, the most deadly monster of Greek mythology, was (among other things) the father of dangerous storms and winds.

exaggerate. But when I compare the grandiloquence of your words with the   140
subject matter, I can hardly restrain my laughter, and I seem to be reading
something that is not far removed from *The Battle of the Frogs and the Mice*.[33]
Can such whirlwinds, such tempests in human affairs, take rise from such
empty bombast?

What you write concerning Toussain was very gratifying to me because   145
it reveals your kindly and peace-loving nature.[34] But there was no need for
these words as far as I am concerned, since all those verses were uttered spontaneously, save that while counselling forgetfulness you recalled the concept
of remembrance and revived painful memories.[35] There was never any close
familiarity between Toussain and me, and neither of us had any personal   150
obligation to the other for some good service rendered, except that I wished
him well as a man of learning who zealously promoted the study of good
letters. Since in this he is not satisfied to equal himself but surpasses himself
each day, it is natural that my good will towards him should also grow in
intensity. Proof that I have no inclination to get involved in disputes is that,   155
far from thanking friends who wrote to me about rumours and suspicions of
this kind, I thought they should be reprimanded for reporting to me the gos-
sip of the rabble-rousers and the nonsense of the schoolmasters, which serve
no purpose but to create and nourish discord. I excused Toussain for having
alluded to me in an unfriendly manner, as it seemed to the hearers, in a pub-   160
lic lecture. Likewise I testified that as far as Budé is concerned I could never
allow any suspicion to enter my heart that would be unworthy of a man of
such steadfastness, honour, and learning, in a word, Budé. What more can I
say? My letters to them are of such a nature that some among them, taking
offence, seem to abstain from the duty of writing altogether. Far be it from   165
me to implore the help of someone to engage in the sport of writing abusive
verses in answer to theirs – not that there were lacking those who were both
able and willing to do so. He is truly a lover of peace who removes from his
eyes and ears anything that can diminish good will.

* * * * *

33 A mock epic from the late Hellenistic period, parodying the *Iliad*. The title,
   Batrachomyomachia, which Erasmus gives in Greek, has come to mean a silly
   altercation.
34 Brie had come to the defence of Jacques Toussain, who in 1528 circulated a
   couplet defending the reputation of Guillaume Budé as a Latin stylist against
   Erasmus' perceived criticism of it in the *Ciceronianus*. See Ep 2340:28–41, 63–73,
   98–101, and cf Epp 2421, 2422:81–2.
35 Erasmus is playing on the Greek words *amnestia* 'forgetting' and *anamnesis*
   'remembering.'

I deemed that they should be discouraged from this pretence since I   170
knew much more about the secrets of this affair than many people think;
but I prefer to ignore what I know. This much I can sincerely confess: that
I expected a little more seriousness and good faith from the French literati
than those have shown who roused up the masses because Budé and Bade
were mentioned on the same page.[36] Such agitation did they stir up that the   175
noise of this panic disturbance, like that of the clanging cauldrons of Dodona,
spread through both Germanies, Brabant, Italy, and finally into the palace of
the king.[37] Certainly this was something worthy of the king's attention, that
Budé had been compared to Bade. Hither and yon these empty rumours flew
about: 'Erasmus is envious of Budé,' 'Erasmus wants to take vengeance on   180
Budé.' The French nation for a long time has had a bad reputation; they are
charged with stupidity and inconstancy. I have always tried to refute this
opinion for no other reason than that I considered it to be utterly false. But
that such inhuman outbursts over nothing at all could arise among learned
men I would not even have believed Cato.[38] What kind of example is it, no   185
doubt to please Budé, to attack in scurrilous epigrams the reputation of one
who praised and continues to praise Budé in the most affectionate and honorific terms in so many published works?[39] I could introduce here the story of
the Indian elephant who did not notice the gnats.[40] But if I reveal the names
of the versifiers to you, they would not wish to be regarded as gnats.   190

But we can pardon the common herd if they misbehaved in a public
uprising. Where were the real friends of Budé sleeping at that time, those
who could control the crude disturbances of insignificant little men? For
perhaps Budé, intent on matters of more grave concern, knew nothing of
this. Otherwise, if Budé did know about it and did nothing to prevent it,   195
with what pretext will you defend his sincerity and honesty for allowing
to be done against a friend what I did not allow to be done against Lee, an
enemy?[41] When the melodrama was at the height of its intensity in Louvain,
and in my absence my supporters mocked Lee in pamphlets and with public

* * * * *

36 See n29 above.
37 The great brass cauldrons in the oracle of Zeus at Dodona were so positioned
    that when one was struck, the reverberation caused all the others to ring out;
    see *Adagia* 1 i 7.
38 See *Adagia* iv v 61: 'Even if [the absolutely trustworthy] Cato were to say it [I
    would not believe it].'
39 For the 'scurrilous epigrams' see Ep 2027:25–8.
40 *Adagia* 1 x 66
41 On Erasmus' feud with Edward Lee in 1518–20 see Epp 765, 998, 1061.

insults, I threatened them all with my enmity if they continued to expose 200
me to hatred through their stupid behavior and obscure my victory through
their ignoble actions. I gave the order through Vives of having this letter read
publicly from the chair of the university.[42] Some persons were indignant at
this action and withdrew from my friendship. Similarly when the Germans
had sent a huge volume of letters in which Lee was castigated,[43] after reading 205
hardly one or two of the letters, I had the fascicle delivered to More to be suppressed.[44] No one was unaware of what Lee's acrimony deserved, but I preferred to take into account what befitted Erasmus. On the one hand I did this
because I did not wish to avail myself of the influence of others even against
an enemy, in which case it was an act of civility. On the other hand I did not 210
want this example of impudence to fall back upon my own head, in which
case it was an act of prudence. Now consider how differently I acted towards
Budé than Lee did towards me; and yet what I did not permit to be done to
a declared enemy, Bude's supporters thought should be done to me. Then
again when a tragic scene was staged against Maarten van Dorp,[45] against 215
whom Jérôme de Busleyden and Thomas More had written sharp attacks,[46] I
calmed the whole commotion, taking care to have those pamphlets in which
I was defended and praised to be withdrawn from publication.[47] I did the
same thing when it seemed that the controversy between you and More was

* * * * *

42 No such letter is extant, and the incident is otherwise undocumented.
43 Erasmus had a hand in provoking the outpouring of volumes of letters by
   German scholars attacking Lee. For a list of them see Ep 1083 introduction.
44 Possibly in August 1520, when he wrote in a letter to John Fisher that he wished
   the Germans would keep quiet about Lee; see Ep 1129:19–24.
45 On the controversy in 1514–16 between Erasmus and the Louvain theologian
   Maarten van Dorp, which ended with the two men being loyal friends, see
   Epp 304, 337, 347, 438.
46 No such attack by Busleyden has survived. More's was the letter to Dorp of
   21 October 1515; summary and discussion in Rummel 1 8–10. It was hardly a
   'sharp attack,' and it did much to bring Dorp back to public support of Erasmian
   scholarship.
47 Even after his reconciliation with Erasmus was known in Louvain, Dorp continued to be treated as an enemy by some of Erasmus' friends elsewhere. In
   the summer of 1519 Nicolas Bérault sent him a letter of reproach for his earlier
   opinions (Ep 994:13–15), and at the same time Wilhelm Nesen lampooned him
   as an enemy of the Muses in the Dialogue of the Two Tongues (CWE 7 341 with
   n42). Erasmus appears to have been taken by surprise by both attacks, but he
   lost no time in coming to the defence of Dorp; see Epp 1002:38–44, 1044:56–7
   with n10.

about to end up in a bitter feud.[48] I prevented the publication of whatever   220
More had written against you, even those things that had already been printed, and I begged More to confide his feelings to me in the matter.[49] Was there
really no one among Budé's many friends to extinguish the growing fire?
And yet he was the only one to be appeased. For just as a spirit of animosity has never existed in me, so I have given no exterior sign of a malevolent   225
spirit. What I conceded to Dorp, by whose pen I was repeatedly provoked,
none of you has conceded to a friend, although there was no lack of those
who were adding oil to the fire. I know for certain that if Budé has acted out
of character in any way in this affair, it was at the instigation of others. But if
they thought this courtesy should not have been granted to me, surely they   230
should have granted it to the reputation of Budé, they should have granted it
to the studies we shared in common, and, finally, they should have granted it
to themselves. What is more criminal or more lowly than this example? You
mention my loftiness of mind and the great glory accruing to my studies;
at the end you urge me to imitate Alexander the Great, who said, 'It is the   235
lot of a king to be maligned when he has acted well.'[50] You remind me that
enmities are mortal, friendships immortal; you plead with me, using many
arguments, to despise the impudence of the wicked and to recover my peace
of mind once this tempest has abated and the halcyon days have returned.

All of these things I admit you express in a learned and highly rhetori-   240
cal manner, but I do not see why it was necessary to sing me this song. I gave
no indication of being upset by such doggerel verse. Is it not sufficient contempt not even to have deigned to read them, far from preparing revenge?
What enmities do you bid me to put aside when I have not declared enmity
against anyone? If the confidence inspired by my merits or my lofty spirit,   245
comparable to that of Alexander, are no guarantee of my tolerance, then my
asinine character is. It is hard to imagine that any ass or beast of burden
could be found whose back is as hardened to the cudgel as my spirit is to this
kind of contumely. We are daily stoned by slanderous books.[51] You might call
it an evil ordained by fate. But it would be fitting that this pestilence be far   250
removed from humane studies.

* * * * *

48 See Epp 620, 1045, 1087.
49 See Epp 1093, 1096:135–8.
50 Plutarch *Alexander* 41; cited by Erasmus in the *Apophthegmata* CWE 37 357 (4.67);
    cf Epp 2340:74–6, 2421:53.
51 Cf Epp 2382:39, 2383:50–1, 2422:83–4, 2443:138–40.

Moreover, you took up Toussain's cause too late, as I said, for I had been purged of feelings of anger against him long ago. And although no pact of friendship has been made with him so far, nevertheless I do not refuse to do what you ask, if he is willing to enter anew into a contest of good will with 255 me, this time, I hope, with more good faith. I have always considered Budé an upright and kind-hearted man, and I would never have suspected anything concerning his *Commentaries*[52] if I had not been warned by the letters of friends.[53] I did not expect that he would not disagree with me in some matters, but if he were to do so without arrogance I declared that it would give 260 me great pleasure. And I am inclined to believe that it would be a mark of greater sincerity to signify his disagreement in a respectful preamble rather than demonstrate his contempt by his continued silence.

If it is permitted to pour out what is on your mind into the bosom of a friend, my dear Brie, I was born with an ingenuous disposition, which 265 has often caused me great harm. But I am not so insensitive as not to detect Budé's annoyance in his *Commentaries*, which I read, at least selectively, when they were published in Basel (I did not have the opportunity to do so previously):[54] as when he writes about those who criticize the talent and style of various writers, or those who recommend the use of forms of speech more 270 recent than those prescribed by Lorenzo Valla, or those whose writings are so watered down that they cannot bear the sun or the passage of time, and many more things of this kind. The friends will deny that the remarks were directed at me.[55] That would be more convincing if in the *De asse* Budé, whenever he felt like digressing, had not already vented his spleen with shafts 275 of this kind against others without naming names.[56] He prefers to test the guesswork of the reader rather than give the name, either because he does not think it is safe not to allow himself some room for denial or because he does not think the one he is attacking is worthy of being named. For this purpose I myself have suppressed or disguised names.[57] 280

But even conceding that Budé had the right to do this, seeing that you do not rebut the accusation but rather demand praise for his honesty,

* * * * *

52 The *Commentarii linguae Graecae*, published by Josse Bade at Paris in September 1529
53 See Ep 2027:31–3.
54 See Ep 2224 n1.
55 Erasmus is nowhere mentioned in Budé's *Commentaries*.
56 *De asse* (1515) was Budé's magisterial treatise on Roman coinage.
57 As, for example, in referring to Gerard Geldenhouwer as Vulturius Neocomus; see Ep 2358:14–15.

it would at least have been more honest and more worthy of his integrity
to remove grounds for suspicion from the reader. And it would have been
more becoming to his generosity not only not to sprinkle his *Commentaries*   285
with suggestions of his resentfulness, but also to remove all suspicion in a
clear statement, not for my benefit, but for other more unfair interpreters of
Budé's writings than I, especially since I had asked this of him by letter.[58] It
was not that I was ambitious for this little touch of glory, for I have been long
sated with fame, but because I thought that this would contribute to tranquil-   290
lity in the world of letters. I perceived what pestilence had taken hold of the
teaching of Christian philosophy. I saw that men's minds were inclined to
discord by some fatal evil. I was afraid that this contagion might spread to
humane letters, and it already seemed to be doing so, thanks to that charlatan
through whom you think Budé was moved to anger against me.[59] No one   295
had conceived this suspicion through me, since I wished to abolish it, but
they had derived it partly from Budé's letter to me (which to them seemed
somewhat contemptuous, but to me simply candid), partly from rumours
spread by him to several people. Budé did not refuse to eliminate this suspicion; he merely said that he was afraid that this was not the opportune mo-   300
ment to name me.[60] For my part, however, I often sought the opportunity to
make honourable mention of Budé in my works. But although in this work,
when explaining a single expression, he makes honourable mention of some
persons, in many passages the opportunity presented itself of mentioning
Erasmus at least in two or three words. Certainly when in his discussion of   305
the word παρηκολουθηκότι in Luke he retracts his former opinion and gives
mine, prompted, if I am not mistaken, by my *Annotations on Luke*, he had
the opportunity to mention me.[61] Again, when he explains what a colophon

* * * * *

58 Ep 1794:11–24
59 Apparently Aleandro; see lines 102–14 above.
60 The letter was Ep 1812. For the rumours and the need to eliminate suspicion,
    see lines 111–21 in that letter.
61 In his *Annotations on the Pandects* (1508) Budé included a translation of Luke 1:3 in
    which he sided with the Vulgate by rendering the difficult word παρηκολουθηκότι
    as *assecuto* 'understood.' In the first edition of his *Annotations* (1516), Erasmus
    objected that the real meaning was *persecutus* 'investigated.' Budé courteously
    acknowledged the criticism but continued to defend his original view; see Epp
    403:89–120, 441:1–16. Erasmus then had to respond to Budé's arguments in the
    next edition of the *Annotations* (1519). Returning to the matter in his *Commentaries*,
    Budé discussed it at length but without really abandoning his original position
    and without mentioning Erasmus; see page 561of the Paris edition.

is, he seems to have borrowed quite a few things from my *Adagia*[62] – not that he does not have the right to do so (it is permitted to use what is published, I admit), but if he had looked for an opportunity, there were any number freely to be had. I would even venture to say that no more convenient opportunity could present itself in any other subject. But this courtesy, small as it is, even though it was solicited in the name of humane studies, not for myself, I had already reciprocated before his work was published. I never feared any offensive abusiveness from Budé even if he had been provoked in some way. But we had to find a cure for men's suspicions. As far as I am concerned, I find nothing in his *Commentaries* that pertains to me, and yet in the meanwhile those who wish me well complain that Erasmus' reputation has been injured, and those who are prejudiced against me charge me with the things he said even in printed books, as if they were aimed at me without any mention of my name. Pierre Danès drew his attention to one passage, urging him to avoid arousing men's suspicions.[63] He adamantly refused, although amends could have been made merely by omitting a single page. What is it, therefore, that induces you to admire Budé's openness in this work? Is it that he did not attack me by name? I neither deserved this nor did I expect it from such a man. It is not good faith not to harm one who has not harmed you in any way, but it is good faith to speak in a friendly manner even of one who is not deserving of it. What difference does it make if Budé is well disposed towards me (and I am convinced of this) if his speech is so modulated that friends and enemies alike understand or at least suspect that his words are aimed at Erasmus? Consequently, if you assess the situation, there is no reason for you to proclaim Budé's good faith to such a degree in this regard. But if you turn your attention to the duplicity of the instigators who take delight in pitting scholars against one another, I confess that I recognize the good faith of a man who gives more thought to his own reputation than to their malice.

The study of the humanities also has its scourges, it cannot be denied. I have found out for myself how these instigators gave support to both sides, something of which Demosthenes was accused.[64] They liked no type of contest better than to set learned men against each other like pairs of gladiators so that they could enjoy the suffering of others. You can learn from those who are not too old that there were people in Paris who would set Fausto Andrelini

* * * * *

62 See page 430 of the Paris edition.
63 No other evidence of such an intervention by Pierre Danès (Ep 2044) has survived.
64 Plutarch *Life of Demosthenes* 15

against Tardif,[65] then against Delius,[66] or Balbi,[67] or Scopus,[68] now against
one, now against another, for the pure pleasure of watching their furious
rage. Then again you will find others so thirsty for glory that – since they can-   345
not acquire any fame in times of serenity – they do what Androcleides was
famed to have done in the Greek proverb, stir up discord.[69] Then after they
have devoted their energies to the one whom they favour, they seek double
praise, taking on the role of peacemakers, and they wish it to appear that
they have settled the disturbance of which they were the authors. I would   350
more justly be angry with such persons than with Budé, for if he fell victim
to some human error, I am one who can turn a blind eye to certain failings in
friends. But the truth is that the morals of men have so deteriorated that today a black swan or a white crow is less rare than a faithful friend; so great is
the cunning in many people of simulating and dissimulating, so great is the   355
art of deception that there is nothing genuine, everything is fraudulent. And
if you do find sincere sentiments in some people, so great is the inconstancy
of their character that you would say they were like Euripus.[70] A little bit of
jealousy is enough to discourage some people from friendship, never mind
hoping to find the sort of people who would die together with you. Others,   360

* * * * *

65 Guillaume Tardif (c 1440–c 1500) lived at Paris from about 1467 and in 1473 was
teaching at the Collège de Navarre. His quarrel was not with Fausto Andrelini
(Ep 84) but with Girolamo Balbi (Ep 23:49n), who in 1486 attacked his Latin
grammar (1470, enlarged edition c 1475) as useless and faulty. Tardif responded
with his *Antibalbica* (1487), to which Balbi replied with his *Rhetor gloriosus*. Two
further editions of Tardif's *Antibalbica* followed (1489/90, 1495).

66 A Paris acquaintance of Erasmus who called himself 'Delius Volscus' (Ep 95:24n),
which was apparently not his real name. The name Volscus may identify him
as an Italian (the Volsci were an ancient Italic people who lived in southern
Latium on the banks of the Liris).

67 A bitter rivalry developed when Balbi and Andrelini (see n65 above), as well
as a third Italian poet, Cornelio Vitelli (CWE 28 583 n640) were simultaneously
admitted to teach poetry at the University of Paris (5 September 1489). By 1493
Andrelini had managed to drive away his two rivals, and by 1496 he had established himself at the court as the poet royal.

68 Evidently the nickname of one of the humanists whom Erasmus knew at Paris;
no identification has been made; see Ep 103:2n.

69 *Adagia* II ii 91: *In seditione vel Androcleides belli ducem agit* 'In civil war even
Androcleides is a general,' said of 'mean and contemptible men' who stir up
division and discord to create for themselves the opportunity to 'rule for a
season.'

70 The tides of the strait of Euripus were proverbial for their prodigiously rapid
ebb and flow; see *Adagia* I ix 62: *Euripus homo* 'Man's a Euripus.'

because of some slight offence, turn from friends into enemies. There are those who, if you do them some kind favour, repay you with leaden thanks, and if you offend them, with leaden anger, as the playwright said.[71]

These considerations, my dear Brie, discovered through long experi- 365
ence, lead me to seek human friendships more carefully, cultivate them less diligently, and lose them with less chagrin. It is safer to rest in the friendship of Christ, who never deserts anyone he has received into his friendship. It is enough for me to exhibit this disposition to men: to wish to be helpful to everyone, to do harm to no one, as far as in me lies, not to spurn the friendship of good men, nor to give anyone good reason to withdraw from friendship 370
with me, nor to be tormented if someone parts company with me through no fault of my own. It is a slight loss if he who was never a true friend should cease to be a friend. I would more rightfully be indignant with such friends than with Budé. But while I continue to take everything in good part and be true to myself, what praise will I earn, I ask you? To those disposed not 375
to think well of me I shall appear timid and cowardly; those who are more fair-minded will approve my moderation. But among those from whom I receive approval for my moderation what praise will Budé have? I would prefer this praise of my innocence to be taken away from me in order that Budé be awarded praise for his courtesy and good faith. When men who are 380
far from stupid perceive in his writings the complete silence reserved for my name, and at times some veiled aspersions, and when, by contrast, they find no oblique allusions in my books but see him so often praised by name and, as they say, with all the stops pulled,[72] what will they think to themselves? What will they say? What else but that he is remarkably sincere and that I am 385
wasting away in the brilliance of his fame? We have long been waiting here for the volume of his *Correspondence*,[73] but in one way or another your France is not very generous in sharing its works of learning with us. For that reason I was never able to lay my hands on the *Commentaries* until Basel made them available, when they were published there.[74]   390

But to finish this letter, I have long ceased to be angry with Toussain, and I do not reject his friendship, if at your behest he invites me to it. I am

* * * * *

71 Plautus *Poenulus* 813
72 Literally 'using all the holes,' said of a flutist playing with all the holes open, which produces a piercing noise; see *Adagia* I v 96.
73 Budé's *Opus epistolarum* would be published by Bade at Paris in February 1531. Cf Epp 2422:86, 2449:76–8.
74 See lines 266–9 above.

not the least bit less friendly to him because he was not able to hold the tiller firm in such a terrible tempest. I have always so despised the nonsense of the petty grammarians that I have not even deigned to look at them when they are presented to me. There seems to be a fatal pestilence in our times that any uncouth individual whatever does not fear to rant and rage in published books against any famous or learned man. Since even the power of the emperor cannot render him immune from this insolence, I would be too self-indulgent if I could not put up with my fate. If it is my peculiar misfortune that so many people take up their pen against me alone, I prefer to undergo this fate rather than stain my pen with the blood of so many foes.

That's enough about Budé, my dear Brie. I have no need of his favours, thanks to the gods, and I have no intention of making him feel obliged to me for any good service. It can benefit my reputation, I admit, but I shall willingly cast off this burden; far be it from me that any others should be added. It can harm my reputation: I have become used to insults, and everyone must suffer his own fate, even though I fear no such thing from him. If it is a question of some slight offence, I am a man. I have learned to make some sacrifice to human feelings, more to friendship, and most of all to the general tranquillity of the pursuit of studies. Moreover I am not so insensitive[75] as not to understand rhetorical figures, nor do I lack the skill to reply in kind if I wish – and most probably material will not be lacking. But it would take a more than vicious insult to make me take up my pen against Budé. I would rather use my eloquence elsewhere. For my part I think Budé is too great a man for a person of my rank to envy. We gladly concede to him the foremost position in belles-lettres, we applaud him when he celebrates a brilliant triumph. We have no desire to remove the crown that clings with much distinction to his head.[76] Nonetheless, though he possesses these superior talents, others have their talents also; everyone does not have the same training, and what is different is not necessarily inferior.[77] Nothing would further understanding in the scholarly world more than the absence of the disease of self-love and sincere admiration on everyone's part of the good qualities of others.

I consider your country of France fortunate on many counts: first because it has laid claim to that ancient glory of letters by the right of recovery

* * * * *

75 Literally 'I don't have such a poor sense of smell,' a phrase of Horace (*Epodes* 12.3) enshrined in Latin letters despite its origin in an obscene context
76 Horace *Satires* 1.10.48–9
77 This phrase (*nec statim deterius quod est dissimile*) is found in Tacitus' *Dialogus de oratoribus* 2.18, where he comments on the different styles of rhetoric among ancient authors. The work had only recently been discovered, and the phrase quickly became popular with Renaissance authors.

of its own possessions; then because it has created a sort of republic of letters, of which it has made Budé prince with all legitimacy; and because scholars collaborate with one another in sharing their writings. Would that the same mentality existed in Germany, where everyone writes for himself and you will scarcely find anyone to whom you can entrust the revision of even a tiny 430 book, and where the association of the Graces with the Muses has been dissolved to such an extent that if there is any agreement between persons, they are brought together by the spirit of faction rather than by sincere benevolence. But I would wish that this republic would be more widespread, so that you would regard whoever cultivates the rites of the Muses as Frenchmen 435 and there would be an alliance of intellects, not of regions. This understanding would be more conducive both to the advancement of humane letters and to the extinction of the enemies of good letters. Barbarism has not yet been completely subdued; it still has its bastions of defence, and somewhere it is planning to renew the war. 440

Controversy among learned men is useful, but all bitterness must be absent from it. What a great source of pleasure it is that there is agreement between Budé and Zasius, who in his most recent book calls Budé the 'prince of humane learning.'[78] I hear that he has come to an agreement also with Alciati.[79] I do not know what to say about Longueil except that I am sad that 445 a young man of such high hopes was so short-lived, to use Homeric language.[80] It is not sufficient that agreement of mind exist among men of letters, but it is important that this be conspicuous and evident to all, especially in the case of those among whom some kind of contention has intervened. So then if Budé wishes to heal men's suspicions, he will perform some action 450 worthy of our long-standing friendship and of his character. But if for some reason he is unwilling to do this, I will take it in good part, even if he publishes books containing slurs against me, as long as they are stuffed full of an equal amount of learning.

Your letter passed through many hands; it was not only unsealed, but 455 almost in tatters. I suspect it was purloined by our Evangelical brethren.[81] Give my best greetings to Jacques Toussain. Please give my respectful greeting to Budé as well, if he is the man I was convinced he was even before you

* * * * *

78 In the second sentence of the *Defensio novissima*; see Ep 2368 n1.
79 See Ep 2329 n14.
80 μινυνθάδιον; Homer *Odyssey* 19.328. Christophe de Longueil (Ep 914), whom Erasmus viewed as a promising scholar who had been spoiled by excessive Ciceronianism, was the immediate target of the *Ciceronianus*; see Ep 1948 introduction.
81 Cf Allen Ep 2487:4–5.

sang his praises to me. If you can persuade both of them, and if they profess
in writing what you promise in their name, you will oblige all of us by the   460
same friendly office. Make show of your rhetoric in this, if you wish. Your
eloquence was not wanting in the cause of the latter, and this, it seems to me,
pertains to the general interest of studies. Rumour had spread here that Bade
has died and that Lefèvre was burned at the stake. I am happy that both were
ill-founded.[82] Similarly Erasmus, according to people in Bourges, had been   465
burned at the stake.[83] But I have died so many times and come back to life
so many times that I think hardly anyone will believe it when I really die.[84] I
wish you continued happiness, dearest Germain.

Given at Freiburg im Breisgau, 5 September in the year of our Lord 1530

2380 / To Guilhelmus Quinonus   Freiburg, 6 September 1530

This letter, evidently the reply to one no longer extant, was first published
in the *Epistolae floridae*. The addressee has never been identified, and the title
'mandator' has never been explained.

ERASMUS OF ROTTERDAM TO GUILHELMUS QUINONUS, MANDATOR,
GREETING

I am pleased that your opinion of Montanus agrees with mine, and I am fully
persuaded that whatever kindnesses you bestow on him you will entrust
to a man of the greatest fidelity.[1] At the same time, while my wishes for the   5
promotion of his studies coincide with yours, we do not have the same resources. Consequently I do not hesitate to act as his surety and I have no fears
that Ate will be the companion of my guarantee.[2]

I do not know what Furies are hounding our friend but he seems to
have abandoned all human feelings.[3] I knew that he was fickle, a drunkard,   10
and a good-for-nothing; I never suspected that so much perfidy and malice
lay lurking in him. Four books he has hurled at my head already under his

* * * * *

82 Josse Bade would not die until 1535. On the rumour concerning the burning of
   Lefèvre cf Ep 2362:21–3; and for his current situation, see Ep 2362 nn15–16.
83 See Ep 2373:3–18.
84 Cf Ep 2209:48–50 with nn13–14.

2380
1 On Philippus Montanus, see Ep 2065 introduction.
2 See *Adagia* I vi 97: *Sponde, noxa praesto est* 'Stand surety and ruin is at hand.' Ate
   was a malevolent deity who prompted men to irresponsible acts.
3 Gerard Geldenhouwer; see Ep 2358:14–20.

own name, two have come out from another author, but at his instigation.[4]
And it seems that he will never put an end to it until he dashes himself
against his own evil genius.   15
     One could say that they are examining the mysteries of the Bona Dea
at the imperial diet, so difficult is it to know what is going on there.[5] If the
emperor makes any concessions to the sects, they will declare themselves
victors, and I do not see how anyone will put up with their insolence. But if
the other side wins, who will suffer the tyranny of the monks?   20
     In your offering to share not only your home but all your resources I
recognize a Pythagorean friendship.[6] Would that I could enjoy them more
close at hand. Farewell.
     Given at Freiburg im Breisgau, 6 September 1530

2381 / To ?   [Freiburg, ? September 1530]

> This letter was first published by Allen on the basis of the autograph rough
> draft, without heading or date, in the Royal Library at Copenhagen (MS GKS 95
> Fol, folio 235). The approximate *terminus post quem* is supplied by the reference
> to Gilbert Cousin (lines 5–6), who entered Erasmus' service in the summer of
> 1530. Allen speculated that the addressee, who was on the move in the service
> of the emperor, might have been Alfonso de Valdés, who later complained of
> the rarity and brevity of Erasmus' letters to him (Ep 2469:2–3).

Cordial greetings. Being a lazy person by nature and busy, I did not want to
waste my time in writing to you, uncertain whether you were there or were
journeying about on missions assigned by the emperor. If there is anything
you wish to know about my personal affairs or about what is happening in
England and Lower Germany, you may learn of them from my secretary, 5
Gilbert.[1]

* * * * *

4 See Ep 2375 n16.
5 Bona Dea was an Italian goddess, worshipped at Rome, where an annual nocturnal ceremony in her honour was held in deepest secrecy at the home of a
  chief magistrate. Men were rigorously excluded from the ceremony.
6 A reference to the dictum of Pythagoras that 'friendship is equality'; see *Adagia*
  I i 2, and cf *Adagia* I i 1 ('Between friends all is common').

2381
1 Gilbert Cousin (Gilbertus Cognatus, 21 January 1506–22 May 1572) was born
  into a family of considerable importance at Nozeroy in the Hapsburg Franche-
  Comté. He was one of ten children, most of whom had military careers. After

Erasmus and Gilbert Cousin
at their work table in Freiburg in 1530

2382 / To Erard de la Marck   Freiburg, 7 September 1530

This letter was first published in the *Epistolae floridae*. For Erasmus' relations
with his difficult patron Erard de la Marck (Ep 738), prince-bishop of Liège, see
Ep 2222 n14. This is the last of the letters in their surviving correspondence. At
this point, Erard was attending the Diet of Augsburg.

ERASMUS OF ROTTERDAM TO ERARD,
BISHOP AND CARDINAL OF LIÈGE, GREETING
One who interrupts those who are exceedingly busy is usually regarded as
an importunate person, but one who disturbs those who are engaged in matters of faith and religion justly runs the risk of being regarded as not only   5
insolent but impious. Therefore in order to be less grievously at fault, I shall
express what I want in a few words.

I shall not ask your Eminence to give proof of his constancy in protecting Erasmus, his protégé of long standing. I know your steadfastness of
character, and you know that I am not in the habit of making importunate   10
demands. But now, contrary to my nature, I shall play the part of a beggar. I
am told that you beautify not only your own region but also the realms of the
emperor with magnificent buildings, which wins you great praise for your
generosity as well as for your devotion to the common weal. All acknowledge that an abundance of resources and honours have justly been heaped   15

* * * * *

studying law for a time at Dôle, he undertook the private study of theology and
medicine. In the summer of 1530 he was in Freiburg, perhaps as a student or
tutor, at precisely the time when Erasmus, having lost the services of Nicolaas
Kan (Ep 2261 n34) and with the departure of Quirinus Talesius already foreseen (Ep 2389), needed a new amanuensis. Cousin's amiable character, fine
memory, absolute reliability, and complete identification with Erasmus' out-
look soon made him a companion and associate in the older man's scholarly
work. On Erasmus' recommendation, he was awarded a canonry at Nozeroy
in 1533. He remained in Erasmus' service until the latter's return to Basel in
1535, at which point he returned to his hometown of Nozeroy. He was planning
to move back to Basel in 1536, but Erasmus' death intervened, so Nozeroy remained his permanent home. Devoting himself to scholarship and the teaching
of paying pupils, he remained a thoroughly Erasmian reform Catholic, eschew-
ing the militance of the Counter-Reformation. From the mid-1550s he repeatedly had to defend himself against charges of heresy and, on the express orders
of Rome, was kept under house arrest from 1566 until his death. For a much
more detailed biography of Cousin, together with a list of his publications, see
Allen's introduction to this letter.

upon a man who does not arrogate to himself the riches and distinctions he has acquired, but contributes them to the public good.

In your wisdom you will be aware, I believe, that the Collegium Trilingue, which was established not long ago at Louvain, is not the least ornament of the emperor's domain.[1] But the revenues are very meagre and barely suffice for necessary expenditures. It was a kingly enterprise, which Jérôme de Busleyden, a man worthy of immortal memory, conceived. If his personal resources had equalled his generosity, there would have been no need of external assistance. He expended his entire fortune on this magnificent undertaking. If your Eminence will deign to show his favour to it, you will earn not only enormous gratitude from the world of studies but also the highest degree of true glory among men, and you will be investing in something most pleasing to God – for how else should I express it? – since for a temporal munificence you will receive in return the recompense of heavenly life. Occasions sometimes present themselves when one can be of immense benefit without incurring any personal loss. I wish merely that at this moment you give thought to the Collegium Trilingue. One who has the confidence of a person who is disposed to do as much good as he can to all men lends a service, in a sense, by advising him where he may best bestow his generosity. You know that I am not in the habit of seeking favours for myself; therefore in your great kindness you will understand that the love of learning has turned me into an importunate petitioner and will attribute it more to a sense of duty than to impudence.

I am being stoned by the pamphlets of these individuals.[2] Already seven have appeared.[3] I send my latest apologia to your Eminence.[4] I must take their impudence towards me in good part, since it does not spare even his Majesty the emperor. Courage will not fail me if the favour of princes does not cease to support me. We are eagerly longing for the Lord to have pity on us and turn this grim turmoil into tranquillity through the piety and wisdom of the emperor and the princes. May the Lord Jesus protect and prosper your Highness.

Given at Freiburg im Breisgau, 7 September 1530

* * * * *

2382
1 On the establishment in 1519–20 of the Collegium Trilingue at Louvain, for which Jérôme de Busleyden (lines 21–2) had made provision in his will, see Ep 691 introduction.
2 Ep 2379 n51
3 See Ep 2375 n16.
4 The *Epistola ad fratres Inferioris Germaniae*; see Ep 2377 n4.

2383 / To Bernhard von Cles   Freiburg, 7 September 1530

This letter was first published in the *Epistolae floridae*. For Bernhard von Cles, bishop of Trent and King Ferdinand's chancellor, see Epp 1357, 2007. He was currently with King Ferdinand at the Diet of Augsburg.

ERASMUS OF ROTTERDAM TO BERNARD OF CLES,
BISHOP AND CARDINAL OF TRENT, GREETING
When will I render thanks to equal to your unheard-of kindness, most reverend prelate, who invite me so often to share your family dwelling?[1] What more could I strive for, or with whom would I more willingly live if my age 5 and my health were not such that I am incapable of living together with anyone, or even of living at all if I did not carefully regulate this little body of mine, known to me from long experience? In the past I had a certain aversion for the life of the court. But when I see that kings themselves study philosophy and that in the courts of princes studies and virtue are given 10 their due honour, I would not be displeased with a life that joins brilliance and distinction with moral rectitude. When Plato expresses the view that countries will be prosperous if either their kings dedicate themselves to philosophy or those skilled in philosophy are placed at the helm of public affairs,[2] he is not thinking so much of a knowledge of the disciplines as of 15 a mind inbred with the highest principles, lofty, and elevated above all human concerns. The greatest part of this philosophy by far is Christian piety. We see an admirable zeal for it in Emperor Charles and King Ferdinand. This gives me no little hope that through them God will turn this turmoil in human affairs into tranquillity. Likewise I consider Caspar Ursinus fortu- 20 nate on many accounts.[3] In addition to his exceptional gifts of intelligence, learning, and eloquence it has been his good fortune, in the flower of his youth and prospering state of health, to have dealings with great monarchs and to have won their recognition of his worthiness. Although he receives a great many honours from them, he in turn is capable of bestowing 25

* * * * *

2383
1 Since 1525 Bernhard von Cles had repeatedly invited Erasmus to come live at Trent; see Ep 2097:13–20 with n4.
2 *Republic* 475C–502C
3 Caspar Ursinus Velius, holder of the chair of rhetoric at the University of Vienna and official historian to King Ferdinand (Epp 1810 n35 and 2008 introduction), was also in attendance at the diet in Augsburg.

honours on those from whom he has received them. Indeed, either I am
mistaken or this man will one day surpass all those who are celebrated
for their learning, eloquence, and writings. What quickness of mind, what
impeccable speech, even when he is speaking extempore. You would think
he was speaking from a written text! What a felicitous style, what a range   30
of knowledge! And then what refined manners, especially becoming to a
courtier! If I could provide such convivial companionship to your most
reverend Lordship, I would hasten spontaneously to such a benevolent patron, more illustrious for his virtue than for his good fortune. In the present circumstances I am at least content to congratulate others. Now that I   35
have reached the last act of the play, I need only be concerned with saying
'Goodbye and give me your applause.'[4] I shall leave the stage with tranquil
mind if, as I hope, the emperor's piety, your moral uprightness, and the
concord of princes will have calmed the troubles in the church and will
have calmed them without great bloodshed. In armed conflict it is often   40
the most unprincipled who emerge victorious, and killing is not the mark
of great intelligence; but to restore peace after a violent storm by prudent
counsel is an action worthy of an outstanding prince. We do not despair.
Under the Christian princes Arcadius and Theodosius the world was shak-
en by much graver dissension when everything was defiled by the Arians,   45
the Origenists, the Manicheans, the Donatists, and the Circumcellions, and
paganism was still alive in many places. And yet thanks to the counsel of
those emperors the tumultuous disturbances were settled little by little,
with no great massacre of human beings.[5]

I am gradually recovering from my illness,[6] but in the meantime I   50
am being stoned by pamphlets of the Evangelicals.[7] Six have already been
hurled,[8] and there will be no end. I still remain here, against my will, but my
friends insist on it.[9] Please God their advice will prove fruitful. I could hardly
survive if the authority of princes did not sustain me. May the Lord grant
prosperity to your most reverend Eminence in all things.   55

At Freiburg, the vigil of the Birth of the Virgin, 1530

* * * * *

4 *Adagia* I ii 35
5 Cf Ep 2366:42–53.
6 See Ep 2360 n1.
7 Ep 2379 n51
8 See Ep 2375 n16.
9 See Ep 2360 n5.

2384 / From Johann Koler   Augsburg, 10 September 1530

This letter was first published as Ep 134 in Förstemann / Günther. The autograph was in the Burscher Collection of the University Library at Leipzig
(Ep 1254 introduction). Erasmus' answer is Ep 2406. For Johann Koler, canon of St Moritz in Augsburg, whose friendship facilitated Erasmus' contacts
with Anton Fugger, Christoph von Stadion, and other influential people in
Augsburg, see Ep 2195 introduction.

Most cordial greetings. You acted very well in hearkening to the good advice
of your friends and in continuing to remain there until we see the results of
this council.[1] What it will be, however, is difficult to judge. Up to now nothing has been neglected by both sides that could lead to an understanding.
Our most reverend bishop of Augsburg, Christoph, while acting opportune-   5
ly as mediator, is suspected of being too favourable towards the Lutherans,
whereas in truth he desires nothing more than peace and therefore cannot
countenance the Judaism of certain individuals who pledge that they will not
depart one iota from the prescriptions of ancient ceremonials.[2]

I wrote to you in my last letter[3] that all controversy concerning faith   10
has been delegated to fourteen men. Since they could not come to an agreement, the number was reduced to six, but they could not reach agreement
either. And now this is being discussed only among the princes,[4] and as far

* * * * *

2384
1 See Ep 2360 n5.
2 Cf Epp 2353A:33–6, 2362 n9, 2419:17–19. On 6 August Christoph von Stadion,
  bishop of Augsburg (Ep 2029), addressed the assembled bishops and princes,
  admonishing them to do 'nothing contrary to justice,' because it was 'not true'
  that the Lutherans held 'views contrary to any article of faith,' and one should
  thus 'seek ways and means of preserving the peace of the church.' He added
  further that the Lutherans were only protesting against the many abuses of the
  Roman church. This led to an unseemly row between Bishop Christoph and
  Elector Joachim I of Brandenburg, who insisted loudly that the Lutherans had
  indeed fallen into heresy. See StL 16 1368–9 (no 1038).
3 Not extant; it would have been written circa mid-August.
4 On 3 August 1530 the *Confutatio pontificia*, a point-by-point rebuttal of the
  Lutheran *Confessio Augustana*, was formally presented to the emperor, who
  declared his satisfaction with it and his rejection of the Lutheran confession.
  The refusal of the Lutherans to accept this decision meant that the emperor's
  personal attempt to mediate a settlement of the religious controversy had
  failed and that, if the Germans were to cooperate effectively against a renewed
  Turkish intrusion into the Empire, some other path to a peaceful settlement

as I understand, the whole controversy is centred on the canon of the mass.[5]
Personally, I have a much different view, for I think we are perfectly in agree-   15
ment on all the articles of faith, provided that we could agree on the restitution of goods that were carried off.[6] On this crucial point everything depends,
in my opinion, no matter what they put forward about the canon of the mass.

I am certain that you receive detailed accounts from your friends here
about the acts and proceedings of the whole diet, but so that you may have   20
my opinion about these things, here they are. All the princes here desire
nothing more than peace, especially Ferdinand, king of Hungary, who will
not be able to achieve his goal by any means unless the situation in Germany
is completely settled and put at rest. But each side seems to have the aim
of prolonging things as much as possible to a future council or another   25
diet so that in the meantime each one can consult his own best interests.
Ferdinand's one objective is that they should grant him aid in his struggle
against the Turks and that at the next diet he be elected king of the Romans.[7]
But he is perfectly aware how difficult this will be, and he can easily discern

* * * * *

had to be tried. The initiative was seized by a group of prominent princes, who
assigned the task of negotiation to a committee of fourteen that was equally
divided between Catholics and Lutherans – four princes, four jurists (princely
counsellors), and six theologians – and was soon reduced to a committee of
six (four jurists and two theologians). Johann Eck and Philippus Melanchthon
were the chief theological spokesmen for the two sides. Negotiations in this
format, which commenced on 16 August, came to an unsuccessful conclusion
on the twenty-ninth. September saw a variety of ultimately futile attempts by
Catholic moderates to keep talks alive and find a peaceful settlement. For the
outcome of the diet, see Ep 2403 nn10–11.

5 Other contentious issues were the marriage of priests, the nature and the limits
of episcopal authority, monastic vows, and the ownership of church property
(see following note).

6 In communities where Protestantism had displaced Catholicism, ecclesiastical
properties (churches, monasteries, and their endowments) had fallen into evangelical hands and been put to the use of the new ecclesiastical establishment.
Bitter contention over Catholic demands for the restoration of such properties
would continue until the Peace of Augsburg in 1555.

7 At the diet the Hapsburg brothers in fact secured the agreement of all but one
of the seven electoral princes (the elector of Saxony) to proceed immediately
with the election of Ferdinand as king of the Romans. The election took place
in Cologne on 5 January 1531, and the coronation in Aachen followed six days
later. To be elected king of the Romans was to be designated heir apparent to
the emperorship and to be authorized to act with full imperial authority in the
emperor's absence from the Empire.

that this cannot be accomplished unless things are settled in Germany and   30
the controversies concerning the faith are resolved. And for that reason efforts are being made with great earnestness and diplomacy to piece together
some kind of agreement using whatever stratagem possible, or to put off the
whole thing until the next diet or the next council, something that will never materialize until Ferdinand, having in the meantime fulfilled his wish,[8]   35
makes some other plan.[9]

There was a rumour that the emperor was going to proclaim another
diet in Cologne on the first of March. Another rumour, but more obscure, was
afoot that John the Voivode, as they call him, after slaughtering all the forces of
Ferdinand in Pannonia recently, invaded the border regions of Austria. What   40
is certain is that all through our regions troops are being recruited to be sent
to Austria as reinforcements and from there if possible to the Pannonians.[10]
There is confusion everywhere. There are those who predict that after the departure of the emperor everything will become more turbulent, more critical,
and more dangerous.[11] That is my worst fear. But that is enough and more   45
than enough about public affairs. As for myself, I have decided to pray for
more prosperous times and bear with serenity whatever may happen.

* * * * *

8 To be elected king of the Romans
9 Pope Clement VII, fearing that a council might prove to be anti-papal on the
  model of the fifteenth-century reform councils of Constance and Basel, was determined not to convoke one. Thus denied a council, and lacking the means
  to eradicate heresy by force, Emperor Charles and King Ferdinand had no op-
  tion but to conclude a series of temporary truces with the 'adherents of the
  Augsburg Confession' in which their right to practise their religion where it
  was already established was recognized in return for aid against the Turks. The
  result was that the 1530s and the early 1540s were a period of rapid expansion
  of Protestantism in Germany.
10 In the wake of the Turkish withdrawal from the siege of Vienna in October 1529,
  Ferdinand had managed to reoccupy some of Western Hungary without, however, getting as far as Buda. In January 1530 efforts got under way to negotiate
  a truce between him and his rival for the crown of Hungary (Pannonia), John
  Zápolyai, voivode (governor) of Transylvania, who enjoyed the support of the
  Turks. Negotiations did not go well, and in the second half of the year Ferdinand
  resumed military operations against John; cf Epp 2396 n1, 2399 n2. A one-year
  truce was finally concluded in December 1530, and renewed for another year in
  May 1531. A final settlement would not come until 1538. Cf Ep 2261 n11.
11 Erasmus understood this to be an expression of fear that after the emperor's
  departure from Augsburg, the tensions between the Catholic authorities and
  the burgeoning evangelical movement would lead to grave tumults; see Ep
  2406:69–71.

For the rest, our friend Anton has delegated me to inform you that you could do nothing more pleasing to him than to betake yourself here some day. He puts not only his own fortunes at your disposal but his house as well.[12] Our reverend bishop of Augsburg promised the same in my last interview with him, and you could deduce it yourself from his frequent letters.[13] I pledge and promise for my part that nowhere in the world could you lead a healthier life or grow old more peacefully than here with us in Augsburg, a most pleasant city, abundantly endowed with every natural blessing. You will not lack a beautiful house, gardens, a place of seclusion if it is needed, benevolent and generous friends. From the moment you arrive, you will find glad welcome from everyone. You will never regret the move, for no matter how things turn out you will never be safer in all of Germany than here. I cannot imagine why you could choose France or Brabant; you are well aware how the people of those regions have long regarded you. Do you think they have changed their attitude? But in your wisdom I am certain you will give proper consideration to all of this and will decide what is best to do in the circumstances. Here you can always count on us as your most faithful and devoted friends. If you make a decision, I beg you to let us know in time.

Concerning the nectar of the gods, Anton is going to look into it at the first opportunity. We do not like aged wines. Within a month's time new wine will arrive from Italy. We will send you a sample, and if you find it agreeable you can decide how much you would like. Anton has no greater desire than to please you in whatever way he can. Along with my last letter I sent a letter of Anton's addressed to a merchant in Antwerp,[14] to whom he wrote that he should retain your English pension and put it at your disposal or entrust it to your agents. If in the future he can be of further assistance, you may indicate your wishes to him and rest assured that it will be done.

I gave a full account to Anton about the animosity of our notorious friend towards you.[15] He replied in few words that he knew he was a nonentity and

* * * * *

12 For Anton Fugger and his earlier invitations to Erasmus to settle in Augsburg, see Epp 2145, 2222:6–10, 2299:46–8.
13 The offer is not documented in a surviving letter of the bishop, but see Epp 2029:98–9, 2145:9–11.
14 Cf Epp 2364:5–8, 2403 n4.
15 Heinrich Eppendorf (Ep 1122 n5), who was in Augsburg pursuing his vendetta against Erasmus; see Epp 2392, 2395, 2400, 2406, 2429, 2438, 2450, 2451, 2452. For the history of Erasmus' feud with Eppendorf see Ep 1934 introduction and CWE 78 370–8.

that he had known the frivolous character of this frivolous individual for some time and was not at all surprised at his perverse actions, etc. Therefore, you have a very true and accurate testimony concerning him, and I approve 80 of your attitude that he must be regarded as if he did not exist. He wrote to me yesterday about some affair with relation to the legate,[16] completely concealing his hatred. I was astounded by his fickleness. But let him get what he deserves; he is an acquaintance of mine but no longer a friend.

Eck laughs at your protest and openly shows it to everyone and boasts 85 about a deed well done.[17] But you know the man's character: the greater the danger the more he makes light of it. Anton Fugger asked me to send his greetings. I pray that you remain in the best of health in Christ.

Given at Augsburg, city of the Vindelici,[18] 10 September 1530

Yours, Johann Koler   90

2385 / From Jacopo Sadoleto   Carpentras, 17 September 1530

This letter, Sadoleto's reply to Ep 2312A, was first published in the *Epistolae floridae*. Erasmus' answer is Ep 2443. For Sadoleto, bishop of Carpentras, see Ep 1511.

JACOPO SADOLETO TO ERASMUS OF ROTTERDAM, GREETING

Your favourable opinion of my Psalm,[1] coming from the most learned of men and a man of great importance, brought great joy to my heart. But since the prestige of your name, my dear Erasmus, is such that a brief commendation of yours is equal to the most singular praise of anyone else, I readily recog- 5 nized that the more your words of praise exceeded what my meagre talent could bear, all of that was entirely owed to your love for me and to your exceptional and preeminent kindness, in which you seem to wish, just as you do in the practice and knowledge of the highest disciplines of learning, to outdo us all. For if you were my blood brother, how could you better demonstrate 10

* * * * *

16 Campeggi (Ep 2366)
17 Erasmus' letter to Eck is not extant; cf Ep 2387 introduction.
18 Koler writes 'Augusta Vindelicorum,' the standard Latin name for Augsburg. In pre-Roman times the Vindelici inhabited an area that corresponded roughly to northeastern Switzerland, southeastern Baden, southern Württemberg, and Bavaria. The Romans gave the name 'Augusta Vindelicorum' to its chief town.

2385
1 The commentary on Psalm 93 (Vulgate numbering); see Epp 2272 n4, 2312A:134–6.

the gladness of spirit that you experienced from the fruit of my slight talent, whatever its worth, or your good will towards me? It is in this very quality that a certain uprightness of character rarely to be found in any age and a moral integrity are seen to exist, uncontaminated by any desire to indulge in malicious criticism. This is the property of true and perfect virtue. Those 15 who possess it, since they are confident in themselves, usually also admire the virtue of others. But I shall think myself unworthy of your testimony to my merits if I allow you to gain the upper hand in your affection for me; for I was not born so slow-witted as not to know what your outstanding qualities demand, nor am I so ungrateful that I do not return equal feelings of benevo- 20 lence for your extraordinary good will towards me.

But since this can be shown more by deeds than by words, enough of mere talk. When your Psalm[2] was delivered to me while I was at dinner in the company of a number of important people, I of course read it through avidly, rapidly, but I could not prevent its being snatched from my hands, so 25 great is the desire of everyone to read your writings. So I am waiting to be able to read it again. As far as I could perceive from my first impressions, two things in it gave me special delight: one was that almost all through it and in every passage I felt that my spirit was moved by your words with feelings of piety and religion, so sweetly and piously did your language flow, soothing 30 all the senses; the other was that in this kind of activity you have certainly become more determined to resist the tiresome chatter of senseless individu-als, which is not so much to be refuted as despised.[3]

When in my last letter I urged you to adopt this attitude, my dear Erasmus, I did it because my devotion and concern for your dignity urged 35 me to do so. For although, as you write, it is sometimes necessary to rebuke harshly those who are deeply asleep in their vices, nonetheless it must be done in such a way that this kind of reprimand does not seem to proceed from rage and frustration; if there is anyone to whom this applies, it is cer-tainly to you. It is very difficult, if not impossible, not to be roused to anger by 40 those whose incessant clamour is exasperating and who, in order to snatch some empty glory for themselves, harass men of great renown with useless discussions as if it were a gladiatorial entertainment. But to the excellence of all your other titles to glory it is fitting that you add this one, that you either ignore them or, if they are to be reprimanded, you chide them in a paternal 45

* * * * *

2 *In psalmum 22 enarratio triplex;* see Epp 2266 introduction, 2312A:134.
3 On this, and on the comment in lines 43–7 of the following paragraph, see n7 below.

manner, since you are the father of us all and of this century in bringing sacred learning back to its antique splendour. In addition, since certain things have been commonly accepted that by their nature are so redolent of piety that one should express some slight censure only for what is in excess, as is the case of the veneration of certain saints and the proliferation of paintings, 50 I would advise that we should not stand in the way of popular enthusiasm. Not that it is not much more correct to fix one's most elevated meditations on Christ, but at the same time these things are not foreign to our faith, and not everyone is capable of rising to those sublime heights.

Perhaps I am rash in writing this to you, not taking sufficiently into ac- 55 count who is writing to whom; but forgive my audacity, my dear Erasmus. My great and incredible love for you drives me to be frank in a spirit of friendship, even to the point of temerity. And yet in your great generosity you will take it in good part. But may I perish if I have anything else in view than your tranquillity and dignity and eminence, which I have always 60 defended, and to the best of my abilities have wished to be honoured and adorned with recompense. Accordingly, I recall that I sought to persuade the present pope to award you with a certain prestigious priestly office in Germany; and with the kindness and favour which he exhibits towards men of learning he would have done so if some people had not opposed it and, 65 directing their efforts against you by the use of calumny, turned the good intentions of the pope in another direction.[4] As for Zúñiga,[5] a learned man, who was preparing certain answers against you, I diverted him from this purpose and opinion through my authority and entreaties; and as long as I remained in Rome he did not dare write anything against you.[6] 70

To come back to the Psalms: in the Psalm you recently sent me, of the two points I singled out I see that one was passed over in complete silence and the other was just lightly touched upon;[7] I was marvellously impressed

* * * * *

4 Erasmus understood 'some people' to be a reference to Girolamo Aleandro and Alberto Pio; see Ep 2443 n34. It is not known what 'priestly office in Germany' Clement VII might have awarded Erasmus.
5 Diego López Zúñiga (Ep 1260 n36)
6 Sadoleto was the secretary of Leo X from 1513 to 1523. This claim that he alone was responsible for banning the publication of Zúñiga's works at Rome is more than a bit exaggerated; see Epp 1213:30–41, 1302:69–71.
7 In Ep 2272, which gratefully acknowledged the receipt of Erasmus' commentary on Psalm 85, Sadoleto had expressed (in lines 39–46) 'one wish' that had two parts: first, that Erasmus should 'back away from all controversies' with his conservative critics, and second, that he should 'glide over certain subjects'

and delighted by your moderation of mind and prudence. Other qualities of yours in it are admirable and not new: splendour of language, solemnity, 75 richness of style, variety and dignity of subject matter, so that it is clearly evident that with you the treasures of speech are not used up but always gush forth. And when I compare my mode of speech with yours I see plainly that I crawl along the ground and treat divine matters in a mundane way while you give them a more mystical meaning and preserve their dignity and maj- 80 esty. And yet whatever we are, you and I, we both receive it all from God, to whom we are bound to render thanks and praise and perpetual obedience.

Concerning what you asked about Hesychius,[8] I had in my possession a book of the Psalms in Greek, a book of remarkable antiquity. In it was a preface of Hesychius, brilliantly written, in which he attempted to 85 prove that all the Psalms were written by David. That book, along with all the others, was lost.[9] What I have left are Greek collections by an uncertain author, written with more elegance than substance, which is what I mostly use. Hesychius is sometimes cited in them. But when I have read them and some books of Latin writers whom you recommend, I do not so much fol- 90 low their explanations as surrender myself totally to the Holy Spirit, and I am carried off wherever he leads me. Would God that the corporal man in me could be as fitting a temple for the Holy Spirit as the spiritual man is. But who knows whether Almighty God, who gives you travails and anxieties and poor health, does not thereby do you more good than if he granted 95 you tranquillity and soft relaxation. For my part, I think that this is so, and it seems to me that in truth nothing can be happier than a life that is laborious and troubled but joined directly to God.

May things turn out well for the German nation, for I love the whole race and think it is entirely worthy of attaining the glory of its ancestors in 100 protecting and propagating the true religion. As for those who prevent this and contaminate the glory of their country, may God bring them back to a good frame of mind.

* * * * *

(religious practices) concerning which ordinary people 'have deeply held opinions.' Here Sadoleto notes that in Ep 2312A, which answered Ep 2272 and was accompanied by a gift copy of Erasmus' commentary on Psalm 22, Erasmus had not responded in sufficient detail to the points raised. Thus prompted, Erasmus would devote the bulk of Ep 2443 (lines 42–261) to an extended discussion of both.
8 Hesychius of Jerusalem, a fifth-century Greek exegete; see Ep 2312A:155.
9 For the loss at sea of Sadoleto's library, see Ep 2059 n8.

Your notes on my Psalm were most gratifying. I intend to remove a great part of those errors.[10] Some of them originated in the best authors. As for me, my dear Erasmus, I wish you to be assured that although I am a man of modest means and punished by Fortune with great losses,[11] I have nothing that I do not wish to be as much yours as mine. Not only in this regard but in all that pertains to preserving your dignity and reputation I am resolved both of my own will and in answer to any recommendation of yours to give proof to you always of my supreme loyalty in friendship and good will. Farewell.

17 September 1530, at Carpentras

2386 / From Johann von Vlatten · · · · · · · · · · Augsburg, 17 September 1530

The autograph of this letter is in the Rehdiger Collection of the University Library at Wrocław (MS Rehd 254.160). A summary with excerpts is found in Horawitz IV 12. The complete text was first published by Dr Franz Wachter in *Zeitschrift des bergischen Geschichtsvereins* 30 (1894) 204. Vlatten (Ep 2360) was in Augsburg attending the diet.

Greetings, Erasmus, so dear to my heart. Even if I have nothing certain to report of which you should be informed, since I perceived that our Quirinus was conveniently available,[1] I wanted to give you a rough description of the diet. You know that purgatory has been under heavy siege now for more or less twelve years, if I am not mistaken, by a great gang of assailants, and that those who tried to defend purgatory have been randomly mutilated, some in the foot, some in the hand, some in the head, to such an extent that if their last hopes had not given them courage in their calamity, they would be in their last agony, worn out by their incredible struggle, overwhelmed by immense suffering, or they would have been forced to deliver purgatory into the hands and authority of their adversaries. But now that they have been given an opportunity to recover their breath, supported by the protection of high-ranking prelates and leading citizens, they seem to be regaining their shattered morale and brandishing their swords and pens, so that it is

* * * * *

10 Erasmus had included with Ep 2312A a list of typographical errors that he found in Sadoleto's commentary; see lines 324–5 of that letter, and cf Ep 2443:427–30.
11 Presumably in consequence of his departure from Rome to Carpentras shortly before the city was sacked in May 1527; see Ep 2059:26–7 with n8.

2386
1 Ep 2367 n3

not clear which side will carry off the victory, so fierce is the fighting on   15
both sides.[2]

Caught up in this siege, our Polyphemus was wounded and suffered
grave injury.[3] But if in both camps they would allow a remedy to be applied
to their passions, emotions, and personal ambitions and distinctions, it is certain that the dispute could easily be settled. In the meantime we must await   20
the outcome of all this, and our Saviour Christ must be implored with all our
heart that after all this turmoil, discord, and wars he may deign to grant us
his Christian peace.

Farewell, most judicious of men, and love me as you do, and take good
care of your health.   25

At Augsburg, on the spur of the moment, 17 September 1530

Your Johann van Vlatten, scholaster

To Master Erasmus of Rotterdam, a man of great learning, respected
and revered friend

2387 / From Johann Eck   Augsburg, 18 September 1530

For Johann Maier of Eck, who called himself Johann Eck, see Epp 386:95n, 769,
2357 n1. First published in the *Vita Erasmi*, this letter is Eck's answer to one from
Erasmus that is no longer extant. For Eck's activities at the Diet of Augsburg,

* * * * *

2 Purgatory was one of the contentious issues (along with papal authority and
   indulgences) that were deliberately omitted from discussion in the Augsburg
   Confession. Accordingly, the matter was omitted from the Catholic Confutation
   of the Confession and – despite the Lutheran theologians' fear that silence might
   be misinterpreted as agreement – it did not subsequently come up in the negotiations between the two sides at the diet; see *Spalatini Annales* 152, and MBW Ep
   1078 T 4/2 695:3–696:19. It was Luther, who was not at the diet, who decided
   to clarify the issue by publishing his *Widerruf vom Fegefeuer* (Wittenberg: Georg
   Rhau, c 20 July), the first copies of which reached Augsburg on 13 August; see
   Spalatini Annales 152, and see also the first paragraph of Luther's pamphlet
   (WA 30/2 367). Johann Eck replied with *Christenliche erhaltung der geschrifft für
   das Fegfeur*, which was printed by Wolfgang Stöckel at Dresden on 26 October.
   Although the details are unknown, it is easy to imagine that the appearance of
   Luther's treatise in Augsburg would have sparked a public (and possibly dis-
   orderly) debate among the supporters and opponents of the Reformation then
   present in in the city. Vlatten clearly found the entire business amusing.
3 Erasmus' wayward servant Felix Rex, known as Polyphemus (Epp 2130 introduction, 2334 n1) was in Augsburg at the time, apparently in the household
   of King Ferdinand. The nature of his suffering and wounds in the battle over
   purgatory is unknown.

Johann Eck, Catholic theologian
and professor at Ingolstadt, at age 43

reports of which annoyed Erasmus, cf Epp 2365 n5, 2371:20–2, 2378:4–5, 2384:85–7, 2392:22–40. No reply from Erasmus is extant, but he comments on this letter in Ep 2406.

JOHANN ECK TO MASTER ERASMUS OF ROTTERDAM, THEOLOGIAN, GREETING

That our mutual friend Ludwig Baer gave you greetings in my name,[1] most learned Erasmus, he did rightly and properly, and at my behest, but that there was some quarrel between us, as you imply, I neither understand nor 5 acknowledge. I confess I was displeased that, although you are more prolific than rabbits,[2] you so long put off launching an attack against the enemies of the faith, which you admit was often asked of you.[3] You state that you have ignored what some friends reported to you, namely, that in one of my works I called you a 'tongue-tied theologian.'[4] I wonder how friends could have 10 told you this, when I always proclaim you the most eloquent of theologians. Perhaps I aimed this barb at someone else, even if they suppose that you were the target. As far as your 'opinions' are concerned (for that is how you refer to them and lay claim to them),[5] I do not withdraw the charge. When I had extracted three thousand articles from the books of Luther and oth- 15 ers, I selected four hundred to be presented at the diet. And I did this even though no one was willing to debate the matter with me despite my repeated protests before the Lutheran princes and the Lutheran preachers who were also present. I had also been given those four opinions, which I included with the other doctrinal questions.[6] They seemed to me then, as they do now, 20

* * * * *

2387
1 On Baer see Ep 2225 introduction.
2 Erasmus says the same thing of himself in Ep 305:249–50.
3 On the slow gestation of Erasmus' decision to take the public stand against Luther that both friends and critics urged upon him, see CWE 10 xii–xviii.
4 For 'tongue-tied theologian,' Eck writes *infans theologus*. The primary meaning of *infans* is 'unable to speak,' 'mute,' 'not eloquent,' but it can also mean 'childish' or 'infantile.' Eck's protestation that he thought Erasmus 'most eloquent' (line 11) indicates that, at least for the purpose of defending himself, he understood the word in the first sense. But what Erasmus heard in *infans* was 'childish.' In Ep 2406:21–2, he cites Eck's words as *infantulus theologus* 'little infant (ie infantile) theologian.' Either way, Eck's complaint was that Erasmus had been culpably silent in the face of a theologian's duty to speak out in defence of the faith. Not surprisingly, Erasmus did not 'ignore' what he regarded as a grave insult; cf Ep 2406:19–25.
5 Cf Epp 2365:19, 2371:21, 2406:11.
6 See Ep 2365 n5.

scandalous.[7] If you are angry with me for bringing them forward, you should be angry with yourself first, since you first proposed them. I shall not conceal from you what displeases me about these four supernumerary opinions[8] when I am free from the diet. I do not seek the favour of the Zwinglians or the Lutherans; rather I am glad and prefer to have displeased them. Your 25 servant presented me with a copy of your apologia against the Capernaites of Strasbourg,[9] a gift which I much appreciated, you may be sure. If you continue to capture the little foxes that are destroying the vineyard of the Lord,[10] you will have me as a son and a disciple ready to be at your service. Keep well in the Lord and our Saviour. 30

At Augsburg, 18 September 1530

2388 / From Pierre Du Chastel   Arc-en-Barrois, 19 September [1530]

> This letter was first published as Ep 96 in Enthoven. The autograph is in the Rehdiger Collection of the University Library at Wrocław (MS Rehd 254.48). Allen supplied the year date on the basis of Ep 2425, which was written at Paris in February 1531, after Du Chastel had arrived there with his bishop. For Pierre Du Chastel see Ep 2213 introduction.

Cordial greetings. When I was about to set out from here, most illustrious of men, and indeed was about to mount my horse, someone told me that Anton would be passing through this region within eight days on his way from Paris to his native town.[1] Therefore, although I had much less time to write than your eminence or the ordering of my affairs and my office allowed, I 5 wished to write to you, even if it was in haste. And although you did not write a word in reply to several letters that your Du Chastel sent you,[2] but meanwhile did write rather frequently to some Germans living in Bourges,[3]

* * * * *

7 See Ep 2406.
8 In the Ingolstadt printing of the 404 Articles, the final eight (397–404) are not numbered.
9 For the term 'Capernaites' see Ep 2374 n4. The apologia was presumably the newly published *Epistola ad fratres Inferioris Germaniae*; see Ep 2371 n20. The servant would have been Quirinus Talesius (Ep 2367 n3).
10 Song of Sol 2:15

2388
1 Anton Bletz of Zug, professional courier; see Ep 1784 n1.
2 Not extant
3 Viglius Zuichemus and Karel Sucket; see Ep 2356.

still my affection and my special regard for you cannot permit me to neglect
any occasion for sending my greetings. Furthermore, you can hardly believe   10
how much importance I attach to your well-being and various undertakings.

I am at present in the service of the bishop of Poitiers,[4] but I do not yet
know under what conditions. If you write something to me, you will have
to send it to Paris, and afterwards to Blois, where the French king has been
residing for many years now. There is nothing I would not do for your sake,   15
whether you prescribe or prohibit something, and nothing would be more
pleasant than if we could see each other. But that, I think, lies at the knees of
the gods.[5] Finally, I pray to almighty and merciful God that you be in good
health and remember your Du Chastel. Farewell.

From Arc-en-Barrois, 19 September [1530]   20
Yours, Pierre Du Chastel
To the most illustrious Erasmus of Rotterdam, my master. At Freiburg
im Breisgau

2389 / From Pieter van Montfoort   Augsburg, 20 September 1530

First published as Ep 135 in Förstemann / Günther, the autograph of this letter
was in the Burscher Collection of the University Library at Leipzig (Ep 1254
introduction). Pieter van Montfoort (documented 1530–7) was the son of Jacob
van Montfoort, who often served as one of the four burgomasters (consuls) of
Haarlem. He was at this time in the service of Albert of Brandenburg, archbishop of Mainz (line 13), but he also enjoyed the favour of the emperor, who occasionally employed him in connection with affairs in Germany. At some point he
had visited Erasmus at Basel. In May 1533 he was sent by the Estates of Holland
to present Erasmus with a gift, and he stayed with Erasmus at Freiburg for six
days. At that time Erasmus wrote highly laudatory letters to Mary of Austria
(Ep 2812) and Nicolaus Olahus (Ep 2813), recommending Montfoort for the
provostship of Haarlem. The friendship between the two men was, however,
destroyed when Erasmus became convinced that Montfoort had cheated him
out of a substantial portion of the gift that he had been sent to deliver (Ep 2922).
No other letter to or from Montfoort survives.

Cordial greetings. Although I have always been apprehensive about writing
you a letter, most learned master, out of a certain awkward sense of shame,

* * * * *

4 Louis de Husson; cf Ep 2213 introduction.
5 Homer *Odyssey* 1.267, cited in Greek

now, at the instigation of our friend Quirinus,[1] I have been emboldened
to write to one whom the whole world reveres. Concerning the book of
Trebizond for which you asked.[2] I do not have it here, but as soon as I return   5
to Mainz, I will send it to you. I must say that I admire your open-mindedness
and restraint, since you are willing to publish personally writings that con-
tradict your own opinions, so that everyone will have freedom of judgment
and the reader will emerge better informed by comparing different opinions.
But leaving this aside, so that I do not appear to be speaking too freely, I will   10
pass on to something else.

When I was in Haarlem recently – for I had been sent on a mission to
Brabant by my gracious prince, the cardinal of Mainz – and while we were
talking about various things in the city council, we happened to mention the
choice of a pensionary (as they are commonly called).[3] For the one who now   15
holds that office is not suitable both because of his old age and because he
often suffers from paralysis. A second person, a young man, whom our burgomasters in The Hague had destined for this position and were encouraging
to learn legal practice, died. Moreover, another young man whom the burgomasters had chosen on my advice to assume this office was solemnly sworn   20
in, but he too is unsuited to this office since, of course, it is a secular one. When
I told our friend Quirinus about this, I perceived that if this office were offered
to him, he would not refuse.[4] On the contrary, he asked that I write about this
matter to my father, Jacob van Montfoort de Hoeff, who is at present a consul
of Haarlem, to see if the council would be willing to assign this function to   25
Quirinus. I think, or rather I dare to say I know, that this will come about easily if Erasmus, who knows Quirinus inside and out,[5] would deign even with
one little word to recommend him to my father and Frans de Witte, the burgomasters.[6] For they would do even much greater things to please you. In addition, they would be even more willing to have Quirinus spend two years in   30

* * * * *

2389
1 Ep 2367 n3
2 Possibly a manuscript of his Latin translation of St John Chyrsostom
3 The pensionary was the chief legal officer of a Dutch city, the secretary of its city
   council, and its principal representative at meetings of the provincial estates.
4 The appointment was made in 1532; on 7 May of that year Erasmus sent him a
   letter of congratulation (Ep 2647).
5 Literally 'underneath and in the flesh'; Persius 3.30
6 Montfoort is mistaken here: Frans de Witte (documented 1518–30), had indeed
   served several times with Jacob van Montfoort as one of the four burgomasters
   of Haarlem, but by this time he was no longer in office, having stepped down
   in 1529.

France at their expense to learn the language, since they intended to support
at their expense young men in France as a preparation for fulfilling this task,
so that through his knowledge of law and the French language he might have
better qualifications. Moreover, I shall first write to my father to have further
information so that I can later pass it on to Quirinus and he will then apprise   35
you so that you will be able to write, if you would, with full knowledge of the
circumstances.7 I would not wish that you ask anything of our city in vain.
Farewell, and lay the blame on Quirinus for my daring to write to you.

    Given at Augsburg, 20 September 1530

    Yours with all my heart, Pieter van Montfoort de Hoeff   40

    To the most learned master of sacred theology and of all humane let-
ters, Desiderius Erasmus of Rotterdam, his master worthy of the highest
respect. At Freiburg im Breisgau

2390 / From Nicolaus Olahus   Augsburg, 20 September 1530

    This letter, Olahus' answer to Ep 2345, was first published in Ipolyi, page
    74. The manuscript is page 225 of the Olahus codex (Ep 2339 introduction).
    Erasmus' reply is Ep 2393. For Nicolaus Olahus, see Ep 2339 introduction.

RESPONSE OF NICOLAUS OLAHUS TO DESDIDERIUS ERASMUS
OF ROTTERDAM
I cannot help expressing my admiration for your outstanding virtues and
kindness, most distinguished Erasmus, since, as you write, you are contemplating the addition of me and my name to your list of your special friends.   5
Thanks to this kindness, virtue, and singular nobility of mind, you have long
deserved that all should honour, revere, and venerate you. Continue, therefore, as you have begun, regard me as one of your friends, and make me feel
that I am dear to you. Farewell.

    From Augsburg, 20 September 1530   10

2391 / From Nicolaus Olahus   Augsburg, 21 September 1530

    The autograph of this letter, first published as Ep 136 in Förstemann / Günther,
    was in the Burscher Collection of the University Library at Leipzig (Ep 1254
    introduction). It would appear that, having already written Ep 2390 in response

*****

7 Erasmus, who had already made efforts to secure a suitable position for
  Quirinus (see Epp 2246:36–7, 2298:18–19), would surely have written such a
  letter if asked, but there is no surviving record of his having done so.

to Ep 2345, Olahus received a farewell visit from Quirinus Talesius (lines 14–15) and, as a consequence, decided to write this letter to accompany a gift (lines 16–17), the delivery of which he entrusted to Quirinus. Erasmus' answer to both letters is Ep 2393.

Greetings. I can scarcely say, most eminent doctor, whether I would have been more delighted by a longer letter from you than I was by the shorter one that Felix delivered to me.[1] For from it I also understood what I would have understood from a longer one, namely, that I will be the recipient of your good will and extraordinary kindness. Therefore, it was most gratifying 5 to me that you employed this brevity. And I have deemed your offering of an apology, expressed in your letter and presented by Felix in your name, as entirely unnecessary. Therefore, my dear doctor, keep your promise to count me among your special friends. I shall make every effort on my part that you will not have reason to regret my friendship. 10

The queen still maintains the kindly and sympathetic disposition towards you that she has always demonstrated in the past because of your outstanding qualities, and I shall diligently undertake to the best of my ability to assure that these feelings increase in intensity. Since your servant Quirinus was returning to you and had already bid me adieu,[2] I did not wish him to 15 return empty-handed, as they say, so that you will remember me when you dine and sup.[3] Farewell and accord me your friendship and know that I am devoted to you.

From Augsburg, 21 September in the year of our Lord 1530

Your Nicolaus Olahus, treasurer of Székesfehérvár, secretary and coun- 20 cillor of the queen, etc

To the most eminent Master Erasmus of Rotterdam, doctor of sacred theology, etc, master and friend worthy of all respect

2392 / From Johann Henckel   Augsburg, 1 October 1530

The autograph of this letter, first published as Ep 137 in Förstemann / Günther, was in the Burscher Collection of the University Library at Leipzig (Ep 1254 introduction). For Johann Henckel, court preacher and confessor to Queen Mary of Hungary, see Ep 1672, and cf Epp 2011, 2100.

* * * * *

2391
1 Felix Rex (Ep 2386 n3)
2 For Quirinus see Ep 2367 n3.
3 The gift was a silver spoon and fork; see Ep 2393:23–5.

The name of Heinrich Eppendorf, which was unfamiliar to me, I have come to know only from your books, most learned Erasmus.[1] Caspar Ursinus Velius,[2] who had known him for a long time, brought him here to my dwelling because his lodgings were adjacent to my hovel. Many people are accustomed to visiting me in my retreat; some are pleasant company, others 5 I bear patiently. The result is that at times I am constrained to put up with insipid conversations. I have become aware of the character of this man more from his boastful words than from anything else. I have frequently caused him annoyance by placing your judgment and erudition above the studious pursuits of all others, for I know how to use rather than abuse associations 10 with this kind of person. You may be sure that no one will ever have enough credibility with me to alter the renown of Erasmus and the opinion I have formed of him. The whole controversy about Eppendorf that you describe to me I learned from him himself, with a few variations (as often happens with those who plead their unjust cause before the judge), so that if I had wished 15 to judge the case, I would have been able to pronounce the judgment that I had already formed on my own on the basis of certain presumptions. He has not seen the letter you wrote me about Polyphemus,[3] but I think he heard me mentioning these things about him. There is not much difference between Cyclops and that Thraso.[4] Whatever the case, no one will ever be able to tar- 20 nish your name in my eyes with his lies. But enough of this.

With Eck I have spoken only once, and in this one conversation in the presence of Fabri he treated me in such a way that I shall not willingly attempt to talk to him again.[5] He aroused my indignation by his furious cries and injurious words. If I had not thought he was drunk, I would have answered him, 25 contrary to my custom. I did, however, give him a very brief answer, more moderate than Fabri had expected. In the end there was nothing he could object to, except that I have had numerous dealings with that heresiarch, Melanchthon.[6]

* * * * *

2392
1 See Ep 2384 n15.
2 Professor of rhetoric at the University of Vienna and official historian to King Ferdinand (Ep 2383 n3)
3 The letter is not extant. For Polyphemus (Felix Rex) see Ep 2386 n3.
4 'Cyclops' was Erasmus' nickname for Rex, 'Thraso' his favourite nickname for Eppendorf.
5 See Epp 2387 (Eck) and 2374 (Fabri).
6 Henckel's contacts with Lutherans at the diet included Georgius Spalatinus (Ep 501) as well as Melanchthon. Both found him to be an honourable and friendly man. He provided them with a list of twenty theologians who had come to Augsburg as their opponents, and he described to them Queen Mary's

I have never belonged to any faction, and I never will. If, however, it were necessary to adhere to any faction, I would prefer to side with Melanchthon than   30
with the unabashed ferocity of Eck. I have heard from someone, a person of
irreproachable credibility, that he collected a hundred heresies of yours, taken
mostly from the *Colloquies*, but that he will keep them secret until he can find
someone who can explain the errors you have made in Greek. He says that you
made annotations in Greek so that even very learned and subtle Aristotelian   35
theologians would not be able to understand them easily in that language,
which does not come within the scope of their profession. Perhaps he is thinking of the colloquy on Echo.[7] I have heard that he has made certain other statements about you that would be more likely to provoke the laughter of sensible
people than the condemnation of the mentally deranged. I read the pamphlet   40
or, as they prefer to call it, the *Epistola apologetica* of the church of Strasbourg,[8]
which was given to me together with your *Epistola adversus quosdam etc.*[9] as
soon as I arrived here. I did not realize that it was written by Bucer. While I was
attentively reading both of them at home, someone brought Bucer and Capito
to my house. He claimed falsely that they were citizens of Nürnberg and that   45
they sought my advice and aid in certain matters. From the beginning of the
conversation I sensed their trickery, but they did not reveal who they were.[10]
When they saw the two *epistolae* on the table, they asked what I thought of
them. I answered that in the *Apology*[11] there was a honied poison and that I regretted that Erasmus was distracted by lies and nonsense of this sort from the   50
more useful activities that we were expecting from him. Both of them smiled,
and after presenting some sham business or other they left. The next day I
learned from the one who had introduced them to me that they were Capito
and Bucer. Capito returned to Strasbourg on the following day; Bucer in the

* * * * *

personal inclination towards evangelical doctrine. On 28 July Melanchthon forwarded to Luther a list of questions, prepared by Henckel on behalf of Queen
Mary, on the propriety of communing in one kind only if one's government forbade communion in both kinds. See *Spalatini Annales* 140–1 and WA-Br 5 510–11
(Melanchthon to Luther, 28 July 1530).

7 In the colloquy *Echo*, all the questions of Juvenis (Youth) are answered by Echo
with a single word or a very brief phrase that rhymes with the last word of the
question. Many of these answers are in Greek. Eck evidently suspected that
heresy lurked in them, but he does not appear to have pursued the matter further. See ASD I-3 555–8, and cf CWE 40 796–801 with n3.

8 Ep 2312 n2

9 Ie the *Apologia adversus monachos* (Epp 1879, 1967)

10 Cf Ep 2374 n5.

11 Bucer's *Epistola apologetica*

end came to see me, and excusing himself profusely for not having revealed 55
who he was, began to discourse at great length on his views about the Holy
Eucharist, wishing also to know my views on the subject and what scriptural
passages I used to support the physical consumption of the host. I answered
him more briefly than he expected. Finally he left, and although he promised
he would return on the following day (for I had an appointment in court), he 60
did not reappear.

Since I have not been in this region previously, I cannot determine the
veracity of the events narrated in the *Epistola*.[12] At any rate they do not seem
very different from the usual tumults and uprisings, etc. It is your duty therefore to disregard the false pretences by which they manifest themselves to 65
the world, and to commend your immortal name to posterity by more useful studies in an unadulterated style and to fulfil the pledge given. 'In what
works?' you will ask. We are awaiting the long desired commentaries on the
Epistle to the Romans,[13] the Method of Preaching,[14] some psalms suitable for
preaching, similar to Psalm 85[15] (I know what benefits they have and bring to 70
those who wish to impart pious teachings to the people). We are also awaiting your collected minor works; your major works will keep their proper
classification and authority in separate volumes. If you do not organize your
minor works, who will be able to do that successfully? We need a single definitive copy that can serve posterity as well. If you do not wish to do this for 75
all of them, do it for those which seem more pious to you.[16] These words will
suffice for a learned man.

A copy of your letter to Lorenzo Campeggi, written on 18 August,[17]
reached me. I showed it to the queen. Your predictions did not displease her;
indeed, she appreciated your advice very much. She will gladly do what you 80
entrusted to her in the letter you sent me.[18] It is rumoured that we are going
to move to Brabant. As soon as I have more certain news about that I will let

* * * * *

12 Again, Bucer's *Epistola apologetica*
13 Erasmus published no commentary on Romans other than the *Paraphrase* (1517).
14 The long-promised *Ecclesiastes sive de ratio concionandi* would finally be published in 1535.
15 Erasmus' commentary on Psalm 85 was written in the form of a sermon; see
Ep 2017 and CWE 64 3.
16 The first edition of Erasmus' complete works was that published by Froben at
Basel in 1538–40. It followed (with modification) Erasmus' own division of his
works into *ordines*, as would LB and ASD in their turn. Cf Ep 2283 n8.
17 Ep 2366
18 Not extant

you know.[19] May the Lord preserve you safe and sound for the consolation of
many good men, my master and dearest friend in Christ.

At Augsburg, the first day of October in the year of our Lord 1530   85
Johann Henckel, your devoted friend
After reading this letter, consign it to the flames.

2393 / To Nicolaus Olahus   Freiburg, 7 October 1530

This letter, Erasmus' response to Ep 2390, was first published in the *Epistolae
floridae*, but Allen based his text on the manuscript found on page 225 of the
Olahus codex (Ep 2339 introduction), which had already been published in
Ipolyi, page 89. Olahus' reply is Ep 2399.

ERASMUS OF ROTTERDAM TO NICOLAUS OLAHUS,
TREASURER OF SZÉKESFEHÉRVÁR, SECRETARY
AND COUNCILLOR TO HER MOST REVEREND MAJESTY

It is no small consolation to me, my dear Nicolaus, that in this century, which
breeds on every side so many monstrous men, and in which fidelity, charity,   5
and humanity not only languish but seem entirely extinct and buried, one
finds some sincere and honest people, which gives us hope that some day
that golden race of mortals will come back to life. I have had some friends so
attached and devoted to me that they seemed ready to consult my interests
even at the cost of their own lives, if the situation demanded it, who are now   10
more than deadly enemies, and to such an extent have they ceased to be my
friends that they have even ceased to be human beings. No memory of former friendship, no regard for loyalty, no sense of humanity holds them back
from their misdeeds. Such a state of affairs has rendered the old friends who
have remained faithful more dear to me, and renders new ones, if any fall to   15
my lot, even more agreeable.

As someone of simple character myself, I am delighted by sincere
friends, of the sort that I have clearly discerned you to be, both by your letters
and by what my Quirinus tells me, not to speak of your beautiful, charming
gifts,[1] for which there was no need. The image of Olahus has been too deeply   20

* * * * *

19 In 1531 Queen Mary would become regent of the Netherlands, but Henckel
would be dismissed from her service at the behest of Charles v, who questioned
his orthodoxy and deemed him too sympathetic to the Lutherans.

2393
1 See following note.

impressed on my mind to be torn away or effaced. Your excessive solicitude was extremely gratifying, since I know that it proceeds from an abundance of love. Your spoon and fork will also be a source of great pleasure,[2] for in this way at least I shall have Olahus as my dinner guest, and often I may say to my friends, 'Here is my famous friend Olahus,' since the Fates have denied   25
us other amenities of close association.

It is pleasing to celebrate the good fortune of us both: yours since you have been privileged to have a place of honour with one who among prince-ly women has no rival for her kindness and holy life; mine for having such a sincere friend at the court of a powerful sovereign, to whom I should like   30
to be warmly recommended, and whose favour I pray may be without end. I learned by experience some time ago how much influence a friendly mem-ber of her entourage can have. And if the old Greek proverb 'Like is friend to like' does not lie,[3] I have no doubt that you are especially dear to her be-cause of the sincerity and openness of your character. And I am not unaware   35
how much influence she has with her brothers, Emperor Charles and King Ferdinand. If their favour should fail me, I do not see how I could hold my own against so many monsters. To this day, certainly, they have afforded me whatever I could expect from princes most devoted to me.

It is left to us to engage, under the auspices of the Graces, in this hon-   40
ourable combat, in which the greater the rivalry we display the firmer our friendship will be. I pray for the greatest happiness of the most holy Queen Mary. Farewell.

Given at Freiburg im Breisgau, 7 October 1530

2394 / From Andrea Alciati   Bourges, 7 October 1530

This letter, Alciati's answer to Ep 2329, was first published in the collection of *Aliquot epistolae selectae* that was appended to *De puritate tabernaculi* (Basel: Froben and Episcopius, c February 1536) 88–94. Erasmus' reply is Ep 2468. The omission of the present letter from the *Epistolae floridae* and the *Epistolae palaenaeoi* was dictated by the freedom of some of Alciati's remarks; see Ep 2468:203–6.

* * * * *

2 Listed among the silver objects in the 1534 inventory of Erasmus' valuables; see Major 42 with n7; Sieber 8.
3 *Adagia* I ii 21

ANDREA ALCIATI TO ERASMUS OF ROTTERDAM, GREETING

It is as you write, excellent Erasmus: Fortune raises up most of those whom
she seems to bring down and, tossing them about by her ebb and flow, makes
them better. But, as I see it, each of us suffers his own demons.[1] I have experienced the avarice of soldiers,[2] you the virulent and bitter invective of cer-   5
tain scholars. But perhaps your situation is better, because you have in your
hands the instrument of revenge; I have not been able to do anything against
my demons other than to console myself with that ancient verse: 'We must
endure the follies of the powerful.'[3]

But come now, most candid Erasmus, let us examine how you also in   10
some way could find your own Rhamnusia[4] more indulgent, or at least could
disregard her. For I see that you are strongly affected by her, so much so
that there is hardly a letter of those that you published in the last four years
from which evident proofs of this concern do not erupt. But why should I
mention epistles when you put together and publish so many *apologiae* in   15
such rich abundance that you seem to be a second Alcinous, in whose garden
fruit upon fruit would grow?[5] But I ask you, what profit did you derive from
it? Were your rivals suppressed? No more than hornets when they are disturbed. Why then do you not learn from experience that either you must find
a more violent deterrent or that not even that will stop them? A more violent   20
deterrent you cannot find, since even those famous writers of old Tertullian,
Cyprian, Jerome, and Augustine could not. Why therefore do you not desist
from these vain efforts and show the middle finger to all those who enjoy
grinding tooth on tooth?[6] You have given to everyone the greatest proof of
your fairness by never having been the first to take up your pen against any-   25
one, but until now you only protected yourself against the attacks of those
who were carping at you, and you never gave trouble to anyone unless he
pulled down the moon on himself, as they say.[7] What need is there, if new

* * * * *

2394
1 Virgil *Aeneid* 6.743
2 See Ep 2276 n1.
3 Euripides *Phoenician Women* 393
4 Another name for Nemesis; cf Ep 2329:6–7 with n1.
5 Homer *Odyssey* 7.120
6 See *Adagia* II iv 68: *Medium ostendere digitum* 'To show the middle finger,' and
   Adagia II vi 32: *Dentum dente rodere* 'To grind one tooth on another,' ie to criticize
   someone who cannot be hurt by it or does not feel it.
7 See *Adagia* IV i 59: *Lunam detrahere* 'To pull down the moon,' said of someone
   whose arrogance invites retribution from Nemesis.

enemies arise, to prepare new defences, and to give in to these captious critics who impose one task after another on you to their heart's content? What   30
an excellent riposte that was of Scipio when, ignoring his accusers, he said,
'Today I have conquered the enemy; it is right, therefore, to postpone litiga-
tions and quarrels.'[8] You triumph daily over your enemies, having published
so many outstanding volumes, such as the *Adagia*, in which you showed how
the barbarians who mount an attack on the Greek and Latin languages can be   35
driven off; like the *Novum instrumentum* and the *Paraphrases*, thanks to which
you have laid the true foundation of theology against those so-called theologians; like the commentaries in your edition of Jerome, with which you pierced
the cowled crow's eyes[9] and showed that those who advertised themselves
to the people as men of great sagacity were nothing but pure Phineuses.[10]   40
     After winning such glory, why do you descend into the arena? Long
ago you were given the right to retire from combat by the consensus of all
learned men. And if you do not wish to invoke your age as an excuse, you
can adduce a much better argument. There is no lack of things with which
you can occupy yourself to everyone's greater advantage than these *apolo-*   45
giae, whose sole goal is, as the poet said, to wound the buffoon Pantalabus
with a malignant verse.[11] Concerning that pamphlet against you which you
complain was like a sample of an apprentice's work,[12] what can I say but that
it did not have much to do with you? It seems directed rather at Luther, from
whom you are a double diapason apart.[13] For the passages that he assembles   50
from your writings to show that they lend an opportunity to heretics will
never convince those who have seen the works of either of you. And even
if we admit that this may have happened sometimes, what fault is that of
yours? A much greater opportunity is provided for them by the Scriptures
themselves, since there is no belief so perverse that it does not falsely put for-   55
ward the Sacred Scriptures as a pretext. Why does he not hold forth against

* * * * *

 8 Livy 38.51.7–8
 9 See *Adagia* i iii 75: *Cornicum oculos configere* 'To pierce crows' eyes,' ie to make it
   clear that earlier generations knew nothing and saw nothing.
10 Phineus, legendary king of Thrace, whose cruelty the gods punished by making him blind and sending the Harpies to torment him
11 Horace *Satires* 2.1.21–2. 'Pantalabus' was the name by which Erasmus referred
   to Luis de Carvajal in his *Responsio adversus febricitantis cuiusdam libellum*; see
   Ep 2110 n10.
12 Alberto Pio's *Responsio accurata et paraenetica*, written in 1526 and circulated in
   manuscript but not published until January 1529 by Josse Bade in Paris
13 Ie separated by a very long interval, in complete disagreement; see *Adagia* i ii 63.

heretics in the same way? There is nothing so pious that it cannot be converted by them into something bad, just as a crafty lawyer dishonours the laws. You could have let this pamphlet run its course without adverse effects, just like many others of this kind, which are more of an onus than an hon-   60
our to their authors. Who would approve the action of a general who, engaged in a dangerous external war, gets involved in internal strife? It seems to me that those famous theologians of old observed this rule: if any works were published that diminished the authority and majesty of orthodox law, they answered them, lest through the wiles of the accusers simple people   65
would be deceived and would stray from the straight path; but if there was some charge that pertained to a personal injury, they did not consider it worthy of a response. It is known that through a simple change of one vowel Cyprian was called Coprian by his enemies,[14] and yet there is no extant apologia against them of that saintly man. Palladius accused Jerome by name of   70
spending too much time with virgins, but he let such a detractor go without refuting him, content with his good conscience alone.[15] Therefore, let us leave these *Anticatones* to the pagans;[16] let us leave such controversies, with the demonstrative genre that is proper to them, to the rhetors, who, if they have no real cases to argue, declaim on invented subjects.[17] Let us on our part imi-   75
tate the example of Christ our Lord, and let us pray for those who persecute us.[18] What opinion do you think serious men of learning have when they take into their hands the books of those who accuse you in this way, if they ever do take them into their hands? Do they say that someone has inflicted a crushing blow on the real Erasmus because Erasmus has some erroneous   80
opinion about religious beliefs? Not at all! Not even envy itself could accuse him of this, him, a man of irreproachable orthodoxy. Is someone attacking him who had previously been wronged by him? But there is no record of a

* * * * *

14 From the Greek κόπρος 'excrement'
15 Palladius (368–c 431) made some disparaging remarks about Jerome's relations
     with the patrician Roman widow Paula, who accompanied him to the Holy
     Land; *Lausiac History* 36. In his *Vita Hieronymi* Erasmus reports that Rufinus
     of Aquileia, Jerome's bitter enemy, had suborned various people, including
     Palladius, to slander Jerome's name; see CWE 61 44. Cf Ep 2468:111–14, where
     Erasmus points out that Jerome did indeed defend himself against these charges, though not to Palladius.
16 Julius Caesar's *Anticatones* was his hostile polemic in response to Cicero's panegyric of Cato the Younger.
17 Alciati refers here to the Roman schools of declamation during the Empire, where
     extravagant fictive themes were taught as exercises in demonstrative oratory.
18 Matt 5:44

vitriolic letter of his except when he is provoked. It follows, therefore, that
they wrote these things driven by vain and pagan ambition, and they reveal   85
their own impiety while they try to expose that of another. You are mistaken,
Erasmus, if you have such a low opinion of the prestige of your name and the
respect of the learned world that you would think that by denigrations of this
kind you can be brought tumbling down from the citadel of learning and uprightness that you have so long occupied. The more learned those who have   90
written against you are, the more stigmatized they are, because they have so
little respect for studious pursuits in general that they are audacious enough
to inflict injury on you, who have done them such good services. What must
we think the common people and the ignorant will say when they see such
flames of controversy burning so intensely among the leaders of the various   95
factions?[19] 'Very well,' they say, 'there is good reason for us to console ourselves on our ignorance when we hear things uttered by them that everyone would laugh at among us.' Don't you see, therefore, how much better it
would be to come to a decision in this matter and in future take vengeance
on them with silence; otherwise what will be the final outcome of this affair?   100
'Vengeance brought forth vengeance, and harm brought forth harm.'[20] You
see how a very short pamphlet contains the seeds for huge volumes, how
from a single dragon so many brothers, sons of Cadmus spring up,[21] how one
person portends a metamorphosis of all church leaders. You showed learned
men what you were capable of when you said that you would deal with that   105
subject; now show them your nobility of mind, your disdain of personal injury, your equanimity. You will bring shame to all these Zoiluses.[22]

I write to you, most kindly Erasmus, not because I wish to give you
counsel, that is, to teach Minerva,[23] but so that I may inform you of my opinion, whatever it is worth. It is possible that there are other reasons I do not   110
know of that compel you of necessity to run to the call of the trumpet. I beg
you to take it in good part if I comport myself towards you with more liberty
than my respect for you should allow me. People have also provoked me, as
you write, but so far I have ignored the simpletons. Those who were more
learned were obliged by my kindness and respect to be reconciled to me. If   115

* * * * *

19 Literally 'the Coryphaeos [factional leaders] of [various] doctrines'
20 Zenobius *Paroemiographi Graeci* 3.28, cited in Greek
21 Cadmus, founder of Thebes, slew a dragon that had devoured his servants.
    Advised by Athena, he extracted the dragon's teeth and sowed them in a near-
    by furrow, whereupon they sprouted and turned into warriors who immedi-
    ately began to kill one another.
22 The name Zoilus was proverbial for a carping critic; see *Adagia* II v 8.
23 See *Adagia* I i 40: *Sus Minervam* 'The sow teaches Minerva.'

Longueil were living, and the Fates had not taken him from us before his time,
I have no doubt that he would restrain those enigmas and allegories inasmuch as they could be prejudicial to our reputation.[24] What need did he have
to appoint himself as a judge between Budé and me when we understand
each other perfectly? And yet he was not the only one to have tried to destroy   120
our mutual good will; there were others also. But when I arrived here I discovered that all these accusations were false, and I found out by sure proofs
that Budé is completely frank and sincere, and consequently I would dare to
give my solemn word that you should have no doubt that he will be favourable to you also.[25] Therefore, I pray you, do not give the impression that you   125
believed your friends, who incite you against him, more than he believes his
friends. It is not possible that among very learned men some animosities do
not arise, but it is in the public interest that they are not transformed into
enmities and last for too long a time.

I shall soon crown your pupil, Karel Sucket, with the doctoral laureate,   130
which will be at the public expense.[26] This has been granted to his learning
and my commendation by the city of Bourges, something that to this day
has been given to very few. Viglius would prefer to have a teaching post in
Germany. Would that Zasius had designated such a successor. You praise
him because he has diligently applied himself to literary studies; I praise   135
him because he has devoted himself with equal assiduity to the study of law,
which is very rare. It is up to you to choose between him and Karel. Both of
them are circumspect, both well trained, both skilled in speaking. It is no
wonder that both are eligible.[27] I would call down every evil on these venomous bedbugs who cause you to lose sleep, if I did not know that together   140
with the Corinthians they had already paid the penalty from the heights of
the Arctic heavens, and to the full.[28]

Farewell, and love your Alciati in return, as you do.

At Bourges, 7 October 1530

* * * * *

24 See Ep 2329:106–13.
25 See Ep 2329 n14.
26 See Epp 2276:34–40, 2329:41–57.
27 In the end, Erasmus offered his support to Alciati's (ultimately unsuccessful) project to get Viglius Zuichemus appointed as the successor of Udalricus Zasius at
   Freiburg; see Epp 2418:6–22, 2468:174–6, Allen Ep 2484:1–5. Viglius went on to a distinguished legal career in Germany and the Netherlands (see Ep 2101 introduction).
   Karel Sucket became a lecturer in law at Turin, where he died in November 1532.
28 In Aristophanes Clouds 634, the Corinthians, the bitter enemies of the Athenians,
   are described as bedbugs. This sentence is an elaborate play on words of similar
   sound: koris 'bedbug,' Corinthos, and koros 'plenty,' 'excess.'

Julius Pflug
Medallion by Friedrich Hagenauer (1530)
Chorherrenstift, Herzogenburg, Austria

2395 / To Julius Pflug   Freiburg, 10 October 1530

First published in the *Episolae floridae*, this is Erasmus' answer to a letter from
Pflug, now lost, which was apparently the first step in the establishment of
contact between the two men.

Born near Leipzig, Julius Pflug (1499–1564) was the son of Caesar Pflug, councillor to Duke George of Saxony. He was educated from 1510 at Leipzig, Bologna,
Padua, and then again at Leipzig, where he received his licence in law in 1525.
After another visit to Italy in 1525–8, he returned to Saxony and the service of
Duke George. An irenically minded but loyal Catholic, he devoted much effort
to the attempt to reconcile the Lutherans with the Roman church, participating
in the collquies with them at Leipzig in 1534 and Regensburg in 1541. In the
latter year he was elected bishop of Naumburg, but could not take possession
of the see until after the defeat of the Protestants in the Schmalkaldic War of
1546–7. In 1548 he was one of the principal authors of the so-called Augsburg
Interim, by which Catholic doctrine and practice (with a few minor modifica-
tions) were imposed on the defeated Protestant estates (1548–52). His efforts to
restore Catholic discipline to Naumburg were fruitless, and he died as the last
Catholic bishop of the diocese.

Finding in Pflug a kindred spirit, and fully aware of his influence with Duke
George, Erasmus responded warmly to his offer of friendship and encouraged
his efforts towards religious reconciliation. Pflug was the dedicatee (Ep 2852) of
De sarcienda ecclesiae concordia (1533).

ERASMUS OF ROTTERDAM TO JULIUS PFLUG,
COUNSELLOR OF DUKE GEORGE, GREETING
It was said wisely by the ancients, distinguished sir, that if there is any good
coming from evil, we must pluck it.[1] From what you write concerning the
Dorpian affair,[2] although in other respects it was full of annoyances, I gained   5
this advantage, that I had the opportunity of making your acquaintance. For
I seem to have perceived in your letter, as in a mirror, your mind, the dwell-
ing-place of the Graces, the Muses, and all honourable learning. First of all,
I admired greatly the marvellous integrity of your spirit and the remarkable good sense of your temperament. This was evident in your exposition,   10
coherent from every point of view, not exhibiting anywhere any harshness,

* * * * *

2395
1 Source unidentified; not in the *Adagia*
2 Ie the controversy with Heinrich Eppendorf; see Ep 2384 n15, and for Pflug's
  role in settling it, see Ep 2400.

disconnectedness, affectation, or ineptitude due to inappropriate petty remarks. You could hardly imagine how much I was displeased with myself
when I contemplated your virtues, but we will leave that to another time.
I am happy to be obliged to you for your good will towards me, since you   15
are so sincerely concerned with my tranquillity. And would that you could
bring about what we both equally desire. For some time now, in the matter
of this good-for-nothing I have the wolf by the ears, as the saying goes,[3] not
knowing either how to let him go or how to hold on to him. If he would only
be a friend to himself as I am to him. But however the gamble turns out in   20
this affair I have full confidence that the friendship that has been entered into
between us will be lasting. If in your singular kindness you do not feel aversion for a poor little friend of lowly condition, I shall earnestly endeavour
not to do anything unworthy of your good graces. I must first ask that you
think well of these improvised pages.[4] I have entrusted them to the prefect   25
of Breisach.[5] I am somewhat afraid that this message may not find you in
Augsburg. If you have to stay there longer, I will write to you a little more in
detail. Farewell.

    Freiburg im Breisgau, 10 October 1530

2396 / From Nicolaus Olahus   Augsburg, 13 October 1530

    This letter was first published in Ipolyi, page 90, on the basis of the manuscript
    on page 93 of the Olahus codex (Ep 2339 introduction). For Olahus, see Ep 2339.

TO ERASMUS OF ROTTERDAM
No doubt you have heard of the atrocities committed in Hungary in the past
few days by the Turk, Mehmed Bey, governor of the citadel of Belgrade,[1]

   * * * * *

3 *Adagia* I iv 25
4 Possibly a draft of the *Admonitio adversus mendacium*; cf Epp 2400:37–8, 2406:59–
  60, 2451:42–3.
5 Cf Ep 2400:24–5, 2406:64–5.

2396
1 The life of Yahya-Pasha-zade Mehmed Bey (d 1548) is not well documented.
  In 1529, when he was governor of Smederevo, he served in the vanguard of
  the Ottoman forces that besieged Vienna. In the late autumn of 1530, when an
  Austrian force sent by King Ferdinand besieged Buda (Ep 2399 n2), Mehmed
  Bey came to the defence of the city, forced the Austrians to withdraw, and then
  made raids into Hapsburg Hungary and into Austria itself. In the 1530s and '40s

which we lost a few years ago in a great disaster for Christianity.[2] They say
that from Belgrade he arrived there, where he devastated and pillaged, with 5
about ten thousand Turks, in so swift a march that they covered the distance of more than fifty Hungarian miles in seven days.[3] He destroyed by
fire that part of the kingdom which we call the domain of Máté,[4] and he
sent fifteen thousand men and youths of a strong and vigorous age as pris-
oners to Turkey. It is said that he had three outposts in certain districts be- 10
longing to Alexius Thurzo.[5] After the departure of the Turks, Thurzo went
to see the scene of their cruelty and reached the second of their outposts,
where he found more than five hundred children, some dispatched by the
sword, some dashed against the ground. Moved by pity for these half-dead
infants and by hatred for the cruelty of the Turks, he chose fifty of them who 15
were still faintly breathing and sent them in two wagons to his stronghold
in Sempthe,[6] in the hope that they might recover their health by some cure
or other.

See, then, my Erasmus, under what heavy tyranny the Christian people
are weighed down, and what great servitude Hungary, which flourished 20
with glorious triumphs and was distinguished by its great courage and the
illustrious accomplishments of its people, now suffers, so that neither by day
nor by night is it safe from the depredations and plundering of the enemies
of the faith.

Farewell from Augsburg, 13 October 1530 25

2397 / To Léonard de Gruyères   Freiburg, 17 October 1530

This letter was first published in the *Epistolae floridae*. For Léonard de Gruyères,
chief judge of the diocesan court at Besançon, see Epp 1534, 2139.

* * * * *

he continued to play an important role in Ottoman actions against Hapsburg
forces in Hungary and elsewhere. In 1543 he was made Beylerbey (governor-
general) of Buda.
2 Besieged by the Turks from 25 June 1521, Belgrade fell to them on 29 August.
3 Allen reports that at the time a Hungarian mile was the equivalent of 1.13 km.
4 Olahus writes *terra Mathiae*, literally 'land of Matthias,' a region of northwest-
ern Hungary (roughly equivalent to the western half of present-day Slovakia
plus a strip of northern Hungary) named after Máté Csák (c 1260–1321), the
Hungarian oligarch who was *de facto* its independent ruler.
5 See Ep 1572 introduction.
6 In the county of Nyitra, in present-day Slovakia

ERASMUS OF ROTTERDAM TO LÉONARD, OFFICIAL IN BESANÇON,
GREETING

Although I am called by some a rhetor out of envy, no doubt I have used every rhetorical plea to excuse my persistence in endlessly disturbing with my
letters of supplication men occupied with other matters from whom, more- 5
over, I have never merited any favours. But what room is there for shame
when that kind of necessity presses on us that often drives man to eat man?
My stomach cannot tolerate German wine. Homer writes that the most atrocious form of death is to die of hunger;[1] I say it is to die of thirst, and we are
close to that danger at the present moment. Some months ago I sent a young 10
Polish nobleman to you; since he did not encounter you there, he returned
empty-handed.[2] Now I send you the pillar of my miserable household.[3] I do
not wish to burden you with any expense, for I have benefitted from your
liberality many times; I have given him a sufficient amount of money. It is
a question of finding a wine that suits me, which can be arranged through 15
your servant. In Montbéliard I do not have anyone whom I know even in the
slightest; otherwise I would not have given your city this disturbance.[4]

On the first of September I was ready to return to Brabant, but I was
ordered by members of the court of the emperor to remain here until the diet
is over.[5] And this is not the first time I regretted my compliance. Now winter 20
is pressing upon us and it is not safe to fly forth from the nest. That is why I
ask you to save Erasmus this time at least; in the future I will take measures
to avoid being compelled to importune you. I shall not keep you any longer.
Regarding the latest new events I wrote to the treasurer, François.[6]

Farewell, my incomparable patron. 25
At Freiburg, the eve of St Luke, 1530

2398 / From Andreas von Trautmannsdorf   Augsburg, 19 October 1530

The manuscript of this letter, first published as Ep 138 in Förstemann / Günther,
was in the Burscher Collection of the University Library at Leipzig (Ep 1254

* * * * *

2397
1 Homer *Odyssey* 12.342
2 The nobleman was Marcin Słap Dąbrówski; for his fruitless errand, see Ep
2348:11–14.
3 Quirinus Talesius (Ep 2367 n3), who had recently been ill; see Epp 2348:19–20,
2349:9–11, 2356:35–7.
4 Montbéliard in the Franche-Comté, not far from Besançon, was an alternative
source of good wine.
5 See Ep 2360 n5.
6 François Bonvalot (Ep 1534 n10); the letter is not extant.

introduction). Little is known about the writer, who was apparently in Augsburg attending the diet in the entourage of the elector of Mainz (lines 29–30). He was probably Andreas (III) von Trautmannsdorf (last documented in 1556), of the branch of that noble family established near Grafendorf, fifty kilometres northeast of Graz in the Austrian province of Styria. He was steward of the archbishop of Salzburg at Leibnitz in Styria and later cellarer of Styria.

A recommendation. Do not be surprised, most learned man, that I, a rather crass Minerva,[1] of no talent, very little ambition, but of great audacity and no less temerity, should accost you, the prince of letters, with my letter. When you know the reason you will cease to be surprised.

It was reported to me by one of our servants that you have need of a 5 secretary at the moment, since you do not have your usual number.[2] Your learning, your wide knowledge of languages, your incredible renown, and the other innumerable gifts of your divine intelligence, with which the whole world resounds, have foisted on me the duty to attend to your interests to the best of my abilities, if you are willing and if my assistance and solicitude 10 find favour with you. There is here in Augsburg at the moment a servant of Georg Rithaimer, etc.[3] He is the assistant teacher of noble children.[4] He is zealous, of good morals, a Latinist – and what is essential in teachers – faithful, discreet, very willing to endure his labours and the anger of his master, humble as well, and since he is not yet twenty years old, he would be easily 15 predisposed to obey your commands. If you think he is acceptable (I hope this will prove to be of great advantage to you), write back quickly. He will go to visit you in Freiburg with the understanding that if, once you have seen him in person, he corresponds to your requirements, you will find him prepared for all tasks, even the most humble; if not, he will return to those who 20 recommended him. You will find more than one guarantor for him. I should be glad if you do not take adversely this ardent enthusiasm I have evinced in your regard. But if this initiative is successful I shall be like a devoted servant to you – to whom I especially commend myself – not just on this occasion

* * * * *

2398
1 Ie a man of little culture; see *Adagia* I i 37.
2 Erasmus had lost the services of Nicolaas Kan, and the departure of Quirinus Talesius was in the works. In the meantime, however, Gilbert Cousin had become Erasmus' secretary; see Ep 2381 n1.
3 Georg Rithaimer of Mariazell in Styria (d 1543), had studied and taught at the University of Vienna where, in 1529, he was appointed professor of Greek. In 1520 and 1521 he had corresponded with Joachim Vadianus (Ep 1314 n5), who spoke highly of his scholarly qualifications.
4 Nothing is known of him.

but in more important matters as well. Farewell, and may he who guides the   25
celestial machine deign to keep you safe and sound as long as possible for the
entire flock of cultured men.

At Augsburg, at the court of my most reverend master, the cardinal and
archbishop of Mainz[5]

19 October in the year of Christian salvation 1530   30

Your most obedient servant Andreas von Trautmannsdorf, etc

To the master of all literature, Desiderius Erasmus of Rotterdam, his
teacher

2399 / From Nicolaus Olahus   Augsburg, 25 October 1530

This letter, first published in Ipolyi, page 96, is Olahus' reply to Ep 2393. The
manuscript is page 99 of the Olahus codex (Ep 2339 introduction). For Nicolaus
Olahus, see Ep 2239 introduction.

TO ERASMUS OF ROTTERDAM

I read attentively and with affection the letter you sent to me. I learned from it
your perturbation, which has affected you in an extraordinary way, caused by
the perfidy of friends of yours who should have been grateful to you. It is not,
my dear Erasmus, that their evil actions and perfidy torment you alone. For al-   5
though one can find many friends endowed with courage, honesty, and other
qualities of the heart, how few they are compared to those who are full of malice, wickedness, and infidelity! Therefore, it is not only you but also everyone
else who can rightfully complain of unfaithful friends. If I am not mistaken,
you will never have reason to regret my friendship. On the contrary, I take   10
such pleasure in your friendship that I would not exchange it for any treasure.

I think you want to know about the situation in Hungary, once flourishing with great feats of arms, now crushed beyond all description. I wrote to
you in some detail elsewhere about what the Turks have done there.[1] Recently
our king sent an army of twelve to fourteen thousand soldiers there, I think.   15
Well equipped with all that is necessary for that campaign and supported
by a naval force, it has advanced, according to reports, as far as Esztergom.[2]

* * * * *

5 Albert of Brandenburg (Ep 661)

2399
1 Ep 2396
2 In late September 1530 Ferdinand sent an army of about 10,000 to reconquer
   Buda. Arriving there on 31 October, the army easily took the city itself but failed
   to capture the citadel, where John Zápolyai, Ferdinand's rival for the kingship,

What it has accomplished there is still uncertain. I fear this one thing: that because of the severity of the weather it may be weakened and lose its morale,
and the enemy forces, being in a country like their own, can withstand the   20
rigorous cold, and being better protected and equipped against other physical obstructions, may emerge superior (may Almighty God avert it). If this
should happen and other difficulties arise, we would have no hope of recon-
quering Hungary. For the Turks, as you know, are very powerful enemies,
and their strength lies above all in their speed.[3] In the meantime, while the   25
princes of the Empire would like to do something against them, they will be
able to lay waste all of Germany by fire and the sword, and I greatly fear that,
because of the internal discord and irresponsibility of Christian princes, that
famous prediction, namely, that the Turks will advance as far as Cologne and
will have to be defeated there,[4] may be verified in our age. There was great   30
hope that the emperor, the king, and other German princes would deliberate
in their imperial diet about what measures should be taken to drive the Turks
out of Hungary. It turned out differently than we thought. For practically the
whole discussion was consumed in altercation, and under the pretext of safe-
guarding our faith and religion everything else was neglected, so that you   35
could say that nothing was thoroughly debated or decided in the course of
the diet except that forty thousand infantry and eight thousand cavalry were
promised for a future general expedition against the Turks, on condition that
the emperor would succeed in pacifying Germany and could reach an accord
with the princes in matters of the faith. No one knows when this will be done   40
and whether it can be done at the present time, so great is the diversity of
opinions and so opposed the intentions of princes. Therefore, as things stand,
and with everything pointing to internal warfare rather than mutual peace,
what else can we expect but peril for Christendom and, after Hungary is lost,
the destruction of all of Germany?[5]   45

The sudden departure of the courier interrupted me, although I wanted
to write more. Therefore, take it in good part, my dear Erasmus, if you were
not able to read the elegant letter you desired.

Farewell from Augsburg, 25 October 1530

* * * * *

had taken refuge. By the end of the year the siege had been abandoned. Cf
Epp 2384 n10, 2396 n1.
3 Cf Ep 2396:4–7.
4 We have no information regarding this 'famous prediction.'
5 Though incomplete, this is a well informed and essentially accurate account of
the failure of the diet to agree on effective measures against the Turks because
of its failure to resolve the increasingly acrimonious religious divisions in the
Empire. For more details see Ep 2403 nn10–11.

2400 / To Bonifacius Amerbach   Freiburg, 26 October [1530]

This letter, in which Erasmus explains his decision to publish the pamphlet that
was to become the final instalment in his controversy with Heinrich Eppendorf,
was first published in the *Epistolae familiares*. The autograph is in the Öffentliche
Bibliothek of the University of Basel (MS AN III 15 20). The decision was made
in response to reports of Eppendorf's intrigues against Erasmus at the Diet
of Augsburg; see Epp 2384 n15, 2406. Accompanying the letter was a copy of
the pamphlet in question, the *Admonitio adversus mendacium et obtrectationem*
(Freiburg: n p 1530), an expanded version of Ep 1992 (see line 37).

Cordial greetings. If you have scant approval for my decision I am not at
all surprised. It was not chosen, but imposed. I had decided to swallow in
silence the outrageous behaviour of this idle debauchee. But he makes no
end of it, and he has no shame. As soon as he arrived in Augsburg, he sought
an audience with Duke George. The duke responded through an intermedi-   5
ary that he would consider the matter carefully. After many days Eppendorf
returned, making the same request. The duke answered that he had charged
Simon Pistoris with the task of hearing what he had to say.[1] Eppendorf answered with annoyance that he had no business with Simon Pistoris, that he
wanted an interview with the duke, to whom he had been falsely accused;   10
whereupon he left in a mood of great indignation. And so he remained quiet
until Pistoris and Carlowitz returned to their native city on business.[2] When
he went on the attack again, the duke gave Julius Pflug the task of hearing
Eppendorf's complaints.[3] Seeing that Pflug was ignorant of the whole affair,
Eppendorf filled both his ears with foolish tales to the point that the duke,   15
concerned for my tranquillity, as it were, wrote to me that I should place trust
in Pflug's letter.[4] Julius himself wrote me a letter that was learned and friendly but showed that he had heard nothing but pure lies from Eppendorf.[5] At
the same time Pflug sent me a copy of the preface I had promised,[6] adding
that, if I acknowledged it, the duke thought it would be wise if I dedicated   20
a book to Eppendorf and get back my tranquillity. The duke asked that I

* * * * *

2400
1 For Pistoris, secretary to Duke George, see Ep 1125 n6.
2 For Christoph von Carlowitz see Ep 1951 n7.
3 For Pflug, see Ep 2395.
4 The duke's letter is not extant.
5 Pflug's letter is not extant; Ep 2395 is Erasmus' answer to it.
6 See Ep 1941, the dedicatory letter to the book that Erasmus had agreed to dedicate to Eppendorf but subsequently refused to produce, and cf Ep 2406:45–52.

respond as soon as possible, since he was already preparing his departure. Cochlaeus told me not to send my reply to him in Augsburg because he thought the prince would be leaving in three days.[7] I answered via the prefect of Breisach but I do not yet have a reply.[8] This trickster purposely arranged that there would be no time to answer before the departure of the princes. He insinuated himself into the company of some of my friends to find out if there was anything to learn from them about himself. He saw the letter I had written to Fabri. He saw the one to Henckel even though there was nothing in it about Eppendorf.[9] And I have no doubt that he did the same with many others.

Immediately after Eppendorf's arrival, the rumour was spread that I was so offended by the book of the Strasbourgers that I went into a frenzy and died from it;[10] and I have no doubt that the rumour was spread by his intrigues. Afterwards he declared publicly before a great number of people that I had begged pardon of him on my knees before the magistrates in Basel.[11] That is why I had this pamphlet published,[12] in which there is not a word of injury against Eppendorf. But after knowing the truth, those who heard him or read his letters will understand how great is the falsity of this man. Farewell.

At Freiburg, the day before the eve of the feast day of Sts Simon and Jude

To the most distinguished Master Bonifacius Amerbach. At Basel

2401 / From Udalricus Zasius   Freiburg, 26 October 1530

This letter was first published in LB III/2 1748 *Appendix epistolarum* no 360. The manuscript is in the Rehdiger Collection of the University Library at Wrocław (MS Rehd 254.166). For Zasius, renowned jurist and professor of law at Freiburg, see Ep 303.

Cordial greetings. I cannot but be extremely grieved, great Erasmus, that you are harassed to such a degree by men of little repute that you have thought

* * * * *

7 For Johannes Cochlaeus, chaplain to Duke George, see Ep 1928.
8 See Epp 2395:25–6, 2406:64–6.
9 The letters to Fabri and Henckel are not extant.
10 See Ep 2324:11–13.
11 This took place at Augsburg during the diet; see CWE 78 393–4.
12 Ie the *Admonitio adversus mendacium* (see introduction)

it necessary to resort to arbitration.[1] For who would not curse those who,
bent on disturbing your serene tranquillity, do not so much desire to bring
a case against you as to continue extorting money from you, you who love   5
peace, who would not wish to provide, let alone give, anyone an opportunity
of disturbing you? But these times of rank injustice are such that the more
unprincipled a person is, the more he is encouraged in his wickedness, while
good men, on the contrary, are humiliated and tormented and defiled by the
filthy mouths of scoundrels.   10

   As to the arbitration by which you have tried to deliver yourself from
the persecution of this restless individual, not only do I approve but I commend you highly. It is true that our Ulpian praises the discreet reflection of
one who abhors lawsuits and is more disposed to be bereft of his savings
and his possessions than face litigation.[2] But let these depraved persons who 15
with no just cause harass illustrious men, of whom you belong to the first
rank, take heed. But you, great Erasmus, why are you worried about these
ignominious creatures or fear them? As far as I am concerned, if those who
wish you evil attacked me, I would so despise them that I would not deign
to talk to them, not to speak of judging them worthy to cross my threshold   20
or to be my guests. You are not in jeopardy, and you enjoy such an excellent
reputation that anyone who would wish to attack your name would be repu-
diated before the trial by the consensus of all learned men. Therefore let your
virtue, preeminent learning, and blameless integrity console, restore, revive,
sustain, and encourage you, and pay no attention to the lies of scoundrels.   25

   I, who revere you like a god, would write longer about this affair but
I do not wish to weary you any longer with my inanities. Farewell and fear
not; let him come, if he dares, this person who threatens to sue you for injuries, and let him make trial of Zasius, your lawyer, to his undoing. You are
in Freiburg, not Basel, under the most just of princes;[3] let your adversary   30
beware of opening his mouth. Again farewell, and be assured that I am the
most obedient of all your servants. I have never heard a word about the
dispute with your adversary, otherwise I would not have maintained silence
so long.

   * * * * *

2401
 1 A clear reference to Erasmus' quarrel with Heinrich Eppendorf, who was once
   again threatening Erasmus with legal action for defamation (lines 27–9 below).
   See Epp 2400, 2406.
 2 Digest 4.7.4.1; the writings of the Roman jurist Ulpian of Tyre (Domitius Ulpia-
   nus, d AD 228) were the source of one-third of the *Digest* (*Pandects*) of Emperor
   Justinian I.
 3 Ferdinand of Austria

From my house, 26 October 1530   35
Yours sincerely, Zasius
To the great Erasmus of Rotterdam, my honoured patron and master

2401A / From Léonard de Gruyères   Besançon 27 October 1530

This is Gruyères' answer to Ep 2397. It was first published by P.L. Lefèvre in
Archives, Bibliothèques et Musées de Belgique 13 (1936) 119–21 on the basis of the
manuscript, a rough draft, in the Archives Générales du Royaume at Brussels
(MS 1625, Fonds des Papiers d'Etat et de l'Audience). Informed of the existence
of the letter by Professor A. Roersch in Louvain, the Allen editors published it
as Ep 2401a in Allen XI xxxi–xxxii.

Greetings, most learned Master Erasmus. Your servant,[1] who is here with me,
delivered your most welcome letter to me. I have long desired to know how
you were, what you were doing, and how things were going there in Freiburg.
All these things were related to me by your servant with great eloquence and
amiability. I was somewhat disturbed that at the beginning of your letter you   5
excuse your importunity. By the immortal gods, how could Erasmus cause me
any inconvenience? Erasmus, I say, whose writings kings and princes without
exception read with keen enthusiasm and cherish for their exceptional wisdom and erudition? Shall I, insignificant man that I am, be so occupied that I
do not have the time to read an occasional letter from Erasmus that I receive 10
once a year? Be assured, my beloved Erasmus, that you are most dear to me
and that there is no one more devoted to your name than I. And what is more,
I consider it the greatest honour when you think fit to write to me. Wherefore
in future do not, I pray you, have recourse to such apologies.

     But as regards the wine, I made you a gift of one cask of new wine be- 15
cause I had no more of the old 'clear' wine, the one I know agrees with your
palate. Take it in good part, I beseech you. If we had had a more abundant
harvest, I could have honoured you with a more worthy gift, as you deserve.
But the truth is that for the last two or three years the grape harvest has been
so meagre that it is not easy to find new wine of the kind we call 'clear,' 20
and everyone, even the leading citizens, settles for a red wine that they call
'thick.' I hope the new wine will be more delicate than the old wine if you use
it after the Christmas holidays. Your servant informed me that he had found

* * * * *

2401A
1 Talesius; see Ep 2397 n3.

some old 'claret' for sale, thanks to Etienne Desprez, the schoolmaster,[2] a
man who loves and respects you very much. That will be more suitable for   25
you. And you will be able to use it until the new wines mature. When your
messenger, the young Pole,[3] was here recently, I was not in town. Otherwise
I would have made sure that he did not return to you empty-handed. I was
at the court of the king of France at the time, on embassy from the emperor.
That office is now filled by Master François, the treasurer.[4] If he were here,   30
being a good friend of yours, he would have given you a cask or two of wine.
I will see to it that your letter reaches him together with the book, namely the
answer to the apology of the Strasbourgers.[5]

Lastly, you write that if you had not been delayed by members of the
emperor's court, you would have set out for Brabant on the first of September.   35
I would be quite distressed if you had to depart so far from us. The rumour
was that from there you would go to Dijon. I was happy to learn this because
I hoped, if that were the case, that you would pass this way and I would have
the opportunity to see you. However it turns out, and wherever you may be,
you will always have your devoted friend, Léonard, from whom you can   40
expect every assurance and the unfailing services of a friend. Farewell, glory
of letters and singular ornament of our age. Farewell.

From Besançon, on the eve of the feast of Sts Simon and Jude 1530

2402 / From Matthias Kretz   Augsburg, 29 October 1530

The manuscript of this letter, first published as Ep 139 in Förstemann / Günther,
was in the Burscher Collection of the University Library at Leipzig (Ep 1254
introduction). Erasmus' reply is Ep 2414.

Born near Augsburg, Matthias Kretz (c 1480–1543) studied in Vienna and
Tübingen (bachelor of theology 1512) before acquiring a doctorate in theology at Ingolstadt under the direction of Johann Eck (1519). In 1521 he became
preacher of the cathedral at Augsburg, but had difficulties because of the rapid
growth of support for the Reformation in that city. At the Diet of Augsburg in
1530 he was one of the theologians charged with preparing the Catholic confutation of the Lutheran Augsburg Confession. In 1533 he became dean of the
cathedral chapter at Munich, where he remained for the rest of his life. For a list
of his publications, see Allen's introduction to this letter.

* * * * *

2 Ep 2140
3 Ep 2397 n2
4 Ep 2397 n6
5 The *Epistola ad fratres Inferioris Germaniae* (Ep 2324 n2)

†

Cordial greetings. If I could not count on your great kindness, most honourable Erasmus, so highly praised by all who know you, I would be shamelessly impudent to dare to write to such a great man, and furthermore, one
whom I have never met. My reason for writing was nothing other than that
I wished to declare to you my complete devotion and deep attachment to   5
you. Practically the whole city of Augsburg is aware of this, since they heard
from my lips in a public church seven years ago the rules of your Christian
soldier,[1] from which they derived no little benefit, I believe. Furthermore, a
testimony to my respect for you is my little book, which I called 'Whether
Erasmus of Rotterdam is a Lutheran,' which I wanted to publish six years   10
ago, when many were still trying to associate you with the party of Luther.[2]
Now there is no need of such an apologia, since obviously the whole world
openly acknowledges that Erasmus is Catholic to the core, or more correctly,
he is the Jerome of our age and the chariot and charioteer of our Catholic
faith and its most courageous defender. I showed this book to Lieven[3] and   15
Polyphemus[4] to read when, out of regard for you, I had invited them to supper recently. I would mention at this point, save that it might be an indication
of flattery, with what admiration my most reverend master in Augsburg, the
vicar-general, Jakob Henrichmann,[5] and I read your works,[6] how much we
love them, how much we venerate them.   20

You must not become suspicious, most worthy sir, if by chance you get
to know that I invited Eck to my home during the course of the diet. I was
also host to Fabri, bishop of Vienna, Cochlaeus, Ursinus, and many others,[7]

* * * * *

2402
1 Found in the *Enchiridion militis christiani*, probably in the edition of 1518
2 In 1938, the date of the publication of Allen 9, fragments of the work still survived in the University Library at Leipzig (MS 0331m). See Allen's note to line 9
of his text.
3 The name in the text is 'Licinio.' Following Allen, we interpret this as most
probably a miswriting of 'Livino.' Lieven (Livinus) Algoet was in Augsburg
at this time; see Ep 2278 n2. The reading suggested by Förstemann / Günther,
'Luscinio' (ie Ottmar Nachtgall), seems unlikely, given that Nachtgall, who had
lived at Augsburg from 1523, left the city in 1528 to settle in Freiburg; see Ep 2166
n3. There is no evidence that he attended the diet in 1530.
4 For Polyphemus (Felix Rex) see Ep 2386 n3.
5 From 1514 until his death in 1561, Henrichmann was parish priest at Zumar-
schausen, west of Augsburg, and vicar-general of the diocese of Augsburg.
6 Kretz's word for 'works' is *lucubrationes*, a term that Erasmus often used as a
generic description of his publications, as in *Loca quaedam in aliquot Erasmi lucubrationibus per ipsum emendata* (Ep 2095 introduction).
7 See Epp 2374 (Fabri), 1928 (Cochlaeus), 2383 n3 (Ursinus Velius).

who are loyal friends of yours. My home was like a public inn for men of
learning. As for Eck, although he was once my teacher, I daringly opposed   25
him to his face, addressing grave reproaches to him in your defence. But that
will suffice. If I perceive that your ears were not offended by my stammering,
most learned of all men, in future I will write more confidently. I pray that
God the Almighty will preserve you unharmed as long as possible for the
whole Christian world. Amen.   30

   At Augsburg, 29 October in the year 1530 of our redemption
   Matthias Kretz, doctor in theology, preacher in the city of Augsburg,
chaplain completely devoted to your Excellency.

   To the most celebrated and learned of all men, Master Erasmus of
Rotterdam, theologian in the true sense of the word, the glory of Germany,   35
his master worthy of everlasting respect. At Freiburg im Breisgau

2403 / To Erasmus Schets   30 October 1530

This letter, Erasmus' answer to Ep 2364, was first published by Allen on the
basis of the manuscript in the British Library (MS Add 38512 folio 48).

Cordial greetings. I received your letter dated at Antwerp on 13 August but
sent here from Augsburg. I thank you for kindly taking care of the letters to
England. I merely wonder how your letter was delayed for so long in the
hands of Goclenius.

   I wish to know for the half of what year Jan de Hondt sent 65 florins.   5
For Pierre Barbier owed me a six-month pension that he appropriated some
years ago.[1] In addition, two pensions were owed from the feast of St John
1529 to the feast of St John 1530.[2] Now a third one will be owed beginning
with the feast of the Purification.[3] I do not know whether Barbier has made
off with some of this too. For, being in debt, he had given my pension as se- 10
curity to Jan de Hondt until he could acquit himself of his debt; he owed him
four hundred florins. I wrote to you about this through my servant Kan, but
he tarried long on the journey and did not go to Courtrai, as he promised.
Afterwards he wrote that he had sent these letters to you. I do not know if
this is true.   15

* * * * *

2403
1 For the difficulties with Barbier summarized in this paragraph see Ep 2404.
2 Ie John the Baptist, 24 June
3 2 February

What you write about the Fuggers I do not quite understand. I did not entrust anything to the Fuggers. I simply asked Quirinus to see if I could have recuperated my money without risk through the Fuggers, for I have a very close friendship with Anton Fugger. But his agents reacted haughtily. Now Anton has written to them, but I do not see what advantage this will   20 be to me. The reason I did this is that the English do not seem to have great trust in Luis de Castro.[4] I will never be able to find a greater friend than you. If the money comes into your hands through Luis, through you into the hands of the Fuggers, through them into the hands of Anton Fugger in Augsburg, and from Augsburg to me, with risk and losses, what good was it   25 to have changed negotiators? To me it seems more reasonable that you keep what is given to you until the opportunity presents itself of getting it to me. I know what I sent to my servant Quirinus; I do not know what he said. He is rather over-confident, and it is the fate of scholars never to have servants whom they can trust. But if there is some reason that you do not want to be   30 burdened with this commission, it is not my habit to demand too much of my friends. How much Luis nibbles off I do not know. You know better. I have a feeling that my friends are not well disposed towards him – or rather do not trust him.

We must act prudently in the case of Haio Cammingha. He is a young   35 man of headstrong character and he owes money to many people. If he is treated rudely he will feign anger and pay nothing. It is hardly to be believed that he has been made a councillor,[5] for he has not lived in Louvain very long. I would more readily believe that he has gone off to war somewhere. I shall send a letter in my own hand to his brother. You can add his name on the   40 back of the letter, since I do not know it, affix a seal to it, and send it.[6]

Concerning the pension from the emperor, since I see no hope, I thought nothing should be done.

At the diet nothing was done except that it was agreed on both sides to attack the Turks if the emperor leaves Germany in peace; otherwise they   45

* * * * *

4 It appears that Erasmus' English friends did not trust Luis de Castro and that Erasmus thought that the Fuggers, with their international connections, might be able to arrange for the English pension to be transferred without losses due to exchange or commssions. He instructed Quirinus to make inquiry about this, but the Fugger agent in Antwerp appears to have responded rudely. Only later did the agent receive from Anton Fugger a letter instructing him to accommodate Erasmus in this matter; see Ep 2384:72–5.
5 See Ep 2364:13–14 with n7.
6 The letter is not extant, and the name of the brother is unknown.

cannot make war on the Turks.[7] Ferdinand was made archduke of Austria, etc with great pomp and ceremony.[8] In Frankfurt he will acquire the crown of the kingdom of the Romans *extra muros*.[9]

There has been long discussion of some sort of mutual agreement between the Lutherans and the Catholics; in many articles they were in agreement in one way or other. But in the end two things were displeasing in the decision of the emperor: first, the word 'sect'; second, that it was added that the foundations of Lutheranism had been effectively refuted by the evangelical and apostolic writings.[10] When the emperor refused to change this, they said with great arrogance in the presence of the emperor that they not only believed but also knew that the doctrine of Luther was based on the gospel. And so they returned home, to the great indignation of the emperor. A severe conclusion is expected, which has not yet been made public.[11] But it will all

* * * * *

7 Cf Ep 2399:33–45.
8 In 1520–1 Charles v had ceded rule over the Austrian lands to his brother Ferdinand, but only now, in preparation for Ferdinand's election as king of the Romans (see following note), did he go through the formality of bestowing Austria on Ferdinand as an imperial fief (4 September 1530). See Schirrmacher 256–7; Karl Eduard Förstemann *Urkundenbuch zu der Geschichte des Reichstages zu Augsburg im Jahre 1530* 2 vols (Halle 1833–5; repr Hildesheim 1966) II 377–9 no 175.
9 Ferdinand was elected king of the Romans in Cologne, not Frankfurt; the coronation took place in Aachen; see Ep 2384 n7.
10 The 'decision of the emperor' was the text of the first version of the articles of the recess of the diet pertaining to religion. Released on 22 September 1530, the 'first recess' declared 1/ that the 'opinion and confession' of the Protestant estates (ie the Augsburg Confession) had been 'refuted and rejected' (in the Catholic Confutation) on the basis of the gospel and the writings of the Fathers; 2/ that the Protestant princes and cities had until 15 April 1531 to reconsider their position and return to the Catholic fold; 3/ that the Protestant estates were to desist from all further religious innovations, and to refrain from inducing or compelling Catholics to join their 'sects'; and 4/ that the emperor would undertake to bring about the convocation of a general council within six months of the conclusion of the diet. See StL 16 1531–5 no 1113. In the weeks that followed, the Protestant princes and cities rejected all attempts to induce them to accept and sign the recess and, in the absence of an acceptable religious settlement, they refused to contribute the aid against the Turks to which they had originally agreed.
11 The final recess of the diet, which was not published until 19 November 1530, reiterated the points summarized in the preceding note, doing so in language that revealed the emperor's anger at the Protestant estates and his disdain for the 'rebellious, deceitful, already condemned doctrine' that was so contrary to

reflect the mind of the pope and the priests. Nothing was done with regard to
the Zwinglians; in fact they were not admitted to express their views.[12] May　　60
God turn this to a better end than what my heart forebodes.

　　　Here, besides enormously high prices, an epidemic is also raging.[13]
Everything is ten times dearer. I would like you to combine the money Pieter
Gillis has with what you have.[14] I wish, my good friend, that you are in the
best of health together with your dear ones.　　　　　　　　　　　　　　　65

　　　Given at Freiburg, the Sunday before All Saints 1530
　　　Yours, Desiderius Erasmus of Rotterdam

　　　I suspect that you are mistaken about the names of the Haios. There
are two. Haio Herman is councillor in Leeuwarden; Haio Cammingha is the
one who owes me money, but you must not provoke him. You must deal　　70
with his brother.

　　　To the honourable Erasmus Schets, merchant. In Antwerp

*　*　*　*　*

the 'old, true Christian faith.' It was further stipulated that the Edict of Worms
(1521), which had outlawed Luther and his followers but had hitherto been
observed in the breach, was still the law of the land, violation of which would
be met with appropriate 'imperial punishment, according to the circumstances
of the case.' See StL 16 1596–1616 no 1155, especially §§8, 62, 66. The Protestant
estates left the diet convinced that the emperor intended to make war on them
because of their religion, and by the end of the year they had taken the preliminary steps towards the formation of the defensive League of Schmalkalden,
which was officially established on 27 February 1531. The emperor, however,
was in no position to make war on the Protestants. For one thing, he could not
deliver on his promise of a council, and the Catholic princes were not prepared
to support him in the use of force against the Protestants in advance of their
condemnation by a council. Even more important was that Charles was still
in desperate need of the support of the Protestant estates in dealing with the
immediate threat of renewed Turkish aggression. To secure that support, he
negotiated with them, starting in 1532, a series of temporary truces that greatly
facilitated the spread of Lutheranism in Germany in the 1530s and '40s; cf Ep
2384 n9. See also Stephen A. Fischer-Galati *Ottoman Imperialism and German
Protestantism 1521–1555* (Harvard University Press 1959) chapter 3.

12 Martin Bucer and Wolfgang Capito managed to have their *Confessio tetrapolita-
na* presented to the emperor, but it was not read to him and received no formal
consideration. Zwingli mailed in his own confession of faith, the *Ratio fidei*, but
it was completely rejected. See Ep 2333 n12.

13 Erasmus often complained about the high cost of living at Freiburg; see Ep 2215
n10. On the plague, see Ep 2426 n3. Both are mentioned again in Epp 2410:55–6,
2450:12–13.

14 For monies entrusted to Pieter Gillis on Erasmus' behalf, see Allen Epp 2494:25–
33, 2511:7–11, 2512:1–2, 2527:5–8, 2530:45–50, 2552:14–15, 2558:28–36, 2578:4–12.

2404 / From Pierre Barbier   Tournai, 1 November [1530]

The autograph of this letter, first published as Ep 77 in Enthoven, is in the Rehdiger Collection of the University Library at Wrocław (MS Rehd 254.15). The
letter is Barbier's answer to one, no longer extant, written by Erasmus on 29 August 1530 (line 2). An earlier letter, written between December 1529 (Ep 2239)
and August 1530, had not reached Barbier (lines 58–9). This letter, along with
Ep 2407, was forwarded to Erasmus by Erasmus Schets in December 1530 (see
Allen Epp 2487:1–3, 2490:8–10, 2494:4–5). The two letters reached Erasmus sometime between 21 April and 11 June 1531 (see Allen Epp 2490:8–9, 2501:1, 4–5).

For Barbier, dean of Tournai, see Epp 443, 1294, 1862 n2. After the introductory paragraph, Barbier switches abruptly to the subject of Erasmus' bewil-
deringly complicated financial affairs, which Erasmus himself had difficulty
understanding, and which still await investigation by a competent scholar. In
the absence of the letter to which Barbier is responding, some of his loosely
worded references to past events are difficult to pin down. The contents of
Ep 2407 provide a certain amount of welcome illumination.

†

Hail, most learned master, my Erasmus! I received your letter an hour ago,
the one sent more or less on 29 August of this year, no earlier, for as the messenger told me, it remained in some way or other with the dean of Bruges for
six weeks or more.[1] To respond to it: as to your saying that I write a very detailed account of the Spaniard, I merely described the actual state of affairs.   5
But let us pass on to other matters.

The chancellor acted as my guarantor in my presence,[2] as you say, and
as guarantor he ordered payment to be made from his account, whether the

* * * * *

2404
1 The dean of Bruges was Marcus Laurinus (Ep 1342).
2 The chancellor was Jean Le Sauvage (Ep 410), and the incident referred to here
   took place in 1517. In July of that year the sum of 300 florins was due from
   Erasmus' imperial pension. The Spanish agent responsible for delivering the
   money (line 5 above) was late in arriving, so Le Sauvage undertook to pay
   the sum out of his own account. According to Barbier, the chancellor assumed
   responsibility for the entire sum but in fact paid only 200 florins, which Barbier
   had passed on to Erasmus by c 10 July (Ep 597:29–30). When the agent arrived,
   he gave Barbier 'barely' 240 florins, 200 of which went immediately as repay-
   ment to Sauvage (Ep 621:10–13), leaving Barbier with only 40 florins towards
   the 100 still owed to Erasmus. At the time Erasmus appears to have had no
   doubts concerning Barbier's honesty ((Ep 652:2–5), but in a letter of February
   1525 to Jan de Hondt (Ep 1548:24–5), he accused Barbier of having stolen 'forty

Spaniard gave him anything or not, and he ordered not part of the pension,
but the whole pension to be paid. Whatever he ordered or did not order, he   10
gave me only two hundred florins which, I think you will not deny, I paid out
to you immediately in the house of Antonius Clava,[3] as you will acknowledge. You add that I said, 'He did not wish to give any more,' or that he did
not give it, and I repeat that now also, but I will never admit that I said, 'We
will bring the rest in an hour.' I wonder, no matter what happened, if I am   15
mistaken or not mistaken about a transaction of fifteen years ago.[4] This much
is certain: whatever de Hondt paid, he paid the whole amount, because he
was my authorized agent in the matter.[5] And it is not surprising if it was
counted out to you at his initiative, since he had been given full responsibility by me in this matter, unless perhaps you wish to require from me that   20
which, during that period, I never dealt with myself.[6] I make an exception of
one term,[7] which de Hondt himself used for my affairs.[8] I do not believe nor
do I disbelieve that it was done by my order.[9] I say that your Excellency once

* * * * *

florins' from his imperial pension ('forty' seemingly an error for 'sixty,' ie XL
for LX) and of harbouring designs on his Courtrai pension as well. Although
Barbier continued to insist that he had not received the money and therefore
did not owe it, Erasmus, who had come to distrust Barbier on other grounds as
well, continued to believe him guilty as charged; see Ep 2239.

3 For Clava see Ep 175:13n.
4 The reference to 'fifteen years ago' agrees most easily with the summer of 1517,
  when the sum of 300 florins was due from Erasmus' imperial pension (see n2
  above). But in Ep 2407:11–15, Johannes de Molendino, who had seen this letter, understood Erasmus to be referring to the annuity that Erasmus received
  in consequence of having ceded a prebend at Courtrai to Pierre Barbier, who
  subsequently ceded it to Jan de Hondt. The annuity had first been offered to
  Erasmus in July 1516 (Ep 436), but the arrangement for its payment from de
  Hondt via Barbier to Erasmus was not completed before 1518 (see Ep 751).
5 All de Hondt's payments to Erasmus were made in his capacity as agent for
  Barbier; see Epp 751:7–8, 1245 introduction.
6 Ie the period in 1516–17 before Barbier and de Hondt had concluded their arrangement for the payment of the Courtrai pension to Erasmus.
7 Barbier uses the word *terminus* 'boundary,' 'limit' in the sense of a period of time
  with defined limits. Here it refers to a period to which the payment of a specified
  sum was attached.
8 Ep 2407:13–18 makes clear that this is a reference to the half-year (summer
  of 1524) in which the Courtrai pension was used to defray the expenses of
  Barbier's suit for the deanery of Tournai, with de Hondt acting as the agent for
  Barbier, who was still in Rome (Epp 1458, 1470).
9 According to Erasmus (Ep 1471:8–9), Barbier told him at the time that de Hondt
  had acted without his instructions.

wrote to me that the same de Hondt had sent you a letter of mine about this
affair. But, whatever the case may be, it should not seem surprising that you   25
were given compensation through the efforts of the person who was taking
care of this matter for me. It should seem harsh to you if I had to pay twice.

. Concerning the exchange, I explained fully in a previous letter that in
no way did I make the same de Hondt legally liable for the pension in perpe-
tuity, as may have been indicated to you,[10] as I could easily explain to you if   30
you were here. But I see there are those who want misunderstandings to exist
between you and me. You say that a new excuse has been invented, namely,
that I said that I do not want to be made financially liable to you in the tribunal either of justice or of my conscience. That is not a new excuse, but the
plain truth. And you were informed about it, and before you decided that the   35
prebend of Courtrai should be given to me, you weighed the pros and cons,
you slept on it, and stayed awake debating it. The matter could not have been
arranged in any other way according to canon law. The prebend could not be
the equivalent of such a large pension, and I did not have priestly benefices
from whose revenues I could pay you. As to the benefices I received as a   40
recompense (and any other benefices that exist in the whole world),[11] I never
asked that any of them be joined to my deanery. You know that nothing was
paid out, no receipt from you for the last two years has been shown to me,
nor are there any now. The money corresponding to this whole period was
kept by this same de Hondt until the month of June. My brother then became   45
mortally ill, and you wished part of the benefices to be relinquished to him.[12]
Then, for fear that he would die, the same de Hondt appropriated the money.
It has been spent and cannot be paid to the account at present, but it will be,
around Christmas time, at least a good part of it, as I wrote to Morillon, and
I hope that he will write to you about it.[13] He had written to me two months   50
ago, or at the least one month ago, that you had written to him with certain
complaints, about which I do not admit any guilt, except that I wrote to him

* * * * *

10 It appears that Erasmus' Courtrai pension, according to an arrangement that
   Erasmus never fully understood (cf Ep 751:11–20), was to have been charged to
   de Hondt's prebend only for period of years, and that thereafter Barbier was to
   bear the full responsbility for it out of the income from his other benefices. In a
   letter to Erasmus Schets of 27 August 1532, Erasmus finally acknowledged the
   validity of this arrangement (Allen Ep 2704:24–5).
11 On the cession of the benefices, see Ep 1094 n6.
12 The brother was Nicolas Barbier (Ep 613), about whom nothing is known apart
   from the few references to him in Erasmus' correspondence. For the cession of
   a benefice to him in 1521 see Ep 1245:31–6.
13 No such letter from Guy Morillon (Ep 532 introduction) is extant.

asking that he beseech you that you would be satisfied with my response (for
I had not yet received your letter and did not know you had written to me). I
ask this favour of you now, Master Erasmus. Even if I had sworn a thousand   55
times, I could not write you anything else.

Concerning my nephews I cannot write anything other than what I
wrote to you then.¹⁴ About your thousand ducats,¹⁵ about which you say
I am joking, this much is certain: that a man who lacks nothing should not
pressure more than is just a man who is needy in the extreme, and especially   60
a servant who in good faith promises that he will pay all that he owes com-
pliantly. I have not received, to my knowledge, any other letter from you besides the one I answered (in another hand than my own, as you write)¹⁶ and
in which it seems you limit the content to a few recent news items. No one
has come here for a year and a half or two years to ask me for your money on   65
your account. If anyone did come, he would have surely found a good part of
the money reserved for you until the month of June, and I would have given
him the money, asking for a receipt.

The courier is in a hurry and we were held up by religious functions on
this holy day, so that I was not able to recopy the letter or correct it adequately. 70

Finally, as to your unwilling withdrawal from the combat to establish
Christian peace, I would rather die than allow myself to be torn away from it
even at the risk of making open enemies. But, I beg you, appraise the situation not only according to your own judgment, but accept another's as well.

I gave cordial greeting to Molendino in your name.¹⁷ He has invited   75
your servant Quirinus for supper.¹⁸ I would have detained him for dinner
tomorrow but he is afraid you will count twice, hour by hour, his delay in
returning. Besides, I have left my house for fear of the plague, as he knows.
When he returns he will be welcomed more generously. May the one good
and omnipotent God keep you safe and sound in mind and body.   80

From Tournai, the first of November

Yours, as your servant, Pierre Barbier

To the most learned Master Desiderius Erasmus of Rotterdam. At
Freiburg

* * * * *

14 Cf Ep 2239:5–9 with n2.
15 It is not clear what this refers to. One thousand ducats was a considerable amount
   of money. The ducat was worth 80d groot Flemish in 1530, so the sum was equivalent to about 35 years' wages of an Antwerp master tradesman at 9.05d per day
   and a year of 253 days (CWE 12 650 Table 3, 691 Table 13).
16 Ep 2239, dated 7 December 1529, in a secretary's hand
17 Johannes de Molendino; see Ep 2407.
18 For Quirinus see Ep 2367 n3.

2405 / From Germain de Brie   From the court [Blois], 8 November 1530

This is Brie's answer to Ep 2379; Erasmus replied to it with Ep 2422. The
letter was first published by Brie in his *Gratulatoriae quatuor ad totidem viros
clarissimos* ... (Paris: C. Wechel 1531). The manuscript, the basis of Ep 140 in
Förstemann / Günther, was part of the Burscher Collection of the University
Library at Leipzig (Ep 1254 introduction). For the location of the court at this
time, see Marichal I 726–7 (nos 3797–8).

GERMAIN DE BRIE TO ERASMUS OF ROTTERDAM

These days have seemed to me the most rewarding and beautiful, if ever
there were any others, and not only for me, but for you. For first of all they
renewed an old friendship with a very important – shall I say person or
prince? certainly a prince, and a great prince – a friendship entered into in   5
Rome when we were both young men, which was dormant rather than ex-
tinguished for more or less twenty years because of our absence from one
another. Next, while those days gave rise in us, that is, in this very renowned
prince and me, to the most pleasant conversations about the outstanding
men of our century, they led us to mention you in such laudatory and hon-   10
orific terms that I can hardly judge which of the two of us found it more
pleasant, more agreeable, more delightful. Truly, he shows such good will
and such ardent devotion towards you that not only in loving but also in
praising and lauding you to the skies and admiring you he does not yield
even to me (I do not think I can say much more than that). As a result, he per-   15
suaded me to acknowledge that I am now under a great obligation to him as
much in your name as in my own (why would I not be? since a good part of
the opinion that certain people hold of you, good or bad, flows in some way
from the great mutual friendship that exists between us). He also enjoins me
to make sure in my first letter to you not to conceal the warm sentiments he   20
entertains for you. I thought it was important for you to know about this so
that when you have the time you will write him a letter that will serve as an
expression and, so to speak, a lasting testimony of your reciprocal good will
and affection towards him. I was not unaware that you would do this of your
own accord (in keeping with your usual benevolent nature), if you happened   25
to hear about it from some source other than my letter. Your letter to him
should be all the more clear and explicit since this news came to you from
Brie, which is to say, from a man closely linked to you by an inveterate loyal
friendship, and therefore free of embellishment. I would think it a sin or even
a crime on your part if you were not to reciprocate the affection of one who   30
has so much affection for you and such a high opinion of you, who speaks so
commendably of all that concerns you, and who acclaims, commends, and
admires you to the highest degree.

But not to keep you in suspense any longer, Agostino Trivulzio, cardinal of the church of Rome, is a man of singular nobility (the name of his fam-   35
ily of itself is proof enough), illustrious for his great humanity, his learning,
and his wisdom.[1] I met him in Rome long ago at the time of Pope Julius when
I was a young man and he was a young man (we are of the same age). I made
a special effort, although that was not necessary, to insinuate myself into his
friendship and his circle of acquaintances for the sake of imbibing elegant   40
learning (which he already pursued with great enthusiasm). He possessed
then as much amiability as he does now, not grafted on and implanted, but
so innate and natural that it was evident to all (I speak especially of men of
learning), frank and undisguised. Afterwards he cultivated, enhanced, and
ennobled his learning, wisdom, and other virtues, which flourish in him   45
in great abundance, so that he was appointed by Pope Leo to the glorious
College of Cardinals and there, as the leader of that sacrosanct college, he
has drawn all his colleagues to love, admire, and venerate him more than
any other person.

   I know that just as only the artist can rightly judge a painter and a sculp-   50
tor, so a learned and wise man can only truly be recognized by a learned and
wise man. Nevertheless, as far as it has been given me to comprehend with
my mediocre knowledge and judgment, so many great virtues appear, stand
out, and shine forth in Cardinal Trivulzio, and shine forth in such a way that
even one who is moderately intelligent is strongly affected. In the few days I   55
spent with him he so beguiled, touched and, so to speak, fascinated me that
no other person holds my attention, has me in his power, and possesses me
more than he alone. And by Hercules! he has great affability, a rare urbanity
in his conversation, and rare too is the pleasantness that radiates from his

* * * * *

2405
1 Agostino Trivulzio (d 1548) was member of a noble family of Milan that was
   devoted to the interests of France in the politics of Italy. While serving as protector of the Cistercian order in Rome, he entered the service of Pope Julius ii
   as chamberlain and apostolic protonotary. Leo x created him cardinal in 1517.
   Following the sack of Rome in May 1527, Trivulzio, who had been closely identified with the pro-French policies of Clement vii, was imprisoned with him in
   the Castel Sant' Angelo before being sent to spend eighteen months in captivity
   at Naples. In 1530 he accompanied Clement to Bologna for the coronation of
   Charles v, and then in March 1530 departed for the French court (and the reunion with Brie celebrated in this letter). In 1531 Francis i made him bishop of
   Bayeux. On the death of Clement vii in 1534, Trivulzio led the French cardinals
   in their support for the election of Alessandro Farnese as Paul iii. Much admired for his erudition, Trivulzio assembled materials for a history of the popes
   and cardinals that he did not live to write. Brie calls him a 'prince,' but he was
   that only in the sense of 'prince of the church.' See illustration 175 below.

face and expression. And all of that is joined to an equal seriousness (which 60
I consider as difficult as it is important). Add to this an irreproachable life, a
charming and sincere manner, which is at the same time upright and worthy of praise and modelled on antiquity in every aspect. What can I say of
his character, lofty, sublime, gracious, varied, penetrating, nimble, learned?
What shall I say of his judgment, shrewd refined, polished, sensitive? He 65
submits to it the writings both of the ancients and of modern authors with
careful precision, in the manner of Aristarchus.[2] Wherefore you must attribute all the more honour and esteem to the benevolence awarded you by a
prince rendered illustrious by his many great virtues, especially since it is
engendered solely by his love of your intellectual abilities and admiration 70
of your learning. I may be mistaken, but I think it is reasonable to believe
that he who is attracted by the virtues of others must have an abundance
of virtues himself. And in addition to those that I have enumerated, which
are attested to and well known, there are many other virtues in him which I
can hardly describe in words. Not to mention those great insignias of virtue 75
that he bears, which in themselves, albeit many have acquired them without
virtue, nevertheless have always been so prized by men of our time that the
person on whom they had been conferred was considered equal in dignity to
the greatest of kings.

At this point perhaps you may think that I have given free rein to my 80
love for Trivulzio and have carried his praises beyond the limits of truth.
But I assure you, so help me God, that his virtues are far greater than I have
described. Certainly, I have great respect and love for him; who would not
love a cardinal endowed with such great virtues? But it is the duty of a friend
to honour him with the eulogies that he deserves, and not to load him with 85
praises belonging to another. So I exhort you, most beloved Erasmus, and
if you will allow me, I pray and beseech you, to accept with open arms, as
they say,[3] such great benevolence towards you of no ordinary cardinal, but
of Trivulzio, in a letter worthy of both you and him as soon as possible.[4] If
you send it to me I shall deliver it into his hands, for he will be staying with 90
us for a few months. Believe me, you will have not only the charming and
agreeable friendship of such an important cardinal but also his most gener-

* * * * *

2 Aristarchus of Samothrace (c 216–144), librarian of Alexandria and literary
critic of proverbial severity, who established the historically most important
edition of Homer
3 *Adagia* II ix 54
4 Erasmus responded to this request with Ep 2423.

ous and honorific patronage. For he enjoys such influence and authority in
his college (I did not wish you to be unaware of this) that you could compare
only a small number of his colleagues to him (I do not wish to say anything   95
too exaggerated about an extremely modest man). I await your letter with
great anxiety.

From the royal court, 8 November 1530

I had already written and sealed this letter when I received three letters of yours all at once, one more than laconic, the second of an acceptable   100
length, and the third more than Asiatic (although the style itself is more redolent of Atticism),5 all dated from Freiburg around the same time.6 One contained I know not how many Greek homilies of Chrysostom on the Epistle to
the Romans, in manuscript, which have not yet been translated by anyone,
which you sent to me so that they would return to you translated into Latin   105
by me and could be published soon thanks to your friend Froben for the
profit of men of letters. For you prescribe and fix the time within which you
wish the task to be finished.7 But I will talk to you more about that at another
time. I am taken up with the noisy turmoil of the court, in the country, not in
the city. So you may understand that I have less freedom, less tranquillity at   110
my disposal. In the meantime, to let you know my feelings about this assignment (that is what you demand of me most urgently), I am not only disposed
but ready to comply with your wishes in this regard if my strength is equal
to the task, as I trust it will be, unless something more profound and abstruse
lurks in the remaining homilies than in the first two. I read them both in   115
their entirety without drawing a breath,8 as well as the preface of the author,
which you will receive translated by me, together with some first drafts that
I have finished. In this way you will see that the weaving of the fabric has
begun, and you can have a taste of the translation of the preface and can expect the rest. For I have conformed myself totally to your will, my dear friend   120
Erasmus, for some time now, and I have so composed myself to carry out all
your commands that there is nothing, especially in this kind of service, that

* * * * *

5 In Greek and Roman rhetoric the simple, direct style was known as 'Attic'; the
  more florid style was known as 'Asiatic.'
6 Of these three letters, only Ep 2379, dated 5 September 1530, survives.
7 The Homilies on Romans had had to be omitted from Froben's Latin Chrysostom
  because of a breakdown in communication with the intended translators; see
  Ep 2359 introduction.
8 'Without drawing a breath' is one word in Greek: ἀπνευστί; there is no equivalent in Latin.

I would not undertake to carry out as soon as you requested, devoting every effort to it with hands and feet.[9]

And certainly I shall not deceive your expectations in this matter. 125
Besides, it would not be at all possible for me to abandon that translation without incurring significant risk to my reputation. I have made known the whole matter to the king, that you had sent me the Greek homilies for me to translate into Latin, and he, because of his own quite remarkable interest in Chrysostom,[10] encouraged me again and again to take on this task, and 130
such was his enthusiasm that he added that he would recompense my labour with some fitting reward. Therefore the fruits of this labour, undertaken not only at your invitation but also with royal compensation, will readily become available before very long although, as far as I am concerned, this one reward motivates me, glory (not my own, but that of Paul and Chrysostom, to both 135
of whom I am most fervently devoted) and also the honour and advancement of sacred letters.

So then, I undertake this labour with all the more vigour and enthusiasm partly because, through daily familiarity with other writings of Chrysostom, I have come to share your view that the Homilies are genuine, 140
not spurious, works, and partly because they have not yet been translated by anyone into Latin. My friends (especially those to whom, by a peculiar vice of nature, the brilliance of another's reputation is usually odious and displeasing) hope that it redounds to my honour that I produce a translation that is entirely mine and not shared with others and in so doing demon- 145
strate to them that I can engage in an arena where no one else has set foot. Nonetheless, I am inclined to the opinion that he who corrects a book that has been badly translated by another is no less deserving of praise in the world of letters than someone who sets himself to translate a book that has not had the benefit of a Latin translation. In the latter case you have only 150
the naked meaning of the author, whereas in the former those who wish to compare the Greek and the Latin text, and have not yet mastered Greek perfectly (how few there are who have attained this) reap a twofold profit, for they both understand the meaning of the author and at the same time are warned to avoid the lapses of the first translator, if ever they themselves 155
are involved in a similar work of translation. It can often happen in practice that the meaning of Greek words is at times so ambiguous that unless you are very attentive, and unless you use extreme caution joined with an equal

* * * * *

9 Ie with diligence (hands) and swiftness (feet); see *Adagia* I iv 15.
10 See Ep 1795:2–4.

amount of learning and natural ability, the similarity of Greek expressions
will drive you into those very same errors into which your predecessor has   160
ridiculously fallen. It is pleasant and helpful when you see the second translator has pierced the eyes of the crow, as they say,[11] so that you will not fall
into the same mistake in the same or similar words. It is a commonplace
that a man forewarned is worth two.[12] In addition, in this way, if I am not
mistaken, these impostors will be more reluctant to occupy themselves with   165
translating. We see them rushing, with no sense of shame or discernment
and to the great bane of serious studies, to obscure with the darkness of
their inarticulateness and ignorance (not to use harsher terms) the clarity of
Greek authors, while at the same time they have a creeping fear that through
the example of another's impudence they may one day be branded with the   170
mark of ignominy and ignorance for their translations.[13]

But more about this another time. I hasten now to that part of your
lengthy letter in which you subtly make work on the homilies appear easier.
What do you mean? You say, 'The name of Germain de Brie is already illustrious and of itself commends the book to the reader; a popular author   175
is a great attraction.'[14] Is it because I appear desirous of some modest glory
that you wish to induce me by this artifice, to allure me by this blandish-
ing, as it were, to the goal for which you have destined me? Certainly I am
not averse to any exhortation of yours, especially to undertake this kind of
work, through which I can make some contribution to learning, but I do not   180
acknowledge or accept the praises you confer on me regarding the two languages. Why do you wish me to be your collaborator? While you assign me
a part of translating the homilies, you write that you reserve part of the work
for yourself so that the exertion will be lighter. Am I to be your collaborator,
Erasmus, you who are so competent in both languages that you seem to excel   185
in whatever you say or write? I sincerely confess, and I am not ashamed of
confessing it, that when I read your writings I sense from the comparison
how badly I write. And yet I am touched that you have such esteem for me
that you would deign to invite me to this collaboration, to involve me in such

* * * * *

11 See Ep 2394 n9.
12 Not in the *Adagia*, but a common proverb nonetheless, with variants in different
   languages. In English the equivalent is 'forewarned is forearmed.' Closest to
   the Latin version used here by Brie is the Spanish proverb 'hombre prevenido
   vale por dos.'
13 A barb doubtless aimed primarily at Johannes Oecolampadius; see Ep 2359
   introduction.
14 See Ep 2379:75–8.

an honourable labour. But as for this association that you have so generously   190
offered me (in your usual kindness), I shall never persuade myself to accept it, for the reason I mentioned. For I am afraid (as I remember I wrote to
you on another occasion) of the association and the comparison of roses and
windflowers.[15] Therefore I shall take it upon myself to translate the Homilies
in their entirety. I would prefer that you allow me this rather than that I be   195
included in this association either of work or glory with you as in the Trojan
horse.[16] If you do not envy me this independent glory, I would like to extend
the time you prescribed. I acknowledge that I can complete the work, whatever it entails, within the prescribed period; I have, nevertheless, wished to
maintain the same care that I brought to other writings of Chrysostom that   200
I have previously translated at your initiative and invitation (although you
object that I was guilty of slowness, if it please the Muses). That is my usual
practice, since I have little confidence in my learning and eloquence. If perhaps some error be committed through carelessness in my translation of the
Homilies, believe me, even greater care will be required; the effort to please   205
you will not serve as an excuse. And then, every time I am about to publish
something, the saying 'The hasty bitch brings forth blind whelps' regularly
comes to mind.[17] Therefore, in this one prescription – the deadline – I would
wish that you allow me to disagree with you with the same vigour that I
usually display in obeying you in all things. For I prefer to preserve my own   210
reputation rather than serve the interests of your friend Froben. A tardy publication of my works makes it more solid than a rushed one. That phrase of
Homer is well known to you: 'Late to come, late in fulfilment, / The fame
whereof shall never perish.'[18]

     Again, farewell.   215

     To Master Erasmus of Rotterdam, by far the prince of eloquence in both
languages in our age

2406 / To Johann Koler   Freiburg, 12 November 1530

This letter was first published in the *Vita Erasmi*. Although it is Erasmus' reply to
Ep 2384, it consists largely of his indignant reaction to Ep 2387 (from Johann Eck).

* * * * *

15 See Ep 1045:141–3 and *Adagia* II vi 41.
16 *Adagia* IV ii 1
17 *Adagia* II ii 35, cited in Greek
18 Homer *Iliad* 2.325, cited in Greek

ERASMUS OF ROTTERDAM TO THE EXCELLENT GENTLEMAN
JOHANN KOLER, PROVOST OF CHUR

Many things have been written and made known to me about Eck's vanity,
arrogance, frivolity, and drunkenness, but I never suspected that he entertained such virulent feelings against me, especially since he sometimes sent 5
me greetings, and we have mutual friends in Ludwig Baer and Joannes Fabri.
How his answer lacks all common sense! He talks as if the articles were
brought to him as though to the emperor, and says that he did not read them
nor did he know whose they were before I asked him. He calls them scandalous, as if the diet came together for nonsense of this sort. He criticizes 10
me for calling them 'opinions,' as if I were stating openly that those were
my sentiments. It was safer to call them 'articles.'[1] What is more shameless
than to condemn in writing what you did not read and did not know who
the author was? I demanded that he indicate the passages; at this point he
became silent. I pointed out to him that there were two articles that are no- 15
where to be found in my writings. He did not respond until recently, although
he should certainly have done so. He merely promises that he will indicate
what he found offensive in them when he is liberated from the diet, as if the
diet depended on him personally. He promises to be a most respectful son to
me if I continue to oppose Luther, as if he had not heard of the *Diatribe*,[2] the 20
Hyperaspistes, and other works and letters of mine. He does not know whether
he hurled that insult, 'infantile theologian,' against me or someone else.[3] What
does this man consider important? I cannot conjecture either whence he conceived this venom against me, unless it is because nowhere in my writings is
Eck celebrated in letters of gold. I suspect the man was stirred up by Heinrich 25
Eppendorf.[4] He seems to have come to Augsburg mainly for this purpose,
that in this great crowd of people he can sow his lies, which he produces from
himself as a spider produces thread. I am surprised that he did not get as
far as you, since there is no place where he has not wormed his way in, this
great master of lies, whose words find credibility nowhere except with those 30
who have no experience. This man, not worth a farthing, thinks he is famous
if people say he is engaged in a controversy with Erasmus. He requested an

* * * * *

2406
1 As Eck had done in his pamphlet *Articulos 404* (Ep 2365 n5)
2 Ie *De libero arbitrio*
3 In Eck's letter the 'insult' is *infans theologus* 'tongue-tied theologian,' but here
   Erasmus changes *infans* to *infantulus*. See Ep 2387:10 with n4.
4 This account of Eppendorf's conduct at the diet is essentially identical to that
   found in Ep 2400.

interview with Duke George. The duke answered that he would think it over.
Not many days later he came back singing the same refrain. The duke did
not receive the man, saying that he did not wish to acknowledge someone 35
who refused to acknowledge his own father (in fact, Eppendorf boasted that
he was a nobleman even though he is a commoner).[5] But the duke handed
the task of hearing him to Simon Pistoris, to whom I had written a detailed
account of the whole affair. Thereupon, Thraso replied,[6] 'I have no business
with Pistoris; I wish to exonerate myself before the duke.' And he departed in 40
a great fit of anger. He kept quiet until Pistoris returned to his native country
with Carlowitz. Finally, in his shamelessness he managed to get the duke to
delegate the case to Julius Pflug, whose ear our friend Eppendorf had filled
with innumerable lies, which was easy enough for him to do because Julius
knew neither Eppendorf nor the case. And so the duke wrote to me asking 45
that I place my trust in Pflug. Julius wrote me a very friendly and learned letter touching on many things,[7] which can be summed up in this way: that in
addition to the preface I should write a short book dedicated to Eppendorf, in
accordance with the agreement, although he violated the agreement in many
ways before leaving Basel and afterwards did not cease writing and speaking 50
about me in a hostile manner, often reciting a raving book that he had written
against me.[8] And he wanted a book for no other reason than that he could
boast again about the conditions to which he had reduced Erasmus. He hoped
to have some profit from the decision of the arbiters; since he failed in this, he
became even a worse enemy. Even though everyone knew that he had done 55
everything contrary to what was agreed upon, he demands his rights, as if he
had fulfilled all the conditions, and he is not ashamed of anything. I had decided to tolerate everything rather than defile my writings for the sake of this
worthless individual, but since he never stops lying, I have written a book in
which I pass cursorily over the subject so as not to exhaust my secretaries.[9] I 60
have moderated my style in order not to harm Eppendorf, but in such a way
that those who have heard the man will realize how brazenly he lies. He made
sure that the letters of the duke and Julius would reach me at a time when I

* * * * *

5 See Ep 1934:94–135; CWE 78 370–1, 377–8, 381.
6 See Ep 2392 n4.
7 Neither the letter from the duke nor that from Pflug is extant.
8 Evidently a manuscript of the still unpublished *Iusta querela* (Ep 1934 introduction), which would not appear in print until February 1531.
9 Ie the *Admonitio adversus mendacium*, which had just been published; cf Ep 2400
n12.

would not have time to respond. I answered via the prefect of Breisach, to whom I had also entrusted letters to other persons,[10] to none of which have I 65 received a response. I am afraid that villain intercepted them. Of Eck he consistently speaks badly; he made abusive use of his name.

How many portentous things are happening in Germany! I am grateful to you and Master Anton for your kind offer of hospitality. But how is it suitable that you invite me to Augsburg when you are also afraid, and it is very 70 possible that after the departure of the emperor grave tumults may arise? There is no one more mild and scrupulous than the emperor, but I fear that the malice of some may abuse his goodness. I see that they treat unimportant things seriously and serious things lightly. In pontifical ceremonies nothing is left out, and now they are discussing the title of king of the Romans.[11] 75 Would that they would calculate how much annual revenue these magnificent titles bring them. But I will cease, since it is not even safe in this age to utter groans. Give thanks to Master Anton in my name, praying that he take care that the letter to Brassicanus be brought to Vienna,[12] and if the diet is dismissed, that it reach Polyphemus and Johann Henckel.[13] 80

Farewell, my beloved friend in the Lord.

At Freiburg, the day after St Martin's 1530

Do not divulge these things that I have disclosed to you.

You will recognize the hand of Erasmus of Rotterdam.

2407 / From Johannes de Molendino   Tournai, 14 November 1530

This autograph of this letter, first published as Ep 141 in Förstemann / Günther, was in the Burscher Collection of the University Library at Leipzig (Ep 1254 introduction). For Johannes de Molendino (Jean Molinier), canon of Tournai and close friend of Pierre Barbier, dean of Tournai, see Ep 371 introduction.

Cordial greetings. If I answer your letter somewhat tardily,[1] Master Erasmus, most learned in all things, the fault, which I do not altogether excuse, should

* * * * *

10 See Epp 2395:25–6, 2400:24–5.
11 See Ep 2384 n7.
12 The letter is not extant. For Brassicanus, professor of rhetoric at Vienna, see Epp 1146, 2305.
13 See Epp 2386 n3 (Polyphemus), 2392 (Henckel).

2407
1 The letter is not extant.

be imputed not so much to me as to our friend Barbier, our dean, who last summer was often absent from the city for long periods of time. I reminded him that he had to write to Erasmus, which he never refused to do. On the contrary, he said, 'After certain business matters are complete, we will write, without fail.' Which he did, and I read his letter,[2] which seems to answer amply your letter to me. I am not familiar, however, with the whole affair in all its details, although he assured me with great solemnity that what he had written to you was completely true and certain, since you complained to me about three things especially. The first concerned the six-month pension sent here of his own accord by Master Jan de Hondt, which was employed when there was a dispute here about the deanery of Tournai.[3] Barbier was then in Rome with Pope Adrian.[4] He wrote to me that he would pay back the six-month pension to you entirely, which he does not retract even now. But, he says, it is harsh of you that you do not allow him to use a small part of the pension that he generously sent to you fifteen or sixteen years ago and which he could have kept for himself. The other two matters concerned the Spaniard and another sum of money recently received by Master Jan de Hondt himself. Since he has had extensive discussions with you about this, I shall not mention it for the moment, so as not to waste my time. Pardon me, I beseech you, since I am unfamiliar with all these matters, which were handled by Chancellor Le Sauvage.[5]

But I return to your letter, which gave me more pleasure than anything that happened to me in the last year. I would have gladly shown it to my friends, as an exceptional gift, had I not given thought to preserving the dignity of one's neighbour. But if I have not written anything to you in the last three or four years, there is no reason for you to accuse me of forgetfulness, negligence, or ill will, for of all learned men I love you especially from the bottom of my heart and with all sincerity, and I honour and respect you, and treasure all your writings, so much so that they are my greatest delight. And I would write to you more frequently, but I am ashamed, believe me, to send these crude trifles to you, such a great hero and champion of all literature.

* * * * *

2 Ep 2404
3 See Ep 2404 n8, and cf Allen Ep 2487:9–12.
4 Barbier arrived in Rome with Pope Adrian in August 1522. By the time of Adrian's death in September 1523, Barbier's appointment as dean of the Tournai chapter had been confirmed, but the lengthy litigation (see preceding note) prevented his taking possession of the deanery until sometime in 1527 or 1528.
5 See Ep 2404 n2.

But if I learn that you think well of them, in your great kindness towards everyone, I will see to it that in a short time you see more silly trifles,   35
if I cannot manage to write anything better. The illness from which I was suffering last month has now become less severe but prevents me from writing
at greater length.

Farewell, most celebrated Master Erasmus.

Tournai, 14 November 1530   40

Yours sincerely, Johannes de Molendino

To Master Erasmus of Rotterdam, celebrated among all nations. At
Freiburg

2408 / From Adriaan Wiele   Augsburg, 16 November 1530

The autograph of this letter, first published as Ep 142 in Förstemann / Günther,
was in the Burscher Collection of the University Library at Leipzig (Ep 1254 introduction). For Adriaan Wiele, secretary to Charles v in the Council of Brabant,
see Ep 1351 n8.

Cordial greetings. I would have deafened your ears with my useless trifles if
my dull stupidity and the perfection of your learning, which does not abide
anything that is not elegant and highly polished, had not deterred me. What
would I, a jackdaw who has not even greeted literature from the threshold,
sing to a parrot?[1] And yet my affection and respect for you (I who was and   5
will always remain the admirer and champion of your celebrity, to the point
of arousing hatred) prompt me to make known to you what a noted Friar
Minor here named Medardus (I would call him Mostardicus),[2] court preacher to the king of Hungary for public assemblies and slanders etc, spat out
against you from the pulpit, either to accuse you of calumny or betray you in   10
some way.[3] In the presence of a rather numerous crowd, in a manner worthy

* * * * *

2408
1 Ie what would a stupid, ignorant man (*Adagia* I iv 37, I vii 22, III iii 97; cf Ep
   2275), who knows nothing of literature (*Adagia* I ix 91), say to an eloquently
   articulate man (*Adagia* II v 59).
2 Ie Mustardy; cf lines 18–19 below.
3 Medardus (whose full name was apparently Medardus von der Kirchen) is documented only for the years 1530–2. At the diet in Augsburg, Johann Henckel
   (Ep 2392) told Melanchthon and Spalatinus that Medardus was 'a big shouter'
   (*ein grosser schreyer*), whose sermons Mary of Hungary, Ferdinand's sister, would
   attend only when she had no choice; see *Spalatini Annales* 140.

of his temerity and virulence, he called you Herr Asinus,⁴ as if you were
hallucinating when, in translating 'He has regarded the *humilitatem* of his
handmaiden' in the Magnificat, you substituted *vilitatem* for *humilitatem*.⁵ To
this he added at the top of his voice that you provided the instigation and oc-   15
casion of all present evils and dissensions. These words aroused the indignation and muttering of the more learned members of the audience.⁶ Therefore,
to make this outlandish fool reef his sails, either pour a jar of spicy mustard
down his throat or, if you prefer, treat him with contempt.⁷

I know besides that every time you write about your pension, which   20
has long been owed to you by his Majesty, you have wasted both oil and toil.⁸
You risk losing the rest of it as well, unless through some friend you make
solicitation for it. In this matter I assure you of my loyalty, if you will but
send me the commission, and of my aid, which is available to all righteous
and learned men.   25

* * * * *

4 Word-play on 'Erasmus' and *Herr Asinus* ('Sir Jackass'). Cf Ep 2468:93, where
  Erasmus mentions 'Erasinus' as one of the comic distortions of his name.
5 Medardus was by no means the first to take offence at Erasmus' translation of
  Luke 1:48, where Mary refers to her 'humble condition' (or, as the King James
  Version has it, her 'lowly estate') rather than her 'humility' (as Erasmus' critics
  wanted it); cf CWE 40 938–9. In the colloquy 'The Sermon,' published in 1531
  (see n7 below), Erasmus answered Medardus' criticism at length, pointing out
  that he had not used the disparaging word *vilitas* 'meanness' but had merely understood the Vulgate's *humilitas* to mean 'lowly social status' (the clear
  meaning of the Greek ταπείνωσις) rather than 'humility' (which would have
  been ταπεινοφροσύνη). See CWE 40 945:10–34.
6 According to Erasmus, these included King Ferdinand and his sister, Mary of
  Hungary; Bernhard von Cles, bishop of Trent; Balthasar Merklin, bishop of
  Constance; and Johannes Fabri, bishop of Vienna. See CWE 40 953:1–5. Fabri
  subsequently informed Erasmus that he had strongly rebuked Medardus for
  his impudence (Allen Ep 2503:1–5). Cles, on the other hand, reported that he
  heard no abuse from Medardus and that he would not have borne it patiently
  if he had heard any (Allen Ep 2504:25–34).
7 Erasmus took his revenge on Medardus in the colloquy *Concio, sive Merdardus*
  'The Sermon, or Merdardus,' first printed in the September 1531 edition of the
  Colloquia; see CWE 40 940–62. Where Wiele had mocked Medardus by turning
  his name into 'Mostardicus' ('Mustardy'), Erasmus turned it into 'Merdardus'
  ('Shitty').
8 Ie money and labour; see *Adagia* I iv 62. For the non-payment of Erasmus' imperial pension see Ep 2364 n8.

There is nothing new here except that in its labour this diet in the end gave birth to tumults and the inextinguishable fires of war, if ever (God forbid!) it comes to war. Be in good health.

In haste from Augsburg, 16 November 1530

If you wish to ask something of me, direct your letter to Antwerp to the 30 house of our common friend Pieter Gillis.[9]

The confessor of Queen Mary,[10] a friend of mine, commends himself to you. I am translating your famous *Christian Widow* into French, to be presented to her Majesty, when it is finished.[11]

Most devoted to your Lordship, Adriaan Wiele of Brussels, secretary 35 to his imperial Majesty in the Council of Brabant, widower of many years, weighed down with eight children (what a burden!), especially four marriageable daughters who must soon find a husband.

To the distinguished and most learned Erasmus of Rotterdam, my most revered master 40

2409 / From Nicolaus Olahus   Augsburg, 19 November 1530

This manuscript of this letter, first published in Ipolyi, page 108, is page 116 of the Olahus codex (Ep 2339 introduction). For Nicolaus Olahus, see Ep 2239 introduction.

Thirteen days have gone by, my dear Erasmus, without any news from Buda. It is certainly astonishing that we have not been able to obtain any news about the city. When we heard that siege had been laid to Buda,[1] from the first attack we conceived the hope that in a short time we would gain possession of the city and that John,[2] as well as the others who are confined in 5 the citadel, would fall into our hands. Now we are far from that hope. And not only do we doubt that we will attain this objective, but we also fear that because of such a long delay things will go badly for us in the siege. But,

* * * * *

9 Ep 184
10 Johann Henckel (Ep 2392)
11 No such translation is known.

2409
1 See Ep 2399 n2.
2 Zápolyai (Ep 2384 n10)

you will say, the captain, Wilhelm von Roggendorff,[3] has not hitherto written
anything because he is awaiting the end of the operation, so that if it suc-   10
ceeds he can unexpectedly write something more joyful. Perhaps this is the
cause of his long silence, but we would prefer to have all the news, good and
bad, in order to make provision in time for every eventuality. If the outcome
were favourable, we would rejoice; if unfavourable, we would take thought
of remedying things by whatever means possible. But however things pro-   15
ceed, we must await the will of God the Best and Greatest, on whom depend
the affairs of all mortals. If something joyous and favourable befalls us, we
must render thanks to him; if it turns out unfavourably, it must be attributed
to our fault, because it is on account of our sins that he has justly inflicted
this evil. You, who are rightly regarded as the most prudent of all people of   20
our times, please continue to keep me informed about the things I discussed
in my letters to you.[4]

Farewell, and consider me your devoted follower.

At Augsburg, 19 November in the year of our Lord 1530

2410 / To Antoine d'Albon   Freiburg, 27 November 1530

This letter was first published in the *Epistolae floridae*. Antoine d'Albon (1507–74),
member of two noble families of the Lyonnais, became abbot of the Benedictine
house at Savigny in 1520, and five years later acquired the same office at the
abbey of Saint-Martin-de-l'Île-Barbe, north of Lyon. In the meantime, he studied theology at Paris. Contact between him and Erasmus may have been established through the good offices of Nicolas Maillard (line 5). In later years
d'Albon was heavily involved, as lieutenant-governor of the Lyonnais (1558–
61) and as archbishop of Lyon (1564–74), in the military and religious struggle
against the Huguenots. Somehow he also found the time to edit and publish a
commentary on the Psalms by the fourth-century Rufinus of Aquilea, using a
manuscript that he had found in the library of his abbey at l'Île-Barbe.

* * * * *

3 Wilhelm Freiherr zu Roggendorf und Mollenburg (1481–1541) was an Austrian
   noble who served with distinction in the administration of the Hapsburg
   Netherlands. He undertook diplomatic missions for Maximilian I, served as governor of Friesland (1519–21), and held a military command in the Netherlands
   before returning to Austria to play a major role in planning and organizing
   the defence of Vienna against the Turks in 1529. He continued to serve as com-
   mander of the struggle against the Turks until fatally wounded in Hungary.
4 Ie the religious and political troubles at the time; see Ep 2399:42–5.

ERASMUS OF ROTTERDAM TO ANTOINE D'ALBON,
ABBOT OF L'ÎLE-BARBE, GREETING

When someone presented himself who was heading for Lyon and was to
return here, I was determined that he would not leave without a letter of
mine for you. And so, rereading your letter,[1] which the theologian Maillard   5
had brought to me,[2] I made a new one out of the old one and drew redoubled pleasure from it. For from beginning to end it breathed both your great
humanity and a certain distinct moral purity characteristic of you. I won't
say anything about myself, since Maillard in his characteristic kindness persuaded you that I was somebody. Moreover, I wasn't able to read what you   10
say about my works without blushing. I would earnestly wish, however, that
they be of such a kind as not to seem altogether unworthy of the ears and
eyes of men like you.

There are two things about which I do not think it is necessary to justify myself in any great detail, if I have adequately perceived your character   15
from your letter. I received Maillard – a man of considerable renown and
highly recommended by you – very coolly, I know. But my present state of
health compels me to abstain from this kind of duty, so much so that when
Christoph von Stadion, bishop of Augsburg, a man not only distinguished
by his noble ancestry but also richly endowed with consummate learning   20
and other virtues worthy of a bishop, who had come for the sole purpose
of seeing Erasmus,[3] bringing with him an honorific gift that would not have
been unworthy for a powerful king to give to a great magnate,[4] I received
him with even greater coolness than I did Maillard. For I neither invited him
to my table nor offered him a glass of wine, and only twice allowed him the   25
opportunity of meeting with me. I detest this – I shall not call it incivility, but
appearance of incivility. But I must either put up with this embarrassment or
regard my life as of no consequence. Sometimes with my feeble strength I try
to play the convivial host, but soon the goddess Ate is at hand.[5]

Concerning the other matter, believe me, I know full well that the excuse   30
is more valid than you would wish. Seven months have gone by since I last
addressed a letter to your Highness. Would God that I could blame this only
on a shortage of couriers or the occupations of my studies! But I had scarcely

* * * * *

2410
1 No letter from d'Albon to Erasmus has survived.
2 For Maillard see Ep 2424 introduction.
3 See Ep 2277:2–5.
4 See Ep 2277:5–6.
5 Ate, goddess of evil, often represented as the bringer of punishment for hubris

recovered towards April from the languor that seized me while Maillard was
here, when suddenly very mild but very noxious winds brought back the   35
malady. First there were griping pains in the belly, a torture more cruel than
death. This was followed by an abscess under the navel. Next I had to deal
with doctors and a brutal surgeon, and there would have been no end to it
unless they had made an incision in my stomach. It was by this type of death
that St Erasmus suffered martyrdom.[6] With this malady I struggled for about   40
five months, from which at last I was released but was left weaker than ever.[7]

Would that I could have been able to visit your Tempe,[8] l'Île-Barbe in
name rather than in reality. I have long been searching for such an abode, in
which my old age, wearied with labours and wrangling, could find peace.
I am invited by many, but for some obscure reason my heart is inclined to-   45
wards France,[9] not only because of the wine, although this is also a factor.
For this summer I came perilously close to dying of thirst, I, a man not at all
addicted to drink![10] I would have emigrated to Besançon, but that was not
expedient because of the dissension between the magistracy and the canons
that was said to be increasing in violence at the time.[11] I often had an eager   50
desire to go to Lyon, but I was deterred from that, partly by the length of the
journey, partly because there was nothing prepared for me there, partly by
war, which was rumoured to exist between the Savoyards and the people
of Bern. I had decided to depart thither by the first of September,[12] because
here, in addition to the extreme cost or shortage of necessities, a dangerous   55
pestilence is raging,[13] and there is fear of an evangelical war, as they like to
call it. But at that moment a letter arrived from the imperial court advising
me not to move anywhere before the end of the diet, and that if there was

* * * * *

6 St Erasmus (St Elmo), who suffered martyrdom under Diocletian (fourth cen-
    tury), was said to have been tortured by having hot iron hooks inserted into
    his intestines. His intercession came to be invoked by sufferers from colic and
    indigestion.
7 See Ep 2360 n1.
8 A valley in Thessaly, much celebrated by the poets as the most delightful place
    on earth
9 For the consideration that Erasmus had given to moving to France, see Epp
    2371:5–7, 2384:60–2.
10 For Erasmus' dependence on wine from Burgundy, see Ep 2348:9–15, 2397:1–17.
11 Cf Ep 2112:5–11.
12 Erasmus had in fact intended to depart for Brabant, not France; see Epp 2370:16–
    18, 2375:57–9, 2397:18–20.
13 See Ep 2403 n13.

risk of war, they would warn me in time.[14] Since many were singing the same song,[15] I obeyed, and I regret my compliance. For in the meantime winter 60 has set in, the plague is spreading at an alarming rate, and it still is not clear what the dénouement of this diet will be. The Zwinglians did not succeed in securing a hearing.[16] The Lutherans were allowed to present their articles and were told that when a brief answer was given to them, the emperor would pronounce his decision. Since there was no agreement, the task was 65 given to several princes from both parties to compose their differences if it were possible. When nothing was accomplished by so many, the matter was entrusted to a select group of six.[17] The dispute was almost resolved, except that the Lutheran princes did not wish to hear anything about restitution and getting rid of the wives of priests. Finally the emperor decreed that the ter- 70 ritories that had accepted the new doctrines were to conform to the rites of the other churches; they have been given six months to comply, that is, until the Ides of April.[18] The evangelical princes were offended by two provisions of the imperial decision: one that their community was called a 'sect' in it; the other that it was added that the doctrine of the Lutherans had been ad- 75 equately refuted by the basic teachings of Holy Scripture.[19] They did not accept this, saying that they not only believed but also knew that their doctrine was based on gospel and apostolic foundations, and this they maintained in the presence of the emperor with great audacity. The emperor received this declaration with great indignation. They returned to their homes. The final 80 recess has not yet been published, although it is no secret what it will be.[20] For it is already known how many princes and cities intend to remain on the side of the emperor and how many will join the sects.

What will come of it God knows, but in the meantime these serious measures are being taken: the emperor received the crown from the pope, 85 with no part of the ceremony omitted except that it was not done in Rome.[21] Ferdinand was formally installed as archduke of Austria,[22] and is soon to

* * * * *

14 Ep 2374
15 See Ep 2360 n5.
16 See Ep 2403:59–60.
17 Cf Ep 2384:10–14 and n4.
18 13 April. The recess of the diet in fact specifies 15 April.
19 See Ep 2403:49–57.
20 The recess had in fact been published in Augsburg on 19 November; see Ep 2403 n11.
21 It took place in Bologna on 24 February 1530.
22 See Ep 2403 n8.

be elected king of the Romans with solemn ceremonies.[23] The Turks have reduced Austria to a pitiful state, and recently also Moravia, planning even greater cruelty, if God does not prevent it.[24] There are those who are threaten- 90 ing the king of England because he is planning to divorce his wife.[25] I am glad that your France is free from these evils, and may it ever remain so. Certainly I would prefer that no other final dwelling place fall to my lot in my old age. In financial matters I am not greatly in need, since I am a man who is content with little. It is a haven of peace that I desire,[26] since God alone will be able 95 to put an end to the troubles in Germany. If you will deign to reply to this letter, you will give me great consolation. If Maillard complains that he has received no letters, let him consider that this was written to him also, since all is in common among such friends. May Almighty God keep both of you free from harm. 100

Given at Freiburg im Breisgau, 27 November 1530

2411 / To Lorenzo Campeggi   Freiburg, [c end of November] 1530

This letter was first published in the *Epistolae floridae* without a month-date. Allen chose the conjectural date on the basis of the remarks in the letter indicating that Erasmus was aware that the Diet of Augsburg had ended. This is consistent with Campeggi's having forwarded the letter to Cardinal Giovanni Salviati on 20 December; see *Monumenta Vaticana: Historiam ecclesiasticam saeculi XVI illustrantia* ed Hugo Laemmer (Freiburg im Breisgau 1861) 71–2. For Campeggi, see Ep 2366.

ERASMUS OF ROTTERDAM TO CARDINAL LORENZO CAMPEGGI, GREETING
We were not such much hoping for the tranquillity of the church as praying for it. I see now that nothing remains but that Christ will awaken and command these waves to be calm.[1] So far, however, I entertain no hope that 5 God will put thoughts of peace into the emperor's mind, especially towards

* * * * *

23 See Ep 2384 n7.
24 Erasmus is remembering the events of 1526–9, from the battle of Mohács (in Moravia) through the siege of Vienna.
25 See Epp 1932 n11, 2211 n14.
26 See Ep 2360 n6.

2411
1 Cf Matt 8:26.

Christians.[2] We know all too well, alas! how great is the brutality of the
Turks.[3] It is no secret what their designs are. Seeing that with all our forces
and resources combined we are hardly equal to them, what will happen if,
disagreeing with each other on so many matters, we venture upon a war   10
against an enemy as powerful as it is cruel? If ever Germany begins to be
thrown into tumult in civil wars, I would not wish to pronounce words of
ill omen, but may God avert what these beginnings portend! If, ignoring for
the moment the matter of the sects, we consolidate our forces to do what is
most urgently needed, I hope time itself will bring some remedy. Already the   15
people of Basel, as I hear, are coming to their senses and are not afraid of publicly taunting their church leaders with insults and sarcasm.[4] For incurable
things there is no more effective doctor than the propitious moment: not to
mention the recent suppression of heretics by force of arms, especially when
the war becomes so widespread. Although it is quite out of fashion, never-   20
theless we must be more concerned with what befits Christian clemency and
what is expedient for the common good rather than what the impudence of
a minority deserves.

I would not have refused to be present there, after my health showed
signs of improvement, if there had been any hope that my presence would   25
have been of help.[5] I knew that there were people there who, judging everything according to their own private viewpoints, seem to be spirited de-

* * * * *

2 The diet, which had convened amidst high hopes that the emperor would preside over a peaceful settlment of the religious controversy, ended with a recess
   that announced the emperor's determination to subdue the Protestants by force
   if they did not quickly abandon their heresy and return to the Catholic faith; see
   Ep 2403 nn10–11.
3 See Epp 2396, 2399.
4 While the majority of the people of Basel supported the Reformation, some
   clung to the old ways and resented the attempt of the city fathers to enforce
   conformity to the new order and its standards of conduct. But the noisiest objections came from ordinary people who accepted the new order but bitterly
   resented having to go on paying tithes and other taxes and levies in support
   of the clergy. The courts had to deal with instances of public abuse of the clergy, including Oecolampadius himself. One woman even announced that she
   wanted to stick a knife into him. See Paul Roth *Durchbruch und Festsetzung der
   Reformation in Basel: Eine Darstellung der Politik der Stadt Basel im Jahre 1529 auf
   Grund der oeffentlichen Akten* (Basel 1942) 80–4.
5 Erasmus had earlier said that he would not attend the diet unless invited by
   the emperor, and that, if invited, he would plead poor health as his reason for
   declining; see Ep 2339 n6. On Erasmus' serious illness, which began to give way
   to slow recovery only in the early weeks of the diet, see Ep 2360 n1.

fenders of the church, although no one harms it more. Whenever I join battle with a squadron of its enemies, someone immediately shows up to inflict a deadly wound from behind. I wrote the *Diatribe*;[6] Zúñiga sprang up with 30 his *Conclusions*.[7] I wrote the *Hyperaspistes*;[8] Béda leapt up with his virulent calumnies.[9] I wrote against Vulturius and Bucer;[10] Alberto Pio sprang up again, adding to his previous publications a whole volume in which he has collected from my writings those things that seem to resemble condemned beliefs.[11] But if one wishes to reprehend things that merely resemble cen- 35 sured beliefs, since the greatest truth is similar to falsehood, I assure you that I will collect two thousand articles from papal decrees and from the works of the most approved Doctors of the church that are not only scandalous but irreverent. And yet the subject matter treated by Pio is such that if I proceed to defend myself with all my strength, I would harm the cause 40 that I support and for the sake of which I have provoked the irreconcilable hatred of two sects.

If any tumult arises, I will be among the first victims of the Zwinglians and the Lutherans; and yet I would prefer to suffer this rather than be compelled to leave the camp of the Catholic church.[12] I have gathered together 45 no disciples, I have attached myself to no sect. As an old man in poor health, I have preferred to suffer much hatred and many dangers rather than depart one inch from the community of orthodox believers. And even if I admit that in many books I may have written some things a little incautiously, my

* * * * *

6 Ie *De libero arbitrio*

7 *Conclusiones principaliter suspectae et scandalosae quae reperiuntur in libris Erasmi* (Ep 1341A:914–27). Erasmus' point is not that Zúñiga's book (published in 1523) was a rejoinder to *De libero arbitrio* (published in 1524) but rather that, despite all published evidence to the contrary, Zúñiga and Erasmus' other hard-line critics refused to take seriously his devotion to the church and his opposition to Luther. The same comment applies to the references to Budé and Pio in the sentences that follow.

8 *Hyperaspistes 1* (1526) and 2 (1527)

9 The *Annotationes* against Erasmus and Lefèvre (1526) and the *Apologia adversus clandestinos Lutheranos* (1529), in neither of which was *Hyperaspistes* a target of criticism

10 *Epistola contra pseudevangelicos* (Ep 2219 n5), *Epistola ad fratres Inferioris Germaniae* (Ep 2371 n20)

11 Pio's *Tres et viginti libri in locos lucubrationum Erasmi*, written in response to Erasmus' *Responsio ad epistolam Alberti Pii* of March 1529, was published at Paris by Josse Bade in March 1531.

12 See Ep 2366 n17.

sincerity deserved a little more indulgence. I know that whatever Pio does   50
it is at the instigation and with the help of Girolamo Aleandro,[13] who has
no reason to wish me ill and several reasons why he should wish me well.
When he had no permanent position, my letters of recommendation were
useful to him,[14] and afterwards I made honourable mention of him on several occasions.[15]   55

It seemed proper to me to pour out these things into the bosom of my
special patron, who has always shown his favour to me. Since previous actions cannot be revoked (for Pio's book is already in press), may you in future
restrain their relentless criticisms, or rather false allegations, which are dangerous to me if I keep silence, and if I respond of no avail in curbing heresies.   60

I am grateful for your kindness in immediately acquitting the preacher
in Thann on my recommendation.[16] It is not the first time I have experienced
your benevolence. I would not have interrupted your very many important
occupations with this letter if you had not asked me to write again.

If I am at fault in this, one must pardon my obedience or the confidence   65
that I have conceived long ago in your exceptional kindness.

May the Lord Jesus preserve your most reverend Lordship in safety
and prosperity.

Given at Freiburg im Breisgau, in the year 1530

2412 / To Hieronymus Froben   Freiburg, 15 December 1530

This letter was first published as Ep 9 in Horawitz II. The autograph is in the
Camerarius Collection of the Bayerische Staatsbibiothek at Munich (Clm 10358
folio 1).

Cordial greetings. If I had judged the *Paraphrase on Valla* worth publishing,[1] I
would have entrusted it to you of my own accord. But the alphabetical order

* * * * *

13 See Ep 2371 n22.
14 Erasmus gave him letters of introduction when he left Italy for Paris in 1508; see
   Ep 1195:59–60.
15 As, for example, in *Adagia* II i 34
16 Nothing is known of this incident.

2412
1 On the unauthorized publication in 1529 of Erasmus' early paraphrase of
  Lorenzo Valla's *Elegantiae* see Ep 2260:70–134. For the authorized edition, see
  Ep 2416.

that was inserted in it by some ass makes it impossible to correct it.[2] In addition there are many things in it that came from that moron, Alaard.[3] I would give it to Emmeus for no other reason than to keep Colines from publishing 5 it,[4] since I think he is my enemy. For he just finished publishing a second book of Pantalabus.[5] When I have the time I will go back over that work, omitting the alphabetical order.[6]

It is not only the Laconian apophthegms but many others as well that have not been published up to now. If you print the work in the format that 10 you used for the *De liberali institutione* there will be more than forty quaternions.[7] You do not always have the time or enough paper in reserve. Moreover, you still have what Glareanus is preparing,[8] and there are only two months remaining.[9] During the Christmas holidays I'll send you part of the work so that you can begin it. If possible, I would like it in large print. For either I am 15 entirely mistaken or the work will sell.

If your press depends on me, it is hanging on a rotten rope.[10] If war breaks out here, I have to flee. If it does not, at my age tranquillity is necessary.

* * * * *

2 The alphabetical arrangement employed in the unauthorized edition meant that words which should have been treated under a single heading (eg, adverbs expressing time) were disconnected from one another; see Epp 2260:107–16, 2416.

3 Alaard of Amsterdam (Ep 433), who was responsible for the publication of the unauthorized edition. Erasmus took particular exception to Alaard's claim, in a letter accompanying the paraphrase, that the work had been written in Paris, when in fact the text he published had been written c 1489 while Erasmus was still a monk at Steyn; see Ep 2260:75–91 with nn16 and 18. A much larger version of the work was produced at Paris; see Ep 2260:91–101.

4 Erasmus has the Paris publisher Simon de Colines confused with his stepson Robert Étienne, who published the first Paris edition of the unauthorized version of the *Paraphrasis* (cf Ep 2260 n15). Johann Faber Emmeus published the first authorized edition of the *Paraphrasis* at Freiburg in March 1531; see Ep 2416.

5 The reference is to the *Dulcoratio* of Luis de Carvajal, published by Simon de Colines at Paris in 1530; see Ep 2110 n10.

6 Erasmus in fact retained the alphabetical order.

7 The reference is to the *Apophthegmata*, which Froben published in 1531 (Ep 2431). The first two books consisted of the *Apophthegmata Laconica* of Plutarch. Despite the reservation expressed here, Froben followed Erasmus' suggestion that the work be published in the same format as *De liberali institutione*, better known as *De pueris statim ac liberaliter instituendis*. For 'quaternions' see Ep 1289 n6.

8 Henricus Glareanus (Epp 440, 2098 n1) supplied the text of Livy's *Chronologia* for the edition of Livy that Froben published in March 1531; see Ep 2435:87–97.

9 Until the Frankfurt book fair

10 *Adagia* I ix 72

You must look for someone else. I will always be with you in spirit. It would, however, be unkind if you were not to allow me to be kind to someone else, 20 especially if that can be done with no detriment to you. You did not want the Greek letters to be commissioned to Bebel,[11] but it has been two years now that you have been preparing your Greek font.[12] I put up with your using me as more than a friend as long as I am not your slave.

Goclenius does not regret taking Erasmius as a pupil, for he writes 25 that he is ready to do anything for my sake. For this reason I am willingly obliged to him for taking the abandoned child as his pupil. By this he demonstrated that he is truly a friend. I do not know what hopes there are for his education.[13] I still think that it is better that one waste effort and expense than that he be in the service of some lowly wholesale dealer.[14] And he will 30 be able to live in Louvain even if he does not live with Goclenius. So far Goclenius has not complained about him in any way. But if he had to be directed towards a sedentary profession, I would prefer that he become a scribe. It is a clean occupation and one that you can exercise at home. It never allows the student to be idle and it is a skill that is appreciated ev- 35 erywhere. With wholesale dealers the corruption of youth is very common, until they get the French pox.[15]

I am sending my servant Quirinius to Holland in April, and perhaps he will not return.[16] If you want Erasmius to stay with me this summer until we make some decision in his regard, he will spend less and will learn as much 40 as the members of my household. Nevertheless, I think it more advisable

* * * * *

11 The Basel publisher Johann Bebel. It is not clear what 'Greek letters' refers to. Allen wondered if perhaps there was a proposal to rival Aldus' *Epistolographi Graeci* (Venice 1499).
12 In preparation since 1528, the new font was first used in the *Epistolae floridae* of 1531; see Ep 2062:23–4.
13 In the summer of 1530, Conradus Goclenius took Erasmus' godson, Erasmius Froben (Ep 2229), into his home when the boy, who had been sent to Louvain in 1529 to study at the Collegium Trilingue, could no longer lodge with Karl Harst. Goclenius was dismayed at Erasmus' poor performance as a student but, to oblige Erasmus, tried to do his best for the boy. See Ep 2352:281–304.
14 One of the plans for the boy considered by the Froben family (and vehemently opposed by Erasmus) had been to apprentice him to the printer Melchior Trechsel in Lyon; see Ep 2231:23–6.
15 Ie syphilis; see Ep 2209 n40.
16 By this time it was already clear that Quirinus (Ep 2367 n3) would leave Erasmus' service and seek his fortune in the Netherlands, where he had applied for the job of pensionary in his native town of Haarlem; see Ep 2389.

that he remain in Louvain. He is not the worst of servants even though he is a troublesome student.

Grynaeus sent me a young man named Claudius, adding that he heard from you that I was looking for a servant. But I suspect that he is an evangelical vagabond. For he admitted to Quirinus that he was on his way to Wittenberg and that he did not come here to be a servant but to obtain money for travelling.[17] I gave him more than two gold florins. I wrote to Grynaeus asking that he keep him in Basel for three months,[18] promising him a crown every month; if he did not wish to do that, he could add two florins for travel

* * * * *

17 This Claudius had come to Basel from Paris, speaking little or no German, and had established contact with Simon Grynaeus and the Froben press; see Epp 2433:5–29 and 2434:8–11. In a letter of 15 March 1533 (Allen Ep 2779:1) Erasmus mentions a 'Frenchman' named 'Claudius Lotharingus' (Claudius of Lorraine), who had carried a letter for him to Andreas Silvius of Bruges. The Allen editors tentatively identify 'Claudius Lotharingus' as the Claudius of Epp 2412, 2433, and 2434, but then cite the text of a letter of March 1534 to Jean de Boysoné at Toulouse (MBW Ep 1426), in which Melanchthon describes a 'Claudius Clivensis,' which at first glance seems to mean 'Claudius from Cleves.' This Claudius had been at Wittenberg in 1533 and from there had travelled via Basel to Paris, carrying with him a letter from Melanchthon to Simon Grynaeus. If Erasmus' description of the Claudius of Ep 2779 as 'Lotharingus' is correct, then he can hardly be the Claudius 'Clivensis' of Melanchthon's letter. But if, as seems clearly to be the case, Melanchthon is describing the Claudius of the three letters in this volume, then 'Clivensis' cannot be read as 'from Cleves,' since someone from there would have been a native speaker of German. The MBW editors have tentatively identified the Claudius in question as Claudius Allobrox (d post 1554), who was born at Moûtiers-en-Tarentaise in Savoy, a town not far from La-Côte-Saint-André, the Latin name for which is 'Clivus S. Andreae.' Allobrox (the name apparently derived from 'Allobroges,' a warlike people who inhabited the the area of Savoy in ancient times) fits Erasmus' description of Claudius as an 'evangelical vagabond.' Within a few years of the visit to Basel recorded here, he was a notorious Antitrinitarian and supporter of Michael Servetus. In 1534 he was expelled from Wittenberg because of his Antitrinitarian views (MBW Ep 1564 [3]) and in 1537 he was banished from Strasbourg for the same reason (MBW Ep 1929 [6]). He is known to have been expelled from Basel, Ulm, and Constance as well. He continued his wanderings, is known to have recanted and relapsed twice, and was arrested in Augsburg in 1554, after which he disappears from the record. See MBW 11 290, and cf Robert Wallace *Antitrinitarian Biography; or, Sketches of the Lives and Writings of Distinguished Antitrinitarians* 3 vols (London 1850) II 4–8 sv 'Claude of Savoy.' CEBR (1 306 sv 'Claudius') states that Allen proposed a tentative identification in Ep 2779:1n, but does not indicate what the proposal was.

18 The letter is not extant.

money.[19] But, as I see, the evangelical vagabond went straight to Strasbourg and from there to Wittenberg. I am not angry with Grynaeus, since I think he deceived him too. May an evil spirit carry off these evangelicals. Anyway I am glad to be rid of him. Keep well together with our mutual friends and give my greetings to Boniface.   55

At Freiburg, 15 December 1530
Answer as soon as you can.
Your true friend Erasmus
To Master Hieronymus Froben. In Basel

2413 / From Erasmus Schets   Antwerp, 18 December 1530

The autograph of this letter, which was first published by Allen, is in the Öffentliche Bibliothek of the University of Basel (ms Scheti epistolae 24). Delayed in transit, the letter appears not to have been received by Erasmus until June 1531; see Allen Epp 2487:1–2, 2501:14. For Schets see Ep 2364.

†

Cordial greetings. I last wrote to you in the month of August.[1] I do not know whether you received my letter, for it is not as convenient for me to send letters to you to Freiburg as it was to Basel.

In two or three letters I am informed by Luis de Castro that he is not receiving any money from your English pensions,[2] although he had your letters   5
safely delivered into the hands of the archbishop long ago and made himself available to receive payment as honourably as he could.[3] Our good friend Luis suspects there is an agreement between the agents of the archbishop and those Italians who are accustomed to nibble away at your money through

* * * * *

19 The 'crown' was probably the French écu au soleil, valued in 1530 at 76d groot Flemish, equivalent to just over the wage of an Antwerp master mason/carpenter for eight days' work. The Carolus florin was worth 42d groot Flemish in 1530; the travel supplement amounted to the equivalent of an additional eight-day wage of an Antwerp master tradesman (cwe 12 650 Table 3, 691 Table 13).

2413
1 Ep 2364, answered by Ep 2403 which, as the following sentence indicates, had apparently not yet been delivered.
2 For Luis de Castro, Schets' agent in London, see Ep 1931 n3. For Erasmus' pensions from William Warham, archbishop of Canterbury, see Ep 2364 n3.
3 The letters are not extant.

interest charges, so that they are more inclined to deal with the Italians than 10
with Luis.[4] But this certainly displeases Luis and me, who would willingly
look after your interests in whatever way we can and whenever the opportunity arises. If perhaps you have made provisions through other parties,
please inform me. I did not fail to write to Luis so that he will know about it.

I have begun to fill your sponge[5] with the double Courtrai pension that 15
Master Jan de Hondt paid,[6] namely, a sum of one hundred thirty Brabant or
Carolus florins.[7] Since you directed me to administer them, I shall not delay
to carry out your orders. Some time ago a package came to me addressed to
Frankfurt and it was given to my agents to be sent to me. No letters from you
came with it, but the man who delivered it to me maintained that it was sent 20
by you. When I opened it I found a bundle of books of Chrysostom on which
was written the address of the bishop of Rochester.[8] When I saw this I sent
it immediately to England to be presented to the said bishop in your name.

I wrote to you quite some time ago, mistakenly, about Haio the Frisian,
who has a seat on the Council of Friesland. I thought he was in debt to you. 25
But after making further inquiries I found out that it is another Haio who
is your debtor, who lives in Louvain.[9] Goclenius is pestering him for your
money as much as he can, but he is beating the air. It is days since I heard
anything from Louvain.

Here there is nothing new. The Diet of Augsburg, as they call it, is draw- 30
ing to an end,[10] but not so happily as the situation of Christianity demands,
seeing that it has produced little or nothing in the way of an agreement. It
seems, however, that dissensions may be abated by convoking a general
council. But I do not know whether the pope will give his approval. It is to be
feared that if a council is not convoked as soon as possible, all the remaining 35
Catholic lands throughout the world will surrender to the evangelicals in a

* * * * *

4 On the Italians cf Ep 2243:20–3.
5 See Ep 2370 n1.
6 See Ep 2364 n4.
7 This sum was equivalent to 5,460d groot Flemish or almost two and a half
  years' wages of an Antwerp master tradesman at 9.05d per day and a year of
  253 days (CWE 12 650 Table 3, 691 Table 13).
8 Presumably a set of the five-volume Latin Chrysostom (Ep 2359) intended as a
  gift for John Fisher, bishop of Rochester
9 See Ep 2364:10–14 with n7.
10 The diet had come to an end with the proclamation of the final recess on 19 November. For the main provisions of the recess see Ep 2403 n11.

turbulent chaos. At Jülich evangelical preachers have been received whom the duke and duchess and all the nobles of the province welcome and listen to regularly; the same is true at Cleves.[11] I see that the phenomenon is spreading far and wide and will become almost indestructible if nothing comes 40 from on high.

From England the news is that the cardinal of York,[12] who lived a long and glorious life, met his death in a most pitiful manner. It seems that, removed from government for many years, he contemplated taking revenge on his king and the kingdom and conspired with the Scots, sworn enemies 45 of the kingdom, in certain actions that were redolent of treason. The plot was discovered, and by order of the king he was captured, together with his followers, to be led by some horsemen to the royal court, but because of the ignominious death that he feared, probably conscious of his crime, it is said that he swallowed some deadly substance. For it was while he was being 50 carried in a litter because of his feigned illness that he met his death, alone and without a word.[13]

* * * * *

11 Schets was poorly informed about the situation in Jülich and Cleves. The marriage in 1510 of John III of Cleves-Mark and Maria of Jülich-Berg-Ravensberg had set the stage for the formation in 1521 of what is usually referred to as the United Duchies of Cleves-Mark-Jülich-Berg. In addition to being difficult to administer politically, this conglomeration of territories was religiously fragmented among adherents of Catholicism (including the duchess and her court preacher), Lutheranism, and Anabaptism. From 1525 onwards, Duke John attempted to deal with this situation by means of church reform based on a calculatedly 'Erasmian' mix of broadly formulated Catholic doctrines, traditional ceremonies, the avoidance of polemics, better training of the clergy, and close government supervision through visitations. Conceived and led by the ducal counsellors Karl Harst (Ep 1215), Johann von Vlatten (Ep 1390), and Konrad Heresbach (Ep 1316), all of them acquaintances, correspondents, and ardent admirers of Erasmus, this effort would come to fruition in the *Kirchenordnung* (church ordinance) of 1532–3, a Latin translation of which was shown to Erasmus for his (unrecorded) comments (Allen Ep 2804 introduction). See also James M. Estes *Peace, Order, and the Glory of God: Secular Authority and the Church in the Thought of Luther and Melanchthon, 1518–1559* (Leiden 2005) 149–50.
12 Thomas Wolsey, who had fallen from power because of his failure to procure papal approval for Henry VIII to divorce Queen Catherine; see Ep 2237 n2.
13 This was all wild rumour. Arrested on 4 November 1530 and charged with treason, Wolsey set out for London to face trial and, almost certainly, execution. But on 29 November, while still under way, he died quietly and of natural causes at Leicester Abbey.

The king is still ardently pursuing his divorce.[14] It seems that he has obtained some decision from French universities by which it was decided that his marriage, to which he has adhered up to now, is contrary to divine and 55 natural law, and that the pope's authority does not have the power to authorize it by a dispensation.[15] I do not know what will come of it; I fear however, that if he tries to accomplish this, he will stir up terrible enmities and perhaps the ruin of his kingdom.

Be in good health, in happiness and prosperity, dearest of friends. 60 Please write back and keep me informed about your health.

From Antwerp, 18 December 1530

Unconditionally yours, Erasmus Schets

† To the incomparable, world-famous Master Erasmus of Rotterdam, my greatest friend. At Freiburg   65

2414 / To Matthias Kretz   Freiburg, 22 December [1530]

First published in the *Epistolae floridae*, this is Erasmus' reply to Ep 2402. Ep 2430 is Kretz's reply. The year-date (cf line 33) has to be changed to 1530 because this is the answer to Ep 2402 and is itself answered by Ep 2430, and because the book of Alberto Pio referred to in lines 12–14 was not published until March 1531.

ERASMUS OF ROTTERDAM TO MATTHIAS KRETZ,
PREACHER IN AUGSBURG, GREETING

I would truly be not only the most discourteous of men but also unworthy of the name of Christian if I did not return the friendship to which you first invited me. For several years now certain persons have wickedly spread the lie 5 that I am in total agreement with Luther, not because they were convinced of this but because they thought this rumour would be suitable for destroying Erasmus. Now, disappointed in this hope, they have devised another pretext, that Erasmus is the seed ground and source of this tragedy. They hold to this

* * * * *

14 See Ep 2410 n25.
15 On 2 July 1530 the efforts of Henry VIII to secure the approval of the Paris faculty of theology for the dissolution of his marriage to Queen Catherine were rewarded when the deeply divided faculty declared, by a narrow margin, that Pope Julius II had acted invalidly in providing Henry with a dispensation to marry his brother's widow and that the marriage between Henry and Catherine was consequently null and void. See James K. Farge *Orthodoxy and Reform in Early Reformation France: The Faculty of Theology of Paris, 1500–1543* (Leiden 1985) 135–50, especially 141.

tenaciously even now.[1] Alberto Pio, former prince of Carpi, who engaged in   10
verbal skirmishing on this subject two years ago,[2] now treats it seriously, hiring menial servants to collect from all my works whatever could be distorted
into calumny.[3] If he did not alienate the good will of the pope towards me,
he at least cooled relations. The book is being published by Bade.[4] It is an
old story about the consul turning into an orator;[5] now we are witnessing a   15
prince becoming, I am tempted to say, a sycophant. The man chiefly responsible for setting the music in motion is a certain Jew,[6] fortunate in his own life,
but deadly for the church, while Pio has brought luck neither to himself nor
to others. I am resolved to remain mute from now on in the face of this kind
of deceptive chicanery.[7]   20

I have learned from experience that the reverend bishop of Augsburg
has more than a heart of gold.[8] Concerning our friend I never cease to wonder.[9] If he has carried this poison around in his heart, I am astonished that
he was able to conceal it; but if he conceived it recently, I wonder where he
imbibed it, since previously he gave no indication of hostile feelings; on the   25
contrary, a number of times he sent his greetings through mutual friends.
Certainly he never suffered harm from me, and indeed I appreciated the
man's talent. But if what my friends write is true, no one ever vented his rage
against me more furiously. There was a certain person among you there, the
greatest of all Thrasos.[10] It is he, I suspect, who has poured oil on the fire. I   30

* * * * *

2414
1 See also Epp 2441:61–3, 2466:93–5. The persons in question are Noël Béda
   (CWE 82 xi–xviii) and Alberto Pio (CWE 84 xi–lvi).
2 In the *Responsio accurata et paraenetica*, written in 1526 but not published until
   January 1529; see Ep 2080 n1.
3 At least since January 1530 Erasmus had known via letters from friends that Pio
   was at work on his *Tres et viginti libri in locos lucubrationum variarum D. Erasmi
   Roterodami*, and that he was being assisted by the Spanish scholar Juan Ginés de
   Sepúlveda; see Ep 2375 n19.
4 It was published at Paris by Josse Bade on 9 March 1531, two months after Pio's
   death on 7 January.
5 Juvenal 7.198. The point is that from birth human beings are at the mercy of
   fortune, which can turn an orator into a consul or vice-versa.
6 Girolamo Aleandro; see Epp 2371 n22, 2375 n19.
7 Erasmus in fact published a lengthy and abusive reply to Pio's book: *Apologia
   adversus rhapsodias Alberti Pii* (Basel: Froben, July 1531).
8 Christoph von Stadion (Ep 2359)
9 Johann Eck; see Ep 2406:3–25.
10 Heinrich Eppendorf; see Ep 2406:25–67.

could barely write these words, accomplished sir; I will write more fully at another time.

At Freiburg, 22 December 1531

2415 / To Johann Koler   [Freiburg], 22 December 1530

> This letter was first published as Ep 14 in Horawitz I. The autograph is in the
> Austrian National Library at Vienna (Codex Palatina Vindobonensis 9737 folio
> 6). On Koler see Ep 2384 introduction.

Cordial greetings. The person who brought me your last letter was one-handed.[1] I think the executioner has the other one. My servant gave him two silver pieces, which are worth eight rappen.[2] Thereupon, as if struck by a club, he indignantly threw them on the ground. This was a lesson to me. You cannot trust anyone. I am happy that the package addressed to Polyphemus   5 reached him.[3] I know what Polyphemus is up to with the bishop:[4] he is looking for someone who will supply him with money for his idleness and drunkenness. He boasts to everyone that he is my servant and disciple, whereas it is quite a different story. If he does not stop doing this, I will see to it that he regrets it. I gave him a serious warning once and for all; let him seek other   10 friends without the appeal that my name provides. I suspect that he detained Lieven there,[5] from whom I hear that certain works of mine have been published.[6] Pretend you know nothing of this, say nice things to Polyphemus, nothing more, for my sake. I like him so much I wish he were in India. He was aware of the bishop of Augsburg's kindness. I would not wish that my   15

* * * * *

2415
1 The letter is not extant.
2 Probably the 'rappen,' a silver penny widely circulated in Freiburg and other
   cities of the upper Rhine and Switzerland after the formation of the *Rappen-
   münzbund* or monetary union of the later fourteenth century (*Von Aktie bis Zoll:
   Ein historisches Lexikon des Geldes* ed Michael North sv 'Rappen').
3 For Felix Rex, known as Polyphemus, see Ep 2386 n3.
4 Ie Christoph von Stadion, bishop of Augsburg (Ep 2362); cf line 15 below.
5 Lieven Algoet (Ep 1091), whom Erasmus had dispatched on an errand to
   Augsburg during the diet (Ep 2278 n2).
6 The meaning is presumably 'published there'; cf Franz Bierlaire *La familia
   d'Érasme* (Paris 1968) 80. Lieven may perhaps have reported seeing a copy of
   D. Erasmi Roterodami über Bäpstliche unnd Kaiserliche Recht von den Ketzern, the
   German translation of Gerard Geldenhouwer's *D. Erasmi Roterodami Annotationes
   in leges pontificas et caesareas de haereticis*, which was published at Augsburg in
   December 1529; see Ep 2219 n4.

friends spend any money on such idlers. I will conceal my feelings, for sometimes we can make use of such brawlers.

Matthias Kretz, the preacher at Augsburg, has written to me.[7] I would
like to know what kind of a man he is, for I have sometimes been deceived
by letters of this kind coming from Dominicans.[8] I would be surprised if the   20
princes had left no good wine behind. But I do not want our friend Anton to
be too concerned about this.[9] Farewell.

22 December 1530. After you have read this letter, tear it up.

Yours, Erasmus of Rotterdam

To the most distinguished gentleman Johann Koler, my much respected   25
friend. At Augsburg

2416 / To the Reader   Freiburg, 31 December [1530]

This is the preface to the authorized version of Erasmus' *Paraphrasis in Elegantias
Laurentii Vallae* (Freiburg: Johann Faber Emmeus, March 1531), where the text
has no date. In the second authorized edition, published by Faber Emmeus in
1534, the same preface is dated 31 December 1533. The autograph rough draft
of the prefatory letter (Royal Library at Copenhagen, MS GKS 95 Fol, folio 248) is
dated simply 31 December. For the unauthorized publication of the paraphrase
see Ep 2260:70–134 and cf Ep 2412.

DESIDERIUS ERASMUS OF ROTTERDAM TO THE READER, GREETING
Men's morals seem to have reached the point, dear reader, that everyone
thinks that he can do just as he pleases; and so great is the freedom to inflict
injury that we are often ashamed to complain while others have no scruples
about doing harm endlessly. When I was a young man, about eighteen years   5
old, I was asked by a beginning teacher to collect some excerpts from Lorenzo
Valla's *Elegantiae* for the use of children without much preparation in Latin.
I complied with his wishes with the twofold affability of age and character
and jotted down what seemed adequate in a very haphazard manner. I delivered the text to the schoolteacher, keeping no copy for myself, thinking   10
no more of publishing it than I was of hanging myself. I now see that it has
appeared and has been distributed in innumerable copies.

* * * * *

7 Ep 2402, answered by Ep 2414.
8 Kretz was not a Dominican. For Koler's assurances that Kretz was a good man,
cf Ep 2437:73–7.
9 Anton Fugger, who had offered to supply Erasmus with wine from Italy; see
Epp 2384:67–71, 2437:29–37.

Let decent people judge whether this was not a heinous crime punishable by law. But this did not seem enough. They added the title *Paraphrasis*, which might be construed as being done for the sake of ridicule. It would   15
have been tolerable to call it an *Epitome*. Not even this seemed insulting enough to them. They mixed in some things that are not in Lorenzo and were not added by me. In addition, they omitted certain things that should not have been ignored. Up to this point it can be called a wrongful action. It is, however, not merely a wrongful action but an act of extreme stupidity   20
that, contrary to the nature of the subject matter, they divided up the work in alphabetical order.[1] This was not arranging things in order, but untying a broom.[2] The whole organization of this work consists in the comparison of similar and dissimilar words. If that is broken up, the method of teaching is rendered useless. For example, when Lorenzo points out the difference   25
between *ut, sicut, velut, tanquam,* and *quasi,* what is more absurd than separating all of these terms in alphabetical order? And at the very beginning of the work you find the meaning of *abstinentia,* but we do not find *continentia* and *temperantia,* even under their initial letter. But Valla compares these three – *abstinentia, continentia,* and *temperantia* – among themselves. What of the fact   30
that they present certain general rules – about datives in *-abus,* gerunds and gerundives, both supines, comparatives and superlatives, words used with both active and passive meanings – which cannot be divided up alphabetically, unless perhaps I have to look for *asinabus* under the letter *a, filiabus* under *f, deabus* under *d,* and so on. It is clear from this that the one who did this   35
was so lacking in judgment that he even lacked common sense. Accordingly, since I saw that after the book had already been published twice, a French printer was preparing a third edition,[3] I did the only thing I could do: seeing that this was not to be prevented, I examined what had been printed and after making many additions, deletions, and changes, I succeeded in getting   40
the book into the hands of young boys in a more correct version.

What is left except to publish also those commentaries I wrote in Paris thirty-five years ago,[4] not for a man, but for a stone, and he swore that he would not share them with anyone else. He kept this oath as if he had sworn

* * * * *

2416
1 See Ep 2260:107–16. But in his edition Erasmus retained the alphabetical order; cf Ep 2412:1–8.
2 Ie doing something completely useless (*Adagia* I v 95)
3 Robert Étienne had published the work at Paris in November 1529 (cf Ep 2260 n15) and reprinted it three times in 1530.
4 Ie the much larger version of the paraphrase, which Erasmus wrote (but did not publish) in Paris; see Ep 2260:91–101, and cf Ep 2412 n3.

that he would share them. I wrote neither of these books with a view to pub- 45
lishing them; nevertheless, what I wrote when I had reached adulthood was
much more acceptable than what I jotted down as an adolescent. But I pray
for a better frame of mind for those who take such liberties with the writings
and reputation of others. If they know neither the laws of men nor the laws of
God, let them at least reflect on whether they would like done to themselves 50
what they do to me. Farewell, reader.

2417 / From Frans Titelmans [Louvain? 1530]

This is the preface to Titelmans' *Libri duo de authoritate libri Apocalypsis* (Antwerp:
M. Hillen 1530). No precise date is possible. Titelmans had sent the work to
Erasmus in December 1529, presumably in manuscript (Ep 2245:56–7), but the
preparation of the book for printing, and therefore the composition of the preface, appears to have taken place in 1530. For the history of the antagonism
between Erasmus and Titelmans, see Ep 2206 introduction. The translation is
faithful to the 'pretentious loquacity' (cf Ep 2275:16–17) of the original.

TO DESIDERIUS ERASMUS OF ROTTERDAM
In recent days, most learned Erasmus, after I finished, by the grace of God,
my commentary on the book of Psalms,[1] I was contemplating turning to that
most sacred book, the Apocalypse of St John the Evangelist. Since my confrères and friends were encouraging me with various reasons and for a long 5
time had ardently desired a commentary on this book, I resolved right at the
very beginning of the preface to treat of the authority of this book and the
author himself before proceeding to the narration. This seemed all the more
necessary in this book, concerning which in these times certain scoundrels,
who have abandoned the authority of the church, say whatever seems right 10
to them and, mentally depraved, blaspheme whatever they do not understand and openly speak disparagingly of this book in many ways and deny it
all credibility. They have not been afraid to assert in published books that this
book is neither apostolic nor prophetic, and more than that, does not seem
worthy of an apostle or the Holy Spirit. And, to be sure, through their bellow- 15
ing and impudent calumnies they have brought it about that a good number
of people have begun to have doubts both about the author and the authority

* * * * *

2417
1 The *Elucidatio in omnes psalmos*, which had been completed in the summer of
1529; see Titelmans' *Epistola apologetica* (Ep 2245) fol в verso.** It was, however,
not published until June 1531 (Antwerp: M. de Keyser for W. Vorsterman).

of this book, especially since, because of the sublimity of the exalted subjects contained in this book, access to the understanding of it is granted to very few. And so (since people are usually not favourably impressed by things they do not understand) the authority of this book of Holy Scripture has come to be neglected and despised by a great many, and it is defrauded of its due honour. Wishing therefore (as far as in me lies) to reaffirm in some way the authority of this book of Scripture, canonically recognized by the church, to counter their madness, I have diligently consulted the opinions of the ancient writers in this matter before proceeding with the commentary, and I have examined carefully and conscientiously what each ancient writer thought of this book and its author.

As I was perusing all these works, diligently scrutinizing the opinions and judgments of each author, both ancient and modern, I arrived eventually at the book of your *Annotations* (not wishing to omit anything that was related to the subject).[2] When I had diligently gone through it, at the end of the work I came upon a lengthy annotation,[3] in which I found a great amount of information concerning the authority of the work and its author, which seemed to be a vehement attack against the authority of the book or the author. I saw heaped up there whatever objections had ever been made or could have been made against it. Each objection, even those which were introduced from the opinion of others, seemed magnified and marvellously enhanced with an astonishing vigour of language and weightiness of opinion, to such an extent that anyone who had read through this annotation could not have remained without grave doubts about the authority of this book and its author. I saw that almost all these arguments, presented with as great skill and abundance of citations as possible, were left unchallenged by you, and no refutation of these objections was put forward. I was dumbfounded when I read these things for the first time, and I did not know what to do, as if terrified at first sight. There was such an accumulation of arguments and ancient testimony that I scarcely hoped that I could find my way out of it. So great was the verbal adornment, so magnificent the rhetorical amplification, that it seemed hardly possible not to follow where they led, namely, to entertain an erroneous opinion about the author or the authority of this most sacred book.

But when I reread that annotation more carefully again and again and pondered each point individually and examined everything more thoroughly, I discovered that everything was far different than it appeared at

* * * * *

2 In the fourth (and definitive) edition (Basel: Froben 1527); see lines 93–4 below.
3 LB VI 1123C–1126A

first sight. After making a comparison with the opinions of the oldest of the church Fathers, I found many things introduced in the annotation that very 55
plainly contradicted the opinions of the Fathers. After examining and carefully weighing the original passages, I found that some things cited by you on the authority of the ancient writers were manifestly false, and the texts were not as you inappropriately had cited them with a contrary signification. Certain things were enveloped in such ambiguous language that one could 60
not understand their purpose or their meaning, but for the simple-minded they provided reason for doubt and for the evil-minded an occasion for malice. For the rest, I found after a closer examination and a more exact appraisal that the remaining parts had very little probability, or that what at first sight seemed very clear could reasonably be refuted with very little effort. 65

Since this book of your *Annotations* was widely consulted by students, it was necessary (if I wished fully to accomplish my purpose and insure that the authority of the book was fully defended) that I examine in detail this annotation of yours and refute in a rational response the arguments against the authority of the book contained in it. This is what we did for several days, 70
scrutinizing each little part of the annotations one by one, refuting the arguments and proving conjectures and suspicions false through the testimonies of the oldest and most respected Fathers of the church, as far as my powers allowed, through the grace of God. Those same comments that I presented orally to my hearers at that time I have determined to pass on in writing as 75
a warning to those who were not present, so that just as with my hearers I had attempted orally to strengthen the weakened authority of canonical Scripture, so even absent, I could do the same for those who could have been assailed by some scruple or harmful doubt or some ill-founded judgment based on an erroneous opinion, since your writings have for some time been 80
made public throughout the world and are dispersed far and wide. And since this matter concerned you more specifically, I wished to transmit this present work to you and to dedicate it to you since it is of special interest to you. At the same time, we did not wish you to complain again (as you are accustomed to do from time to time) that we are secretly undermining your 85
reputation or forming conspiracies against you. For that reason we have examined in great detail each part of this annotation, so that even from this one passage you may understand how dangerous it is to call into question what all the faithful hold firm and certain together with the church of God, which is the foundation, pillar, and support of truth[4] (a practice to which you are 90

* * * * *

4 1 Tim 3:15

more than sufficiently inclined, as we have shown in other passages). I also engaged myself in this task so that you would consider how much work of revision the entire book of your *Annotations* is in need of (even though it is in its fourth edition) after you have discovered in one annotation so many weak points, some even containing manifest falsehoods and certain others either 95 badly understood or given the opposite meaning.

We have thought it best to divide the results of our research into two books. In the first we will try to confirm the truth of our conclusions from the testimonies of the early Fathers of the church and then establish them firmly so that any pious member of the church can know what he should 100 think and believe about this book of the Apocalypse and so that all doubtful ambiguities may be removed from the hearts of the faithful (who are willing to submit to reason and authority). In the second book, confiding in the grace of God and the benign help of the Holy Spirit, we will attempt to abolish through appropriate rational arguments all those explanations, conjectures, 105 suspicions, and authorities that are opposed, or could be opposed, or could seem to be contrary to the truth, so that we will not consciously omit anything that pertains to the question but will make it public in order to testify the perfect certitude of the truth. And so that each point may stand out more distinctly and clearly to the reader we decided to divide the book into chap- 110 ters. In addition, since opposite points of view stand out more clearly when placed in juxtaposition to each other, it seemed worthwhile to us to present immediately to the reader at the beginning of the book that aforementioned annotation of yours in its entirety, just as we found it in the fourth edition, the most recent to date. In this way those who with pious mind and sincere 115 judgment will have the opportunity of reading our writing will more easily grasp the meaning of the argument and will understand the arrangement. You, on your part, most learned Erasmus, once you have read and carefully pondered all this, and after coming to know and discern the truth, will do that which befits a good man who wishes well to the church and everything 120 pertaining to it, and will reaffirm with a strong assertion of faith those things you wrongly doubted. But now, first of all, let us present the text of your annotation.

2418 / To Udalricus Zasius [Freiburg, 1530–1]

This letter was first published by Allen. The autograph, with the bottom of the page torn off and at least one line missing, is in the Öffentliche Bibliothek of the University of Basel (MS G II 13a 56). The address (line 25) is on the verso. The approximate date is indicated by the reference in lines 6–7 to Alciati's letter of 7 October 1530; the reference in line 3 to the Froben Chrysostom, published in

August 1530; and the reference in line 2 to the death of a friend, almost certainly
Willibald Pirckheimer, who died on 22 December 1530.

Cordial greetings. Most distinguished sir, you sent me a truly Laconian scytale.[1] What a friend I have lost! About nine days ago I had sent him as a gift
five volumes of Chrysostom;[2] generous as he was, I suspect that he had prepared a gift for me in return. But what good is it to cry. From his example I
will expend myself with more moderation in my studies.   5
    Alciati, a great admirer of your talents, in one letter and again in another,[3]
is astonished that you are not preparing someone who, if something should
happen to you, which we pray will be late in coming, will be able to succeed
to the position in the administration of which you have acquitted yourself in
such a way that no one could easily take it on unless he is either extremely   10
learned or extremely brazen. There are two contenders from our region,[4] one
of whom, Karel Sucket, is already giving public lectures in Bourges, and that
with great success, to such a degree that the magistrates are prepared to pay
from the public treasury his expenses for a doctoral degree, if this has not
already been done, as I think. The second candidate, Viglius, a Frisian by   15
nationality, not only has an equal competence in your discipline, but also
has frequented the green swards of the Muses with considerable success. He
writes letters perfectly and extempore in the style of Poliziano.[5] I can show
you an example, if you wish. It seems that he is coming here just to see you.
Please God he can be kept here on agreeable terms. For if we can place our   20
trust in Alciati, and if I can make any judgment from his letters, that young
man could bring more lustre to this school and a greater enrolment. I hear
that because of the death of one of the professors a chair is vacant. For my

* * * * *

2418
1 The scytale (σκυτάλη) was a device used by Spartan (Laconian) military com-
   manders to send encrypted messages to one another. It consisted of a strip of
   papyrus wrapped around a dowel of precise diameter and length. The message
   written on the strip while it was on the dowel could only be decoded when it
   was wrapped around an identical dowel after delivery. Otherwise it looked
   like a meaningless jumble of letters. The Greek word came to mean any Spartan
   message, ie a message characterized by laconic brevity, and that is the sense in
   which it is used here.
2 See Ep 2359 and cf Ep 2413:21–3.
3 See Ep 2394:134–9, the only one of the two letters extant.
4 See Epp 2394:130–4, 2468:166–91.
5 Angelo Poliziano (Ep 61:154n), the great fifteenth-century Tuscan humanist whom
   Erasmus admired enormously; see, for example, Ep 471. In *De conscribendis epistolis*,
   Erasmus included many examples from Poliziano's letters for imitation.

part, I live a snail's life.[6] Recently just by poking my head out, like the ass,[7]
I nearly died from breathing in some cursed little breeze.[8] ...   25
.To the most illustrious Udalricus Zasius

2419 / To Wolfgang Rem   Freiburg, 2 January 1531

This letter was first published in the *Epistolae floridae*. Wolfgang Andreas Rem
(1511–88), son of the jurist Wolfgang Rem (Ep 2269 n2), received his early education at Augsburg, learning Greek and Latin from Ottmar Nachtgall (Ep 2166
n3). After studies at Ingolstadt, Padua, and Tübingen, he received a licentiate
in law at Dôle (January 1529), and then a doctorate in both laws at Bourges
(June 1530). Already the recipient of ecclesiastical preferment at Augsburg, he
became a canon of the cathedral chapter in 1531, rising eventually to the provostship in 1580. He served successive bishops of Augsburg as legal adviser.
In 1531 he was made councillor to King Ferdinand, and in 1545 councillor to
Emperor Charles. From 1545 to 1547 he represented the bishop of Augsburg,
Otto Truchsess von Waldburg, at the Council of Trent. This is the only surviving
letter in Erasmus' correspondence with Rem, but there are friendly references
to Rem in letters to other correspondents in Augsburg (Epp 2475, 2565, 2527).

ERASMUS OF ROTTERDAM TO WOLFGANG REM, GREETING
I consider it not the least part of my good fortune that I have such sincere
friends as your distinguished father and you, a young man who resembles
his excellent father in every way. But to respond in a few words to your letter,[1]
which was no less elegant than courteous, I am at present overwhelmed with   5
work as hardly ever before; I merely wish that my vigils will have produced
something worthy of such talent. In an age bereft of culture, I may perhaps
have stimulated study among the young, especially among the Cimbrians
and Batavians;[2] now times have changed so that it may be justly said of my
works, 'acorns have had their day.'[3] For me nothing could be more desirable   10

* * * * *

6 'Said of those who live frugally and on little' and never leave the house;
  Adagia IV iv 57
7 *Adagia* I iii 64
8 A reference to the serious illness in the spring and summer of 1530, which
  Erasmus thought had been caused by gentle but deadly winds; see 2360 n1.

2419
1 Not extant
2 Ie the Germans and the Dutch
3 *Adagia* I iv 2

than that my second-rate wheat should become worthless in comparison
with the produce of a richer harvest.

I could not have made my way there without exposing my life to extreme peril, and so I preferred to live. Moreover, I had foreseen that if I had
gone,[4] I would more quickly have drawn some new tragedy upon my head 15
than appease inveterate dissensions. I knew whose opinion the emperor relied
on,[5] and I was not unaware of what kind of theologians were there,[6] for whom
anyone who dares to open his mouth for the cause of piety is immediately
branded as more than Lutheran.[7] And I am by nature one who speaks frankly
and is intolerant of hypocrisy. If I had conformed to the sentiments of certain 20
people, I would have had to say many things contrary to my own conscience.
For that reason I am almost grateful to my bad health, since because of it I
could absent myself.[8] The Lord will not allow his small bark to be engulfed by
the waves, no matter how this sea rages.[9] It is of no great importance where
this poor little body is buried. Augsburg has been highly recommended to 25
me.[10] It is just that I fear that if the storm were to break out there, it would not
be possible to flee as easily from there as from here, where France is nearby,
and it would of course be easy to return to Brabant, taking advantage of the
Rhine. In this state of affairs it is difficult to decide anything with certainty.
Since all is uncertain, I must, like the gladiator in the arena, make sudden 30
decisions. In the meantime, dearest Wolfgang, let us enjoy an exchange of letters between the two of us. I ask that you be sure to give my greetings to your
father, a man of great distinction. If you invite Polyphemus for a drink,[11] it is
just like the horse to the plain.[12] If you try to fill him with wine, you will be like
the Danaids in hell.[13] This is all I had to say for the moment. 35

Farewell. In Freiburg, 2 January 1531

* * * * *

4 To the diet at Augsburg
5 The papal legate, Cardinal Campeggi (Ep 2366), who counselled harsh treatment of the Protestants
6 See Ep 2357 n1.
7 Cf Ep 2384 n2.
8 For Erasmus' illness in 1530 see Ep 2360 n1.
9 Cf Luke 8:24.
10 See Ep 2384:48–60 with nn12–13, and cf Ep 2430:9–10.
11 For Felix Rex (Polyphemus) see Ep 2386 n3.
12 Ie encouraging him to do the thing he is best at and most enjoys doing (*Adagia* 1
   viii 82)
13 Of the fifty daughters of Danaus, mythical king of Egypt, forty-nine killed
   their husbands and were condemned to spend eternity carrying water in per-
   forated jugs.

2420 / From Bonifacius Amerbach   Basel, 27 January 1531

First published by Allen, the manuscript is a much corrected autograph in the Öffentliche Bibliothek of the University of Basel (MS C VIa 73 45 verso).

Cordial greetings. I recently sent a letter from Sadoleto addressed to you,[1] most illustrious Erasmus. But there happens to be a priest[2] here just now who has a diploma, to use the language of jurisprudence, and he is travelling to Freiburg, and other letters are coming from Paris. If you wish to answer them, you may do so within eight days,[3] for the messenger assures me that 5 he will remain for that period of time. I have no time at the moment to write further, unless you want to hear that old refrain 'I am yours, and yours I wish to be.'[4] There is nothing that I would not gladly do for your sake. But since, as I hope, you have been long convinced of this, it would be superstitious to insist on it again: all superfluous things are ill timed.   10

Farewell, most illustrious Erasmus, and love me, as you do.
At Basel, 27 January 1531. Many greetings to Glareanus.[5]
Yours sincerely, Bonifacius Amerbach

2421 / To Jacques Toussain   Freiburg, 30 January 1531

This letter was first published in the *Epistolae floridae*. For Toussain, since March 1530 royal lecturer in Greek at the new Collège de France, see Ep 2119.

ERASMUS OF ROTTERDAM TO JACQUES TOUSSAIN, GREETING
For the good will Brie bears us we are both equally in debt; for his service in restoring good relations between us neither you nor I are greatly indebted to him.[1] I had never conceived any dislike for you, since it is my nature that I cannot dislike learned men who have rendered good service to the world 5 of study, even if they bore me to death. Several persons of good sense had

* * * * *

2420
1 Ep 2385
2 For 'priest' (*sacerdos*) Bonifacius originally wrote 'Fichard,' perhaps a relative of the Johann Fichard who was studying with Zasius in Freiburg (Ep 2306 n2).
3 Epp 2421–3
4 Cicero *Ad Atticum* 10.17.4
5 Epp 440, 2098 n1

2421
1 See Ep 2379:253–63.

JAMES TUSSAN.

Jacques Toussain
From *Contemporary Portraits of Religion and Letters,*
Being Facsimile Reproductions of the Portraits in Beza's 'Icones' (Geneva 1580)
and in Goulard's Edition (1581) London 1906
Centre for Reformation and Renaissance Studies
Victoria College, University of Toronto

written to tell me about this, not as if it were some rumour being circulated, but as something verified in every sense;[2] and to admit it frankly, they had convinced me. I felt no bitterness towards you, but I interpreted it as something proceeding from a certain exaggerated devotion to Budé; and I would   10
like to have such friends myself, but certainly I was not jealous of Budé. Proof of that was my letter of mild complaint,[3] although at that time a truly frenzied panic was raging. No other words come to mind to better express this. But before Brie wrote to re-establish good relations between us,[4] my heart was already totally cleansed from impurities to the point that not even   15
a trace of it remained in my memory.

Concerning what you write about the splendid position of which you were deprived because of me, and about your being publicly disgraced,[5] I do not quite understand what it is all about. For I do not think that one very brief letter could have so much weight with the king's entourage that be-   20
cause of it you were in danger of not obtaining the post of teaching Greek with a royal stipend,[6] especially since you had your friend Budé, whose vote in that matter was worth more than all the others. But no matter what happened, it is better to dismiss it. It is much more pleasant to congratulate you, my dear Toussain, on having been chosen for this most prestigious appoint-   25
ment, that is, your having been led out on to a vast stage, from which you can give evidence of your far from ordinary learning, not only to the French but to the whole world. I have no doubt that in virtue of your skill and vigilance you will give a performance that will win the applause of all the companies of scholars, and that you will fulfil the expectations of the most excellent   30
prince who is the creator of this celebrated institution; I would exhort you, moreover, to assume a state of mind equal to the eminence of the office.

I greatly congratulate you also on your friendship with the distinguished Bishop Ludovico Canossa,[7] whom I had the opportunity to meet in

* * * * *

2 Ie that Toussain was the author of a poem ridiculing Erasmus for his supposed denigration of Budé as a Latin stylist; see Ep 2291:31–4.
3 Ep 2119
4 Ep 2340, answered by Ep 2379
5 The letter is not extant.
6 Toussain had endured years of uncertainty between the promise of a royal appointment in 1526 and the final achievement of it in 1530; see Ep 1842:26–32.
7 Canossa was bishop of Bayeux and a diplomat in the service of Francis I; see Ep 489 introduction. Toussain had entered his service in 1529, but in November of that year Francis I arranged for his release so that he could be appointed to the new Collège royal.

England,[8] when he was endeavouring by the authority of Pope Leo to calm   35
the discord existing between the kings of France and England. I admired his
adroit intelligence. I was extremely grateful to him for his singular favour towards me, which he manifested both at that time directly and later by letter.[9]
I think that the good fortune which his generosity afforded me then would
have been more properly bestowed on you. But then how could fortune be   40
lacking to a person with your qualities? We must only pray that it does not
carry you off in its flood and does not lay its hand on you after you have been
torn away from your studies.

Because you showed yourself a vigorous shield-bearer for me against
certain lovers of abuse,[10] I truly admire your courage greatly, but I would   45
not wish you to contend too stubbornly with this kind of people, lest you
not only defeat them but also make them more moved to anger against me.
It is better that they desist, worn out with fatigue, when they have no opponent. Many of them are returning to their senses, even if some of them
are ashamed to admit it. Now they have looked for another subject. They   50
go around saying that I have provided the seedbed for this whole tragedy.[11]
The world has always had this kind of creature and will always have them.
It is the mark of kings to be badly spoken of although they have done good.[12]
What we have to attend to, ignoring these wasps, is to see to it that good will
among those who cultivate good letters is maintained. For even this certain   55
Italians are trying to destroy.[13] This is the usual strategy of those who strive
after tyranny, to increase their power through the discord of others. As far as
a lasting friendship between us is concerned, I will have no need of Brie, either as a hostage or as a witness, once you are committed to me by sealed tablets. I wish also that this letter written extempore in my own hand will have   60
the authority of a legal document. I had heard that the teaching of Greek had
been assigned to Danès, unless it is possible that two professors have been

* * * * *

8 There is a vivid description of this meeting, which took place in 1514, in Allen
   Ep 2599:1–63.
9 Ep 489
10 Seemingly an acknowledgment of Toussain's effort to restore good relations
   between Erasmus and Budé; see Ep 2449:47–51.
11 This was the theme of the controversy between Erasmus and Alberto Pio, for
   which see Ep 1634 introduction, and cf Ep 2414 n1.
12 See Ep 2379 n50.
13 Probably a reference to Erasmus' belief that Girolamo Aleandro was behind
   Pio's attacks on him; see Ep 2371 n22.

assigned to one language.[14] If my little letter that was made public harmed
you in any way,[15] we can easily remedy this blemish. It would give me great
pleasure if you would write me often. Farewell, my good friend.   65

At Freiburg im Breisgau, 30 January 1531

2422 / To Germain de Brie   Freiburg, 30 January 1531

First published in the *Epistolae floridae*, this is Erasmus' reply to Ep 2405.

ERASMUS OF ROTTERDAM TO GERMAIN DE BRIE, GREETING
I am glad that the days during which you were away from Paris turned out
to be so happy and auspicious for you, even though your long absence was
no small discomfort for me, not only because during this time I was unable
to enjoy your letters, which always give me such pleasure, but also because 5
the matter of translating Chrysostom, which for many reasons we wished to
bring to a conclusion, has been put off until now.[1] Things have now come to
such a pass that I do not know what decision to make. Hieronymus Froben
insisted with great urgency that I should undertake the translation of the
commentaries.[2] When I persistently refused, I persuaded him that the first 10
part should be sent to you and that at the same time we should test your
feelings about undertaking the whole work. Since in the meantime he was
exerting pressure on me, and no response at all came from you,[3] we commissioned the second part of the work to Simon Grynaeus,[4] the very learned
young man who had supplied what was lacking to the homilies on the First 15
Epistle to the Corinthians.[5] I am not certain whether he has begun it and how

* * * * *

14 Both Toussain and Pierre Danès (Ep 2044) were simultaneously appointed to
   royal lectureships in 1530.
15 Ep 2119

2422
 1 A number of Chrysostom's works had been omitted from the original five-
   volume Latin edition because no translations were available; see Ep 2359 introduction and cf n2 below. Erasmus soon contacted Brie to secure his help with a
   supplementary volume; see Ep 2379.
 2 Ie the Homilies on Romans, the principal work omitted from the five-volume
   Chrysostom of 1530. On Froben's 'insistence' see Ep 2379:37–8.
 3 See Ep 2405.
 4 For Grynaeus see Ep 2433.
 5 Ie the last fifteen homilies; see Epp 2226 n19, 2359:61–2.

far he has progressed.[6] On the other hand, if he has not begun the work, and if you do not allow any time limit to be imposed on you,[7] I am not certain whether the schedule of the printers will permit it. I approve your preference, as you write, to look to your own reputation rather than to the financial advantage of the printers. Would that I had also followed that advice! But they prize profit as much as we prize reputation. Apart from this, it is not for me that one sows or reaps in this matter except that I am making accessible to them gratis a copy made at my considerable expense. At this point you must decide whether you wish the work to be printed there[8] at your discretion or that Froben print the whole work translated by others at a time suitable to him, for he has decided on the next autumn fair. I am only informing you of this as if it were before the tribunal of your good judgment. I cannot make any definite pronouncement myself without the opinions of both of you. Nevertheless, whatever you decide is best for your interests and dignity, you may be certain that it will not damage our friendship.

Concerning Chrysostom, let us leave aside the commonplaces that you accumulate in great abundance and with brilliant eloquence, especially the reasons that would motivate you to undertake this work – that you have been invited to undertake it not only by the approval but also the generosity of the king, that these commentaries are without question authentic, that they have not been touched up to now by Latin translators – may all these considerations have enough influence on you to make you disregard other occupations of less importance and turn all your attention to finishing this work as soon as possible. I do not disagree with you in what you discuss en passant, that those who translate anew works that were poorly translated by others perform a very useful task, revealing the lapses of their predecessors and rendering the meaning of the author with greater fidelity. I see that Thomas Linacre, who translated more correctly the *Sphere* of Proclus, which had been translated haphazardly by someone else, was of this opinion.[9] Then

* * * * *

6 Ie with the Homilies on Romans. It seems that he had made no progress at all. At any rate, the only translations in Froben's supplementary volume were by Brie and Erasmus. Grynaeus' only contribution to the Chevallon Chrysostom of 1536 was Homilies 30–41 on First Corinthians, the Homilies on Romans having been done by Brie and Wolfgang Musculus.

7 See Ep 2405:197–214.

8 Ie in Paris, words indicating that the Chevallon Chrysostom of 1536 (see Ep 2359 introduction) was perhaps already under consideration

9 For Thomas Linacre see Ep 119:27n. His translation of Proclus' *De sphaera* was published in *Astronomi veteres* (Venice: Aldus 1499). The work is no longer attributed to Proclus.

he translated Galen's books *On Hygiene*,[10] and lastly Aristotle's *Meteorology*, which I do not think has appeared yet.[11] I suspect that Budé was of the same mind, since he translated, after others had done so, Basil's little book *De studiis*, and the *Placita philosophorum*,[12] translated by Giorgio Valla with not too much success,[13] and finally the book *On the Universe* attributed to Aristotle.[14] 50
Who would not be discouraged from translating if he had such a successor? But if there is someone who likes this labour, immortal God! how much opportunity is available in Aristotle, in Plato, in Herodotus and Thucydides, in the *Lives* and the *Moralia* of Plutarch? It would be very fruitful for scholars if, as you did in the *Babylas*, the errors of previous translators were pointed 55
out.[15] For at present there are very few who have the time or the energy to compare various translations. But there is an inconvenience associated with these advantages. He who deals with works with which others have occupied themselves is looked upon by many as being envious and not very honest. He hears people saying: 'It's no great accomplishment to sew something 60
on to what others have discovered and hunt for things to criticize in someone else's work.' Then if the one who finds fault makes errors of his own, which can well happen, there is no room for pardon. This was the case with Raffaele Regio, who translated the *Apophthegmata* of Plutarch after Filelfo and recorded some errors in the previous translation but in the meantime made some 65
conspicuous errors of his own.[16] In my opinion Filelfo deserves more credit, since he was the first to tackle the work with his own resources. It went badly for Thomas Linacre, who dedicated his new translation of Proclus to the father of the present king. Bernard André, tutor of Prince Arthur (who would

*****

10 *De sanitate tuenda* (Paris: G. Le Rouge 1517); *Methodus medendi* (Paris: G. Hittorp 1519)
11 It was never published.
12 Budé's translation of Plutarch's *De placitis philosophorum* was published by Josse Bade at Paris in 1505. The only work of St Basil translated by Budé was the *Epistola de vita per solitudinem transigenda*, included in a volume of *Plutarchi Cheronei ex interpretatione Gulielmi Budaei ... tria haec opuscula*, also published by Bade (for Olivier Senant) in 1505.
13 See Ep 1341A n118.
14 *Aristotelis ... De mundo libellus, Gulielmo Budaeo interprete* (Bade: [Paris 1526])
15 See Ep 1817 n10.
16 Allen's note confuses Raffaele Regio of Bergamo (Ep 450 22n) with his contemporary Raffaele Maffei, known as Volaterranus (Ep 2446 n23). It was the former who made the translation of Plutarch referred to here; cf Ep 2431:71–4. For Francesco Filelfo, see Ep 23:77n, and for his translations of Plutarch see Ep 2431 n14.

have succeeded to the paternal throne if death had not intervened), a stupid 70
flatterer, and not only a flatterer but a villainous informer, told the king that
this little book had been translated not long ago by someone or other (which
was true), but poorly. For this reason the king both withheld his gift and conceived an implacable hatred for Linacre, as if he were an impostor.[17] But all of
this is a digression. Besides, as to that verse of Homer that you like to quote 75
– 'Late to come, late in fulfilment, / The fame whereof will never perish'[18] –
although I entirely agree with you about the sentiment, I strongly disagree
about fate. I cannot bring forth anything; everything I write is an abortion.
And this vice of my character does not seem curable by any remedy. I see
what is best, but I follow what is worse.[19] 80

I have replied to Toussain, and no one need be worried about our mu-
tual good will and trust.[20] What you write about Budé pleases me very much,
and I am thankful to you. Here there are bearers of ill tidings who boast that
Budé stoned Erasmus by name in published books,[21] his letters I suppose.
But you forbid me to have any faith in rumours of this kind, and I do not. 85
Yet I wonder why his *Opus epistolarum* is not available here.[22] Concerning
Trivulzio I see that you are transported with joy like Chaerea in Terence's
Eunuch, when he enjoyed the favours of the young woman.[23] I am not sure if
he is the person I saw in Padua, a young man of rare and astonishing talent.
But when you entreat me to address him in my letter as if he were a great 90
prince, look carefully, my dear Brie, where you are leading me. For I depend
on your will to such a point that if you order me to lead the dance in the
middle of the square, I will readily do your wishes. In what guise shall I present myself to him? What subject do you suggest? What am I to make of your
requiring a brilliant letter from me, as if I had nothing at all to do? What leads 95
you to believe that I have such leisure? Does Erasmus usually lead a life of
leisure? For most of the whole summer I was afflicted with a terrible abscess,
and you would find it hard to believe how slowly my health, impaired by

* * * * *

17 From 1496 to 1500 Bernard André of Toulouse (Ep 243:6on) was the tutor of
   Prince Arthur, the older brother of the future Henry VIII. Erasmus' dislike of
   him is documented elsewhere (cf Ep 1490:7–9), but there is no independent
   confirmation of the accusation made here.
18 Homer *Iliad* 2.325, cited in Greek
19 Cf Ovid *Metamorphoses* 7.20–1: 'Video meliora proboque / deteriora sequor.'
20 Ep 2421
21 For the image of being 'stoned' by the books of opponents, see Ep 2379 n51.
22 See Ep 2379 n73.
23 *Eunuchus* 550

so many illnesses, regained its feeble strength.[24] For several months because
of unceasing torment I could not sleep or take nourishment; afterwards my   100
mind was so averse to study that although I frequently tried to work on *De
ratione conciandi*,[25] I was frequently forced to put it down. Finally, my mind
recovered its enthusiasm in another project, which now is now being ham-
mered out by me and issuing from the press.[26] You know my habits. But it
grew so quickly as I worked on it that I am forced to be totally engaged in it.   105
Therefore I have not yet decided whether it is expedient to put off this duty
until another time.[27] I enjoy, to be sure, being called Asiatic by Brie,[28] who so
often complains of my laconicism. Make sure that Bernhard Bletz brings me
a letter from you.[29] Farewell.

Given at Freiburg, 30 January 1531   110

2423 / To Agostino Trivulzio   Freiburg, 30 January 1531

> This letter was first published in the *Epistolae floridae*. For Agostino Trivulzio
> see Ep 2405 n1.

ERASMUS OF ROTTERDAM TO CARDINAL AGOSTINO TRIVULZIO,
GREETING

In these circumstances, most distinguished prince, another person would be
apprehensive lest he incur the charge of temerity or impudence, but I shall
not be plagued by that concern. For if it can be deemed a transgression that I,   5
a person of such little account, should write to such an important personage,
that I should do so with no specific subject and with no appropriate occasion,
and finally that, though much preoccupied, I should address an unpolished,
impromptu letter to a man of such distinction – this charge must be transferred, I think, to Germain de Brie so that he may plead the case in my defence   10
or, if it seems just, pay the penalty. It is not my custom to deny anything, even
in other circumstances, to a person so dear to me, even if he only suggests it.
In this case he urged me with such earnest entreaties, supplications, and even
threats that he almost swore his enmity unless I acted in conformity with his

* * * * *

24 See Ep 2360 n1.
25 Ie the *Ecclesiastes*, which would not be published until 1535
26 The *Apophthegmata*; see Ep 2431.
27 Erasmus wrote to Trivulzio on the same day; see Ep 2423.
28 See Ep 2405:101–2 with n5.
29 Bernhard Bletz was perhaps the brother of the messenger Anton Bletz; see
    Ep 2065:12–16.

Agostino Trivulzio
Artist unknown

wishes in this matter. To this he was driven by a certain admirable admiration   15
and love for your Highness. He sent me an appropriate letter,[1] celebrating
from beginning to end the extraordinary virtues of Trivulzio, in which I seem
to detect a kind of marvellous, ardent exaltation and joyous inebriation, so to
speak; such is his elation and satisfaction because he had the good fortune to
enjoy the company of Trivulzio for a few days.   20

    But it did not occur to him that the more he exalts the dignity of your
rank and your divine qualities of body and mind, the more he deters me
from what he was striving to persuade me to do, especially when he extols
your consummate learning and sound judgment. And what of his requiring a letter that is simultaneously worthy of you and of me? With one shaft   25
he laid me low, because while he writes that with remarkable kindness you
show favour to my name and my writings, whatever their worth, he also
threatens to try me for ingratitude if I do not make known in a letter that I
acknowledge the benevolent disposition of such a great man towards me.
What was I to do? I was more than overwhelmed by necessary labours, and   30
by chance a courier was available who was preparing to leave soon.[2] Lastly, I
learned from the letter of my friend Brie that you will not remain there very
long, and it is not always possible to find those to whom we can entrust a
letter. Therefore I abandoned all shame and decided to address a most distinguished prince in an unpolished letter.   35

    First of all, I count it as a supreme measure of my good fortune, if I
have any, that my talent and my writings are not altogether displeasing to a
great man who is accomplished in every way, whose single judgment I consider equal to that of a crowded theatre. What shall I say of the fact that the
support of men of this calibre is to me as a staff on which I can support my   40
often flagging and collapsing spirit at this age and in this state of health, in
these unceasing and excessive labours, and finally in the dreadful condition
of this extremely ungrateful world. If we cannot deserve the applause of everyone, it is something to have pleased those who are seated in the orchestra.
I would congratulate you, most distinguished sir, on all the advantages, all   45
the distinctions, all the riches of the spirit, if you possessed them only for
yourself, but since whatever Almighty God has conferred on you, you dis-
tribute for the benefit of all, publicly and privately, I congratulate rather the
holy church, I congratulate the Christian religion, I congratulate the world
of humane letters on having such a patron, champion, sustainer, and friend.   50

* * * * *

2423
1 Ep 2405
2 Probably the messenger who delivered Ep 2420

After a long tempest the desired tranquillity has been granted to Italy; after the dispersing of the clouds serenity has returned to France.[3] Good letters flourish again happily everywhere, though nowhere more prosperously than in France, through the happy auspices of an excellent king. If Germany could shake off this fever, I would hope for a kind of golden century, and I 55 would like, if it were possible, to become young again. I see an almost inextricable labyrinth, but I have not abandoned all hope, especially when certain persons, like you, appear like birds of good augury, promising better things and not allowing us to lose courage. I pray that Christ will grant that this tranquillity will long endure for the Most Christian King, and that he will 60 deign to increase constantly his munificence towards you. I shall ask but one thing of you, that you enrol this poor old man in the number of your clients, and if you think anything can be accomplished by his help, I shall endeavor to prove to you that I could be lacking in everything except my zeal and ready will to gratify you. 65

Given at Freiburg im Breisgau, 30 January 1531

2424 / From Nicolas Maillard   Saint-Bel 1 February [1531]

The autograph of this letter (= Ep 143 in Förstemann / Günther), was in the Burscher Collection of the University Library at Leipzig (Ep 1254 introduction). Together with Erasmus' reply (Ep 2466), the letter was first published in a tiny volume entitled *Mallarii Epistola Musarum Graecarum apologetica ad Erasmum. Erasmi ad Mallarium Epist.*, printed anonymously with the date MDXXX. It is an extremely rare volume, copies of which Allen found in Bern and Autun. Both in the book and in the manuscript, the date of the letter is given as 1530, but that has to be read as 1531, reflecting the French practice of beginning the new year at Easter. Since the book includes Erasmus' letter of 28 March 1531, one must conclude that the printer took his MDXXX from Maillard's letter. Maillard's enthusiasm for Greek and for Erasmus is not invariably joined to eloquence or clarity of expression or accuracy of scholarship. For his part, Erasmus, always pleased at any sign of support from a Paris theologian, wrote an eminently good-natured response. There is no evidence of further correspondence between Erasmus and Maillard.

Nicolas Jérôme Maillard (documented 1508–65) was born in the diocese of Rouen. After briefly studying canon law at Paris he switched to theology, completing his doctorate in July 1522. In the years 1523 and 1524 he was active in

* * * * *

3 As a result of the Peace of Cambrai (1529); see Ep 2207 n5.

the affairs of the Paris faculty of theology. Delegated to examine an unnamed work of Erasmus, he spoke in favour of the limited use of translations of the Bible and publicly advocated the necessity of Greek and Hebrew as well as Latin for theological study. After being challenged and rebuked for this by Noël Béda and threatened with a faculty investigation of his views, Maillard disappeared from the proceedings of the faculty until 1533. In the interim he studied Greek for several years and lived at least part of the time at the château Saint-Bel near Lyon, the home of Antoine d'Albon, abbot *in commendam* of Savigny and l'Île Barbe, a letter from whom he delivered to Erasmus early in 1530 (Ep 2410:5–6). Resuming his active role in the faculty of theology in 1533, Maillard served in many important capacities and became dean in 1558. In 1562 he led the first and only delegation of Paris theologians to the council of Trent. Cf Farge *Biographical Register* 292–6 (§323).

JESUS[1]

NICOLAS JÉRÔME MAILLARD TO ERASMUS OF ROTTERDAM,
HIS TRUE FRIEND, GREETING

From the letter you sent not long ago to my patron,[2] which in your great kindness you addressed also to me, most learned Erasmus, I had more than 5 adequate testimony of the affection you bear towards me, so that I cannot justly voice any complaint about you. Nevertheless, I have always fervently desired that such letters would come forth from such a learned and kindly person, for reading them often brings no less profit than pleasure. But since you did not receive a single letter from me since I left the Breisgau, you have 10 more just cause for complaint. Yet if you examine more carefully the facts themselves and the sequence of events (not to plead any excuses in the meantime), there will surely be no reason for you to complain. And so, if you have time, listen to this brief account about the performance of the play – as it is now called. I am certain that as it will not be bothersome for me to relate, it 15 will not be unpleasant for you to hear.

I had scarcely returned to Lyon towards the beginning of April, when suddenly a friend of mine met me by chance at the first milestone who obviously had something on his mind, so I asked him if everything was going well with him. He informed me that while I was with you in the Breisgau there 20 were quite a few people who were insidiously disparaging my reputation

* * * * *

2424
1 Greek in the text, which is liberally sprinkled with Greek words and phrases throughout
2 Ep 2410

in my absence for the sole reason that I had gone to visit Erasmus, to whom
I was joined by a close friendship, and that already among those who have
great respect for me I began to have a bad, even tragic reputation, so much so
that I almost came to regret my initiative. See, then, my dear Erasmus, how   25
perverse men's judgments are, how corrupt their morals, how evil-minded
and vicious they are! In the meantime, to devise their calumny more skilfully, there was not lacking a know-it-all little friar, hooded and masked,
whose name I will not deign to mention, who, observing a vacancy in our
court (as one may conjecture), boldly arrogated to himself, like a cormo-   30
rant open-mouthed in search of prey,³ the office of preaching the gospel,
although he was really a mime, and, if reports about the man are accurate,
he performed his role in such a way that he seemed more like a buffoon than
a preacher, not without frequently rousing loud laughter from the women.
His sole purpose was to make the name of Erasmus more hateful to the ig-   35
norant and undiscriminating crowd and to blacken my name with the false
charge of siding with this new clique and impious sect, from which Maillard
is a double diapason removed and diametrically opposed,⁴ and will remain
opposed until Lachesis herself unwinds her allotment of wool.⁵ There were
those present also on stage who wished to add the colophon⁶ to the last   40
act, among whom was one who was worthy of exceptional glory and new
annals, the Calliopius of the play,⁷ who is above all pleased with himself
and convinced that he is something, who is regarded as the censor of morals, although in other respects he is deserving of censure by everyone. If
you allow me to put it briefly: he is a tragical ape.⁸ As soon as he became   45
acquainted with the plot of the play, which was known only to one or two
others, he began immediately to inveigh against Erasmus, to slander one
who was absent, to kindle new fire, and what did he not do? He rendered
my name odious even in the eyes of my patron and divulged to the crowd
through mendacious rumours what should have remained water-tight in-   50
formation, and finally affirmed as fact things of which he knew nothing;

* * * * *

3 *Adagia* II x 48
4 *Adagia* I ii 63 (double diapason), I x 45 (diametrically opposed)
5 In Greek mythology Lachesis was the second of the three Fates; she measured
   the thread of life allotted to each person.
6 Ie to add the finishing touch (*Adagia* II iii 45)
7 Ie the main actor of the play, a use of the name Calliopius that reveals a misun-
   derstanding of its occurrence at the end of several manuscripts of the plays of
   Terence; see *Adagia* I v 45, and cf CWE 26 421 with n259.
8 Ie a rascal pretending to be something better than he is (*Adagia* II viii 95)

in a word there is nothing he did not do which a man of good sense would
not attempt even against a dangerous criminal. Little was wanting for this
comedy to turn into a tragedy or, contrariwise, from a *fabula togata* to a *fabula
palliata*,[9] but thanks to Christ, greatest and best, in the end it turned out well   55
and ended more happily than if I had tried to avert the calumny by prayer.
And so it happened to us as it once happened to the Athenians: the owl takes
flight.[10] First, behold, our clownish actor, turned suppliant, proffered grass[11]
and honourably sang a palinode,[12] after summoning witnesses for the purpose. Then the tragic Momus, not without some embarrassment, pretended   60
to be Harpocrates himself;[13] both of them will become devotees of the name
of Erasmus and mine from now on.

That is the outcome of the play, such was the sequence of events, such
was the performance. Although this whole affair is trivial and seems to be
of no importance and is known only to a few, nevertheless I decided not to   65
conceal it and pass over it with a deaf ear, as they say, partly so that it will be
clearer to the reader of this letter under what auspices and with what intention I set out to pay you a visit and at the same time to defend my innocence;
partly also, if perhaps there are some evil-minded people who might interpret
the matter differently than it is and judge it unfavourably, that they may have   70
assurance from your letter and may learn thereafter that it is not the mark of a
pious Christian to stigmatize without cause the reputation of a brother on the
basis of another's malicious report; and, moreover, having been so warned,
that they do not arrogate to themselves greater freedom for doing harm, de-
plorably unleashing their ferocity against any upright and learned man and   75
thinking that they can do whatever they wish with impunity; and being thus
warned they may return to their senses. For my part I do not think there is
any mortal possessed of any intelligence who would willingly tolerate being so openly incriminated and excoriated by ranting scoundrels of this sort,
sometimes even to the detriment of his reputation. Certainly they should   80
have judged everything fairly and justly, whatever it was, and interpreted it
in the best light rather than censure the action beforehand, and they should

* * * * *

9 A *fabula togata* was a play in Roman dress and in a Roman setting. It was generally more serious than the *fabula palliata* with a Greek setting, as in the plays of
   Plautus and Terence.
10 Ie things turned out well (*Adagia* I i 76)
11 Ie acknowledged defeat (*Adagia* I ix 78)
12 Ie recanted (*Adagia* I ix 59)
13 Momus was the god of carping criticism (*Adagia* I v 74), Harpocrates the god of
   silence (*Adagia* IV 1 52).

have assessed the whole matter carefully and not ruthlessly fabricated new rumours and predicted the final outcome. For them and the little crows[14] who resemble them I pray in the meantime for a sound mind and a recogni- 85 tion of past errors. Let them practise piety in another way. And though day after day they were deriding our enterprise in this way and criticizing people behind their backs, and though nothing is exempt from their calumnies and nothing is untouched by their poison, still, there were not lacking in Paris (if my belief is not groundless) men of perfectly good faith, by God – like Ruel, 90 Toussain, Bérault, Danès,[15] with whom I had long-standing ties of friendship, even Budé himself – paragons of equilibrium of judgment in literary matters, all intimately known to you, who on the contrary were fully aware of our enterprise and praised, admired, and esteemed it. Nevertheless, a good num- ber of our theological confrères, including some of the highest rank, were 95 said to have been in complete accord with the views of our foes. And I have never thought there was any lack of those who, even before we embarked on our enterprise, protested (as they are accustomed to do) that it was a scandal- ous action solely because of the name of Erasmus.

However the matter turns out, I have no regrets about my visit to 100 Erasmus. On the contrary, I greatly rejoice that I have finally met Erasmus, a man who in the judgment of the learned is regarded as unequalled in tal- ent and by reason of his renown and extraordinary erudition has long been celebrated. And I was able to know him not only face to face but also in a more than cordial literary conversation and to have been his guest at table, 105 and placed myself under a closer bond of friendship with him. But if perhaps I seem to have attracted only the envy of many for my reputation because of my meeting with you, it gives me pleasure that in the opinion of many, solely through this opportunity, whatever its consequence, of meeting with you, I have acquired no little glory, 'fates to fates always opposing.'[16] It is 110 so difficult to adapt oneself nowadays to the wishes of men, since it is quite evident that not even Jupiter pleased everybody. For how often did I see with my own eyes, both at home and abroad, that whenever mention was made of you in private conversations, which occurs often and brings delight to ev- eryone, and frequently there is talk of my journey, certain persons renowned 115 not only for their noble birth but also for their merits are tormented by a

* * * * *

14 Ie 'those who croak like crows for no good purpose' (*Adagia* i vii 16)
15 Jean Du Ruel (Ep 346:13n), Jacques Toussain (Ep 2421), Nicolas Bérault (Ep 925), Pierre Danès (Ep 2044)
16 Virgil *Aeneid* 1.239

great desire to see Erasmus. How often have I seen people who, lifting their
eyes to heaven and often uttering a heartfelt sigh, said that they would have
already attained a great part of happiness in this life if it had been their good
fortune either to see Erasmus just once or to enjoy his conversation for the   120
briefest moment. How often have I heard others beg, from the bottom of their
hearts in their prayers, that even at the cost of their fortunes and their health
they could greet Erasmus, even if it were only from their doorstep. How
many people, finally, have I known who blamed their own apathy for having
passed their whole lives in indolence, hiding in their nests like the dead in   125
their tombs, even though they were attracted by the delights of literature, and
never left their native land to seek an education. I know some others, so help
me God, who place before themselves, as if it were the original, the printed
image of your little body, skilfully reproduced on sheets of paper,[17] and merely by looking at it are immediately inspired and inflamed with great ardour   130
to take up the study of literature. They are like those who now ingeniously
search after ancient gold, silver, and even bronze coins of the emperors because they think they are of no little usefulness or rather of great advantage
for the study of historical truth because of the circular inscription they bear,
which immediately indicates to what age they belong. They also claim that   135
many were incited to virtue by the images of their ancestors. I predict that
the same will be true of that image of yours, skilfully cast in bronze,[18] on the
reverse of which appears the engraved image of Terminus with this Latin
inscription: 'I, Terminus, yield to no one,' a true symbol of human life, with
which you often seal letters to your friends if at times you wish to give more   140
certain and well-attested evidence of your friendship. Recently a wily pedant
rashly used it as an opportunity to calumniate you, a clear indication of his
error, ascribing it with clever rhetorical embellishment to the arrogance of
Erasmus.[19] I saw one or two samples of it; the renowned scholar Glareanus,[20]

* * * * *

17 Possibly a reproduction of the image of Erasmus on the Metsys medallion (see
   following note), or perhaps one of the Dürer drawings; see CWE 8 28 (Ep 1132),
   CWE 12 262 (Ep 1729). There are many possibilities.
18 The medallion done by Quinten Metsys in 1519; see CWE 7 260 (Ep 1092), CWE
   14 242 (Ep 2018).
19 The wily pedant was Luis de Carvajal (Ep 2110 n10) in his *Apologia monasticae
   religionis diluens nugas Erasmi* (see the Paris edition of 1529 [n pr] folio 9 verso).
   Erasmus answered the accusation in the *Responsio adversus febricitantis cuiusdam
   libellum* (LB X 1676F–1677B), only to have Carvajal repeat it in his *Dulcoratio ama-
   rulentiarum Erasmicae responsionis* (Paris: S. de Colines 1530 folios 67 verso–68).
20 Epp 440, 2098 n1

a man eminently versed in Greek and Latin literature and staunch follower 145
of yours, gave me the opportunity of seeing it in Freiburg.

I should not wish that these words were inappropriate in the effort to
make these sycophants cease harrassing all good men with their worthless
stupidities, their raillery, and their surreptitious detractions, deafening the
ears of learned men with their falsehoods and complaints, bellowing shame- 150
lessly, babbling, and using their ingenuity to torture the virtuous, to benefit
no one, to harm everyone. May they cease, at least, to be surprised that I, at
the risk of my life, paid a visit not long ago to Erasmus, a model of perfection,
a man worthy of admiration in every way and of being exalted with every
distinction. Those who do nothing worthy of praise rend with their teeth the 155
name and reputation of the learned and flay them with words for no reason,
under such an evil genius were they born. That is why, dearest Erasmus, I
have delayed until now writing this one letter to you, and perhaps at greater
length than you would wish. I had to defend myself and refute the charges
made against me, seeing that this chicanery had to be rebutted quickly or I 160
would have to risk the ruin of my reputation.

'But what is the object of all this fine talk, Maillard?' you will say. 'Whence
comes this great hatred for Erasmus?' Among other things, I think, it is because the Erasmian Muse always sings in Greek.[21] These loud-mouthed
windbags, complete strangers to the Muses,[22] hate the melodious Muses and 165
those who cultivate them with fervour, especially if they do so in Greek. They
are as removed from the Graces and the Muses as a pig is from marjoram;[23]
their only concern is to cause trouble to the refined and sacred Muses by
interfering with them, to drown them out continually, and to envy them, all
the more so when the Muses utter more melodious sounds. And it seems that 170
it is for this reason alone that they are opposed to Erasmus and to those who
aspire to the Greek Muses, each of them raging with impunity to his heart's
content against anyone at all, lending proof to the Greek proverb 'Man is
a wolf to man.'[24] And yet, on the contrary, it is no less a true and splendid
saying that 'Man may be a god to man,'[25] as is solemnly confirmed by the 175
sacred oracle of Christ.[26] It would be an arduous task to muzzle slandering

* * * * *

21 See LB X 1677B–C (*Responsio adversus febricitantis cuiusdam libellum*).
22 *Adagia* II vi 18
23 *Adagia* I iv 38
24 *Adagia* I i 70
25 *Adagia* I i 69
26 John 10:34

scoundrels and rabble-rousers like this unless some Hercules rid us of this
pestilence or they quickly return to a better way of life. I know some people
who are so pleased with themselves – I am ashamed to say it – that as soon
as I had decided to knock at the door of the Greek Muses and had not yet   180
crossed the threshold but was merely trying to approach it, they so discouraged me from my endeavor, so diverted me from it that I almost shame-
fully stumbled on the threshold.[27] There were those also who harassed me
in a very disagreeable manner, exhorting me to abandon my initiative and
strongly urging me to desist, to the point that I almost lost courage.[28] Such are   185
men of this taste,[29] if we can call them men, who ingeniously, not to say, mercilessly, persecute with great hauteur the wise and those who know many
languages for the sole reason that they either strive diligently to embellish
the language of the inarticulate or lend it more expression. They do this, first
of all, because they are persuaded that ability in several languages does no   190
little harm to the piety and morals of the young (a completely erroneous
opinion) since only men, because of their variety of languages and diversity
of knowledge, were called μέροπες by Homer,[30] that source of inspiration.
What a disaster for studies would soon befall the whole republic of letters
if they were to convince their hearers of what they are trying with oars and   195
sails[31] to inculcate in them. No one would really believe this, not even the
most illiterate person. At the sound of this word they scent something bad.
If you utter the slightest sound in Greek, they twitch their ears like the ass at
the sound of the lyre.[32] And they show intolerable aversion for what does not
please their palate, and reject whatever seems dissonant to their ears. I don't   200
know what they would do if someone were to spit out Hebrew – perhaps it
would rouse their bile.

* * * * *

27 *Adagia* I v 77
28 Probably a reference to the opposition that he encountered in 1524 from Béda
   and other members of the Paris faculty of theology in response to his contention that theologians should know Hebrew and Greek as well as Latin; see
   Farge *Biographical Register* 297.
29 Literally, 'men of this saliva,' ie men who dislike anything that tastes different
   from what they are used to (*Adagia* II iv 19)
30 *Iliad* 2.285. The meaning of the Homeric epithet *meropes*, used for the most
   part in the plural with *anthropoi*, is not known. Maillard is probably relying
   on a gloss in the lexicon of the fifth-century Greek grammarian Hesychius of
   Alexandria, who derives the word from *meiromai* and *ops*, 'dividing the voice,'
   ie 'articulate.' See *Hesychii Alexandrini lexicon* ed Moritz Schmidt 5 vols (Halle
   1858–68; repr Amsterdam 1965) III 92.
31 Ie with maximum effort (*Adagia* I iv 18)
32 Ie they pretend to understand but do not really hear (*Adagia* I iv 35)

Therefore I would call them Muse-lashers and Muse-haters rather than Muse-lovers. Since they have no lofty goals in mind, they secretly envy the successful efforts of others, conscious, perhaps, of their own ignorance. Since they have nothing that could win them a reputation and render them eternal, they pitifully support themselves on the fame of others, trained as they are in these disreputable skills, and whatever they cannot attain they immediately condemn. They give advice to others, but do nothing to benefit good letters or pious erudition, not one iota; they have nothing more learned to say about literature than a blind person about colours, so cursed was the brood they came from. These days we see some who have lapsed so far into insanity that without any literary discrimination they make judgments about the works of others in a supercilious manner and mark with the critic's stroke things that do not meet with their approval; and there are those who, taking up the lyre upside down, like that famous lyrist,[33] sing merrily to themselves; there are those too who with a ruler, visually impaired, like those who look through differently coloured glass, judge others; they are keen-sighted on the outside but completely dim-sighted on the inside, true vampires;[34] and finally there are those who are so drenched in self-love that they judge others by their own standards. Imbued with this taste,[35] they think with great assurance that there is nothing that should not be subjected to their criticism, even though they never learned or perhaps never understood what they presume to judge. Estimating everything by this criterion, they examine others severely. They are never more ungrateful than towards those who with incomparable exertion continue tirelessly to cultivate the sacred temple of Pallas Athena, and who, overwhelmed by almost Herculean labours and ceaseless vigils, have striven throughout their whole life to adorn the Pandora of literature with their panoply.[36]

I wonder greatly and never cease to wonder what Homeric Ate drove them to this and so deranged them,[37] and how it could have come about that they deviated to such a degree from the straight plumb line of truth.

* * * * *

33 Ie the ass in the adage cited in the preceding note. The adage applies to asses who try to play the lyre as well as those who merely listen to one being played.

34 Maillard uses the word *lamiae*, which in classical mythology were vampire-like monsters who fed on the blood of children and had the power to remove and replace their own eyes. The word is etymologically related to *lemures*, troublesome nocturnal ghosts with enormous but sightless eyes. Cf *La correspondence d'Erasme* trans and ann Alois Gerlo and Paul Foriers (Quebec 1967–84) IX 166 n22.

35 Cf n29 above.

36 There is no telling what Pandora is doing here.

37 Ate was the goddess of mischief, delusion, and folly.

But let them shout, clamour, and strike the heavens with their cries because
I am more favourably disposed to Erasmus than perhaps even is fitting. I
have every right to raise my voice against them, because they babble against   235
Erasmus unfairly, sometimes even rave against him from the pulpit, or rather
they are so out of their minds that they have no just conception of the man.
I gladly favour Erasmus, and I follow him in those matters that are considered worthy of Christ and the name of Christ, which were decreed long ago
by so many teachings of the orthodox church, which have come down to us   240
sanctioned by the holy Fathers of the church and the established practice of
religion, so that I would not depart from my ideals of piety. But if anyone
preach anything to the contrary, even if it were Jerome, Augustine, Ambrose,
Erasmus, or the angel of light,[38] I would not listen to them. I do not think,
however, that any doctrine is ever so perfect and independent through its   245
own resources without skill in languages that it is not often maimed and mutilated by the lack and ignorance of them. While they are of no little help for
other disciplines, they are especially important for Sacred Scripture and for
those who teach Christian philosophy, even in the opinion of our ancestors.
So far are they from being opposed to piety and good morals.   250

Learning is certainly a great and magnificent thing, piety is greater, but
the greatest thing is learning joined to piety and good morals by a common
bond. Posterity will undoubtedly acknowledge a great debt to you, and the
assembly of learned men of our age openly recognize it, partly because good
letters, previously hidden in the darkness and almost buried, are reborn and   255
emerge more polished under the leadership of the French, or if you prefer,
the Dutch Hercules,[39] namely, Erasmus; and partly because the knowledge
of both languages, not long ago accessible only to the few, is flourishing and
sprouting up again more and more, to the chagrin of certain idle chatterers,
but with great applause from the world, since the present progress in the   260
study of Greek and Latin is attributed with one accord to you. For when long
ago the barbarians insolently seized possession with great tyranny of that
noble Palladium of the Muses,[40] which almost collapsed and portended ruin,
and the Muses themselves feared that good letters might be doomed, you
gloriously rescued them from their grasp, zealously driving these drones,   265

* * * * *

38 2 Cor 11:14; cf Gal 1:8–9.
39 'French Hercules,' which would make no sense applied to Erasmus, is presumably a reference to Guillaume Budé. Erasmus ignores it in Ep 2466.
40 The Palladium was a sacred image of Pallas Athena in the citadel at Troy. The
   safety of the city was believed to depend on it. Odysseus stole it, and later it
   was taken by Aeneas to the site of Rome.

this unproductive herd, away from the sacred apiary of the bees.[41] A beautiful victory, by God, a literary skirmish not to be rejected, for while in other
victories the palm is granted only to the victor, in this encounter the loser
receives from the victor a prize not at all to be despised.[42]

Therefore let these supercilious little quibblers depart; let them de-   270
part, I say, and like crocodiles, let them be quiet;[43] let them keep a respectful
silence,[44] and let them cease warring with the tongue,[45] since they are completely incapable of utterance. I beg them to stop assaulting Greek literature,
protesting against it, muttering against it, barking at it, grunting against it.
If they are incapable of learning it, to their own detriment, that is no reason   275
why they should persecute it and those who cultivate it with such visceral
hatred. Let them learn, I implore them, that Greek literature is not only not
harmful to piety but contributes greatly to a true and genuine knowledge
of the Sacred Scriptures. It is as if the famous standard-bearers of Christian
philosophy, principally St Paul, Basil, Chrysostom, Nazianzus surnamed   280
the Theologian, Gregory of Nyssa, Athanasius, Cyril, and Theophylact, had
taught us in Greek a doctrine different from the one that their equals in the
defence of our faith, Jerome, Augustine, Ambrose, Hilary, and Cyprian, had
treated no less eloquently and copiously in Latin.

Consequently, greatly inspired by these incentives to learn Greek, and   285
strongly motivated by your encouragement, I took up the study of Greek
with great enthusiasm (and may it be with equal success), and I have been
studying it now for about six years without the aid of any teachers except
mute ones. And although for many years my heart yearned to acquire the
knowledge of that language, and though I knew that human efforts are often   290
in vain, I calculated that I had done well and had consulted my own best
interests in directing my course of action towards an objective that would
result in no little glory for my name and would always yield a fruitful return

* * * * *

41 Virgil *Georgics* 4.168
42 The sense of this barrage of cumbersome imagery seems clear enough, namely
    that, by reviving the knowledge of languages Erasmus has rescued the sacred
    cause of learning from the 'barbarians' (the scholastic theologians), who in de-
    feat will benefit from the fruits of the victory of their opponents.
43 Cf Pliny *Naturalis historia* 8.37: '[The crocodile] is the only terrestrial animal that
    lacks the use of a tongue.'
44 Maillard uses the religious formula *Favere linguis*, which imposed silence dur-
    ing the performance of sacred rites. He clearly has in mind its famous use by
    Horace, who, assuming the role of high priest of the sacred realm of the Muses,
    invokes silence and drives away the profane (*Odes* 3.1.2).
45 *Adagia* II 10 47

to the one who cultivated it. I was encouraged in this, first, because I was
certain that the study of Greek literature did not detract at all from one's   295
good character but rather that one derives much fruit from it if it is joined to
the reading of the Sacred Scriptures; and then, because your example and my
emulation of you spurred me on immensely, even though I was already running with a will,[46] seeing that in occupying yourself with these studies you
had already won eternal renown with posterity, constantly drawing from   300
them nothing that was not learned, not polished, not refined. But although
your literary abilities have manifested themselves in many works both of the
pagans and of our own writers, it is above all in the works of Chrysostom,
recently translated into Latin with great zeal,[47] that you seemed to reproduce
so skilfully that truly golden tongue with your golden and elegant tongue,   305
and to present it so appositely in an artistically structured style that he seems
to speak now to the Romans as he once preached to his parishioners from
the pulpit. I am in the habit of passing time agreeably reading him among
others and find it both pleasant and useful, because he possesses an elegance
always joined with piety and an exuberant richness of language worthy of a   310
Christian, to say nothing more. Immensely stimulated by these studies, I decided this year to make trial of translating some of his works myself, and take
a chance for the first time at translation, and I was so pleased with the results
that the idea of producing a preliminary sketch appealed to me more and
more with each succeeding day, because it seemed that I had not spent my   315
time idly turning it on the lathe. But when I became aware that a good part of
these works had already been put into Latin, I ceased from my attempts, but
with the conviction that there was no reason to regret my labours.

I am anxious to know from you whether that work entitled 'The Comparison Between Royal Powers, Riches, and Authority and a Monk' by John   320
Chrysostom exists only in Greek,[48] because if I were to translate it, I would
publish the first example of my apprenticeship, whatever its worth. If I learn
that it has already been translated,[49] it will immediately be consigned to the
sponge together with the Ajax of Augustus,[50] so that we will not seem to have

* * * * *

46 *Adagia* i ii 47
47 See Ep 2359.
48 The title that Maillard assigns to the work is in Greek. It is more commonly
    known under the title *Comparison of a King and a Monk.*
49 The Froben Chrysostom included a translation of the work by Johannes Oeco-
    lampadius; see Ep 2359 introduction.
50 Suetonius (*Augustus* 85) relates that Augustus wrote a tragedy about Ajax
    (who died by falling on his own sword) but then destroyed it because its style

wasted our time. I have preferred to put my talent to the test in this Greek   325
exercise rather than to make no commitment at all. It is always better to be
occupied than idle, and to be envied rather than pitied.

But you hold all admirers of you and your works in a state of great
expectation, if what is said about you here is true. I hear that you are preparing with great care, after the example of Augustine, a book of retracta-   330
tions[51] which, they say, deals with certain passages that either through a
lapse of memory, seeing that we are only human, or through indiscretion escaped your attention, or were not too clear and for that reason may have offended the reader, or perhaps seemed unworthy of your style.[52] I praise this
Christian initiative, one most worthy of a Christian man, one who aspires   335
after nothing but piety itself and the sincere practice of the faith. For while
such a proposal would not be unfitting for a man of any condition or any
age, it is particularly apt for the present age, as formerly that great bishop of
the Christian religion did for his own advantage as well as that of everyone,
spontaneously deleting or correcting whatever he found needing revision.   340
I advise you in a friendly manner to do the same and I exhort and beseech
you with particular emphasis to do so through Jesus Christ. And I have no
doubt that you will do it, provided God always keep you safe and sound
and always happy. I would not wish that you be angry with me for this,
most beloved Erasmus. For just as the devotion and love of our heart cannot   345
but be pleasing to you, so this pious exhortation cannot be displeasing to
you, since it proceeds from a loving heart, so close is the bond of love that
exists between us. You will devote your attention to this, my dear Erasmus,
and will do so earnestly, so that for the future I will not have anything that
I can justly ask of you even if I would wish to. That will be done without   350
difficulty if you will not consider it a burden to answer this letter, which is
a defence of the Greek Muses. If you will do so, as I hope, know that it will

* * * * *

dissatisfied him. When asked what had become of Ajax, he replied that his
Ajax had fallen on his sponge, ie had been erased.
51 In the *Retractationes*, written at the end of his life (c 427), Augustine revisited his
previous works in chronological order. As Erasmus points out in Ep 2466:206–
17, the work does not consist of 'retractions' in the modern sense of the word
but rather of 'retreatments' or 'reconsiderations' of his works, with corrections
and explanations and his final thoughts on the topics considered. The work
remained incomplete. Erasmus placed it first in his edition of the *Opera omnia*
of Augustine published in 1529.
52 Maillard is evidently referring to the *Loca quaedam emendata*, which had already
been published with the second edition of the *Apologia adversus monachos* in
1529; see Ep 2095 introduction.

be a very great favour to me. Farewell and remember Maillard. But I shall
not put down my pen until I add this distich as a colophon,[53] which Maillard
dedicates to the eternal memory of Erasmus.   355
      In Latin:

      May Erasmus be protected from the noisy rabble
      So that he may enjoy a long old age.

      In Greek:

      May the goddess Nemesis protect Erasmus, avenger of the Muses,   360
      as she graciously has given him length of years.[54]

      Once again, farewell and long life.
      At Saint-Bel, the calends of February 1530
      To Erasmus, great in every regard. At Freiburg im Breisgau

2425 / From Pierre Du Chastel   Paris, 2 February [1531]

      The autograph of this letter, first published as Ep 144 in Förstemann / Günther,
      was in the Burscher Collection of the University Library at Leipzig (Ep 1254
      introduction). The date 1530 (line 33) reflects the French practice of beginning
      the new year at Easter. For Pierre du Chastel see Epp 2213, 2388.

Cordial greetings. That I write to you so frequently, O most remarkable of all
mortals, is not because I think my letters are suitable for you by their style or
charm or because they bring anything worth knowing or pertaining to your
affairs. But the assurance of your kindness gives me the courage to render
homage to you in this manner, and my love for you and my feelings of ven-   5
eration prompt me to prefer by far to give proof of an untimely or even presumptuous assiduity rather than appear guilty of negligence or ingratitude,
which is the only, or the most grave, offence a protégé can commit. For it is
neither evident nor easy for me to know what are my obligations towards
you in return for all your benefits to me, and what degree of enthusiasm   10
would be appropriate.

                * * * * *

53 See *Adagia* II iii 45: *Colophonem addidit* 'He added the colophon,' ie he added the
      finishing touch, without which a bit of business cannot be concluded.
54 This transformation of Nemesis into a benign goddess is surely unprecedented,
      not to mention unwarranted.

I write, therefore, or rather write back to you quite often, but nonetheless the extraordinary abundance of your answers does not succeed in vanquishing this rustic obstinacy. Indeed I have never thought that in return for my innumerable letters you owed me a single letter. For though I am lacking   15
in many of the other things – learning, talent, cleverness, ability, merits – by which I could rival the magnitude of your kindness and excellent qualities, I consider myself not the lowliest admirer of your high station, if something of this importance could be demonstrated by affection and esteem, not only actions. I would prefer, however, that all of this could be substantiated by   20
anything other than the testimony of a letter.

In the meantime, if you would like to know something about your friend Du Chastel, we are now in the entourage of the bishop of Poitiers in Paris,[1] awaiting with everyone else the entry of the new queen, which will be a well-attended event in keeping with the solemn observances of the French,   25
and all of France is looking forward to it.[2] If I had had the opportunity to see it before I sent this letter, I would have sent you an exact account, content to give a simple and unembellished description of the events and, in addition, a reliable one. Conscious of my deficiencies, I would not even have attempted the other adornments of style and expression. Concerning my future activi-   30
ties I will inform you of the time and the occasion. In the meantime, farewell, glory of your age.

From Paris, 2 February 1530

Yours, Pierre Du Chastel

If you wish to write back, your letter may be addressed to Paris, to the   35
Ecu de Bâle,[3] and it will be brought to me with no difficulty.

To Master Desiderius Erasmus of Rotterdam, my lord. At Freiburg im Breisgau

* * * * *

2425
1 For the bishop see Ep 2388 n4.
2 The new queen was Eleanor of Austria (1498–1558), sister of Emperor Charles v and widow of King Manuel i of Portugal. In accordance with the terms of the Peace of Cambrai (Ep 2207 n5), she was married to the widowed Francis i of France on 7 July 1530. She was crowned queen in the basilica of Saint-Denis on 5 May 1531, and her 'joyous entry' into Paris took place two days later; see Knecht 223, 237, and cf Ep 2427:24–5.
3 The Ecu de Bâle was the famous bookstore in the rue Saint-Jacques founded by Johann Schabler (1504) and subsequently (1515) taken over by his nephew Konrad Resch, who in 1526 sold the store to Chrétien Wechel and moved to Basel, where he ran a bookshop on the Fischmarkt. Louis de Berquin had also used the Ecu de Bâle as his Paris address. See Epp 1692 n15, 1733 n16.

2426 / To Bonifacius Amerbach   Freiburg, 6 February [1531]

Since this is Erasmus' response to Ep 2420, the date (line 10) has to be interpreted as 1531. For Erasmus' observance of the Freiburg custom of using Easter
as the beginning of the year see Ep 2268 introduction. The autograph, first published in the *Epistolae familiares*, is in the Öffentliche Bibliothek of the University
of Basel (MS AN III 15 14). It has also been published as Ep 1497a in AK V 6.

Cordial greetings. 'I am yours, I rejoice to be yours.' There is nothing sweeter
to me than this refrain. There is, however, no need to sing that which is too
deeply engraved in the heart for it ever to pass away. And I do not think that
I have to sing in my turn: 'I am yours, and I rejoice to be yours.'

I am thinking of answering Sadoleto and Alciati;[1] if anyone shows up,   5
let me know.[2] Here there is nothing new save that the plague has eased off,[3]
whereas I hear it is starting up where you are. I hope that you and all of yours
are in the best of health.

Give my personal greetings to Basilius.[4]

At Freiburg, 6 February 1530   10

Yours, Erasmus of Rotterdam

To the most illustrious Doctor Bonifacius Amerbach. In Basel

2427 / To Pierre Du Chastel   Freiburg, 7 February 1531

First published in the *Epistolae floridae*, this is Erasmus' reply to Ep 2425. Since
Erasmus states clearly in line 33 that he is observing the Paris custom of taking
Easter as the beginning of the new year, his year-date '1531' is evidently a mistake
for '1530.' If the month-date is correct, then one is confronted with the remarkable circumstance that Erasmus in Freiburg is replying to a letter written only
five days earlier in Paris.

* * * * *

2426

1 Erasmus responded to Sadoleto's Ep 2385 with Ep 2443, and to Alciati's Ep 2394
  with Ep 2468.
2 The meaning is presumably: 'if a messenger shows up, let me know.'
3 The plague appears to have broken out at Freiburg in the spring of 1530; see
  Epp 2320:15–16, 2322:13.
4 Basilius Amerbach, Bonifacius' older brother

I see and I am glad, my dear Du Chastel, that you are completely dedicated
to polishing your style and that you take Budé as your model,[1] whom many
scholars strive to imitate. I would not be averse to making this effort myself,
if I hoped for any success. But it is no less true than generally acknowledged
that it is very difficult for an old man to change his style. When you repeat- 5
edly sing the praises of my friendliness, kindness, and I know not what services I have done for you, I am so conscious of the paucity of my deserts that
I am ashamed every time I recall how little regard I paid to your excellent
worth when you were with us. But such is men's nature that even if we do
not hate virtue when it is present to us, as Horace said,[2] we certainly neglect 10
it, but when it is removed from sight we enviously seek it, or if not enviously,
certainly thoughtlessly. I admire the singular goodness of your character all
the more since you loudly proclaim my kindness again and again when you
could with good cause accuse me of Scythian incivility.[3] And I shall not hesitate to mend this fault as best I can, if the occasion presents itself or if you 15
indicate to me how I can be of service to you.

I am happy that you had the good fortune of finding a benevolent prelate, but I will be even happier to hear that you have been honoured with the
two-horned mitre,[4] or if this kind of honour does not attract you, I wish for
you a young woman with a rich dowry. Then again, if you recoil from the 20
halter, I pray that you may have the fortune of Baïf, who, as he has signified
in his letter,[5] has received dignified leisure as his lot.[6] I think you must await
the right moment. What Horace says is too true: 'Alas! the fleeting years,'

* * * * *

2427
1 This is not mentioned in Ep 2425 or in any other surviving letter.
2 Horace *Odes* 3.24.31–2
3 *Adagia* IV ix 85
4 Only after Erasmus' death would Du Chastel embark on the ecclesiastical career
under royal patronage that made him the bishop of several dioceses; cf Ep 2213
introduction.
5 No letter of Lazare de Baïf to Erasmus survives.
6 In 1529 Francis I had made him resident ambassador in Venice; see Ep 1962
introduction. The phrase translated as 'dignified leisure' is *otium cum dignitate*,
which Cicero coined (see eg *De oratore* 1.1) to describe an honourable, well-
earned retirement from public life or, as in the case of Baïf, an appointment to
high office that left one with sufficient leisure to pursue scholarship. In Venice,
Baïf not only produced scrupulous diplomatic dispatches but also continued
his philological and architectural research, corresponded internationally with
learned colleagues, and even began to study Hebrew; cf Ep 2447:16–20, 27–8.

Pierre, 'slip by in silence.'⁷ I anxiously await the description of the triumphal entry.⁸ You have a letter in my own hand, so that in this too I square accounts   25
with you, and my bad handwriting, I think, is no worse than yours.⁹ But wait, this other matter almost escaped my attention. What is it that you say about the comparison of countless letters with one? I think there was hardly a letter of yours that arrived here that I did not answer, except for the last one,¹⁰ in which you informed me that you were leaving Paris, and you did   30
not clearly indicate where I should send my answer, and I did not know what friends you had there. Farewell.

7 February 1531,¹¹ according to the Parisian method of calculation

2428 / To Konrad von Thüngen   Freiburg, 21 February 1531

> This is the preface to *Enarratio psalmi 33* (Basel: Froben, March 1531). Ep 2457
> was presumably the letter that accompanied the presentation copy. For Konrad
> von Thüngen, see Epp 1124, 2361. A translation of this letter by Emily Kearns
> has already appeared in CWE 64 273–4.

TO THE MOST DISTINGUISHED PRELATE AND MOST ILLUSTRIOUS
PRINCE KONRAD, THE MOST REVEREND BISHOP OF WÜRZBURG,
DUKE OF FRANCONIA, FROM ERASMUS OF ROTTERDAM, GREETING
I consider it a stroke of exceptional good fortune, most distinguished prelate, that such a great prince as you has deigned to admit this insignificant man of   5
lowly condition among your clients and even, such is your great kindness, into your friendship, and have wished that this be attested by extraordinary proofs. And yet I did not take as much pleasure in having obtained the favour of a man who exerts great power and influence in both spheres, and who is distinguished by the very ancient origins of his ancestors, as I did in being   10
given new hope that one day this tempest that the Christian religion is currently experiencing will be turned into tranquillity, because I saw stationed at the helm of the church men of the first rank who had at heart sacred literature and true piety. But I would, with good reason, seem to be ungrateful if through my own negligence I allowed to fall into disuse so desirable a blessing, which   15

* * * * *

7 Horace *Odes* 2.14.1–2
8 See Ep 2425:24–6.
9 Cf Ep 2213:30.
10 Ep 2388
11 Cf introduction.

you in your singular generosity – responding to a subtle suggestion on an unimportant occasion rather than to a request – so graciously offered to me. For
just as benevolence among persons first becomes cold through long silence,
or as it is expressed more elegantly in Greek, ἀπροσηγορία,[1] and then little by
little dies out, so in the exchange of letters and small services, which act as go-   20
betweens back and forth, it is nourished and thrives.

But in order not to address your Eminence with a useless letter, which
merely fulfils the function of a simple salutation, I have enclosed a Psalm with
commentary in a recent modest work, so that it may not only remind you of
your client but also may be stored away as a gift and, whenever you feel like   25
taking it out, may serve either as a source of pleasure when you are exhausted
by cares, or may be of some use when you withdraw from external affairs to
more sacred occupations – if, that is, it can serve any useful purpose at all to a
prelate of your dignity. At any rate, I hope that through you others may draw
some profit from it. I do not doubt that as the best of shepherds you count   30
among your gains anything that in any way aids or stimulates the piety of
the Lord's flock. And I pray that as you watch over and protect it the supreme
Prince of shepherds will keep you safe and sound as long as possible.

It is a very ancient custom that clients and freedmen testify to their
grateful good will towards their patrons by sending them a little gift from   35
time to time. Consider therefore that this modest gift comes from a client of
meagre fortune but devout heart.

At Freiburg im Breisgau, 21 February 1531

2429 / To Bonifacius Amerbach   Freiburg, 21 February [1531]

The autograph of this letter (= AK Ep 1501) is in the Öffentliche Bibliothek of the
University of Basel (MS AN III 15 16). It was first published in the *Epistolae familiares*.

Cordial greetings. Nicolaus Episcopius gave me some feelings of anxiety when
he informed me that you have been ordered to remain there for eight days,[1] although you were preparing to travel here. Then he said something about a letter
that was intercepted by someone engaged in this hunt. I hope everything will
turn out all right. But let us hope that I am wrong in the presentiment that has   5

* * * * *

2428
1 'Prolonged absence' or 'lack of contact'; cf Aristotle *Nicomachean Ethics* 8.5.

2429
1 For Episcopius see Ep 2233A n4.

always given me reason to fear that you were not happy in that commonwealth,[2] with whose rulers you have had differences of opinion in religious matters.[3] In such a situation you must not be concerned about your possessions. God often compensates with interest for financial gains that have been abandoned for good reason. I know your nobility of character, and I am not unaware of the 10 criminal stratagems in which certain people put all their confidence.

I do not know whether I wrote to you about our Thraso,[4] who writes to me that he has been forced to take up his pen and respond to our little book,[5] 'but with more moderation than the atrocity of the affair demanded.' What makes him so disturbed is that there is mention there of ten florins. To this 15 accusation he responds: 'Who told you that I had asked for ten florins?[6] Tell him that he is a depraved scoundrel and an abominable informer.' He seems to have forgotten what he said to you and Beatus. I will pretend that I did not receive his letter. What do you do with such a monster? But Germany nourishes too many of this type. 20

If you come here, this house will rejoice to have such a guest. From now on we have beds.[7] I pray that you and yours are in excellent health. Give my fond greetings to Basilius.[8]

At Freiburg, 21 February 1530

To the most distinguished doctor of laws Bonifacius Amerbach. In Basel 25

2430 / From Matthias Kretz   Augsburg, 22 February 1531

First published as Ep 145 in Förstemann / Günther, this is Kretz's reply to Ep 2414. The autograph was in the Burscher Collection of the University Library at Leipzig (Ep 1254 introduction). Ep 2445 is Erasmus' reply.

* * * * *

2 Erasmus uses the word *respublica*, which in this context means 'free or self-governing city.' Cf Ep 2145 n11.
3 At issue was Bonifacius' persistent resistance to official pressure to participate in the reformed celebration of the Lord's Supper, a matter that dragged on until 1534; see Ep 2248 n6.
4 Heinrich Eppendorf (Ep 2384 n15)
5 The letter is not extant. The 'little book' was the *Admonitio adversus mendacium* (Ep 2400 introduction), to which Eppendorf responded with his *Iusta querela* (Haguenau: Johann Setzer, February 1531).
6 In the *Admonitio* Erasmus states that Eppendorf had asked for 'ten ducats' (*decem aurei*) for his travelling expenses; CWE 78 391.
7 Perhaps because Nicolaas Kan had left Erasmus' service and Quirinus Talesius was in the process of doing so. On the other hand, Gilbert Cousin had in the meantime moved in; see Ep 2381 n1.
8 Basilius Amerbach, Bonifacius' older brother

Cordial greetings and personal regards. Polyphemus presented me with your first letter, distinguished sir, and a notary public the second, very late.[1] Master Koler recently transmitted your friendly greeting.[2] I was delighted more than I can say by those letters, I, a man who in other respects is often sad. I keep both letters hidden, I kiss them fondly, and venerate them 5 more than gold and topaz. I have absolutely nothing to give your Lordship in return except the grateful heart of one who loves and respects you in the highest degree. And surely I would give concrete proof of this if the occasion presented itself. I recently recommended Augsburg to you, but now, contrary to expectation, it has become worthy of reproach. The emperor is 10 an object of ridicule. The promises made to him are little observed.[3] New preachers are called in from Strasbourg who are profaning almost all the monasteries with their sermons.[4] Recently they even assaulted the church of St Moritz, a place that the Fugger family had kept uncontaminated up to now.[5] The city council is divided into Lutherans and Zwinglians with sharp 15 dissensions.[6] The Anabaptists hold well-attended assemblies inside the city and out,[7] and clearly the situation is getting worse. I do not know what will

* * * * *

2430
1 Only one of these letters, Ep 2414, is extant. For Polyphemus, see Ep 2386 n3.
2 Cf Epp 2415:18–20, 2437:73.
3 Following the imperial diet held in Augsburg in 1530, the city council summoned back to the city the evangelical clergymen whom the emperor had banished from the city during the diet, refused to accept the final recess of the diet (Ep 2403 n11), and proceeded cautiously to support evangelical reformation.
4 The preachers, appointed by the city council in 1531 on the recommendation of Martin Bucer, were Wolfgang Musculus, pastor at Holy Cross, and Bonifacius Wolfart (or Wolfhart), pastor at St Anne's.
5 Cf n14 below.
6 As was the case in most of the free cities of southwest Germany, early sympathy for Luther soon gave way to increasingly strong popular support for Zwingli and his views on the Eucharist and forms of public worship. Tensions between the two evangelical factions complicated the struggle between the advocates of reform and the socially powerful Catholic minority remaining in the city; cf n8 below.
7 In the wake of the Peasants' War (1524–5), Anabaptists fleeing from persecution elsewhere settled in Augsburg, where the city council for a time pursued a hands-off policy. An important Anabaptist synod (known as the Martyrs' Synod) was held there in August 1527. Only when the city fathers became fearful that Anabaptist teachings (on secular authority, taking oaths, military service, and communal property) were a threat to social peace and public order did they order expulsion, starting in the autumn of 1527. By 1530 the few Anabaptists who remained in the city had to meet in secret.

happen;[8] I do not predict anything good unless God favours us with a special gift. I have recently been invited by the prince of Bavaria to an honourable position,[9] which I will assume if permission is granted me by my superiors,   20 the Augsburg chapter. For a year I have been urging them to let me go, and recently I sought the intervention of the royal court for this purpose.[10] I hope that soon my prayers will be answered.[11] When that comes about, I will be happier than many of my predecessors and colleagues here. Urbanus and Oecolampadius have defected from the church.[12] Ottmar Nachtgall, on the   25 contrary, who from Lutheranism and Anabaptism returned to the church,

* * * * *

8 Fear of retaliation from powerful Catholic neighbours (the Hapsburgs, the Wittelsbachs of Bavaria), who were capable of doing fatal damage to the economic well-being of the city, long prevented the city council from taking decisive steps towards the establishment of a confessionally unified evangelical church. Not until July 1534, encouraged by Musculus and the other preachers sympathetic to Bucer, did the council ban Catholic preaching and restrict the celebration of mass to the eight churches directly controlled by the bishop, thus accelerating the decline of Catholic practice in the city. In January 1537 the council gave Catholic clergy and nuns still living in the city the choice of turning Protestant or emigrating. The eight churches still in the hands of the Catholics were turned over to the Protestants, who 'cleansed' them in a campaign of iconoclasm, which, together with the introduction of a starkly simple form of worship, marked the complete victory in Augsburg of the style of reformation inspired by Strasbourg rather than Wittenberg.

9 The prince was Duke William IV.

10 Kretz uses the word *regia*, which, strictly speaking, refers to the court of a king. One wonders, however, why Kretz would have requested the intervention of the court of King Ferdinand, who had no interest in the matter, rather than that of the duke of Bavaria, who was offering him the job.

11 In 1533 he became dean of the cathedral chapter at Munich. Cf Ep 2445 introduction.

12 Urbanus Rhegius (Ep 1253) and Johannes Oecolampadius (Ep 1538) were Kretz's predecessors as cathedral preacher. Oecolampadius was appointed to the post in 1518 but resigned in 1520 to embark on the path that would by 1523 make him the leader of the Reformation at Basel. Rhegius succeeded Oecolampadius, but in 1521 he was dismissed by the chapter because of a sermon attacking indulgences, and Kretz was appointed in his place. In 1524, however, the Augsburg city council appointed Rhegius as preacher at St Anne's and the Franciscan church, and he soon emerged as the leading spokesman of the reform party. In the summer of 1530 he accepted the call of the dukes of Braunschweig-Lüneburg to be a preacher in their capital city of Celle, and from that base he became the principal Lutheran reformer of northwest Germany. His departure helped tip the scales in favour of the Zwinglian faction among the evangelicals; cf n8 above.

was in the end driven out of the city.[13] Johann Speiser is out of his mind;
he is totally delirious and in his second childhood.[14] Johannes Faber, the
Dominican, died before his time, miserably, in exile.[15] I have acted as preacher here in the cathedral longer than any of my predecessors – indeed this is   30
my tenth year. I will leave, I hope, with good conditions, on friendly terms,
with an annual salary that is very substantial, and in reasonably good health.
I would not be able any longer to shout in such a large church. I relate these
things, most eminent Erasmus, without any boastfulness, glorying in the
Lord, and acknowledging gratefully all his benefits.   35

Polyphemus has returned to the king;[16] if you intend to send him a
letter, he wishes that you send it through Koler.[17] I have great affection for
the man, both on your account and also because of his good nature and integrity; he has little in common with the rest of that courtly crowd, with the
exception of his love of wine. Since I had bought some lately that was not   40
decanted, but was rather thick and harsh, he bade me to be of good cheer for
he would see to it that the cask would quickly be empty. He is so devoted
to you that he would readily risk his life for you. We are very anxious to see
your Chrysostom and the *Apophthegmata*.[18] Your recent dialogues are not for

* * * * *

13 Ottmar Nachtgall was never a Lutheran or an Anabaptist. Indeed, it was his leadership of the Catholic faction in Augsburg and his vehement denunciation of
   Luther and the Anabaptists from the pulpit of St Moritz's church in 1528 that
   caused the city council to forbid him to continue preaching, thus precipitating
   his move to Freiburg; see Ep 2166 n3. From Ep 2437:45–52 it appears that he had
   sought unsuccessfully to be appointed as Kretz's successor as cathedral preacher.
14 Johann Speiser (documented 1504–31) was Nachtgall's predecessor as preacher
   at the church of St Moritz, a position in the gift of the Fugger family (1512–24).
   By about 1520 he had become identified with the pro-Lutheran party in the
   city, which led to efforts by the bishop of Augsburg to have him removed. He
   was protected by the city council and his parishioners, but when in 1524 he returned to preaching in clear accordance with Roman Catholic doctrine, his parishioners rebelled and Jakob Fugger replaced him with Nachtgall, though he
   appears to have remained in Augsburg. This letter is the only extant evidence
   concerning his mental health.
15 On Johannes Faber, OP, see Epp 1149 introduction, 2205:206–11, and 2445:117–
   23. In Augsburg Faber was so determined an opponent of the reform movement that in 1525 the city council forbade him to preach and and expelled him
   from the city. Little is known about his life thereafter. He apparently went to
   Rome (Ep 2205:210), but there is no information about when and where he died.
16 Ie to the service of King Ferdinand; see Ep 2386 n3.
17 Ep 2384
18 See Epp 2359 (Chrysostom), 2431 (*Apophthegmata*).

sale anywhere here, although many would like to have them.[19] May the good   45
God preserve you happy for us as long as possible.

At Augsburg, Ash Wednesday, 22 February 1531

Matthias Kretz, chaplain, entirely devoted to your Lordship, preacher
in Augsburg

To the true theologian, most illustrious and learned of all men of this   50
century, Erasmus of Rotterdam, honour of Germany, his master and teacher,
worthy of the highest veneration

2431 / To William v, duke of Cleves   Freiburg, 26 February 1531

This is the preface to the *Apophthegmata* (Basel: Froben, March 1531). On 11 March
Erasmus was expecting the book to appear within a week; see Ep 2445:157–8.
Ep 2458 (c 18 March 1531) accompanied a gift copy of it to Duke William. Two
other Froben editions of the work appeared in Erasmus' lifetime, one in 1532
and another in 1535. For the 1532 edition Erasmus added two new books of apophthegms (bringing the total to eight) and added a new letter to Duke William
(Ep 2711) as preface to them. The 1532 edition already contained a few minor
additions to the text of this letter; that of 1535 included two new sentences and
a whole new paragraph; see nn17, 21, 28. An annotated translation of this letter
by Betty I. Knott is found in CWE 37 3–18. In a number of places the final version
of the text and notes offered here has benefitted from the careful consideration
of Dr Knott's version.

For Duke William v of Cleves see Ep 2189 introduction.

TO THE MOST ILLUSTRIOUS YOUNG PRINCE WILLIAM,
DUKE OF CLEVES, OF JÜLICH, OF BERG, COUNT OF MARK
AND RAVENSBERG, ERASMUS OF ROTTERDAM SENDS GREETINGS
Since you accepted so amiably, most illustrious young Prince William (and
not only you, but both of your renowned parents),[1] the two little books I sent   5
you previously as a pledge of my loyalty to you,[2] it seemed proper to add to
them something more worthy of your noble rank and more useful, if I am not

* * * * *

19 There was a recent edition of the *Colloquies* (Basel: Froben, September 1529) that
   included three new colloquies as well as the *Ciceronianus*. No further edition
   with added content was published until September 1531.

2431
1 See Ep 2413 n11.
2 *De pueris instituendis* (Ep 2189), a volume to which two shorter works were appended with a preface addressed to Duke William (Ep 2190).

in error, for your studies. Accordingly, I collected from all the best authors what the Greeks call *apophthegmata*, that is, terse sayings, since I thought that no other subject would have been more suitable to a prince, especially   10 one so young. Certainly what philosophers have written concerning morals, the governance of the state, and waging war is eminently worthy of being known. But how few people, even private citizens, have enough leisure time at their disposal to make their way through the intricacies and labyrinths of the Socratic subtleties, ironies, and manner of introducing arguments to be   15 found in the works of Plato. Aristotle wrote copiously about moral conduct,[3] but he seems to have written for philosophers, not for a prince. What he wrote about economics and politics is clearer,[4] but this man requires the constant attention and free time of the reader. In addition, since he lacks passion, he does not hold the attention of one occupied with princely responsibilities.   20 As for his philosophical works, and the books of Cicero on philosophy, they are for the most part of a nature that is not directly related to what a prince should know. An example of this type are the discussions in *On the Ends of Good and Evil*,[5] which are more subtle than profitable. They are suited to the education of those who spend their lives merely discussing right conduct.   25 But for one who is born to rule, virtue must be immediately at one's disposal, not discussed at leisure. That leaves history, which seems to be more appropriate for great men, since it presents, as though in a picture, actions deserving of fame and their contrary, and provides pleasure at the same time. But even supposing a prince had the time to read through an infinite number of   30 volumes, who could remember it all?

But as those who engage in wrestling have certain well-defined methods of holding or disengaging from their opponent, so those who are involved in matters of peace and war must have at their disposal certain rules that apprise them of what should and should not be done in any given cir-   35 cumstance. On this account we see that learned men have tried by their diligence to allay the cares of princes. Some of them, like Theognis and Isocrates, wrote maxims;[6] others, like Valerius Maximus and Julius Frontinus, who

* * * * *

3 Chiefly in the *Nicomachean Ethics*
4 In the *Oeconomica* and the *Politics*. The former is now considered spurious (cf Ep 2432:103–4). Erasmus was at this time much preoccupied with Aristotle, having undertaken to provide the preface for a new edition in Greek (Ep 2432).
5 Cicero *De finibus bonorum et malorum*
6 The 1400 verses attributed (about 1100 of them falsely) to the Greek elegiac poet Theognis of Megara (fl c 550–540 BC) feature ideas about life, friendship, fate, death, and much else. Certain works of the Athenian orator Isocrates (436– 338 BC), like the *De institutione principis ad Nicoclen*, contain maxims regarding

indicates that others did the same, gave an account of the stratagems and apophthegms of famous men.[7] It is no leisurely enterprise to search for gold 40 in the veins of the earth or look for precious stones in the sand or in the sea. He renders the prince a welcome service who presents pure and refined gold, who offers select and cleaned precious stones, mounted in gold or encrusted on goblets. This friendly office has been attempted by many, but in my opinion by no one with more success than Plutarch, who, after publishing an ex- 45 ceptionally useful work, *The Lives of Famous Men*, in which he recorded both their deeds and words all mixed together, collected the memorable sayings of various individuals for Trajan, the most esteemed of the Caesars,[8] because in them the mind of each person is reflected as in a faithful mirror. For in deeds the counsellor, the general, and the soldier claim a good part of the praise, 50 but the greater part belongs to Fortune, through whom we sometimes see that the best-laid plans have the worst results while, conversely, the thoughtless temerity of certain persons turns out very successfully. This is illustrated in the story of the Persian Siramnes (a general, I believe), who when asked why his deeds did not correspond to his fine words, responded, 'What I say 55 is in my hands, what will happen depends on the will of Fortune and the king.'[9] Yet good counsels are not without their efficacy. Plutarch is superior to other writers, not only in his choice of maxims but also in his explanations. The *Apophthegmata* have a special quality and character of their own in that they express each man's qualities concisely, cleverly, wittily and urbanely. 60 Just as each individual has his own traits of character, so do individual nations, whence it comes about that some things are fitting for Alexander, others for Philip or Antigonus,[10] some things are fitting for Phocion,[11] others

* * * * *

politics and government that came to be regarded as aphorisms. Erasmus' translation of the work was included with his own *Institutio principis christiani* in 1516.

7 Valerius Maximus' handbook of examples of *Memorable Deeds and Sayings*, dedicated to Emperor Tiberius, was published around 31–2 AD. The *Stratagemata* of Sextus Julius Frontinus, consul in 74 AD, was a collection of military anecdotes featuring maxims on the art of generalship.

8 The dedicatory letter to Trajan (r 98–117) is in Plutarch *Moralia* 172B–E.

9 Plutarch *Moralia* 172D.

10 Philip II of Macedon (382–336 BC) was the father of Alexander the Great (356–323 BC). Antigonus I, the 'One-eyed,' a general prominent under Philip, ruled Greater Phrygia for Alexander and, after the latter's death, was one of the generals involved in the struggle for power in the Greek world.

11 Athenian statesman and general (402–318 BC)

for Alcibiades.[12] Again, some things accord with a Spartan, others with a
Scythian or a Thracian, others with an Athenian or a Roman. In expressing   65
these things Xenophon seems a little watered down, Herodotus a bit frigid,
Diodorus and Quintus Curtius too loquacious,[13] to say nothing of the rest.
Plutarch is perfect in every detail. For that reason I thought it best to follow
him in preference to all the others.

Whatever he wrote in the work that he entitled *On Apophthegms*, there-   70
fore, you will find here in its entirety. I discovered that this work had been
translated twice into Latin, first by Francesco Filelfo and then by Raffaele
Regio, whom I met in Padua.[14] Filelfo made some slips in several passages,
which Raffaele corrected, but then he stumbled himself here and there. No
wonder, they were both human. But each of them wished only to be a trans-   75
lator; I preferred for many reasons to emulate Plutarch rather than interpret
him, to explain rather than translate.

First of all, I wanted the language to be clearer, less tied to the Greek
words. For this is not written for Trajan,[15] a man versed in both literatures
and trained by long experience, but for a young prince, and through you for   80
all boys and young men who are pursuing liberal studies. And it is not written for that age when words and actions of this kind were circulated in little
stories in the baths, at banquets, and in groups of people in the forum. I also
wanted to have the freedom to indicate the subtlety of a saying if I encountered an obscure passage – and there are a great many that give difficulty not   85
only to the uninstructed but also to those with more than ordinary learning.
I myself often had trouble divining the meaning, and perhaps my intuition
failed me at times. In more than one place I had to struggle with the errors of
the manuscripts, which the translators also ran into, inevitably. It is hardly
credible what liberties copyists or certain half-learned persons permitted   90

* * * * *

12 Athenian general and politician, protégé of Pericles, pupil and friend of Socrates
    (c 450–404 BC)
13 Diodorus Siculus (fl 60–30 BC) is the author of the *Bibliotheke*, a universal history
    from mythological times to 60 BC. The first-century Roman historian Quintus
    Curtius Rufus wrote a history of Alexander the Great in ten books.
14 For Francisco Filelfo, see Ep 23:77n; for Raffaele Regio see Ep 450:2n. Filelfo's
    translations of Plutarch's *Regum et imperatorum apophthegmata* (1437) and *Apo-
    phthegmata Laconica* (1454) were published together in 1471, and from the 1480s
    were added to editions of his *Orationes*. Regio's translation of the *Regum et impera-
    torum apophthegmata* was published at Venice in 1508, the year in which Erasmus
    met him in Padua. For details see ASD IV-4 14.
15 Cf n8 above.

themselves in the case of this author, to whom a kind of religious awe is owed. No Greek writer is more venerable or more worthy of being read than Plutarch, especially with regard to morals. And yet this very quality, which should have acted as a deterrent, invited those thirsty for glory and profit to corrupt, add, and remove. As a matter of fact, the more likely a writer is to 95 win applause and renown, the more he is corrupted for the sake of gain.

Proof of this is the very disparity among the Greek manuscripts. Leaving the other works aside and speaking only of the work that we have in hand, Filelfo has certain things that Raffaele did not touch on, and vice-versa. Furthermore, although Plutarch declares in the preface that in his *Lives* he 100 reported the words and deeds of famous men indiscriminately, while in this work, for the sake of concision, he assembled only apophthegms, we still observe that many things are mixed in that are merely clever sayings. Moreover, do not the numerous repetitions in the same work openly proclaim that this subject matter has been tampered with by someone else, not 105 to mention that the apophthegms are reported under the name of the person to whom the words were said, not by whom they were said, as in the case of Lysimachus and Philippides?[16] In Plutarch's collections the answer of Philippides to Lysimachus is included under the heading of Lysimachus.[17] It was more audacious that from one work they made two. Whereas Plutarch 110 chose from the many Spartan apophthegms that remain to us only those that seemed to be sufficient for a very busy emperor, someone, whoever it was (if indeed it was just one person), dedicated a separate book to the sayings of the Spartans, following the order of the Greek alphabet, which Raffaele transposed into the order of the Latin alphabet. This was the worst of the 115 three. Valerius and Frontinus arrange the sayings according to religion, patriotism, fortitude, and justice, and so forth, assigning each of them to its proper class. The most sophisticated order was that followed by Plutarch, adhering to a sequence of regions and kingdoms, and giving the age and rank of each individual; to each king he joins his generals, and to each general his 120 colleagues. From the Persians he goes to the Egyptians, from the Egyptians to the Thracians, from the Thracians to the Scythians, from the Scythians to the Sicilians, from the Sicilians to the Macedonians, and from there to the Athenians, then to the Spartans, following for each of them a chronological,

* * * * *

16 Plutarch, *Moralia* 183E, 508C. Lysimachus asked the comic poet Philippides, 'Which of my possessions can I share with you?' The poet answered, 'Whatever you wish, except your secrets.'
17 This sentence was added in 1535.

not an alphabetical order. From the Spartans he goes to the Thebans and from   125
the Thebans to the Romans, so that through the words of a few the reader
may know the succession of events in the whole history. This was wretchedly
jumbled by whoever excerpted the Spartan apophthegms while at the same
time retaining those that Plutarch had collected for Trajan. Although this is
found more frequently in the previous work, it occurs so many times in both   130
that this inattention cannot be ascribed to Plutarch, a writer of scrupulous
precision. In addition, this second book has no preface, and the preface to
Trajan in the first book is not applicable to both. I will not discuss at this point
what thanks are owed to those who corrupt the books of famous authors in
this way, but it seems to me that it is a kind of sacrilege. Nevertheless, except   135
for some Spartan apophthegms, which are all taken up again in the second
series, I have not left out anything that goes under Plutarch's name, partly so
that the avid rather than the discriminating reader would not find something
lacking, partly because I saw nothing there that was not worth knowing,
even if it is not mentioned in its proper place.   140
     But in a certain sense I have made the whole work my own, since I
make the Greek text clearer, interjecting at times what I had found in other
authors, adding many things which were not contained in this work, and
explaining in the notes the meaning and the application of the apophthegms,
especially those that required some clarification; I did this, however, in a   145
few words, without departing from the true nature of the apophthegm. But
the arrangement in my own work is even more confused than what I found
there, because at first I had decided to enumerate only a few outstanding authors, but the enthusiasm engendered by the work incited me to change my
mind and extend my comments further; and there would have been no end   150
to it unless the immense sea of subject matter that presented itself to me had
not compelled me to sound a retreat. For just as Quintilian places among the
virtues of a teacher of grammar not to know some things,[18] so in this kind of
subject it would seem that a part of thoroughness is to pass over some things.
I would rather be a judicious host rather than an annoying one, especially   155
because if something has been omitted in this supper, it can be served at
another after this one has been digested. We compensated for the inconvenience of neglecting the order by including an index. We need not be concerned about the title, since among the things Plutarch collected under the
name apophthegms there are many things that someone else might prefer to   160
call jests, abuse, witticisms, repartee, banter. But after Marcus Tullius toiled

* * * * *

18 Quintilian 1.8.21

in vain to distinguish among these,[19] and the very learned Marsus did not satisfy Quintilian,[20] and even Quintilian himself, more learned than Marsus, was not pleased with his own command of the subject, I did not think it was worthwhile to expend too much effort on this, thinking it sufficient to indi-   165
cate in passing the type of saying or jest.

In what I added, at least, I was careful not to confuse clever sayings with apophthegms and not to use anything at all except from the most ap-proved writers of both languages, taken from the ancient writers. It is not that I am unaware that many witty and amusing sayings can be found in   170
recent writers, but those consecrated by antiquity have more authority, and I had to impose a certain limit on the work. We should not be disconcerted that sometimes the same saying is attributed by one writer to one author and by another writer to a different author. It is not so important by whom it was said as what was said, even if a celebrated and popular author adds   175
some authority and charm to the sayings. This happens too often to have to be proved by examples.[21] But sometimes it happens through a lapse of human memory, although nothing prevents the same thought from origi-nating from different authors, whether this be the result of imitation or of chance, as in the iambic trimeter 'Converse with the wise makes monarchs   180
wise,'[22] which is said to be a verse of Sophocles,[23] yet it is cited by Plato as a verse of Euripides.[24] Again, the verse 'As one old man leading another, I will escort you like a child' is found in both the *Philoctetes* of Sophocles and the *Bacchae* of Euripides.[25] Similarly, this verse, 'Keeping silent when silence is called for and speaking when it is time to speak,' although it is in Aeschylus'   185
Prometheus,[26] is found in Euripides with two words changed.[27] Many times authors do not agree on either the facts or the name.[28] For example, the per-

* * * * *

19 Cicero *De oratore* 2.217–89
20 Quintilian 6.3.102–112. Domitius Marsus, an Augustan poet, was the author of elegant epigrams, only a few fragments of which remain.
21 This sentence was added in 1535.
22 Aulus Gellius *Noctes Atticae* 13.19.3
23 Nauck fragment 13; see *Adagia* III v 97
24 Plato *Theages* 125B
25 Euripides *Bacchae* 193. Erasmus has mistakenly changed the name of Sophocles' play from *Phthiotides,* as cited by Gellius (see n22 above), to *Philoctetes.*
26 Not in the *Prometheus Vinctus,* but the lost *Prometheus Pyrphorus* fragment 208. It is also found in the *Choephoroi* 582.
27 Euripides *Ino*; Nauck fragment 413
28 The passage beginning with this sentence and ending with 'Lucius Crassus' in line 196 below was added in 1535.

son who made fun of Fabius Maximus because he had recaptured Tarentum by his own efforts is called Livius Salinator by Marcus Tullius,[29] Marcus Livius by Livy,[30] and Marcus Lucius – or, as the Greek manuscripts give 190 the name Μάρκιος Λεύκιος – by Plutarch.[31] Likewise Flavius Philostratus tells us that the sophist Leon was the laughing stock of the Athenian people because of his extraordinary corpulence,[32] but Plutarch says it was because he was thin.[33] What differences there are between Valerius Maximus and Pliny in their account of the dispute between Gnaeus Domitius and Lucius 195 Crassus![34] The most tedious stories are the ones invented for characters from myth, such as those written by the sophist Philostratus when he makes up whatever tales he likes about Palamedes,[35] Ulysses, and others like them; they are twice as boring when you explicate them. I have never mentioned myths of this sort. Like these are the characteristics attributed to various 200 personages in dialogues invented not to be faithful to the truth, but to entertain. Less insipid are the things said in comedies and tragedies; they have great charm when used at the right moment, even if they do not fall under the name of apophthegm unless a famous author accommodates them to a contemporary event, but they are more satisfying if they are distorted a 205 little to give them a different meaning, as, for example, when Aristotle uses a Homeric verse – 'Swift will be your death, my son, uttering such words as

* * * * *

29 Cicero *De senectute* 11; *De oratore* 2.273
30 Livy 27.25
31 Plutarch *Moralia* 195F. The story, recounted by all three writers, is that Marcus Livius Macatus (not Marcus Livius Salinator, as Cicero mistakenly calls him) had lost the town of Tarentum to the Carthaginians in 212 BC but managed to hold onto the citadel for five years until Fabius Maximus Cunctator recaptured the town. When it was suggested that Fabius Maximus was indebted for his conquest of the town to Macatus because he had held onto the citadel, Fabius remarked, 'Indeed, for if he had not lost it, it would not have had to be recaptured.'
32 Philostratus *Sophists* 1.2
33 Plutarch *Moralia* 804A–B
34 Gnaeus Ahenobarbus Domitius and Lucius Licinius Crassus were censors together in 92 BC. Each rebuked the other for living lavishly, which as censors they were not supposed to do. Two very different versions of the dispute are given in Valerius Maximus *Memorable Deeds and Sayings* 9.1.4, and Pliny *Naturalis historia* 17.1.2–4.
35 Philostratus *The Life of Apollo of Tyana* 3.22.2, 4.13.2–3, 4.16.6. Palamedes fought at Troy on the side of the Greeks but he is not mentioned in Homer. There were many stories about him, good and bad. He was said to have invented writing.

these'[36] – to warn Callisthenes, who was acting more freely than was expedient with Alexander.[37]

I had no desire to select many things from Herodotus, because a great 210
part of his stories seems to be the product of the writer's ingenuity. Of the
same type are the sayings that we find in speeches that historians devise,
each in his own way, for their personages, although these can contribute to
critical judgment and a fluent style. The best kind of apophthegm is one that
in a few words suggests rather than expresses an uncommon meaning that 215
no one could easily imagine by force of study and that gives more pleasure
the more and the longer you meditate on it. Taken as a whole, this genre,
which comprises proverbs, wise sayings, things said and done in a remarkable way, is very appropriate for princes, who, because of the affairs of state,
do not have a great amount of time to devote to books. These are learned 220
with pleasure and easily fix themselves in the mind, but deep down they
have far more philosophy than meets the eye. We read that whenever Caesar
Augustus happened upon any teachings of this kind he would make sure to
have them copied down and distributed among his household.[38] We see that
the famous sages of old made it their particular practice to instil into young 225
minds things worth knowing by making them attractive, so that at a young
age they would learn what would be of great use throughout their lives. For
this purpose they interspersed cosmography, astrology, music, and natural
moral philosophy with cleverly devised fables and stories.

In my selections, however, it will seem that there are some that con- 230
tribute nothing to good morals, but only rouse laughter. I do not think that
occasionally relaxing a mind wearied by cares is to be regarded as a vice, provided that the humour is witty and in good taste. Such things cheer and en-
liven the spirit of the young and contribute in no small way to graciousness
of manners and urbanity of speech. What lends more sweetness to the style 235
of Cicero than his seasoning it with bons mots of this sort? And what are the
Moralia of Plutarch but tapestries variegated with colours of this same kind?
Further, things that seem supremely ridiculous become serious when you
examine them more closely. What is more ridiculous than Diogenes walking

* * * * *

36 Homer Iliad 18.95. The words are spoken by Thetis to her son, Achilles.
37 Callisthenes, d 327 BC, nephew of Aristotle and member of the entourage of
   Alexander the Great. Plutarch (Moralia 458B) recounts an episode when, at a
   banquet, Callisthenes provoked Alexander by refusing a strong drink called
   'Alexander's loving cup,' saying: 'I do not care to drink of Alexander and then
   have to call in Asclepius [the god of healing].'
38 Suetonius Augustus 89.2

around at midday with a lantern in the crowded forum, repeating that he is   240
looking for a man?[39] But meanwhile we learn by laughing that those who
look like men (as statues do) are not necessarily men, but to find a man you
must search for his mind. If you allow yourself to be led by reason rather
than by passion, then you have found a man. Similarly, what is as laughable
as the story about Phryne, who made all the other women at the banquet do   245
what she did: she dipped her hand twice into the water and rubbed her face
with it, by this ruse revealing the make-up of the other women in the midst of
general laughter, while she seemed even more beautiful?[40] But this laughter
teaches us what Socrates said in a more serious vein,[41] that we should strive
to be the way we would like to appear to others so that when the make-up   250
is removed we will not reap ignominy instead of the glory we had ineptly
tried to attain. It also teaches us not to rely on external and transitory things,
which are easily taken away from a person through various circumstances,
but to prepare the true riches of the spirit, over which fortune has no claim.
So much serious philosophy is illustrated in the act of a lowly courtesan. To   255
give another example, although Lycurgus educated his citizens with severe
rules, yet he not only allowed them urbane jokes, but even prescribed them.[42]
He instituted, in fact, a kind of meeting place, which he called Λέσχαι,[43] to
which older men now retired from public functions came; they passed their
time pleasantly, exchanging clever sayings and urbane jokes that were con-   260
ducive to praising virtue and blaming vice. He even set up a statue to the god
Γέλως (Laughter),[44] because he thought it was very useful to restore people's
spirit by discreet witticisms and inspire them with enthusiasm for honourable labours, since in human affairs work 'without alternating repose will
not endure.'[45] Even Cleomenes, who was so severe that he never admitted   265
mimes, cithara players, and flutists into the republic, still thought it beneficial for citizens to vie with one another in urbane jokes and pungent witticisms.[46] Finally, whenever there is free time from occupations or the occasion
itself calls for light-heartedness, how much more becoming it is to amuse

* * * * *

39 *Apophthegmata* 3. Diogenes 63; CWE 37 291 (3.226)
40 *Apophthegmata* 6. Stratonicus 83; CWE 38 756 (6.576). Phryne was a famously
    beautiful courtesan who was used as a model by both Apelles and Praxiteles.
41 Xenophon *Memorabilia* 1.7.1; Cicero *De officiis* 2.43
42 Plutarch *Life of Lycurgus* 20.1–6
43 *Life of Lycurgus* 25.1
44 *Life of Lycurgus* 25.2
45 Ovid *Heroides* 4.89
46 Plutarch *Life of Cleomenes* 12.3

ourselves with this kind of pleasantry than to delight in unseemly, ignorant, 270
and obscene tales! It seems to me somewhat more advisable that children
be trained in this type of subject in the grammar schools rather than in the
banal themes of uninteresting content that shed no light on the mysteries of
the Latin language, provided that the teacher point out the ways in which
what has been said in a few words can be expanded and what has been said 275
to rouse laughter can be converted to a serious context. I will also add this:
perhaps it is not suitable to mix pleasantries with the divine Scriptures in
sacred sermons, but it is more excusable for preachers to use them to wake
up those who have fallen asleep than to interpose without warning, as they
often do, old wives' tales taken right from the dregs of the populace.[47] Julius 280
Caesar, who had to endure many hardships, both civic and military, was
accustomed to shake off his weariness by reading witty sayings, in which
he found such pleasure that he even approved that they be hurled against
himself, provided they were clever.[48] There was hardly any emperor who
was more upright or more occupied than Caesar Augustus, yet who was 285
more refined in this genre?[49] I shall say nothing of Marcus Tullius, who in
the opinion of some seems to forget all moderation and decency when he
indulges in pleasantries.[50] The philosopher Xenocrates was a man of rather
somber character, though otherwise a great man, but Plato often advised him
to make sacrifice to the Graces.[51] Zeno, a complete Stoic, used to call Socrates 290
the clown of Athens because of the ceaseless banter of his conversations;[52] yet
no one would deny that he was the more venerable of the two. I will not mention that no one's words have more currency than those that are seasoned
with wit; certainly Socrates or Diogenes or Aristippus would be more useful
for the education of young boys than Xenocrates or Zeno. 295

But if very wise men were right in thinking that the young should be
enticed to the love of a more austere wisdom through certain forms of amusement, then it is even more appropriate for a young prince, who must both
be vigilant and, at the same time, should neither be depressed himself nor

* * * * *

47 Erasmus' *Ecclesiastes* includes a long passage on the use of jests and stories in
    sermons to awaken sleepy listeners (CWE 68 504–9; cf CWE 67 439–41).
48 Suetonius *Julius Caesar* 73
49 Macrobius *Saturnalia* 2.4.1–18
50 Quintilian 6.3.2–3
51 Plutarch *Moralia* 141F; Diogenes Laertius 4.6.246–7
52 Cicero *De natura deorum* 1.93. Cicero ascribes this saying to the Epicurean phi-
    losopher Zeno of Sidon, whom Erasmus here confuses with Zeno of Citium, the
    founder of Stoicism.

send anyone away from his presence cast down in spirit. The mind formed   300
by pleasant studies is made more vigorous in dealing with all problems and
is more congenial in dealing with others. On the basis of these arguments I
could have defended myself if I had collected nothing but witticisms, but in
the work, at any rate, other ingredients have been mixed in, like the condi-
ments at a banquet. If I sense that you find pleasure in this genre, I will not   305
regret having written this work, although some perhaps will judge it insignificant. Others write for those more advanced in age; I nurture a prince of
more tender years. But if one day these entertainments will be unsuitable for
your progress in learning (as I hope will be the case), I know it will not be displeasing to you if through you they will have contributed something useful   310
to the general studies of young men. And perhaps some day I will provide a
more serious work, after you have learned these sayings thoroughly. For they
must be learned by heart so that they will always be at hand.

And yet, what need do you have of my works, since you have at home
Konrad Heresbach,[53] a man of consummate learning in every branch of lit-   315
erature, who I see is so devoted to you that, as befits an excellent teacher, he
is more delighted in the progress and distinctions of his students than in his
own? As he has formed your youthful age, so he will be able to assist you
when you are older by his faithful and prudent advice. For me also it will
have been no less a pleasure than an honour to have developed even in a   320
small way your gifted nature through my assiduity. For the rest I pray to the
good and great God that he deign to guard, preserve, and increase the gifts
he has generously bestowed upon you so that you may live up to the wishes
of your esteemed parents, show yourself worthy of the illustrious images of
your ancestors, and be equal to the glorious rule for which you were born and   325
destined. I shall not end without saying this brief word: while you are dwelling on these matters, remember that you are not reading the apophthegms of
Christians but of pagans, so that you will read with discernment.

At Freiburg im Breisgau, 26 February 1531

2432 / To John (III) More   Freiburg, 27 February 1531

This is the prefatory letter to *Aristotelis … opera quaecunque impressa hactenus
extiterunt omnia, summa cum vigilantia excusa,* the edition of Aristotle in Greek
edited by Simon Grynaeus (Ep 2433) and published at Basel by Johann Bebel,
13 May 1531. The letter, which is Erasmus' sole contribution to the edition,

* * * * *

53 Duke William's tutor; see Ep 1316.

ΑΡΙΣΤΟΤΕΛΟΥΣ ἍΠΑΝΤΑ.

ARISTOTELIS

SVMMI SEMPER VIRI, ET IN QVEM VNVM
uim suam uniuersam contulisse natura rerū uidetur, opera,
quæcunq; impressa hactenus extiterunt omnia,
summa cum uigilantia excusa.

PER DES. ERAS. ROTERODAMVM
φιλολόγε καὶ βιβλιοπώλυ διάλογ@.

ΦΙΛ. Τί νέον κομίζεις; ΒΙΒ.λογ; ΒΙΒ.ὺδ' ἀμῶς. ΦΙΛ.τί δή;
ΒΙΒ. Χρυσὸ βιθρα. ΦΙΛ. Ναὶ σὺ πλυσίως λίγεις,
Ραχύτερον ἐστί. ΒΙΒ.ῆρ Στεγδρίτω λέγω,
Ὃς ἐλαθὸν εὐέλη τῶ μαθημάτων μόσθ@,
Ούτος γ' αίνέησ' ὡς πρὸ τὸ πελὺ κάλλιον.
ΦΙΛ.Λιγ.σε ἀλυθῶς τ' ἀμαλθώας κέρας.
ΒΙΒ. Οὐ μὰ γ' ὁπώρας μισέη, ἀλλ' ἀμφνόκῳ.
ΦΙΛ.Καὶ τίς ἱσῶσιν πλούτον ἡμῖν εμφορή;
ΒΙΒ.Τοῦ τῆρ γὰ παρίχε φιλόπονος ΒιΒίλι@.
ΦΙΛ.Χρυσῷμπτερος γαῶ θ'ιρ, ὰ λογίμπερ@;
ΒΙΒ.Ναί.κέτι χυσὸ @ λίθων προφιρεσερον,
Θῶτς ἃ Ϛφίτε οὐδὲν ἰς αντάξιον.

Indicem librorum. id est. longum diuitis thesauri
catalogum, octaua pagina continet.

BASILEAE, APVD IO. BEB.
ANNO M. D. XXXI.

Cum gratia & priuilegio Cæsareo.

Title-page of the Greek edition of Aristotle
(Basel: Johann Bebel 1531)
Austrian National Library

appears to have been written at the request of Bebel, who doubtless reckoned
that the name of the most famous scholar in Europe would sell more copies
than that of the still relatively unknown Grynaeus. (It is Erasmus' name, not
that of Grynaeus, that appears on the title-page of the volume.) The letter is addressed to John More (Ep 999 n28), the only son of Sir Thomas More, and it is
on the father rather than the son that Erasmus bestows extravagantly generous
praise. This doubtless served the purpose of helping to secure a good reception for Grynaeus, who in the spring of 1531 embarked with Bebel on a visit to
England, bearing generous letters of introduction from Erasmus; see Ep 2433
introduction. (In 1534 Grynaeus dedicated his Greek edition of Plato, published
by Johann Walder at Basel, to John More, making clear that this was a gesture of
thanks to John's father for having helped him gain access to important manuscripts in Oxford.) The present letter is also noteworthy as an astute attempt
by Erasmus to establish an accurate canon of Aristotle's works by identifying
the spurious items in the list of works commonly attributed to him. See Jill
Kraye 'Erasmus and the Canonization of Aristotle' in *England and the Continental
Renaissance: Essays in Honour of J.B. Trapp* ed Edward Chaney and Peter Mack
(Woodbridge, Suffolk and Rochester, New York 1990) 37–49.

DESIDERIUS ERASMUS OF ROTTERDAM TO JOHN MORE, GREETING
Most distinguished young man, Aristotle, indisputably the most learned of
all philosophers, including Plato and Cicero, when asked by a certain crass
and uncultured individual what was the difference between learned and unlearned persons, promptly responded, 'The difference that exists between   5
the living and the dead.'[1] He was perfectly right, esteeming that those who
enjoyed only the life of the body (which we have in common with asses,
swine, and ducks) and who saw the sun only with the eyes of the body
(which eagles see more distinctly), and with their minds (to which, as that
same philosopher said, philosophy gives light and life) saw nothing, were   10
not worthy of the appellation of man and were more truly dead than alive
and differed from stone statues only in the slightest degree; they are even
inferior, because statues are a delight to the eye, speak ill of no one, and
harm no one. He also is accustomed to say that the roots of the liberal arts
are a little bitter but the fruit very sweet.[2] Homer seems to signify the same   15
thing more exactly, inasmuch as he is a poet, when in depicting *moly* – the
most extraordinary and effective herb against any kind of sorcery – he said

* * * * *

2432
1 *Apophthegmata* 7. Aristotle 16; CWE 38 824 (7.234)
2 *Apophthegmata* 7. Aristotle 8; CWE 38 822 (7.226)

that it had a black root but a milky white flower.³ Moreover, liberal learning
assures not only that we are human beings and that we are dissociated from
the race of beasts, thus living fully and truly, but also that we live happily   20
and agreeably. But I have no doubts, my dear More, that having absorbed
long ago the more bitter parts of learning, if there were any, you pluck the
fruits of philosophy, seeing that you were born of such a father and, since
your nails were soft, as they say,⁴ were educated, formed, and developed
by him as much in the disciplines of both languages as in Christian piety   25
and good morals. Certainly that man, as pious as he is learned, had no more
heartfelt desire than to mould a son more similar to him through education
than he had brought to birth through nature, so that indeed he would both
be a complete father and have in you a truly well-bred son. On this account
you are surely little less fortunate than if it was your lot to be born to a king   30
or an emperor. If you acknowledge this good fortune of yours, as I believe
you assuredly do, you cannot but give great thanks to God, the author all
good fortune, and strive with all your might to measure up to the divine generosity so lavishly bestowed on you and the outstanding piety of an excellent
father. For if anyone was given the good fortune to have the opportunity to   35
learn at home, as the comic writer said,⁵ and suck in learning and piety with
his nurse's milk, this was given to you in a striking manner. And you are not
unaware that it was said famously about this same Aristotle (not to depart
from him) that we owe more to those by whom we were taught than to those
from whom we were brought into the world, because from our parents we   40
receive only the gift of life, but from our teachers the gift of living well.⁶
Your excellent father gave you both gifts in great abundance, and you owe
him a twofold gratitude. Since this is the case, I would seem to be assuming
a superfluous task if I should try to spur on a willing runner. I merely like
to applaud and acclaim energetically the one who is hastening towards the   45
goal of perfection, leaving many behind, so that you will run more briskly.
For I think that now that you have completed the easier disciplines and have
entered into the more august mysteries of philosophy, you may join Wisdom
to Eloquence, the queen to her attendant. For it seems to me that those who
do nothing else all their life but learn how to speak correctly are acting quite   50

* * * * *

3 Homer *Odyssey* 10.203–5. Moly was the magical herb given to Odysseus by
  Hermes to protect him against the magic of the sorceress Circe.
4 Ie 'from earliest childhood'; *Adagia* I vii 52
5 Terence *Adelphi* 412; cf *Adagia* I x 49.
6 *Apophthegmata* 4. Alexander 42 (cf CWE 37 360 [4.77]); Plutarch *Life of Alexander* 8.4

foolishly, and they do not attain the one thing they are seeking, since wisdom
is the beginning and the source of good speaking.[7]

As I reflected on these things, dearest John, I resolved on dedicating
to you this Aristotle, the prince and paragon of all philosophy, as if he were
reborn just now, so that by absorbing yourself in his intricacies you may   55
complete the whole cycle of learning. He was the one, in fact, who restored
order to philosophy, which had been handed down by various authors in
fragments, in a scattered and mutilated way, and organized it into one body.
Beginning with poets and rhetoricians, he leads it to logic; then, after carefully arranging morals from every perspective, he leads it through all the parts   60
of nature; lastly, he elevates it to those things that surpass more humble nature, to that highest intelligence that surpasses all understanding. Therefore
Marcus Tullius, no mean judge of talent, calls him alone a river of gold,[8]
although in my opinion it would be more apt to call him a very rich world
of all wisdom. But Chronos, most envious of the gods, not content with eat-   65
ing away marbles and bronzes, images of the body, also devours or destroys
the monuments of geniuses. So rich and inestimable a treasure would have
perished for us if it had not been rescued from Orcus by Lucius Sulla,[9] who
by that benefit alone could have defended himself from the hateful reproach
contained in rude verses in which he was called fortunate for himself, not for   70
the state.[10] For by bringing the works of Aristotle to light again he deserved
to be called fortunate not just for Rome but for the world. But Nemesis tempered this joy in the rediscovery of Aristotle with no small sorrow when we
think of how many monuments of this philosopher perished of those that ancient writers tell us were composed by him; they say that he wrote more than   75
three hundred books. Diogenes estimates the total to be more than 533,000
lines.[11] (Ancient writers are accustomed to number volumes by the number
of lines, since it is a more precise figure, because books are frequently unequal in size according to the quantity of the subject matter.) But they diminish the sadness of this loss with a partial consolation, saying that those that   80

* * * * *

7 Horace *Ars poetica* 309
8 Cicero *Academica* 38.119
9 When the Roman general Sulla conquered Athens in 86 BC, he brought the
   works of Aristotle back to Rome with him, thus allegedly saving them from
   extinction. Cf Plutarch *Life of Sulla* 26. Orcus was the Roman god of the under-
   world, his name synonymous with death.
10 Suetonius *Tiberius* 59. The reference is to Sulla's adopted surname Felix, Latin
   for 'fortunate.'
11 *Apophthegmata* 5. Diogenes 27

have survived intact are few but they are the best. They divide them into four classes, of which the first contains works that treat of the method of speaking and persuading. In this class we can include those that he wrote on poetics, music, and proverbs, or anything similar to those. The second is composed of those that teach the science of discussion and reasoning. The third comprises 85 those that tell of moral and civil discipline. In the fourth are the works that treat of natural and supernatural things. Now I shall describe to you, as in an inventory, what has perished or is extant in each class.[12]

In the first category, which, as I said, is concerned with the teaching of rhetoric, the extant copies in Greek are: three books of rhetoric to Theodectes, 90 although Laertius enumerates only two, but he testifies that the author dealt with rhetoric twice in two volumes. *To Alexander* on public speaking, one book. *On Poetics*, one book.

In the second category, which treats of dialectic, these are extant: *On the Ten Predicaments*, one book; *On Pronunciation*, one book, which is now 95 divided into two. *Prior Analytics*, nine books, although only two are extant, unless perhaps the two books that Laertius calls by the title *Syllogisms* belong there. *Posterior Analytics* or *Demonstrations*, two books. *Topics*, eight books. *Refutations*, one book, which someone or other divided into two.

In the third category, which contains moral works, these are extant: 100 The *Ethics to Nicomachus*, ten books. The *Ethics to Eudemus*, eight books, (or so it seems, since the seventh book is very long). The *Ethics* called *Magna*, two books. *Politics*, eight books. *Economics*, two books, of which the second is spurious.

In the fourth category these works are extant: *On Natural Things Heard*, 105 eight books. *On Meteorology*, four books. *On the Heavens*, four books. *History of Animals*, ten books. *Parts of Animals*, four books. *Generation of Animals*, five books. *On Generation and Corruption*, two books. *On the Universe to Alexander*, one book. *On Colours*, two books. *On Plants*, one book. *Sense and Sensibility*, one book. *On Youth and Old Age*, one book. *On Sleep and Waking*, one book. 110 *On Dreams*, one book. *On Divination in Sleep*, one book. Many sections on *Problems. On Life and Death*, one book. *On Respiration*, one book. *On Breath*, one book. *On Physiognomics*, one book. *On the Soul*, three books. *On Memory and Remembering*, one book. *On Mechanics*, one book. *On Indivisible Lines*, one book. *On the Opinions of Xenophanes, Zeno, and Gorgias*, one book. *Metaphysics*, 115 fourteen books.

* * * * *

12 This following list of Aristotle's works is an almost exact reproduction of that found in Diogenes Laertius *Lives of the Philosophers* 5.22–7.

This much is extant, in Greek. Now learn what works are missing in each category.

In the first category these are missing: *On Poets*, three books. *On Rhetoric*, one book, whose title is *Gryllus. Nerinthus*, one book. *On Rhetorical* 120 *Enthymemes*, two books. *Treatise on the Art of Poetry*, two books. *On Counsel*, one book. *On Ambiguities in Homer*, six books. *On Liberal Disciplines*, two books. *Parables*, one book. *On Indeterminate Things*, twelve books. *On Olympic Victors*, one book. *On Pythian Victors*, one book. *Lists of Pythian Victors*, one book. *Victories at the Dionysia*, one book. *The Theory of Music*, one book. *On* 125 *Tragedies*, one book. *On Learned Studies*, one book. *Proverbs*, one book. *Poem to Philoxenus*. He also wrote elegies. To these may be added: *Mathematics*, one book. *On Grandeur*, one book. *On Music*, one book.

In the second category these are lacking: *The Sophist*, one book. *Menexenus*, one book. *On the Sciences*, one book. *Solutions of Controversial Arguments*, 130 one book. *Divisions of Sophistry*, four books. *On Opposites*, one book. *On Genera and Species*, one book. *On Properties*, one book. *Arguments for Purposes of Refutation*, three books. *On Instance*, one book. *On the Various Meanings of Terms, either through Addition or Subject Matter*, as the translator of Diogenes rendered it, although the Aldine edition has κατὰ πρόσθεσιν,[13] one book. *On* 135 *Science*, one book. *On Divisions*, seventeen books. *On Divisibles*, one book. *On Questioning and Answering*, two books. *On Propositions*, one book. *On Controversial Propositions*, four books. *On the Syllogism*, one book. *On Questions*, one book. *Methodology*, eight books. *On Syllogisms*, two books. *Syllogisms and Definitions*, two books. *On the Desirable and the Contingent*, one book. *Preface* 140 *to Commonplaces*, one book. *Topics Criticizing Definitions*, two books. *Divisions*, one book. *On Definitions*, three books. *On Epicheiremata*,[14] two books. *Controversial Questions*, twenty-five books. *Enumeration of the Arts*, two books. *Art*, one book. *A Second Book on Art*, two books. *Compendium of Art*, one book. *Compendium of the Art of Theodectes*, one book. *Divisions of Enthymemes*, one 145 book. *On Diction*, three books. *On Epitomes*, two books. *Against Gorgias*, one book. *On Problems from Democritus*, six books. *On Learning*, one book. *Against the Maxims of Zeno*, two books. *On General Education*, two books.

* * * * *

13 The phrase κατὰ πρόσθεσιν is a technical term meaning the way in which a predicate may fail to be true of the subject because of an addition. Cf Aristotle *Metaphysics* 1029b30. The Lives of Aristotle and Theophrastus were the first part of the Greek text of Diogenes to be printed, as part of the Aldine Aristotle (Venice 1497).
14 An epicheirema is an attempted proof that is not conclusive.

From the third category the following were lost: *On Justice*, four books. *On Philosophy*, three books. *On the Republic*, two books. *On Lovers*, one book. *The Banquet*, one book. *On Riches*, one book. *On Exhortations*, one book. *On Noble Birth*, one book. *On Pleasure*, one book. *Alexander* or *On Colonies*, one book. *On Kingship*, one book. *On the Good*, three books. *On the Laws of Plato*, three books. *On the Republic of Plato*, two books. *On Friendship*, one book. *What It Is to Be Affected or to Have Been Affected by Emotion*, one book. *Principles concerning Virtue*, three books. *On Fits of Anger*, one book. *On Authority*, one book. *On What Is Better*, one book. *On the Passions*, one book. *On Free Will*, one book. *On the Beautiful*, one book. *Questions concerning Friendship*, two books. *Politics*, two books. *On Just Actions*, two books. *On Justifications*, two books. *Rights*, one book. *Law of Recommendations*, one book. *On Laws*, four books. *Constitutions of States*, one hundred twenty books, and separately, *On Democracy, On Oligarchy, On Aristocracy, On Monarchy*. To these may be added the *Letters to Philip*, the *Letters about the Selymbrians*, four to Alexander, nine to Antipater, one to Mentor, one to Olympias, one to Hephaestion, one to Themistagoras, one to Philoxenus.

From the fourth category these were lost: *On Elements*, three books. *On Motion*, one book. *On Form*, one book. *Questions about the Soul*, one book. *On Nature*, three books. *Physics*, one book. *On the Philosophy of Archytas*, three books. *On the Philosophy of Speusippus and Xenocrates*, one book. *Excerpts from the Timaeus and Archytas*, one book. *Against the Sayings of Melissus*, one book. *Against the Pythagoreans*, one book. *Against the Opinions of Alcmaeon*, one book. *Against Xenocrates*, one book. *On the Pythagoreans*, one book. *On Dissections*, eight books. *Excerpts from Dissections*, one book. *On Composite Animals*, one book. *On Mythological Animals*, one book. *On Sterility*, one book. *On Plants*, one book. *On Medicaments*, two books. *On Signs of Storms*, one book. *The Speculative Astronomer*, one book. *On Motion*, one book. *On Problems That Have Been Examined*, two books. *General Exposition*, fourteen books.

You see, my dear young man, what the world of studies has lost and what remains to us; it seemed right to me to set both before you so that we may profit by what has survived through God's favour and may preserve them more avidly and more carefully. However, there are more books translated into Latin than exist in Greek, and in both there are books concerning whose author there is a justifiable ambiguity. First the small works *On Life and Death, On Memory and Remembering, On Longevity and the Brevity of Life*, and many of this sort may appear spurious, because in Diogenes Laertius, who carefully lists the works of this man, there is no mention of them, although there is practically nothing in them that is not learned and worth reading. It is clear that a book *On Fruit* is by a Christian. The person who wrote the preface to the book *On Vegetables* says that it was translated from Arabic, and

it probably was written by an Arab, because he cites a certain Abruculus un- 190
known to the Greeks.[15] Yet all books of this nature were ascribed to Aristotle
because they are lectured on by those who teach Aristotelian philosophy
in the schools. The book called the *Magna moralia* seems to have been composed of excerpts from the *Ethics to Nicomachus*. The first book of the *Ethics
to Eudemus* reflect clearly the vigour and acumen of Aristotle; the following 195
books seem to have been added by someone else, since the same things are
repeated there in the same words. The subject matter itself of *On Marvellous
Things Heard* reveals that it was sewed together by various authors and does
not have the character of Aristotle. The book of *Problems*, highly learned,
seems to have been adulterated by scholars, which can be seen by the rep- 200
etition of the same things so many times. I am not certain whether this is
the book that Diogenes mentions under the title *Six Books of Problems Taken
from Democritus*. Two other books of *Problems That Have Been Investigated*, one
of *Everyday Problems*, others on *Theses and Propositions* are also mentioned,
from which a good part of the excerpts we possess were extracted. As to the 205
Economics, Laertius enumerates only one book, although Leonardo Aretino
translated two, the second of which is not found.[16] (In its place Aldus substituted a fragment of *Stratagems*, which has nothing to do with economics.)
The first is very authentically Aristotle, but would that it were complete; the
second, which Leonardo gives in translation, has no relation with the first 210
and is not redolent of the character of Aristotle. Laertius mentions one book
On the Soul, but some scholar must have divided it into three. As for the
Rhetoric to Alexander, although it is extremely learned, its authenticity can
be questioned for two reasons: first, because in the manner of orators it has
a preface, which is never the case otherwise (Aristotle always goes straight 215
to the subject matter); next because Diogenes does not mention it. The book
On Plants is not a separate work, but a part of, or if you prefer, the third book
of *On Colours*. The book *On the Universe* to Alexander is by a learned man,
but is very inconsistent with the style of Aristotle. The book *On Indivisible
Lines* is by a very learned man, but it does not have the distinctive quality of 220
Aristotle, and Laertius makes no mention of it. I have presented my opinion
in these matters in such a way that each one is free to make his own judgment
without being influenced by my remarks.

* * * * *

15 Abruculus is an Arabic adaptation of the Greek name Empedocles.
16 Cf Ep 2434:41–3. Leonardo Aretino is better known as Leonardo Bruni
(Ep 173:115n).

It remains for me to touch briefly on what has been added to the knowledge of scholars by this most recent edition by Bebel. First of all, I acknowl-　225
edge that we owe a great debt of gratitude to Aldus,[17] who was the first
through his diligent enterprise to make available to the public in Greek characters an author more worthy to be read than hardly any other. For previously we had him, but so translated that you would need a Delian swimmer,[18] as
they say, to make sense of him, with the exception, if you will, of the transla-　230
tions of Theodorus Gaza,[19] who was most successful in this endeavour, and
Leonardo Aretino.[20] For I think Argyropolous tried his hand at this after the
Aldine edition.[21] The Aldine volumes were very expensive, which deterred
impecunious students of philosophy, and they were unavailable except in
Italy; afterwards there were hardly any to be found, all or at least the great　235
part of them having been sold. But Johann Bebel saw to it that anyone, no
matter how modest his means, could buy this inestimable treasure printed
in very elegant type for a moderate price.[22] Moreover, we have not produced
the same Aristotle, but one much more free of errors than before, thanks
especially to the zeal, vigilance, and trustworthiness of Simon Grynaeus, a　240
young man uncommonly learned in every branch of literary studies and not
without the resources of reliable manuscripts. For example, in the *Dialectics*
a very accurate manuscript was used in which there was hardly a page
that did not present something of value. In the *Physics* the commentaries of
Simplicius were consulted,[23] and in the seventh book of this work, in place of　245
the paraphrase of Themistius,[24] the words of Aristotle himself were restored
on the authority of Simplicius, so that we can be certain that in these two
works there will be nothing or as little as possible for the reader to desire. In
the books *On Animals* many passages have been corrected with the help of

* * * * *

17 The *editio princeps* of Aristotle was published by Aldo Manuzio at Venice in
　　1495–8.
18 Ie a powerful swimmer, an expert who would not drown in depths of abstruse
　　prose; *Adagia* I vi 29
19 Ep 234:12n
20 See n16 above.
21 Johannes Argyropolous (Ep 456:117n)
22 In early April 1531, Bonifacius Amerbach reported that he had paid 12 crowns
　　for the Aldine Aristotle, but only 2 crowns for the Bebel edition; AK Ep 1518:25–7.
23 Simplicius was a sixth-century Neoplatonist known for his commentaries on
　　three works of Aristotle: *De caelo*, *Physics*, and *Categories*.
24 Themistius (c 317–88), Greek philosopher and rhetorician, wrote explanatory
　　paraphrases of many of Aristotle's works, including the *Physics*.

the translation of Theodorus.[25] The text of the *Metaphysics* contained a very   250
slight number of contaminations, except that it seems that the author himself
did not apply the finishing touches. The *Ethics to Nicomachus* were in good
condition and had no great need of the attention of a corrector. Would that
we could fill all the lacunae in the minor works, and fully restore what had
been corrupted. Even more to be desired would be the recovery of all the   255
works of this great man that have been lost.

At any rate everything published by Aldus is available in its entirety in
this edition in a much more correct version and at a cheaper price. I would
not hesitate to guarantee this at my own peril, and the attentive reader will
easily put my good faith to the proof if he will take the time to make com-   260
parisons. If anyone were to estimate how many vigils, how many exertions,
how many expenses were involved in preparing this useful volume for all
students, he would recognize that much applause and gratitude are owed to
Johann Bebel, who, although he could, following the example of others, have
sought immediate profit with frivolous and ephemeral little books, preferred   265
to risk a great part of his resources in publishing outstanding authors. That
famous Spartan paid no attention to riches hanging by ropes:[26] but I am not
sure whether profits that depend on paper are more certain. It is right that
all who study literature should support the industry of such men, and by
supporting them encourage them to dare similar initiatives. That will come   270
about if those who need such a great treasure snatch it up with an avidity
equal to the zeal of the one who offers it. And really, who does not have need
of it? For it is more for their own good than for Bebel's.

But to return to you, most excellent young man. I know you like to
promenade with this Peripatetic;[27] and you will promenade with even   275
greater pleasure when you discover that everything is more free of error.
Consequently, though I am late in exhorting you, I do not think it is necessary to incite you to continue, seeing that you are goaded and stimulated on
every side by so many examples in your own household that even the most

* * * * *

25 Ie Theodorus Gaza (n19 above)
26 *Apophthegmata* 2. Anonymous Spartans 45; CWE 37 167 (2.45). 'Hanging by
    ropes' is a Spartan variant of 'hanging by a thread,' recorded by Plutarch in the
    Moralia 234E–F; see *Adagia* I ix 72.
27 Erasmus puns on the Greek verb *peripatein*, meaning to 'to promenade' or 'take
    a walk' (as in the Lyceum, where Aristotle strolled with his pupils while teach-
    ing them), and 'Peripatetic,' the name customarily applied to Aristotle and the
    school of philosophy that he founded.

indolent and lethargic temperament would be instigated to the study of   280
wisdom. Our Aristotle is reported to have said that it was shameful for him
to be silent and let Xenocrates speak;[28] it would be far more shameful for
you not to study philosophy when you see your excellent sisters, Margaret,
Alice,[29] and Cecilia, occupying themselves with such diligence and success
with writers of both languages. Besides, the most acute stimulus of all for   285
every virtue must be the man who is the paragon of perfection, your father,
Thomas More, who begot you more by education than by nature and in
whom you see as in a mirror that what Aristotle used to say is absolutely
true, 'The best provision for the journey in old age is education.'[30] In fact,
it is in great part owed to literature that he is not only equal but superior   290
to that office, than which there is none more august after the royal majesty
or none more difficult to administer competently.[31] Yet, unless I totally fail
to recognize his character, he would have gladly renounced this post if he
thought it was permissible not to do the will of an excellent prince or to
refuse obedience to the country calling on him with unanimous votes and   295
universal sentiment. He also owes it to philosophy that such a high dignity
did not add to him the slightest bit of pride, nor did the waves of public
engagements clamouring around him on all sides diminish in any way his
inveterate affability.

I see that my letter is getting too long, but I shall let you go after I   300
have mentioned one more Aristotelian apophthegm. To a certain citizen
who boasted that he was a citizen of a large and famous city he said: 'Do
not consider that, but judge whether you are worthy of an illustrious city.'[32]
Likewise, my dear John, you also deserve to glory that you were born of such
a father if, as you are doing, you continue striving to show yourself worthy   305
of such a father.

Given at Freiburg im Breisgau, 27 February in the year of our Lord 1531

* * * * *

28 *Apophthegmata* 7. Aristotle 1; CWE 38 820 (7.219). Xenocrates of Chalcedon was
   a Platonist and head of the Academy from 339–314 BC. Aristotle found much to
   criticize in his teachings.
29 More's second daughter was named Elizabeth. Erasmus made the same mistake in Ep 999:188.
30 *Apophthegmata* 7. Aristotle 27; CWE 38 826 (7.245)
31 On 25 October 1529 Thomas More had succeeded Cardinal Wolsey as lord
   chancellor.
32 *Apophthegmata* 7. Aristotle 18; CWE 38 825 (7.236)

2433 / From Simon Grynaeus   [Basel, c February 1531]

This letter and Erasmus' reply to it (Ep 2434) were first published in *Grynaei epistolae* 121–2, 123–5. The approximate date of both letters is established by the references to Epp 2412 and 2422, and confirmed by the indication in lines 30–2 that the title page of the Bebel Aristotle was already printing. The colophon of the Aristotle is dated 13 May 1531, and the preface (Ep 2432) is dated 27 February 1531.

In June 1529 Simon Grynaeus (Ep 1657), who had been teaching Greek, Latin, and mathematics at Heidelberg, moved to Basel to occupy a chair in Greek. While his theological views, which made him an ally of Oecolampadius and the Strasbourg reformers, recommended him to the city fathers, his established reputation as a humanist scholar and editor of classical texts made him more than welcome to the circle around Erasmus and the Froben press. Although Erasmus disliked Grynaeus' religious views, and in November 1529 was horrified at the thought that Grynaeus might become the tutor of his godson Erasmius Froben (Ep 2231:34–7), he had great respect for the younger man's scholarship and was wont to exploit it freely and praise it generously; cf Epp 2359:61–2, 2379:71–4, 2432:238–42. When in the spring of 1531 Grynaeus and the publisher Bebel undertook a journey to England, Erasmus supplied Grynaeus with letters of introduction to Baron Mountjoy and Petrus Vulcanius (Epp 2459–60).

SIMON GRYNAEUS TO ERASMUS OF ROTTERDAM, GREETING
I rejoice that I am given many tasks by you, I rejoice in your admonitions, I rejoice in your criticism, I rejoice that I am yours, most excellent Erasmus, as long as you will be willing to put up with my modest talents and inexperience. First of all, I had intended on my own to confer with you concerning   5
Claudius, and for this purpose Hieronymus and I met on the day before yesterday, so that we would not inadvertently make any arrangements that did not meet with your approval.[1] I shall give you my view of the matter. If I am not mistaken, the boy will not be suitable because, confident in his abilities, he has formed an exaggerated opinion of himself. That is why he is hesitant.   10
He is aware that it would be impressive for him to have been in your service in any capacity, but at the same time he is worried that he may be too constrained or, if he enters your service, may perhaps not be able to retain your good will. In short, he already regards himself as sufficiently godlike, and only this is on his mind since you showed him this singular favour. And so,   15

* * * * *

2433
1 See Ep 2412 n17.

Simon Grynaeus
From Theodore de Bèze *Icones, id est,*
Verae imagines virorum doctrina simul et pietate illustrium ... (Geneva 1580)
Thomas Fisher Rare Book Library, University of Toronto

elated by this favourable breeze, he is eager to accelerate his studies as soon
as he can and as best he can. I am in doubt myself in what direction I should
push the young man. For I do not have a sufficiently clear idea about the kind
of employment you envision for him and still less about his talent. Moreover,
I do not think we should in any way permit that anyone be designated by   20
you for a confidential function who is not motivated by many lofty incentives. I sent him to you with the intention that he might eventually assume
the role of secretary. As far as I know at present, he would gladly spend the
winter with us. Therefore let us know what you wish us to do. If you wish
that he be sent back, it can be done in this way: I shall tell him that he will be   25
looked after at your expense, so that he can wait until you summon him, for
the boy seems to shy away from that. If you wish him to stay, I will be able
to keep him here without the condition that you proposed until you make a
decision or until we get to know the boy's character better.

Concerning our limping iambs,[2] know that I make no pretences but   30
have appropriated and exploited every poetic license to satisfy the haste of
the printers. There is an example of τοῦ πολὺ καλλίων [much more beautiful]
in Isaeus,[3] or πολὺ μᾶλλον ἑτοιμότερον. Budé translated it 'much more accessible.' I am less familiar with χρυσῶν ῥέεθρα [rivers of gold things];[4] I would
say χρυσοῦ ῥέεθρα ἢ χρύσεια ῥέεθρα [rivers of gold or golden rivers]. Regarding   35
your criticisms of the Chryosostom,[5] I owe it partly to my nature and partly

* * * * *

2 Grynaeus is referring to the Greek verses printed on the title-page of Bebel's
  1531 Aristotle. The word he uses to refer to them is 'scazon' (from the Greek *ska-
  zein* 'to limp'), which literally means a certain type of iambic trimeter in which
  a trochee is substituted for the last iamb, thus creating a 'limping' effect. In this
  case, however, Grynaeus is apologizing for the 'lameness' of the verses and
  not referring to the metrical designation. The poem is a conversation betwen a
  literary scholar and a bookseller. The speakers of the lines are indicated in the
  poem, which is in ordinary iambic trimeter, not of the best quality.
3 A Greek orator (c 420–340 BC), who ran a school of rhetoric at Athens and wrote
  many judicial speeches for others (only eleven of which survive). Demosthenes
  is said to have been his pupil and to have profited from his help in the preparation of public speeches.
4 This was the reading as adopted in the verses as printed.
5 The reference is presumably to the Homilies on Romans, which Erasmus had
  entrusted to Grynaeus for the Froben Chrysostom. See Ep 2422:13–16, where
  Erasmus tells Brie that he does not know whether Grynaeus has begun his translation or progressed very far with it. From this passage, however (lines 35–7),
  one infers that Erasmus had already criticized examples of a translation that
  Grynaeus had shown to him.

to my haste. As regards the periodic style, I fall into that by nature; and concerning my seizing eagerly upon the first words that come to me, that is owed to my haste. I will amend both to the best of my ability. In the meantime I send you a decade or a decade and a half of proverbs. I do not know   40
whether they are to be found among yours.

2434 / To Simon Grynaeus   [Freiburg, c February 1531]

For the source, the date, and the addressee of this letter, see Ep 2433, to which
this is Erasmus' reply.

ERASMUS OF ROTTERDAM TO SIMON GRYNAEUS, GREETING
To answer your letter in a few words and out of proper order, I wish you
to know that I return your feelings of joy that you are my friend. This law
is inscribed on the tablets of the Graces: I have not reached such a degree
of impudence that I would dare to criticize Grynaeus; I could hardly allow   5
myself to give you a word of advice. Far be it from me to burden with many
tasks a friend occupied in very holy labours.[1]
      Concerning Claudius, I had written, if I am not mistaken, that if he
could be of use to you in some way, such as explaining authors to your students, or proofreading, he could remain there for three months. I had written   10
something similar to Hieronymus Froben.[2] If not, you could give him two
florins from me and let him go wherever he wishes. I do not see why there
is any need of subterfuges to send him away. He told me honestly that he
was looking for free time to pursue his studies. Since he asked my advice on
this subject, I convinced him that he should have a purse full of gold pieces,   15
procure for himself an adequate library, and betake himself to Louvain or
Nürnberg or any other place where sufficiently learned men are teaching
and give himself entirely to the Muses with all his heart. He smiled. I would
wish him a rich Maecenas, who would provide him with leisure at his expense. As for his service, I persuaded him to ask for nothing but money for   20
the journey. I was motivated solely by Christian charity. Here the pestilence
was raging, and I saw before me a young man in a foreign country, ignorant
of the language, known to no one, destitute, without a farthing, and it was
winter. What could I do? He seems to have been treated kindly by those with

* * * * *

2434
1 A possible reference to the expectation that he would translate Chrysostom's
   Homilies on Romans; cf Ep 2422:8–14.
2 Ep 2412:44–54

whom he lived, and if he really wanted to enter my service, I would take   25
counsel to see if he was acceptable. He knew only one language, he came
here from Paris, in poor physical condition, without a word of recommendation from anyone. Now that he seems little inclined to be employed, we need
not deliberate about him. The only possibility is that he either leave, if he is a
burden to you, or remain, if he is not an inconvenience for you. But if you are   30
moved by evangelical charity to nourish someone who is without resources
until some better fortune shines forth from somewhere, I laud your piety, but
I would not countenance that you include his name in your journal. I sensed
his self-love also, but it was when I was dismissing him. That is the report
on Claudius. If you dismiss him, I think it should be done in a friendly way.   35

I was convinced, although I do not know from what source I learned
it, that in Greek you say ὄρη χρυσῶν [mountains of gold], but I was not able
to find an example of it. Χρυσῶν ῥέεθρα / rerum aurearum flumen [river of gold
things] could be justified, but I prefer χρυσοῦ ῥέεθρα [river of gold], which,
since it is certain, does not deed a reference.   40

Aretino translated two books of the *Economics*, of which one does not
have the style of Aristotle. Only the first one bears the stamp of the Greek
author; the second one contains a far different subject matter.[3] Budé translated *On the Universe;*[4] it is not by Aristotle, nor is the *Rhetoric to Alexander*. I
thought it good to bring these things to your notice, in case you wish to point   45
them out to the reader in your preface.[5] You must pardon me for not having
had the time to read this over, since I am overwhelmed with a great number
of labours.

Farewell, distinguished sir, and my dear friend.

Yours, Erasmus of Rotterdam   50

2435 / To Charles Blount   Freiburg, 1 March 1531

This is the preface to *T. Livii … Historiae* (Basel: Froben 1531), the edition of
Livy in which the first use was made of the manuscript of the first five books

* * * * *

3 'Aretino' is Leonardo Bruni; see Ep 2432:205–7. Both books of the *Economics* are
   now considered spurious.
4 See Ep 2422:50.
5 The only preface to the Bebel Aristotle is that by Erasmus, Ep 2432. But in
   March 1533 Grynaeus would publish an edition of *De mundo Aristotelis* with
   his own preface and commentary (Basel: Johann Walder). Since he says in the
   preface that he had lectured on *De mundo*, it is possible that in 1531 Erasmus
   already knew of his intention to publish the work.

of the fifth decade that Simon Grynaeus had discovered in 1527 at the abbey
of Lorsch. Grynaeus sent the manuscript to Froben, with the stipulation that
it be published with a dedicatory letter from him to Philippus Melanchthon.
Froben, however, chose to publish this letter from Erasmus to Charles Blount,
fifth Baron Mountjoy (Ep 2367). The same letter was used in a new edition of
1535, with notes by Beatus Rhenanus and Sigismundus Gelenius (reprinted by
Johann Herwagen in 1539, 1545, and 1549). Grynaeus' rejected dedicatory letter
of 8 September 1527 to Melanchthon is still extant (MBW Ep 587).

DESIDERIUS ERASMUS OF ROTTERDAM TO
THE YOUNG NOBLEMAN CHARLES MOUNTJOY, GREETING
Even though I have not yet had the opportunity of seeing your face, my illustrious young man, I see in your letter to me[1] – remarkably limpid, learned,
subtle, friendly, sincere – the best part of you, your mind, depicted in such   5
a way that no Apelles could represent the likeness of your body any more
clearly.[2] I greatly admired with genuine pleasure and delight your rare and
varied gifts of nature, especially at this age. Certainly, I expected nothing but
outstanding qualities of the son of William Mountjoy, but indeed, I confess
that you have far surpassed the hope that I had conceived of your progress. I   10
shall preserve this letter so that I may not only take delight in thinking about
you from time to time but also, by considering it a formal document signed
and sealed by you, I may urge you to continue on the path you have chosen
until you have put the finishing touch on such a beautiful undertaking. You
write that because of the letter I prefixed to the *Adages*[3] you were brought   15
out onto the stage and were forced, willy-nilly, to play your part well and
satisfy the eyes and ears of the multitude. I do not regret having laid this
charge upon you, my dear Charles, but I willingly relieve you of the other
burden that you say weighs more heavily upon you, apprehensive as you
are about how you will make requital for the services I have rendered you.   20
I have no fears that you will disappoint the expectations of your parents; on
the contrary, these splendid beginnings, or should I say the first act of the
play, give us the hope that, just as you exceeded my expectations, so you will
also exceed the expectations of others. But if you distinguish yourself, I shall
consider that if I have rendered you some service, you have recompensed me   25

* * * * *

2435
1 Not extant
2 Apelles (flourished fourth century BC), reputedly the greatest painter of ancient
  Greece
3 Ep 2023

in full and even with interest. The true affection that I never ceased to bear
for your father and that I have now transferred to you as if it were him himself does not expect any other reward than to see you as it wishes you to be.

But lest I seem to be nothing more than one who exhorts and applauds
you as you enact the play, I have, to lend a helping hand, deemed it appropri-   30
ate to dedicate to your name Titus Livius, the prince of Latin history, already
published many times, to be sure, but never more magnificently or more perfectly, and as if this were not enough, augmented with five recently discovered books. Guided by some good genius, Simon Grynaeus, a man learned
in every branch of literature, devoid of arrogance, and gifted in promoting   35
the liberal arts, found them in the library of the monastery of Laurissus, or
as it is called in the vulgar tongue, Lorsch. This monastery, which is situated in the region of Worms or Berbethomagus, across the Rhine, was built by
Charlemagne more than seven hundred years ago and furnished with an immense quantity of books.[4] For this was once the chief concern of princes, and   40
it usually constitutes the most precious treasure of monks. The manuscript
was of astonishing antiquity, written in the old style in a continuous sequence
of letters so that it is very difficult for anyone but a learned, accomplished
man, trained for this work, to distinguish one word from another. Thus it was
no easy task to prepare a copy to be delivered to the printer. All care and vigi-   45
lance was exercised so that there would be no deviance from the manuscript
in copying the text. If the fragment that Mainz once gave us was received with
great rejoicing by scholars,[5] though it was in poor condition, with how much
more acclaim should this great addition to Livy's history be welcomed?

Would that Almighty God might bring it about that this author be re-   50
stored to us in his entirety. Rumours flying about in the mouths of certain
people offer some hope of this prospect: with one man in Denmark, another
in Poland, and yet another in Germany boasting that there are still some unpublished fragments.[6] Certainly, after fortune, beyond all hope, has placed

* * * * *

4 It was founded in 764 by the Frankish count Cancor and his widowed mother.
  Favoured by popes and emperors, it became immensely wealthy and by the
  middle of the ninth century had achieved the status of *Reichsabtei* (imperial abbey), ie a sovereign political territory subject only to the emperor.
5 Now lost, the manuscript contained book 33.17–49, and book 40.37–59. It was
  used for the 1518 Livy published at Mainz by J. Schöffer; see Ep 919, which is
  Erasmus' preface to that edition.
6 Ever since the time of Petrarch, humanists had from time to time become ex-
  cited by rumours that there was a complete Livy in some North German or
  Danish monastery. In 1517 Pope Leo x, following the example of his predecessor

these remnants at our disposal, I do not see why we should despair that more   55
will appear. And in the present circumstances, princes would in my opinion
accomplish something worthy of themselves if with the promise of compensation they would encourage men of learning to track down so great a treasure,
or even urge them to publication – if perhaps there are some people who, to
the grave loss of learning, suppress or hide something intended for public   60
use. It seems exceedingly absurd that men dig into the bowels of the earth almost to hell itself, at great expense and great danger, in order to find a little bit
of gold or silver, while they entirely neglect treasures of this kind, more valuable to them as the soul is more important than the body, and do not think
them worthy of being explored. This is the mind of a Midas, not a prince, from   65
which I know your nature is far removed, and therefore I have no doubt that
you will avidly pursue this kind of gain. Lest anyone should doubt that this
half-decade is truly a part of Livy's history, two factors, in particular, provide
proof: first, the style itself, recalling the author in all its characteristics; second,
the arguments or epitomes of Lucius Florus, which correspond in all details   70
to these books.[7] Therefore, since I knew that no reading is more appropriate
for great men than historians, among whom (I am speaking of Latin writers) Titus Livius easily holds first place, especially since we have nothing of
Sallust's *History* besides two fragments;[8] and when I consider how insatiable
a glutton, so to speak, of histories your father always was, whom I am certain   75
you resemble in this trait also, I thought I would not be acting incongruously
if these five books, properly dedicated to you, should see the light of publication. And yet I would not wish you to be too similar to your father in this,
for he is accustomed to be bent over his books every day from supper until
midnight, not without causing some annoyance to his wife and his attendants   80
and eliciting loud murmurs from his servants. Although he has been able to
do this up to now without detriment to his health, I do not think it wise that
you should run the same risk, for it might not turn out so favourably, When
your father, while still a young man, shared in the studies of the present king,

* * * * *

Nicholas v, had sent an agent to Germany and Scandinavia to find the fabled
treasure (Pastor 8 266–8). Grynaeus' discovery of the Lorsch manuscript appears to have given new life to such rumours. See *Konrad Peutingers Briefwechsel*
ed Erich König (Munich 1923) 408–9 n2.
7 The second-century Roman historian, Lucius Annaeus Florus, wrote an *Epitome
of All the Wars of Seven Hundred Years* that was drawn largely from Livy.
8 Of the various fragments that remain of this work, the speeches of Marcus
Emilius Lepidus and Lucius Marcius Philippus were the best known and are
probably the ones referred to here.

they had a passionate interest in history, with the unqualified approbation of   85
his father, Henry VII, a king of singular judgment and prudence.

The chronology of Henricus Glareanus,[9] a man of exquisite and multi-
farious learning, has been added to this edition. His indefatigable industry
embellishes, enriches, and adorns not only our celebrated college in Freiburg
but also the entire region with humane learning. This chronology illustrates   90
the sequence of times, the characteristics of wars, and the names of persons,
in which previously there was great confusion, owing to the fault of scribes
and half-learned amateurs. Yet that was the only light of history. If this polar
star were lacking, the navigation on the sea of history would be completely blind; and if this thread were not present, the reader, even the learned   95
one, would be enveloped in inextricable error in the labyrinths of historical
events. If you think your letter has been well compensated by this gift, it will
be your turn to impart a letter to me. Farewell.

At Freiburg im Breisgau, 1 March 1531

2436 / From Johann von Botzheim   Überlingen, 1 March 1531

> First published as Ep 146 in Förstemann / Günther, the autograph of this let-
> ter was in the Burscher Collection of the University Library at Leipzig (Ep 1254
> introduction).
>   For Botzheim (1480–1535), canon of the cathedral chapter of Constance,
> which in 1527 had moved to Überlingen, see Ep 1285.

Greetings. I was away from Überlingen for four months, and I do not think I
will return to it before April with the intention of staying. I am, however, in
the habit of going there sometimes when circumstances demand it. The har-
rowing pestilence was the cause of my flight; although it has remitted in its
fury, some fear that spring will bring back a recrudescence of this evil. I shall   5
let you know this coming month. You sent me two little books, which, as you
write,[1] had been sent to you from Augsburg. I was convulsed with laughter
reading them, but they could not be made public here. There are one or two,
however, who I knew would laugh at them. I secretly gave them the books to
read, which prompted their gratitude. That both parties suspect that you are   10

* * * * *

9 Epp 440, 2098 n1

2436
1 The letter is not extant.

an adversary is nothing new. Moreover, I frequently hear those who profess to be on the side of the pope and the church (that is, of the emperor) casting slurs on Erasmus at the instigation of theologians who have stirred up, in leading noblemen for the most part, feelings of aversion towards you, since you are in the habit, they say, of attacking here and there with a very free pen both monks   15 and also the ordinary way of life of the clergy, whereas you should rather have defended all that pertains to us, no matter how abominable (if you please!). I would have written to you several times if ever a messenger had been available. I did not think you would remain in Freiburg in such great danger from the plague.[2] There is, I think, no news here worthy of your attention that you   20 have not already heard. In vain we await the aid of the emperor, who is going to leave Germany, if what certain people say is true.[3] I am anxious to know how you are, what you are doing, and what you are publishing, and I urge you to remember that Botzheim remains faithfully devoted to you. Farewell.

From Überlingen, 1 March 1531   25

Yours sincerely, Johann von Botzheim

To the incomparable champion of true theology and good letters, Master Erasmus of Rotterdam, his protector and teacher, worthy of veneration in every regard. At Freiburg

2437 / From [Johann Koler]   [Augsburg, 2 March 1531]

The manuscript of this letter, four pages in Koler's hand with the final page or pages missing, was in the Burscher Collection of the University Library at Leipzig (Ep 1254 introduction). It was first published as Ep 147 in Förstemann / Günther. The date is established by the references in Ep 2438:1–4. For Koler, see Ep 2384.

Cordial greetings. The letter carrier brought me your delightful and friendly letter,[1] which gave me more pleasure because it seemed more familiar than

* * * * *

2 See Ep 2426 n3.
3 At the end of the Diet of Augsburg in November 1530, Charles had departed for the Netherlands, which Botzheim doubtless considered part of (Lower) Germany (cf Ep 1998 n6). At the beginning of 1532 Charles made his way from Brussels to Regensburg to attend the imperial diet (April–July) and then went to Vienna to supervise the defence of the city against a Turkish attack that did not materialize. In November 1532 he departed for Spain and would not return to the Empire until 1541.

2437
1 Not extant

earlier ones and seemed to emanate from a heart brimming with friendship,
a letter in which you wished freely to confide your cares. I am happy and
rejoice that you consider me someone to whom you can pour out freely all   5
the emotions of your soul and deal with me with the same frankness that
you see I have employed in my relations with you. Therefore, most venerable Erasmus, I pray you ardently that you continue to maintain this openness of mind towards me and this same opinion and judgment of me. I in
turn promise you that I shall always maintain the loyalty you have observed   10
from experience until now, that of a sure and faithful friend, free of artifice,
on whom you may rely in all things and can be assured of whatever can be
asked and expected of a good man.

As far as Polyphemus is concerned, I explained in my last letter why
I allowed him to set out in your direction with the wine.[2] But we must ren-   15
der thanks to the gods that he has already left your house. He said he was
heading for the king's court;[3] I am happy that he left. I was very much afraid
that his behaviour might stamp some mark of disgrace on your reputation.
He certainly took considerable advantage of your name among many of the
people who may show too much favour to your rivals. In any case, he was no   20
burden to me, but for your sake I am happy that he left. He left the enclosed
letter with me,[4] and entrusted me with the task of saving any letters that
might arrive for him from you until he returns. I shall be sure to do this and
shall save the last one you sent.[5]

I am returning to you the pages, delivered to me by Polyphemus, that   25
you wrote against that Thraso.[6] I think they should be suppressed and not published, unless that braggart were to make some other new threats against you.
Then I would think you would have to counter him with this kind of answer.

Anton Fugger is extremely sorry about the loss of the last shipment of
wine,[7] but he is more sorry that all the care and diligence spent on transport-   30
ing it by his own coachman were absolutely worthless. He therefore wished

* * * * *

2 The letter is not extant. For Polyphemus (Felix Rex) see Ep 2386 n3. Concerning
   the wine, cf lines 31–3 below.
3 Ie for the court of King Ferdinand
4 Not extant
5 Not extant
6 Along with Ep 2438:2–3, this passage indicates that Erasmus had circulated his
   Admonitio against Eppendorf (Thraso) in manuscript before having it printed.
   The printed version is first mentioned in a letter to Bonifacius Amerbach of 26
   October 1530; see Ep 2400 introduction and line 37.
7 See Epp 2384:67–71, 2415:20–2.

to send you another consignment in place of the wine that was spilled, in the hope that this time things would go better and you would receive the wine, which we trust has reached you together with this letter.[8] It rests with you to inform us whether it was delivered to you in good order. I have made it clear 35 that the coachman has been paid here for the transportation, so that you will have no expenses to pay.

Concerning that friend of ours who is staying with you,[9] you write that he has wind of something and thinks that I may have communicated your letter to certain persons who may not have kept quiet and that what you 40 wrote to me about him was reported to him. For my part certainly I would like you to be fully persuaded that I communicated your letter to no mortal except Anton Fugger. I did that solely because I wished Anton to know with more certainty his character and morals, although they were already well known. It is rather I who divine what he suspects, for when he had learned 45 that Matthias Kretz intended to withdraw from his post as preacher here,[10] he appealed to me by letter to intercede for him with the canons so that this office would be handed over to him, saying that he was anxious to return here. But I, who had long been familiar with the man's behaviour, did not conceal what kind of reception he would have here and for that reason ad- 50 vised him against continuing to seek this position, openly indicating to him that I would not intercede for him. It is clear how badly he took this because he never wrote another letter to me, even regarding those matters in which my help would have been of great importance. I am not unaware (such is his goodness and equanimity) that he is bursting with envy because he un- 55 derstands that you have such great ties of friendship with the most reverend bishop and with our friend Anton, and that you have been invited to come here by them with such great eagerness.[11] He must know that they have sent you gifts from time to time, which, as anyone who has any acquaintance with the man will know, will make him smart with resentment and irritation. And 60 since he has no one else within easy reach, he pours out all his indignation on you, thinking that you are the cause for his being less courted. Whereas he, on the other hand, never spoke well either of you or of Anton himself, or of me (even when he was living here), and he frequently accused me, while

* * * * *

8 Cf Ep 2438:25–32.
9 Ottmar Nachtgall, who occupied the ground floor of the house in which Erasmus lived at Freiburg; see Ep 2430 n13.
10 See Ep 2430:19–24.
11 See Ep 2384:48–53 with nn12–13, and cf Ep 2430:9–10.

imbibing with his drinking companions, of belonging to the Lutheran fac- 65
tion, and tore me apart with his teeth, although he was often a guest at my
table, and numerous important honours were heaped upon him from day to
day. And although I was warned by my friends, I did not cease loading him
with benefits, stupidly persuading myself that through the numerous services performed for him I would overcome the malice and perversity of the 70
man. I learned more than enough from my experience how much my efforts
were in vain.

I relayed your fond greetings to Kretz.[12] I gave ample proof in my last
letter testifying to what kind of man he is: a good, simple man, not without
learning, a good friend of Eck and Faber also.[13] He will reconcile Eck to you 75
whenever you wish. He is a man totally dedicated to literature and scholastic
theology, and a good friend of mine too.

We wish, if at all possible, that you would come here, and we have no
doubt that once you come here you will not regret having moved. There is
absolutely no reason for you to fear either Eck or even the more influential 80
duke of Bavaria.[14] If they had any power in this city, they would have driv-
en many people out and would not have allowed them to live here. If you
are here you will without doubt enjoy the same privileges and protection as
Anton himself and all of us. Nevertheless, I dare not importune you any further with my invitation since I know how difficult the journey seems to you. 85
If any trouble should arise here (may the gods avert it), I would not want all
the blame to fall upon me, for I desire and wish nothing more than to consult
your best interests and provide for your comfort and safety to the best of my
ability. I would rather suffer the worst evils than that the slightest adversity
befall you. Therefore, my dear Erasmus, you will do whatever seems most 90
advantageous to you. As far as we are concerned, in our desire to have you
with us we are driven by no greater consideration than that it seems perfectly
clear to us that you will be better off and safer with us than anywhere else.
If you think otherwise, you will nevertheless think well of our affection for
you. Our friend Anton asked me to send his best greetings. He too is at your 95
complete disposal and devoted to you ...

* * * * *

12 See Ep 2430:3.
13 For Eck see Ep 2387; for Faber Ep 2430 n15.
14 Duke William IV (r 1508–50), staunch defender of the Catholic church against
    the spread of the Reformation. He was the most powerful prince in the region,
    but he had no jurisdiction in the free imperial city of Augsburg.

2438 / From Johann Koler   Augsburg, 3 March 1531

> First published as Ep 148 in Förstemann / Günther, the autograph of this letter
> was in the Burscher Collection of the University Library at Leipzig (Ep 1254
> introduction).

Cordial greetings. Yesterday I gave my letter to you to the chaplain,[1] to whom
you had entrusted your letter to me.[2] I included with it those pages that you
had written against your Thraso,[3] together with a letter of Polyphemus that
he had left with me when he departed.[4] I hope that by now you have all
received all of them in good order. The chaplain seemed to me (unless his   5
language and his countenance deceive me) to be a good man, and I have no
fears that he delivered the letter to you faithfully.

However that may be, from the letter that the courier brought me from
you I understood that Eppendorf had already responded to your little book.[5]
I am profoundly sorry that you have to deal with these shameless scoun-   10
drels, whom I would not consider worthy of a single word from you, not to
say a response, if I did not think that it is very important for your honour
and reputation that a response be made (lest they abuse your patience in the
future). If, therefore, you are going to respond to the sycophant,[6] I ask you
to paint him in his true colours, so that he be adorned with his virtues, and   15
deal with him in such a way that those like him will understand what it is
to challenge Erasmus; otherwise you will never be free of charlatans of this
sort. I, for my part, would have recommended that your pages be withheld
from circulation, if he were not looking for trouble again with his response.
But from now on I propose that you treat this villain as he deserves, so that 20
malignant spirits of this sort will not bother you in the future. I ask you also
that as soon as Thraso's responses reach you, you give us the opportunity to
become thoroughly acquainted with the malevolence and malicious talk of
this man.

* * * * *

2438
1 Unidentified
2 Not extant; cf Ep 2437:1–2.
3 See Ep 2437 n6.
4 See Ep 2437:21–2, 25–7.
5 Eppendorf's *Iusta querela*, his response to Erasmus' *Admonitio adversus mendacium*, was published in February 1531 (cf Ep 2429 n5).
6 Erasmus did not respond. Thanks to the intervention of Julius Pflug, counsellor at the court of Duke George of Saxony, the long-standing feud between
  Erasmus and Eppendorf was laid to rest; see Epp 2450–1.

Last of all, we are astonished that you have not written to us about the 25
wine that some time ago, thanks to some coachmen of Freiburg who had
brought here some wines from your region, we sent you for a second time,[7]
and together with them some bottles that Johann Baumgartner,[8] a citizen of
Augsburg, had sent to Zasius. It is strange if they have not reached you in
the meantime, since we sent them a fortnight before you sent your first letter 30
to us.[9] I ask that you let us know whether it was delivered or not. If you have
not received them, it would be worthwhile to inquire from Zasius. Our letter
will be in no less danger. Do relieve us of this worry and let us know whether
you received the last shipment of wine.

Anton Fugger asks me to send his warm greetings; he misses you very 35
much. You will see what it is expedient for you to do. Farewell, Erasmus,
worthy of homage and respect in every way.

Given at Augsburg, 3 March in the year of our salvation 1531

Yours, Johann Koler

In my haste to dispatch the courier I failed to look at the other side of 40
the page. Please pardon my haste.

To the most eminent and learned doctor of sacred theology, Erasmus of
Rotterdam, worthy of singular respect. At Freiburg.

2439 / From Nikolaus Winmann Speyer, 3 March 1531

The autograph of this letter, first published as Ep 149 in Förstemann / Günther,
was in the Burscher Collection of the University Library at Leipzig (Ep 1254
introduction). Erasmus' reply is Ep 2486.

Nikolaus Winmann (documented 1520–50) was a native of Fribourg (the capital of canton Fribourg), which lies astride the boundary between German- and
French-speaking Switzerland. In 1523, after having attended schools in Zürich
and Wrocław, Winmann matriculated at the University of Vienna, where Caspar
Ursinus Velius (Ep 2383 n3), who arrived in 1525, became his teacher. In 1528
he matriculated at Tübingen to study Hebrew. In the spring of 1533 he moved
to Ingolstadt, where he taught Greek from 1534, and both Greek and Hebrew
from 1536 until 1538. In later years he is documented as head of the college of

* * * * *

7 Cf Ep 2437:29–37.
8 Ie Johann (ii) Paumgartner, merchant of Augsburg and brother-in-law of Anton
  Fugger. Paumgartner was to become a significant figure in Erasmus' correspondence starting in 1532; see Allen Ep 2603 introduction.
9 Not extant

St Nicholas at Vienna (1539–41), master of a school at Nysa in Silesia, and rector of a Protestant school at Elbłag, east of Gdansk (1548). The last record of him is the preface (dated 23 April 1550 at Speyer) to his account of a sea journey from Gdansk to Amsterdam in 1549: *Navigationis maris arctoi ... descriptio* (Basel: M. Isengrin [1550]). In *Syncretismus* (Cologne: J. Gymnich 1541), an earlier work devoted to the issues of religious concord and resistance to the Turks, he had taken the opportunity to express his great admiration for Erasmus.

I am not unaware, Erasmus, supreme ornament of this age, how importune and how brazen, or to put it more exactly, what an intruder I would be if, unknown and insignificant as I am, I should write to you, who are never not fully occupied, and now the victim of a twofold malady: old age, from which may the Fates permit Erasmus to return to us rejuvenated, and the stone,[1] a tyrant to which I would wish to be subjected in your place. Indeed I would not refuse this torment – the Lord knows that I speak in all sincerity – if only you would be safe and sound (but alas! nothing is attained by wishes). I am possessed by such great devotion and love for you, which are the only things I can boast of to you and the only things that can recommend me in your eyes. For the remaining things in this humble creature are of the sort that are not worth mentioning. If I have any learning (which is either non-existent or very meagre), I owe it entirely to you. I shall always be grateful to you for that, both now and forever, although I cannot repay you for it except by praying constantly to the Lord Jesus for your health and safety. A proof that you are most dear to him is that he has lavished so many great gifts upon you, which you do not keep hidden from your brothers but which, though half-dead, you never cease to pour out unstintingly for the good of the world, so that I have always on my lips these words, 'Our Erasmus will cease to live before he ceases to benefit others.' And as you do this, you are mindful of the Lord's words, which you will hear one day, 'Well done, good servant.'[2] It is because of this that, for many years now, having come to know you more and more through your writings, nothing offends me more than if I find someone who shows little gratitude to Erasmus or bellows out words of opprobrium and detraction against his reputation. This always leads me to open my mouth, although you have no need of anyone to come to your defence. How many little scenes I could relate to you, in which I played such

* * * * *

2439
1 On the history of Erasmus' affliction with calculus ('the stone') see Epp 1989 n4, 2263:11–12, 2271:3–4, 2277:12–13, 2278:10–12, 2290:54–5.
2 Matt 25:21, 23

a role that, if you knew about them, you would certainly acknowledge that Nikolaus cedes to no mortal man in his love for you. The aim of all this is that you will not be vexed, as I said, that I, a stranger to you, should weary 30 you with this nonsense. I shall add that, a few years ago, when I left Vienna to revisit Fribourg in Uechtland,[3] which is my native city, I had turned off towards Basel in order to see you, but I was deluded in my hopes and was forced to tear myself away from there. But then I returned there two days later, and when I stopped at a public inn, I finally saw you on a Sunday in 35 a convent, where you were attending a religious ceremony.[4] As you were returning home from there, since many people were accompanying you (among whom were Beatus Rhenanus and your good friend Froben), I did not dare address you. I followed you, therefore, but when you arrived at your home, a young man appeared and opened the door. After you entered, 40 I sat down on the milestone, and seated there, facing the house, I at least de- lighted my eyes together with my heart in contemplating your house, since there was no other opportunity afforded to me. And then suddenly it oc- curred to me how stupid I had been not to have procured a letter from your friend Ursinus in Vienna and in that way seizing the opportunity of speaking 45 to you. But however it turned out, I can say in all sincerity that I achieved a notable success in having seen the great Erasmus.

I have borne witness up to now of my feelings towards you, but I shall finish shortly, for you do not have the time to read these trifles. It is amazing how your letter to Vulturius as well as the one in which you answer the preach- 50 ers in Strasbourg has won some over to you, but alienated others.[5] You seem to some to be more well disposed towards the state of the church than you were previously, when in reality you are always the same and always lean

* * * * *

3 In Latin, German, and French, Winmann's native city and Erasmus' place of residence have the same name: Friburgum, Freiburg, Fribourg. So, as is some- times still done today, he adds the traditional name of the region of Switzerland in which Fribourg/Freiburg is located, Uechtland (or Üechtland), in order to distinguish his Freiburg from Freiburg im Breisgau.
4 As Allen observes, the date of this visit to Basel is uncertain. It cannot have been later than 1526, the year in which Beatus Rhenanus (line 38) left the city, nor earlier than 1524, when Erasmus' friend Ursinus Velius (line 45) settled in Vienna as professor of rhetoric. In his answer to this letter, Erasmus' mistak- enly connects Widmann's visit to Basel with a prank involving Konrad Brunner (Ep 313:26n), who died in 1519; see Allen Ep 2486.
5 The letter to Vulturius (Gerard Geldenhouwer) is the *Epistola contra pseudevan- gelicos* (Ep 2358 n6); the other work is the *Epistola ad fratres Inferioris Germaniae* (Ep 2371 n20).

in the same direction. I am ashamed to go on at greater length. As for you, greatest Erasmus, courageously despise the carping and insults of wicked 55 men, at peace with your conscience, sparing your old age, which God grant you may pass in peace and serenity. I beseech you, pardon my importunity. It would be unfair for me to ask you to write back. I say only this, that one letter sent by Erasmus would be more pleasing and precious than many treasures. Farewell, and be of good cheer.   60

In Speyer, in the house of the noble gentleman Otto von Falckenberg, custodian and canon of the cathedral church,[6] 3 March 1531

Nikolaus Winmann

To Erasmus of Rotterdam. At Freiburg

2440 / To Grunnius   Freiburg, 5 March 1531

This letter and Ep 2441 are printed at the end of the edition of the *Epistola contra pseudevangelicos* published at Freiburg by Johann Faber Emmeus in 1531. First published by Faber Emmeus in 1529, the *Epistola* had been reprinted several times by other printers in 1529–30, but the inclusion of the two letters in the 1531 volume indicates that it was the second edition to be authorized by Erasmus himself.

The letter responds to a letter or pamphlet written by someone to whom Erasmus assigns the pseudynym 'Grunnius,' presumably derived from *grunnio* 'to grunt like a pig.' Erasmus supplies no clue to Grunnius' real identity. All that is certain is that he was someone identified with the circle of reformers in Strasbourg. Martin Bucer appears to be ruled out: Erasmus had already responded to his *Epistola apologetica* in the *Epistola ad fratres Inferioris Germaniae*, and this letter does not add anything at all, much less anything new, to the discussion of any of the points that Bucer had raised. In Ep 2615, in which Erasmus, addressing Bucer by name, reviews at length his confrontation with the Evangelical brethren, there is no reference to Grunnius or the contents of this letter. Other candidates for identification with Grunnius include Wolfgang Capito and Caspar Hedio, but there is no supporting evidence; Grunnius remains unidentified.

* * * * *

6 Otto von Falckenberg (d 1532) had been canon of the cathedral at Speyer since 1517 when, in March 1530, he was appointed *custos*, in which capacity he was much preoccupied with the legal business of the chapter. Nothing more is known of his connection with Winmann.

ERASMUS OF ROTTERDAM TO HIS FRIEND GRUNNIUS, GREETING

What is it you say, most wise Grunnius? 'Erasmus has taken up his pen against all those who profess Christian piety; therefore, against all Christians.' And yet, I have not taken up my pen against you, but have given you friendly advice, for fear that through the reckless temerity of certain people what hap- 5 pened to peasants may happen to city dwellers.[1] There are many in your fraternity of such depraved minds that you must trick them if you wish to do them a good service. If I were as eager to take revenge as I see you are, you would see what I am capable of. But I shall never cease to act as I have acted up to now so that, if possible, it does not come to armed warfare, but that 10 with the compliance of both sides the church may be restored to tranquillity without any impairment of piety.

Are princes, convinced as they are that you are more than heretics, not to be exasperated when they hear, 'Do not kill the innocent. Do not stand in the way of the gospel?'[2] But, you say, Pharaoh, venting his fury upon the 15 people of God more and more, did not prevent Moses from saying what God had prescribed. Pardon me, dear Grunnius, to this day I have not believed that Vulturius talks to God.[3] But if he is to be compared to Moses, let him perform miracles and by his prayers drive away from us these calamities, wars, famine, and pestilence. Are you not ashamed of this man's grandilo- 20 quence? Do the brethren wish him to stand up to me face to face? Does that mean to play the buffoon in his comments?[4] He will successfully stand up to me if he recalls his confrères to a type of conduct that does not aspire to any of the things that I deplore in their behaviour. You say that nothing can be

* * * * *

2440

1 Cf *Epistola ad fratres Inferioris Germaniae* CWE 78 299: 'I mentioned the example of the peasants lest those who pursue their object by disorder should end up with a similar outcome.' The reference to the peasants' protest is found in *Epistola contra pseudevangelicos* CWE 78 228–9.

2 In 1529 Gerard Geldenhouwer had published three pamphlets in which he cited passages from Erasmus' works in support of the proposition that princes had no right to inflict capital punishment on heretics; see Ep 2219 n4. Angered at being thus associated with the views of a group that he detested, and dismayed at the danger of being discredited in the eyes of Catholic princes, Erasmus responded angrily and at length in the *Epistola contra pseudevangelicos*; see CWE 78 224–8.

3 Vulturius was Erasmus' name for Geldenhouwer; see Ep 2358 n6.

4 Geldenhouwer had published an unauthorized edition of Erasmus' *Epistola contra pseudevangelicos* 'with added comments [*scholia*], in other words, with the addition of scurrilous abuse'; see Ep 2321:26–7, and see also Epp 2219 n4, 2238, 2293.

undertaken without God's counsel. So did his comments appear thanks to   25
divine inspiration?

Do I so thirst for money because I am an old man of shattered health
who may not have enough to provide for the needs of his feeble body? In the
meantime neither age nor fragile health force me to lead a life of idleness, but
I work with my hands so that I will not be a burden to anyone and will have   30
enough to give something to someone who is in need, contrary to what many
of your fraternity do. But I shall cease responding to your inanities. I wish for
you a somewhat sounder mind, or at least one more worthy of the gospel.

At Freiburg, 5 March 1531

2441 / To Eleutherius   Freiburg, 6 March [1531]

Like Ep 2440, this letter was appended to the second authorized edition of the
Epistola contra pseudevangelicos (see Ep 2440 introduction). Again like Ep 2440,
which was addressed to 'Grunnius,' this letter is addressed to a correspondent identified by a pseudonym. From the letter we learn that Eleutherius,
like Grunnius, is a partisan of the Evangelical reformers in Strasbourg, who
agree with Luther 'except regarding the Eucharist'; that it was at Eleutherius'
instigation that Gerard Geldenhouwer published his unauthorized, scur-
rilously annotated edition of Erasmus' *Epistola contra pseudevangelicos*; and
that Eleutherius has since written to Erasmus, taking him to task for his criticisms of Geldenhouwer and Bucer. Erasmus says he calls his correspondent
'Eleutherius' (one who is free, liberator) in the same way that he had called
Gerard Geldenhouwer 'Vulturius.' One wonders if it might be relevant to this
choice of name that Ulrich von Hutten had used the pseudonym 'Eleutherius
Bizenus' and that 'Eleutherius' sounds a bit like 'Lutherus.'

In view of the above, one must regard as untenable Allen's identification
of Sebastian Franck as the addressee of the letter. It is true that Franck (1499–
1542) had been living in Strasbourg since 1530 and that (after his death) the
pseudonym 'Augustinus Eleutherius' was applied to him (as, for example in
Sebastian Castellio's *An sint persequendi haeretici*, 1554). On the other hand, by
the time he arrived in Strasbourg, Franck was already a radical Spiritualist who
had rejected all religious parties – Catholic, Lutheran, Zwinglian, Anabaptist,
or any other – and all efforts to organize churches that imposed conformity
on individual consciences. Indeed, the Strasbourg authorities would soon expel Franck from the city because of the unorthodox views in his writings (for
that expulsion and Erasmus' role in it, see Epp 2587, 2590, 2615, 2622). In brief,
Franck was not a supporter of the Strasbourg reform establishment and he
had no motive to side actively with Gerard Geldenhouwer in his dispute with
Erasmus. Unfortunately, while it is thus possible to affirm that Sebastian Frank

was not Eleutherius, it is not possible to say who was. Pending discovery of the identity of the person who, according to Erasmus, prompted Geldenhouwer to publish his annotated version of *Epistola contra pseudevangelicos*, Eleutherius, like Grunnius, remains unidentified.

The date of the letter (line 121) is either a typo or an example (in contrast to Ep 2440) of the Freiburg custom of beginning the new year at Easter.

ERASMUS OF ROTTTERDAM TO HIS FRIEND ELEUTHERIUS,
GREETING

What say you, charming Eleutherius? Has Vulturius laden me with so many kindnesses?[1] He loved me, I confess, reciprocating my affection for him; in services rendered I think I am even with him. But supposing that I am in- 5
ferior to him in merits, why do you remonstrate with me? He is being de-
rided undeservedly, you say, by the multitude. On what account? that he is an Evangelical? He has not allowed this to remain obscure to anyone in the numerous pamphlets he has published.[2] Proof of this is that in the comments with which, on your advice, he contaminated (I almost said befouled with 10
shit) my *Epistle*, he used his real name instead of Vulturius.[3] What is more, what you cite as an indictment is the duty of no ordinary friend. Is it not the duty of a friend to recall a person from error? 'But he is not in error,' you say. Would that it were so! But it is also dutiful to warn someone not to make a bad play out of a good one by bad acting. This kind of friendly admonition is 15
just what I gave him, it seems to me, in a courteous and even friendly man-
ner. You will say, 'He should have been warned secretly.' I did that, and not just once. But the pamphlets he sent around that contained no little hatred for my name are proof of how tranquilly he reacted to my admonitions.

But what 'evilangelist,'[4] I ask you, told you that I had first secretly sent 20
that letter to Vulturius to the physician Simon,[5] so that it could be printed

* * * * *

2441
1 Gerard Geldenhouwer; see Ep 2358 n6.
2 See Ep 2219 n4.
3 On the verso of the title-page of Geldenhouwer's unauthorized edition of Erasmus' *Epistola contra pseudevangelicos* (Ep 2440 n4) it is stated that the *scholia* are by Gerardus Noviomagus (Gerard of Nijmegen), the name by which Geldenhouwer was commonly known; see the illustration in CWE 16 238.
4 Erasmus writes *cacangelicus*, substituting for 'ev-' (the Greek prefix *ev-* 'good,' in *evangelicus*) 'cac-' (from *kakós*, the Greek adjective meaning 'bad'). 'Cac-' also calls to mind, however, the words *kak* in Dutch and *kacke* in German, both meaning 'shit,' as well as *cacare* 'to shit' in Latin. Cf Ep 2261 n30.
5 Simon Riquinus (Ep 2246 introduction)

in Cologne before it had been received by the person to whom it was written? Is that how those who profess truth indulge themselves in lies? On
the contrary, it was first sent, in manuscript, to Vulturius to warn him that
perhaps it would be printed.[6] Then it was printed in Freiburg, long before it   25
arrived in Cologne – where it was brought, without my knowledge, by my
servant. Truly I did not want it to be printed there again, and thereby have
my printer suffer loss. Therefore there was no need of your service in sending a copy to Vulturius and all his associates and inciting him to war by such
a horrible message.   30
    Concerning your doubts about Bucer, I shall have you know that I do
not know the man, not even by sight, far from there being any close friendship between us. I was under the impression that there was a little more civility and prudence in him than appears in that book, which seasons poison
with a lot of honey.[7] Did that action of Hutten in publishing the bull of Leo   35
seem so clever to you that you could invite Vulturius to imitate him?[8] While
you are at it, why don't you invite him to imitate all the stratagems Hutten
has employed by land and sea?[9] What was accomplished in those clownish
comments?[10] Does he have a better knowledge of the gospel from this? A
little worse, in my opinion. The magistrates in Strasbourg threw the printer   40
into jail, a clear indication of how much they approved Vulturius' work.[11]
But revenge is sweet – even if it was bought at the price of your cause? What
evangelical forbearance! Where did I say that you are all like little birds shut
up in a cage? Are there not many in hiding through fear? Is it not true that
most people do not go anywhere without the safe-conduct of princes? Who   45
was that imbecile who said that I do not dare leave Freiburg? I can return to
Basel if I wish and live in Strasbourg if it suits me. 'Why,' you say, 'does he

* * * * *

6 Ep 2238 appears to indicate that, having received the letter referred to here,
   Geldenhouwer wrote a letter to Erasmus that arrived after the *Epistola contra
   pseudevangelicos* was already in print.
7 The *Epistola apologetica*; see Ep 2312 n2.
8 In 1520 Ulrich von Hutten (Ep 365) published a heavily glossed version of the
   text of the bull *Exsurge Domine*, in which Pope Leo x had condemned as heretical forty-one articles drawn from Luther's writings and given him sixty days
   to recant: *Bulla decimi Leonis, contra errores M. Lutheri, & sequacium* [Strasbourg:
   Johann Schott].
9 Ie 'with great effort and eager desire'; *Adagia* I iv 25
10 See lines 9–11 with n3 above.
11 See Ep 2321:28–9.

not set out for Louvain? Why not Cologne? Why not Paris?' Why don't you add 'Why not Toledo, Rome, or Jerusalem?' I moved to Freiburg reluctantly,[12] so far is it from my mind travel to various cities. What am I going to do in   50 Paris or Cologne?

But suppose that it is not safe for me to travel anywhere: where does the danger come from except that I was more lenient towards you than they desired? Obviously it was right that this charge be made against me by fair-minded men. Do I maintain that the gospel has perished? By now my ears   55 have become inured to hearing 'Gospel, Gospel, Gospel.' But who among the angels revealed to you that I write against you for the purpose of reconciling myself with the sophists?[13] As if I did not know what and in what manner I must write if, disregarding my conscience, I had nothing else in mind but to return to their good graces.   60

I am not unaware that, as you say, the sophists are crying out that I am the instigator of this tragedy. But these same people previously shouted until they were hoarse that I was in league with Luther.[14] Since no one believed that any more, they found another subject for their shouting. But although you know that both of these accusations are false, you still rejoice   65 that troubles are created for Erasmus. What sanctimonious souls! Alberto Pio of Carpi, who while released from his own affairs occupies himself with the affairs of others,[15] tried in a published book to persuade people of what these men grunt. I responded to it, but he, hiring several assistants, renewed the fight. By now the huge work is being rushed into print in Bade's printing   70 shop. Being in poor health, he had turned away from writing, but he wrote it to please members of the Franciscan order. Unfortunately he died before it was finished.[16] That is surely, according to the proverb, to flee after planting the dart.[17] I hope nonetheless that his soul is frolicking among the seraphic spirits. For his body was adorned with the Franciscan habit three days before   75 his death, and once dead he was transported in that same paraphernalia on the shoulders of Franciscans in a pious procession through the middle of the

* * * * *

12 See Ep 2090 introduction.
13 Ie the scholastic theologians, Erasmus' conservative detractors
14 See Ep 2414 n1.
15 Allusion to a well-known line in Horace *Satires* 2.3.19–20
16 See Ep 1634 introduction.
17 Ie to shoot and run; *Adagia* I i 5. Cf Ep 2443:345–6.

city to the monastery, and nothing was omitted from the ceremonies that are usually devoted to the genuine children of Francis.[18]

What is this I hear? In that letter to Vulturius I show favour to Luther   80
because I hope that he will lose his cause? What kind of reasoning is this? Do we show favour to those we hope will fail? But since you hold common cause with him, except regarding the Eucharist, how does it come about that in writing against you, as you say, I show favour to him? You say, 'The preface to the works of Augustine offends the sophists to such an extent that they   85
will never be favourable to him.'[19] For my part I consider that I so moderated my style that no one could have reason to be offended. Or is it you who continue to exult if Erasmus does not placate the sophists? If there is anything in that preface that offends some of you, I suspect it is that I say that the blessed Augustine fought with heretics only with the sword of the word of   90
God. Although this is advantageous for you, you are happy that it turns out badly for me. Amazing charity, really! And what of your ingenuous interpretation of Vulturius' name, as if I were accusing him of avarice. I knew that the charge of extravagance would more easily fit him than that of avarice. But if you did not know that 'Vulturius' is a throw of the dice,[20] you were at   95
least able to know that I alluded to his real name in German.[21] I did it so that he would be exposed to scorn among fewer people. I called him Vulturius just as I now call you Eleutherius; and as he preferred to be known by his proper name instead of Vulturius,[22] so I allow you to be called by your name instead of Eleutherius. Finally, you even threaten Vulturius that if he really   100
wishes to be a disciple of Christ, he should hasten to erase this stigma. Are those who immediately prepare vengeance true disciples of Christ? And did those famous comments bring it about that everyone would have an excellent opinion of Vulturius? If he had not published them at your instigation, he would have the same reputation as I. What is that? An insatiable desire   105

* * * * *

18 Cf Epp 2443:324–49, 2466:93–116, and Allen Ep 2522:66–9. The colloquy *Exequiae seraphicae* 'The Seraphic Funeral,' first published in the edition of September 1531, includes a mocking description of the burial by Franciscans in Paris of 'Eusebius,' which is Greek for 'Pious' or 'Pio.' See CWE 40 1000–1.
19 The preface is Ep 2157.
20 See Plautus *Curculio* 357: 'He threw four vultures' (*iacit vulturios quattuor*), ie he made a throw of the dice of very low value.
21 The first three letters of Geldenhouwer's given name, Gerard, look and sound a bit like the Dutch *Gier* and German *Geier* 'vulture.' See Ep 2358 n6. But *Gier* in German means 'greed' or 'avarice.'
22 See n3 above.

for money! Mention just one person from whom I, I shall not say extorted, but asked for anything, and I will produce many from whom I did not accept things spontaneously offered to me, many with whom I shared my few resources, meagre though they be. I accepted something from Johann Froben – rather I did not accept it, but he thrust it upon me, as something I merited 110 – but I accepted barely a third of what he offered;[23] and in your eyes Erasmus has an insatiable appetite for money? By that vice I think I am less defiled than Vulturius. I am less free of other vices, I admit, but avarice never laid its hands on me. The Evangelicals encourage each other to piety by *Epistles* of this sort, in which there is a great deal of vanity and not a crumb of sincere 115 feeling. I cultivate a long-standing friendship with many with whose beliefs I disagree. You, if someone disagrees with you, from being friends become fierce enemies. And, of course, you had to write such pious things, so much in keeping with the Evangelical cause, even defying the orders of doctors. I wish you health of body and soul.   120

At Freiburg, 6 March 1530

2442 / To Franciscus Cassander   Freiburg, 6 March 1531

This letter was first published in the *Epistolae floridae*. For Cassander, see Ep 2296 introduction.

ERASMUS OF ROTTERDAM TO FRANCISCUS CASSANDER, GREETING
If, in return for your devoted affection for me, most distinguished Cassander, I did not have a great love for you, I would seem to have been born from stony reefs and nurtured by a tigress. After the abscess was opened with a lance, I came back to life little by little, but I did not regain my strength until the ap- 5 proach of winter.[1] For a long time afterwards my mind shrank back from studies and like some Proteus changed into all possible shapes to extricate itself from its bonds, but I, on the contrary, tenaciously drew the bonds ever tighter. Now and again I tried to kindle enthusiasm in my spirit for the work on the method of preaching.[2] I had no success. In the end I was able with great effort 10

* * * * *

23 Froben's generosity to Erasmus is described in Ep 1900:54–70.

2442
1 See Ep 2360 n1.
2 Ie the *Ecclesiastes sive de ratione concionandi*, which was not published until 1535. Cf Allen Epp 2483:53–4, 2508:7.

to continue my work on the apophthegms.[3] This is a subject that, besides affording much pleasure, is congenial to my nature. Whether I accomplished something worthwhile you will be the judge. I wrote a commentary on Psalm 33 to gratify the eminent prelate of Würzburg,[4] who had rendered me many favours, though it was commissioned by someone else,[5] and I cannot divine   15 for what reason. I hardly did anything else this winter except for a preface to a Greek edition of Aristotle and one for Livy, augmented by five books.[6] I wrote numerous letters to the leading men at the Diet of Augsburg, but it is not expedient to make them public in the present state of affairs.[7]

So much for those two topics: the state of my health, and what I achieved   20 under the auspices of the Muses. I would not wish to conceal from you that nothing was delivered here except for your first letter,[8] in which through the opportunity offered by some little question you offered me your friendship, and the last letter, written on 13 November. You see therefore, that five were lost. For my part, I have no doubt that in your prudence you do not commit   25 anything to a letter that would expose either of us to any danger if it were to fall into the hands of others. You must be attentive to whom you confide them, so that your effort in writing them and the special pleasure I take in reading them is not lost.

Be sure to recommend me to the reverend lord bishop of Sénez and his   30 brother, the viscount;[9] and at the same time return the friendly greetings of the provost of Saint-Désiré[10] in my name. Farewell.

At Freiburg im Breisgau, 6 March 1531

2443 / To Jacopo Sadoleto   Freiburg, 7 March 1531

First published in the *Epistolae floridae*, this is Erasmus' answer to Ep 2385. The surviving manuscript is an autograph rough draft in the Royal Library at Copenhagen (MS GKS 95 Fol, folio 201).

* * * * *

3 See Ep 2431.
4 See Ep 2428.
5 Unidentified; cf Ep 2443 n5.
6 See Epp 2432 (Aristotle), 2435 (Livy).
7 Still extant are: Epp 2328, 2341, 2366 (to Cardinal Campeggi); Epp 2332, 2362 (to Christoph von Stadion); Epp 2343, 2358, 2363, 2365 (to Philippus Melanchthon).
8 The one answered by Ep 2296. Neither it nor the letter of 13 November (line 24) is extant.
9 For both the bishop and his brother see Ep 2296 n13.
10 Unidentified

TO JACOPO SADOLETO

Throughout practically the whole summer, most distinguished bishop, I was occupied with doctors and surgeons because of a hard and dreadful abscess that had assailed my navel. And while the assiduity of doctors and surgeons aggravated more than alleviated the evil, at the same time I happened upon a surgeon who would seem savage even among the Scythians.[1] For that reason it came about that the part of the year that is usually the most productive for me was sterile and did not permit me to participate in the diet of princes in Augsburg, although I had been invited there by letters from very important personages.[2] The winter was a little more fruitful. In addition to a good-sized volume of apophthegms,[3] which I took up as a pleasant distraction to restore gradually to its former vigour the feeble strength of body and spirit that had been so severely impaired and shaken, I wrote an exposition of Psalm 33.[4] It was not chosen by us but commissioned by others, as were the last two.[5] Although the words of the Holy Spirit are always marvellously fecund, I think there are few that seem more sterile by comparison, since the title disconcerted me with its ruts, bogs, and ravines.[6] But seeing that my previous audacity turned out successfully twice, my courage grew, and I have dared to submit this laborious effort to your judgment, whatever its worth. I shall be astonished if anything in it meets with your approval, if you are willing to put aside for a moment the role of an excessively benign friend and take on that of a judge. In any case, I have never been more displeased with myself. First of all, I do not doubt that you will condemn my more than impromptu temerity, which I myself condemn and detest strongly, especially on a sacred subject. But it is an irremediable evil, so deeply ingrained that it cannot be torn out except together with life itself. If your clemency will grant me pardon for this one fault, in all else I shall gladly strive in the future to conform to your judgment, which, as you write, I have already begun to do

* * * * *

2443
1 For Erasmus' illness in 1530, see Ep 2360 n1. On the proverbial cruelty of the Scythians see *Adagia* IV ix 85.
2 See Ep 2353A n12.
3 Ep 2431
4 Ep 2428
5 It is not known who suggested that Erasmus compose the exposition of Psalm 33; cf Ep 2442:15. That of Psalm 22 was written at the behest of Thomas Boleyn (Epp 2232:7–12, 2266), while those of Psalms 4 and 85 were requested by John Longland (Epp 1535, 2017).
6 The psalm bears the heading: 'A Psalm of David when he feigned madness in the presence of Abimelech, who drove him out, and he went away.'

to some degree. As for my being such a cautious and, I might say, grudging assessor of your virtues, while you lavish so much praise, by the handful, as they say,[7] on my mediocrity, do not think that you are wasting your efforts altogether, for as a result I admire you more and more and displease myself more profoundly, recognizing that you leave me far behind, no less by your moderation of mind than by all your other good qualities. But it is best to dispense with all these things to avoid overburdening your modesty, especially since, as you write with as much truth as piety, whatever we are or do we must ascribe exclusively to divine munificence. For though your words of praise, which reveal a certain extraordinary kindness of character, far from corrupting me, contribute to rousing my apathy and pusillanimity to action, yet from your sincere and friendly admonitions I perceive more clearly your good will towards me and I derive much more abundant profit.

There are two points, as I seem to have inferred from your letter to me, concerning which you have expressed the wish that I be either more cautious or at least more restrained, namely, in my harsh criticisms of those practices which, though not examples of perfect piety, do not conflict with true religion, like the invocation of the saints and use of images; second, in my refutation of calumnies, no matter what the source, which you advise me should either be entirely eliminated or conducted in such a way that it does not appear that I have given in to anger.[8] Certainly I shall never deny that I have sinned in both cases, and I would earnestly desire that in many instances what was done could be undone. At any rate, since it is the only thing that is possible now, I either correct or temper many things in my published works, for I am a much more severe critic of my writings than St Augustine (who is often offered to me as an example by my friends) was of his. And would God that you or someone like you were at my side to give me timely advice, for now at last I have learned by experience how little benefit was derived from the applause of some people and the cries of those shouting 'Bravo! Bravo!' Nevertheless, certain calumnies are of such a kind that it would be impious to remain silent, as when in crowded assemblies or published books I am portrayed as the author of impious dogmas, a destroyer of the papal dignity, a falsifier of the inviolate Scriptures, a contriver of schisms. One who would tolerate such things in silence would not seem to me to be a pious man in any way. Leaving aside altogether any consideration of my reputation, what was

* * * * *

7 *Adagia* ii i 16
8 See Ep 2385 n7.

less expedient for the tranquillity of the church than for a great number of
people to have been persuaded by what my enemies were concocting in their   65
conspiracy of hatred? I had no serious contention with anyone who found
fault with my intellectual ability or found something lacking in my conduct.
I readily cede renown for learning to anyone; in moral conduct I admit that
I am only a man. But to remain speechless before a manifest calumny of supreme impiety, what is that but to admit to a crime? while to answer mildly   70
and placidly would not fail to arouse the double suspicion of either not having a good conscience or being in deceitful collusion with the betrayers of
the church. One would run the risk that someone might recall to himself that
saying of Cicero, 'If you were not feigning,' Erasmus, 'you would not act like
that.'⁹ And yet even in this regard I did not use my tongue or my pen against 75
everyone. Certain people, because they deserved it, I laughed at rather than
confuted, but never was I not more restrained than those by whom I was
attacked, in my opinion at least. It is possible, and it often happens, that my
emotions deceive my judgment, and I am the type of person, I admit, who
can flare up when I am provoked, but it is not a lasting anger, and I forget   80
injuries as much as anyone else. But when it is a question of printed books,
I usually do not give way to anger. You would probably not entirely disapprove of what I have said if you had time to read both their calumnies and
my apologies. But may the gods grant you better things than that you take
away so many good hours from your holy occupations and devote them to   85
unpleasant trifles. How disinclined my temperament is to these worse than
gladiatorial combats is manifested in that I have hitherto written many apologies, but nothing else than apologies, not one invective. Yet Cato is considered a good man although he brought charges against others more often than
he himself was summoned to appear in court.¹⁰   90

     What makes the matter even more outrageous is that while I am hold-
ing the net and the sickle against those whom these people wish with all their
prayers to see annihilated as mortal enemies of piety, they attack me from
the rear as I do battle for them at great risk to my life and fortunes. They do
this repeatedly, now Zúñiga, now Sancho, now Latomus, now Béda, now   95

* * * * *

9 Cicero *Brutus* 278
10 Marcus Portius Cato, commonly known as 'Cato the Censor' (234–149 BC), was
   a major figure in the political and cultural life of republican Rome. He is re-
   membered for, among other things, being constantly engaged in court cases,
   both as prosecutor or prosecution witness and as defendant.

Cousturier,[11] now Eck,[12] now Clichthove,[13] now the buffoons of Vincentius,[14] now the squadrons of Spanish monks,[15] now Alberto Pio,[16] now Titelmans,[17] now Carvajal.[18] I do not mention those whose books are passing from hand to hand, not yet circulated by the printers; I do not mention the virulent and viperous denigrations that do not spare my name either in public or in private. With what personal danger I do battle with originators of new doctrines it is not safe to commit to a letter, my dear Sadoleto. And I would desire at this point that my trustworthinesss has some weight with you, and that you believe that there is no one whom they hate more or for whom they set more traps. If you read my *Diatribe* or the two *Hyperaspistes* against the very violent volume of Luther,[19] or the *Spongia* against Hutten,[20] or the pamphlet against Leopold,[21] or the letter to Vulturius,[22] or the book against the preachers of Strasbourg,[23] in your prudence you will easily surmise how important it is for me not to be willing to withdraw from the community of the church of Rome.[24] I omit here as well the pamphlets, charged with bitterness, that I did not deem worthy of a response or that have not yet been issued by the printers; I do not mention the threatening letters seasoned with profuse poison;

100

105

110

* * * * *

11 See Epp 1260 n36 (Diego López Zúñiga), 1277 n8 (Sancho Carranza), 934 (Jacobus Latomus), 2375 n23 (Noël Béda and Pierre Cousturier).

12 The manuscript has 'Eccius,' ie Johann Eck (for whom see Ep 2387), but the *Epistolae floridae* and all subsequent printed editions substitute 'Eustathius,' ie Eustachius van der Rivieren, whose *Apologia pro pietate in Erasmi Roterod. Enchiridion canonem quintum* was published in 1531; see Ep 2264 introduction, and cf Allen Epp 2500:21–7, 2522:79–92, 2566:186–9, 2629:20–30. In Ep 2570:94–101, Revieren is paired with Frans Titelmans (n17 below) as an example of monks whose books sell by the thousands only because they attack Erasmus.

13 Josse Clichtove; see Epp 1609 n8, 1642:8–10, 1679:91–6.

14 Vincentius Theoderici and his supporters; see Ep 1196 introduction.

15 See Epp 1742 introduction, 1786 n5, 2094.

16 Ep 2371 n22

17 Ep 2417

18 See Ep 2110 n10.

19 Luther's *De servo arbitrio* was his vituperative response to Erasmus' *De libero arbitrio* διατριβή (Ep 1419 introduction). Erasmus responded with *Hyperaspistes 1* (Ep 1667) and 2 (Ep 1853).

20 See Ep 1378 introduction.

21 Ie Leo Jud, against whom Erasmus wrote the *Detectio praestigiarum*; see Epp 1708 nn1–2, 1737 n1.

22 Ep 2358 n6

23 Ep 2371 n20

24 See Ep 2366 n17.

I do not mention the accusations and the suborned spreading of malicious reports that could rob any man, no matter how noble, of his tranquillity.

What it is like to struggle with so many monsters of wickedness you   115
will be able better to understand than to feel, since you have not experienced this kind of outrageous behaviour. For your moral integrity, about which even fame fears to lie, your incomparable learning safely protected beyond the reach of the shafts of envy, and finally your dignity and authority keep at a distance the stings of hornets and the barking of dogs, to which my   120
mediocrity, or to speak more truly, my humble condition, exposes me. First of all, an inordinate love of liberty imposed it on me. I saw that a high office could not be assumed and administered without a heavy burden of cares. In seeking that honour it was I who fell short, not fortune. I would have had to flee the celebrity of fame for the same reason that I fled a position of dig-   125
nity. I began to sense this failing of mine too late, when it became apparent that this miserable little body was so afflicted that I was not equal to living at court, to which I had been constrained to go, or to any high office. And in the meantime this tempest within the church arose, which would have completely overwhelmed me if the favour of other princes, but especially   130
of Emperor Charles, had not sustained me to a certain degree. For men of this type, once they had begun to rave, would not be deterred from raving by either the emperor or the sovereign pontiff. As a result, on the one hand I cannot placate my old enemies, who were roused up against me because they were convinced that the study of good letters has been revived in my   135
country largely due to my efforts, while on the other hand, I am driven by the new doctrines into the arena to fight against those to whom I was joined by the common bond of the promotion of studies. Thus I am stoned from both sides,[25] with impunity, as one might expect, since I am equipped with neither exceptional learning nor splendour of fortune nor authority. I would be a   140
little more secure (I refer to external concerns) if I had gone over to the camp of the new doctrines or had put up with the slavery of the court; piety held me back from the one, while partly my temperament and partly my health withdrew me from the.other. Before this gladiatorial combat of opinions took rise, I enjoyed great favour with the initiates of humane letters, especially in   145
Germany, and I seemed sufficiently protected by this one defence. Now my most bitter enemies are those who once were my most ardent champions. And so it happened that, like a weak, defenceless little animal crawling on the ground, I was exposed not only to dogs, pigs, magpies, crows, grackles,

* * * * *

25 See Ep 2379 n51.

asps, and vipers, but also to wasps, bedbugs, and fleas. And those who were   150
engaged in an implacable war among themselves but were of one accord in
mangling me joined forces. Nor was there any lack of Italians, who incited
the emperor and all his court to bring about my death.[26] And they would
have persuaded him had I not, with the assistance of humane letters, dissuaded princes possessed of more equitable judgment. And yet against the   155
phalanxes of robed and cinctured men of loose morals neither the emperor
nor the pope has the power to render anyone completely safe.

What was I to do? A horse protects itself with its hooves, a dog with
its teeth, an ox with its horns, a porcupine with its needles, a bee with its
sting, an electric ray with its poison, the dove's protection is its quickness of   160
flight. I had only the pen, which I had always wished would remain forever
unbloodied. Since this was denied by the Fates, I took refuge with what was
closest to it: I merely answered those who harassed me the most violently
and gladly refrained from naming them. I took sedulous care not to offend
any order, always being more moderate than my assailant, in brief, using the   165
shield more than the sword. In answering Cousturier I seem not only to others, but also to myself, to depart from my character. No one wrote against me
more ignorantly or more intemperately than he when from a theologian at
the Sorbonne he became a Carthusian monk.[27] I regret having answered certain people, especially Cousturier, for it would have injured my reputation   170
very little if I had ignored his inanities. And I would have done that except
that when I was hesitating to write, a certain influential person impelled me
otherwise.[28] I often implore them with paternal or rather fraternal affection,
I ask and advise them to revert to more sensible courses of action and cease,
while they are trying to crush me, to cause grave unpopularity and disgrace   175
to themselves and their orders, especially among learned and reasonable
men. A man very much like you shares your opinions, Cuthbert Tunstall,
an English bishop, first of London and now of Durham; and he sings the
same song as you do.[29] But he also does not have the time, because of affairs
at court and in the church, to pay close attention to the pamphlets of those   180

* * * * *

26 Doubtless a reference to Girolamo Aleandro, who was nuncio to the imperial
   court in 1520–2; cf nn37 and 43 below.
27 Cousturier was a *socius* of the Collège de Sorbonne while he was studying theology (1502–10), but his functions at the college were those of proctor, librarian,
   and prior. The acquisition of the doctorate made him eligible for membership
   in the Paris faculty of theology, but he did not participate actively in it.
28 Nicolas Bérault; see Epp 1591 introduction, 1893:19–20 with n5.
29 See Ep 2226:13–38, and cf Ep 2468:1–17.

who attack me and my apologies from the opposing side – for it is not safe to
believe the stories and the accusations heard at banquets. Nevertheless, I respect his judgment very much and I have moderated many things according
to his advice. On this account I admit that I owe him more than I do anyone
else, although I owe him much for many other reasons.   185

So much for the part of your letter in which you advise me either to
treat the barkings of the rabble-rousers with contempt or to refute them in
such a way that I appear to have given in very little to my anger. I would not
wish you to think, most excellent prelate, that I am completely free of fault
and that your advice is in vain or contrary to what I deserve, but only that   190
you be more fair to me and more readily pardon the errors I have committed
up to the present. I come now to the other part of your letter in which you
prudently advise me not to object too vehemently to popular devotions that,
although they do not have the marks of true piety, yet are not to be regarded
as impiety, such as the veneration of the saints and the proliferation of paint-   195
ings. I do not know what was reported to you, but far be it from me to have
condemned the veneration of the saints or the use of images in my books.
In some places I criticize the superstitious or exaggerated cult of the saints.
I think it is superstitious for a soldier about to set out on a mission of plundering to count on returning safe and sound if he has greeted the statue of   200
St Barbara on bended knee and has recited some little prayers in her honour
that are very similar to magic incantations; I think it is out of place when we
venerate the saints with little candles and painted ex-voto tablets while our
whole life contradicts their morals, although it would be very gratifying to
the saints if someone would imitate their piety. I have never been of the opin-   205
ion that paintings and statues should be destroyed, since they are special
ornaments in a person's life, although I would wish that nothing should be
seen in churches that is not worthy of that place. There is a great controversy
about the invocation of saints and the adoration of images. First, it is evident
that there is no place in the divine volumes that permits the invocation of   210
saints unless, perhaps, one wishes to twist the meaning of the passage in
which the rich man in the gospel parable implores the help of Abraham.[30]
Although in such an important matter it may seem justifiably dangerous to
make innovations without the authority of Scripture, nevertheless I nowhere
disapprove of the invocation of the saints, nor do I think it ought to be disap-   215
proved, as long as superstition is absent, which I sometimes censure, and not
without reason. For I interpret it as superstition when we ask for everything

* * * * *

30 Luke 16:24–31

from the saints, as if Christ were dead; or when we implore the help of the
saints in the conviction that they are more liable to hearken to our prayers
than God; or when we ask particular things from each saint, as if Catherine   220
can grant something that Barbara cannot; or when we invoke them not as
intercessors, but as the authors of those goods that God dispenses. I do not
think such advice would seem impious to you and I am quite sure it would
not even seem excessive to you if you knew the immense superstition that
exists in our regions in this regard. A more grave danger is presented by the 225
adoration of images, to which Scripture does not encourage us but gravely
warns us against it. If we approve the subtle fiction of Scotus that images
are to be adored with the same adoration as that which those whom they
represent should be adored,[31] then those early Fathers who opposed that
any statues should be allowed in the churches of Christians were very slow-   230
witted. If the same kind of adoration does not befit the images of God and of
the saints – when the people with equal devotion uncover their head before
the images of the saints, prostrate themselves on the ground, crawl on their
knees, kiss their hands after they have touched an image, rub them with
their bandages – by what sign will you recognize different kinds of adora-   235
tion? And what shall I say of those who talk to the images just as if they had
sensation, and who do not behave in the same way with all the images of
Christ and of the saints but hope to obtain from statue what they would not
dare to ask of another?[32]

Although this is all too true, I shall not beg to be excused from any   240
penalty if anyone can show anywhere in my writings that I condemn the
invocation of the saints and the adoration of images pure and simple. If you
would think fit to be my guarantor also with others, I promise you will be
able to do so without disadvantage or harm to yourself. But if someone has
convinced you of the contrary, or if you have little faith in me, I ask that you   245
bid those who give you this information to show you the passages. Once you
have examined them attentively, you will see that their tragic calumnies are
nothing but mere smoke and mist. Although in themselves these things are
trivial and your admonitions about them so lenient and affectionate, nonetheless you express disapproval of my audacity and temerity as a friend –   250
with extraordinary forbearance, distancing yourself to the utmost from the
behaviour of some individuals who, though they themselves stray from the

* * * * *

31 The attribution of this 'fiction' to Scotus is doubtful; see CWE 84 233–4 n764.
32 For the classic statement of Erasmus' views on the adoration of the saints and
    images, see *Enchiridion militis christiani* CWE 66 63–5, 71–5, 79, 102–3.

path of virtue at every step, cry schism and heresy with every other word.
For myself, my dear Sadoleto, I will bear with resignation being admonished
by those like you, whether it be with reproofs or even blows; far from being 255
offended by such mild remonstrances, I am offended that I am not rebuked
more frankly. For Cuthbert Tunstall, like you in other things, surpasses you
in this one aspect, that he reproves me freely, if something displeases him in
my writings, because he knows my character more intimately and has a more
precise knowledge of my way of life, since we lived under the same roof at 260
one time.[33]

Concerning the prestigious ecclesiastical honour that Pope Clement
was ready to give me on your recommendation if he had not been led to
change his mind by the calumnies of certain men,[34] I am fully conscious of
my debt to you for your favourable disposition, but nonetheless, as far as 265
my future plans are concerned, I consider that my affairs have suffered no
damage. If I had been intent on such ambitions, the benevolence of the emperor, the king of England, and the king of France offered me more than I
could wish, even if I had been extremely avaricious. After fortune gave me
enough to nurture this poor little body, I deemed that I needed nothing more 270
than leisure and tranquillity both for my old age and my studies, in which
I decided to pass peacefully the rest of the life that the gods would give me.
What they persuaded Clement of I do not know.[35] Of this I am totally persuaded: if my state of mind and what I have done and suffered were as clear
to the sovereign pontiff as they are to God, the knower of hearts,[36] he would 275
be somewhat better disposed to Erasmus than to certain parties who made a
noisy uproar. If I had sought after mitres and benefices, I would now regret
the time consumed uselessly, but I do not think at present that I have suffered any disadvantage if I have won approval for my zeal from the supreme
superintendent of the games. Furthermore, just as I cherish the marvellous 280
and spontaneous kindness of your character, so I cannot sufficiently wonder
at the nature of these people who tried to provoke the feelings of the supreme
pontiff against me, and it is no secret to me who they are.

* * * * *

33 In Brussels in 1516; see Epp 476:4–5, 480:13–14, 483:20–2.
34 Cf Ep 2385:64–9 with n4. Lines 284–349 below indicate that Erasmus under-
    stood 'certain men' to refer to Girolamo Aleandro and Alberto Pio.
35 See Ep 1987.
36 Acts 1:24; 15:8

With one of them I shared in Venice not only board and lodgings but bedroom also and a common bed.[37] He suffered no injury from me; indeed, 285 when his conditions were rather straitened he received some help from my letters of recommendation,[38] and nowhere in my writings is he mentioned except in the most honourable terms.[39] His sentiments towards me are clearly visible in a little book in which he explains the meaning of the Hebrew word 'racha,' a copy of which a friend of mine sent me in good faith, when it was 290 passing from hand to hand at the papal court.[40] In it, completely out of context, he writes to the pope that he is extremely surprised that when in the peasants' revolt so many thousands were slaughtered in Germany, Erasmus, who was the leader and standard-bearer of this whole uprising, who stirred up this violent tempest, who churned up the seas from their very depths, was 295 still living. As if I had anything to do with this mad and deplorable revolt of the peasants, or as if I were not the first to protest against this seditious course of action – in a more subdued but prudent way, in my opinion, and more conducive to preserving the concord of the church, than that of those who thought this fire would be put out immediately through their vocifera- 300 tions, their threats, and their violence. I will refrain from mentioning names, for among them are certain persons joined to me by a close friendship. But we see that up to now they have made no headway except that more and more territories allied by more and more binding compacts have become firmly united and continue to be united day by day.[41] May Christ, all great 305 and all powerful, bring it about that I am a vain prophet. And yet, if (which I

* * * * *

37 Aleandro; see Epp 256, 1195 n14.
38 See Ep 2411 n14.
39 For the transformation of friendship into enmity as a result of 'the Luther affair,' see Epp 1256 n11.
40 For the 'little book,' which was never published, see Ep 1717 n18.
41 At this point the Catholic princes of Germany had still taken no significant
   steps to equip themselves with the means to effect their frequent threats to
   crush the Reformation by force. Ever since 1526, however, evangelical rulers
   had been working towards an alliance in defence of their religion. These efforts,
   spurred on by the unfavourable outcome of the imperial diet at Speyer in 1529
   (see Ep 2219 n10) faltered for a time because of the Eucharistic controversy between the Lutherans and the Zwinglians, but took on new urgency in the wake
   of the hostile recess of the diet at Augsburg in 1530 (see Ep 2403 nn10–11). The
   result was the formation of the League of Schmalkalden, the founding treaty for
   which was signed in December 1530. Membership was open to adherents of the
   Augsburg Confession. The original members were few: four princes, including the elector of Saxony and the landgrave of Hessen, and ten imperial cities,

pray God will avert) you see terrible world revolutions arising, not so much destructive to Germany as fatal to the church, you will remember that it was predicted by Erasmus. First of all, we should have ignored Luther with his theses about indulgences and not poured oil on the fire. Next, we should not 310 have dealt with the matter through monks, almost universally hated, nor by means of uncontrolled outcries among the people, nor through the burning of books and human beings, but through books meant to circulate only among the learned. Finally, we should have turned a blind eye to them and put up with them for a while, as we have thus far put up with the Bohemians 315 and the Jews.[42] Time itself often brings a remedy to incurable evils. Despite these continuous exhortations, I was not heard, so much so that, willingly or unwillingly, I was the supporter of sects. That famous 'bull-bearer' thought he was performing a magnificent exploit, since wherever Charles went he filled everything with the smoke and bonfires of books, omitting no one in 320 his threats.[43] It was not his fault that he did not succeed in silencing me: Erasmus would have perished if he had found princes who were well disposed towards him. I was provoked by this fellow beyond endurance.

The other man, whom I never saw face to face but who was known and dear to me through the renown of his learning and culture, inveighed all over 325

* * * * *

including Strasbourg. But during the 1530s its membership grew rapidly, and it was a potent force in the politics of the Empire until its disastrous defeat at the hands of the emperor in 1546–7.

42 By 'Bohemians' Erasmus presumably means the Utraquists, the moderate Hussites who constituted the majority church in Bohemia and Moravia. On the *modus vivendi* between them and the Catholics in Bohemia, see Ep 2366 n16. As for the Jews, most of them had been expelled from Germany in the century and a half following the Black Death in the middle of the fourteenth century. But they were still officially tolerated in the imperial cities of Frankfurt am Main and Worms, and they maintained a precarious existence in a few other places, including Bohemia.

43 *Diplomatophoros* 'bull-bearer,' ie 'bearer of [papal] bulls,' was Erasmus' mocking nickname for Aleandro throughout his *Responsio ad epistolam Alberti Pii*, and he later noted with satisfaction Aleandro's anger at the epithet; see CWE 84 42 n206. As papal nuncio to the imperial court in 1520, Aleandro was charged with the dangerous and thankless task of publishing and executing the bull *Exsurge Domine* (Ep 2441 n8) in the Low Countries and the Rhine region of Germany (Johann Eck was similarly responsible for regions further east). He presided over the burning of Lutheran books at Louvain and Liège in October 1520 and (in the face of much hostility) at Cologne and Mainz in November; see Epp 1141 n11, 1158:5–9, 1166:57–66.

Rome against Erasmus, calling him childish,[44] unlearned, and devoid of all judgment. After I had remonstrated with him in a letter written in a friendly and respectful manner,[45] he responded in a medium-sized, carefully composed volume, which he sent to me before it was printed.[46] From that I was easily able to deduce that the man had not read my works but wrote things that   330 he had heard or that had been reported to him and, worse yet, did not write except by using hired labour. When the work, published in Paris, with a few things added, was brought to me, I responded, but politely and respectfully,[47] taking great care, as far as the nature of the situation allowed, that nothing be said that might injure his character or cause harm to his reputation, even   335 offering mutual friendship, as he had done at the end of his volume. But the instigator of the whole thing did not desist from his efforts, and there was no lack of people in Paris to egg him on, especially Franciscans, whose sacred habit he put on three days before his death and was buried in, with the solemn rites of that order, before the printed volume was finished.[48] I had not yet   340 had the opportunity to see it, but those who had seen it said that it was huge. In it, with the help of many hired writers, whatever might have the slightest resemblance to unapproved doctrines was collected from all my works. How much wiser it would have been to cull those things that openly oppose such doctrines, which are without number! So that good man fled after planting   345 the dart, as the expression goes.[49] I implore God's mercy on his soul, hoping that he will find better defenders before the supreme Judge than he himself provided for the French king against the emperor, or for the pope against the forces of the emperor, or for himself in the defence of his principality.[50]

With great pleasure I express my indebtedness to you for restraining   350 Zúñiga,[51] who I know was forbidden also by Pope Adrian to write anything against me, but only after, in addition to the *Annotations* published in

* * * * *

44 The word is *infans*; on the difficulty of translating it see Ep 2387 n4.
45 Ep 1634, the introduction to which surveys the entire controversy between Pio and Erasmus
46 The *Responsio paraenetica*, written in 1526 but not published until January 1529; see Ep 2080, in which Erasmus urged Pio not to publish it.
47 *Responsio ad epistolam Alberti Pii*, published by Froben in March 1529
48 See Ep 2441 n18.
49 See Ep 2441 n17.
50 A reference to the complicated history of the shifting alliances and affiliations with two kings of France, two emperors, and two popes that ultimately (1527) saw Pio deprived of his principality of Carpi and forced to take refuge in France as Clement VII's ambassador at the court of Francis I. See CWE 84 xxv–xxix.
51 Cf Ep 2385:67–70.

Spain, which he sold in Rome, he raged against me to the full in five or six pamphlets.[52] Even now he is threatening something or other, no longer on dogmas of the faith but, as he says, on grammar. Besides this type of calumny, Germany possesses certain monsters of a fiendish and incredible obstinacy, who by insidious ruses succeed in exposing Erasmus to thieves or overwhelming him with grief. But up to now, by the grace of Christ, they have not been able to shake my resolution and they have not caused much damage to my studies.

I return to the Psalm that you praised.[53] From now on I will try diligently to ensure that what I write, without exception, will merit your approval, which I fear I did not achieve in this Psalm.[54] Certainly, I shall never abandon hope of achieving it now that I have begun to make progress at your instigation. And yet, at least in this type of writing, I yield to emotion more sparingly, obviously because in the presence of such great mysteries I prepare myself in an attitude of religious reverence. On this point I am in complete agreement with you that the reading of many interpreters presents difficulties, especially to one who is treating this kind of subject matter; and it would turn out much more successfully if, after surveying the general sense, one would surrender oneself totally to a mystical spirit, calling oneself away in the meantime not only from vices but even from external and lowlier concerns, and withdrawing into some sublime retreat, tranquil and quiet, far from the turmoil of worldly passions. And the interspersing of a prayer again and again is of no slight importance, since it marvellously revives the vigour and alacrity of the spirit. Immortal God! How great would be our happiness if, putting aside differences of opinion and feelings, we exercised ourselves with one mind in the fertile fields of the Scriptures and frolicked in their pleasant meadows – if one may use that word in a matter that has little to do with play. But, conscious of my uncleanness and knowing what an unsuitable and refractory instrument I provide for the work of the Spirit in treating these subjects, in which he wished those abstruse mysteries of divine philosophy to be hidden as in a hallowed sanctuary, I am in the habit of approaching them not without trembling. The tranquil purity of your heart was described to me by Niccolò Leonico,[55] an upright man, as it appears, and

* * * * *

52 See Ep 1341A:912–23.
53 Psalm 22 in Ep 2385
54 Psalm 33; see lines 13–14 above.
55 Niccolò Leonico Tomeo (Ep 1479 n70), whom Erasmus had evidently known at Venice. He died on 31 March 1531.

well trained in Platonic philosophy. He described this quality of yours in a dialogue in which he presents you discussing prayer in a very saintly manner.[56] If I had read this dialogue (I would have read it if my friends sent it to me in time), my little book on praying[57] would have been a little less jejune and crawling along the ground.[58] But the purity of heart I saw sketched there was represented much more clearly in your splendid interpretation of the Psalms,[59] especially the last one, which I read more attentively and breathlessly (as the Greeks say);[60] I would have seen to the publication of both if someone else had not anticipated me. 390

You would hardly believe how much I admire you for this judgment of yours, which agrees very much with my own: 'Almighty God who gives you travaïls and anxieties and poor health perhaps does this for your greater good than if he offered you tranquillity and soft relaxation.'[61] You seem to have looked deep into me so that I do not know myself better than you do. In the unending sequence of calamities I alleviate my spirit with no other reflection more than the conviction that this is advantageous to my salvation. For God in his unspeakable wisdom purifies men in various ways and renders them worthy of himself; like a stage director he introduces actors of all kinds into the theatre of this life, and he has prepared a reward for everyone who plays the part assigned to him in a fitting manner. St Paul the Hermit is famous for the sole reason that, confined to one place, he remained obscure all his life.[62] Blessed Hilarion, while he fled from fame, became famous everywhere.[63] St Anthony divided his time between the desert and the cities.[64] None of them suffered any kind of adversity. And how much difference there is between Jerome and Augustine, between Chrysostom and Basil, between 395 400 405 410

* * * * *

56 *Sadoletus seu de precibus*, one of Leonico's *Dialogi* (Venice: Gregorius de Gregoriis: September 1524)
57 *Modus orandi Deum* (Ep 1502)
58 Horace *Epistles* 2.1.251, speaking of the lowly style in his satires, as compared to that in other categories of his works
59 Psalm 50 in 1525 (Ep 1586) and Psalm 93 in 1530 (Ep 2385 n1)
60 Cf Ep 2405 n8.
61 Cf Ep 2385:94–6.
62 Also known as St Paul of Thebes (d c 347), traditionally regarded as the first Christian hermit
63 St Hilarion (c 291–c 371), the first recorded hermit in Palestine, known chiefly via the biography of him written by St Jerome
64 St Anthony the Great (c 251–356), regarded as the founder of Christian monasticism

Athanasius and Gregory the theologian,[65] not to mention others very different in character, fortune, and way of life, but equal in piety. But if the stage director has imposed on me a humble and beleaguered role, should I murmur against him or should I not rather sustain the part assigned to me to the best of my ability? He at whose will human affairs are conducted will give a good dénouement to this play. This meditation induces me not yet to abandon all hope about these tumults in Germany, which may result in a great boon for the church. He knows how to turn even our evils into his glory and the well-being of his elect. But though in your exceptional goodness you pray for Germany, I think we should pray for many other regions, in which this fever rages with no less intensity, although it has broken out less violently. But if this matter had been attended to by men like you, the troubles would be more tolerable everywhere. The ferocity of certain people, who look out more for themselves than for Christ, has aggravated and continues to aggravate the malady. But when it seems good to our stage director, all these things will turn to the advantage of the Christian cause.

You are true to yourself, most modest Sadoleto, when you thank me for my notes on your Psalm.[66] But I did not criticize any errors of yours (far be it from me to have such arrogance), but those of the printers; and I did that for no other reason than that you take note of them. In reading the concluding passage, I barely restrained myself from crying for joy. It is all the more pleasant to repeat these words here. You say: 'My dear Erasmus, I wish you to be assured that, although I am a man of modest means and punished by fortune with great losses, I have nothing that I do not wish to be as much yours as mine. Not only in this regard but in all that pertains to the preserving of your dignity and reputation I am resolved both of my own will and in answer to any recommendation of yours to give proof to you always of my supreme loyalty in friendship and good will.'[67] Whenever I read these heartfelt words coming from such an eminent prelate I like to call to mind the words of the old man in the comedy: 'I'm glad to see him, as I'm always glad / To see that such men still exist.'[68] I am very distressed that you have suffered such a diminution of your fortunes since, as they were held in common with other excellent people, it was not your loss alone but that of many others.[69] As far as

415

420

425

430

435

440

* * * * *

65 Gregory of Nazianzus
66 See Ep 2385 n10.
67 Ep 2385:105–11
68 Terence *Adelphi* 445–6
69 See Ep 2385:106–7 with n11.

I am concerned, I consider myself abundantly enriched thanks to you, since it is permitted to me to enjoy such an incomparable friendship. My domestic re- 445
sources are quite limited but, as they say, little birds do not need many feath-
ers.[70] I am content with very little, and if anything is lacking, there are always
those who are anxious to satisfy my needs quickly and cheerfully. I give more
importance to your letter, if you will believe me, than if you had sent me a talent of gold. And I say this not because I do not want to be indebted to you on 450
this account. Rather, I state openly that I am no less obliged to you for these
things that you offer than for the services you have already rendered me.

Bonifacius Amerbach, on whose friendship I principally rely, a man of
such integrity that you would not find a single blemish in him save that he is
immoderately modest, is the father of two children and a professor of law at 455
Basel, although he would prefer to be here. I wanted you to know this so that
you will be more indulgent with him if he writes you more seldom than you
would wish. But I do not think he is ever so occupied as not to have the time
to write to you, whom he loves particularly; it is rather that there is rarely
anyone available to whom we can entrust the delivery of a letter. Whenever 460
after a long delay we receive your letters, we think we have made an acceptable sacrifice to good fortune. It is a great consolation whenever he comes
to see me in Freiburg. He does that more rarely now for fear of the plague,
which sported with us quite impertinently all through the autumn and winter, and even now does not wish to end.[71] I wonder how it is that, although 465
the number of human beings has decreased, the dearness of commodities
nevertheless increases from day to day. Farewell.

At Freiburg im Breisgau, 7 March 1531

2444 / To Quintinus   Freiburg, 9 March 1531

This letter was first published in the *Epistolae floridae*. Allen tentatively identified the addressee as Jean Quintin of Autun (c 1509–61), who by 1536 had become professor of canon law at Paris. There is no evidence either to corroborate
or to invalidate that identification.

* * * * *

70 This is similar to the Dutch proverb 'Cleen voghelkens hebben cleene nest-
   kens' (small birds have small nests), which Erasmus refers to in *Adagia* i vii 62:
   Efficimus pro nostris opibus moenia 'We build the walls we can afford.' See Ari
   Wesseling 'Dutch Proverbs and Expressions in Erasmus' Adages, Colloquies,
   and Letters' *Renaissance Quarterly* x (2002) 81–147, here page 129.
71 See Ep 2426 n3.

ERASMUS OF ROTTERDAM TO HIS FRIEND QUINTINUS, GREETING
Montanus has fulfilled his duty: he mentioned you to me and gave me your
greetings.[1] But what is the point of this? Is it that you want me to know nothing else but that you wish to be acknowledged as my friend? Not a word
about your studies or how things stand with you. What you ask of me was 5
done by me long ago; I wrote to you, but I do not know whether you received my letter. How can I declare you my friend, when you do not wish
me to know anything of your affairs? If you wish to be loved, show yourself
worthy of being loved; and if you wish that I acknowledge you as a friend,
have me understand clearly that I am your friend. I do not write this because 10
I suspect something hostile in you, but to stimulate you to your obligations.
This mad tumult that my *Ciceronianus* has stirred up makes me have less
trust than usual in the French temperament.[2] Farewell.
    At Freiburg im Breisgau, 9 March AD 1531

2445 / To Matthias Kretz   Freiburg, 11 March 1531

This letter, Erasmus' reply to Ep 2430, was first published in the *Epistolae
floridae*. The surviving manuscript, a copy in an unknown sixteenth-century
hand, is in the University Library at Munich (MS Fol A Lat a 18). Allen used the
salutation found in the manuscript: 'Desiderius Erasmus of Rotterdam to the
consummate theologian Matthias Kretz, dean and preacher in Munich.' That
salutation, however, is clearly the anachronistic invention of the person who
made the copy. The letter, written in response to a recent letter from Augsburg,
addresses the situation in that city, where Kretz was still cathedral preacher (cf
line 168) and had not yet been able to accept the appointment in Munich that
had been offered to him (Ep 2430:19–24). We have therefore restored the salutation that Erasmus himself used in the *Epistolae floridae*.

ERASMUS OF ROTTERDAM TO MATTHIAS KRETZ, PREACHER,
GREETINGS
I read with great sadness of spirit what you write about the revolutionary
changes there, but you are not the only one to tell me these things. I fear that
something that we would not want will happen to this city, which stands out 5

* * * * *

2444
 1 There is no evidence of Philippus Montanus (Ep 2065 introduction) having visited Erasmus at this time, so it is possible that he may have included the greetings in a letter that is no longer extant.
 2 See Ep 1948 introduction.

among German cities for its nobility and its opulence. The emperor is bitterly incensed and King Ferdinand is also quite vexed. It is said that there will be a treaty with the Turks.[1] There are those who secretly pour cold water on the king and his brother, who are already more than enough exasperated, and are pouring oil on the fire. I think that with your good judgment you know   10 whom I mean. In the immediate vicinity there are the dukes of Bavaria: with what more impressive claim can they augment their authority than to have crushed heresies and defended the Catholic faith?[2] I do not know if certain purple-robed men of whom you speak have not contributed to this evil,[3] who although they are not unaware that this hatred originated and was nurtured   15 mostly by the luxury and ostentation of priests, yet, according to written accounts, have led there a life of incredible extravagance, banqueting and passing the whole night gambling, not without the knowledge of the popu- lace. I shall pass over in silence the cruelty of some of them, who by threats, insults, and torture are confident that this fatal evil can be put to sleep or   20 rather suppressed. The most efficacious remedy of all is entirely neglected. 'What is that?' you say. That the leaders of the church, converted to a better life, remove the seedbed of this tumult from the world. In that way Christ would lend his aid.

Now, as if it were a purely human predicament and not rather a divine   25 punishment, irritated by the uncontrolled growth of men's crimes, we look to worldly safeguards. The self-indulgence, not to say the tyranny, of cler- ics increases, wealth and luxury increase, while lustful desire does not de- crease. It is not my place to pass judgment on the pope, but those who come here from Italy tell of things that we cannot hear without great sorrow. How   30 inclemently did Clement treat Florence?[4] It seems to me that he intends to smother this conflagration of the world with the favour of princes and a great number of cardinals.[5] But what is this but to anger God even more? As if the world could defeat the world. Only Christ said truthfully, 'I have conquered the world.'[6] If profane monarchs love riches and glory, we must bear it one   35 way or another, and I hardly know whether it is fitting or expedient for any

* * * * *

2445
1 No treaty with the Turks was in the offing, but in May 1531 Ferdinand and John Zápolyai, who was allied with the Turks, would extend for one year the truce they had concluded in December 1530; see Ep 2384 n10.
2 See Ep 2437 n14.
3 'Purple-robed men' is presumably a reference to cathedral canons; cf Ep 2430:20–1.
4 See Ep 2366 n11.
5 See Ep 2375 n11.
6 John 16:33

of them to drive a hard wedge into a hard knot. But if those who occupy the
first ranks in the church offer themselves to monarchs not as teachers and
counsellors but as slaves and ministers to their desires, what hope, I ask you,
is there for this dove who is the sole love of its spouse?[7] Some sound the   40
trumpet to drive out heretics by force of arms, but their purpose is to arrogate riches, leisure, and authority for priests. I fear, however, that while some
princes attack us and others protect us, we are despoiled by both sides, and
that a war undertaken for pious motives will be no less fatal for the church
than destructive for Germany. May Christ, all-good and all-great, bring it to   45
pass that my prediction be proved vain.

And yet, up to the present time, what I have divined has been truer than
I would wish. First of all, when Luther's theses on indulgences appeared, the
best thing was to keep silence. Prieras responded quite arrogantly,[8] and was
the first, as the Greeks say, to take the grasshopper by the wing.[9] Another an- 50
swered in Saxon.[10] At this point Jacob of Hoogstraten, in order to come to the
aid of the Dominicans, left no stone unturned to rouse up the universities,

* * * * *

7 Song of Sol 6:8
8 The Dominican Silvestro Mazzolini, known as Prierias, was the papal official
responsible for examining books for heresy. In that capacity he published in
1518 a denunciation of Luther's Ninety-five Theses in which he maintained that
papal teachings and practices were infallible and that by questioning them
Luther had made himself guilty of heresy. See Ep 872:19n.
9 Just as taking a grasshopper by the wing causes a noisy creature to make even
more noise, so provoking an articulate and disputatious man will cause him to
make an even louder noise than before; see Adagia I ix 28.
10 The Latin for 'in Saxon' is Saxonice, the most obvious meaning of which is 'in
the Saxon language' (ie in the variety of German spoken in Saxony and employed by Luther when he wrote in German). If this is the intended meaning,
the reference may well be to Johann Tetzel, the Dominican whose preaching of
indulgences had elicited from Luther his Ninety-five Theses (October 1517). Both
the Theses and the initial responses to it were in Latin. But in March 1518, Luther
published A Sermon on Indulgence and Grace, which summarized in German the
chief ideas of the Ninety-five Theses and was the first of Luther's books to be a
best-seller. About a month later, Tetzel, who had earlier denounced the Ninety-
five Theses in Latin, responded to Luther's Sermon with a pamphlet written in
Luther's Saxon idiom: Rebuttal of a Presumptuous Sermon ... on Papal Indulgences
and Grace ..., published by Melchior Lotter in Leipzig. In so doing he became,
it seems, the first person to publish an attack on Luther's Ninety-five Theses in
German, doing so moreover at about the time that Erasmus is referring to here.
The work did not sell well or attract much attention, but Erasmus could easily
have learned of it via his contacts at the court of Duke George of Saxony.

namely, those of Paris, Cologne, and Louvain. The last two, in any event, he stirred up to the point that they published two relatively moderate articles against Luther,[11] on the advice, I think of Adrian, who later became   55 pope.[12] This expedient, though not unworthy of theologians, aroused nothing but laughter in most circles, especially the articles of Cologne. But when certain people, without reading Luther's books, began to raise their voices among the ignorant crowd, especially a certain Carmelite of very peevish character,[13] I warned that in this way the evil would spread rather than be   60 eliminated (for the common people were glad to hear that there were those who taught that confession was not necessary and that satisfaction was completely superfluous).[14] I advised that they should either ignore the man or that specialists should discuss the matter among themselves in writing. This advice was disregarded, and by way of thanks I received the reward of being   65 referred to as a Lutheran, although I was the first to voice my objections in this matter and oppose it as best I could. What I predicted came about: the fire gained ground day by day.

In the end the Carmelite thought it was best to resort to jails and the stake and, to tell the truth, the outrageous behaviour of many of those who   70 favoured the new beliefs provoked this reaction. Aleandro arrived with a terrifying bull threatening everyone, and wherever the emperor went, he left smoke and the burning of books in his wake.[15] When these actions ex-

* * * * *

11 Hoogstraten (Ep 1006), a graduate of Louvain, was prior of the Cologne Dominicans and inquisitor for the archbishoprics of Cologne, Mainz, and Trier. For his role in the condemnation of Luther by the universities of Cologne and Louvain, see Ep 1030 n7. Those chiefly responsible for the condemnation of Luther by the University of Paris were Guillaume Duchesne and Noël Béda; see Ep 1188:33–5 with nn15–16.
12 By the time the Louvain faculty condemned Luther's views (November 1519), Adrian had long since (1516) gone off to Spain in the service of Charles v, and he remained there until his election as Pope Adrian vi in 1522.
13 Nicolaas Baechem, known as Egmondanus (Ep 1254 n6)
14 Satisfaction is the part of the Catholic sacrament of penance (following contrition and confession) that requires the performance of meritorious acts to satisfy any temporal punishment for sin remaining after absolution from eternal punishment has been granted. Luther taught that private confession, though salutary, could not be forced, and that public, general confession was sufficient; that a penitent's faith in the priest's words of absolution brought complete forgiveness of all his sins; and that full satisfaction for all penalties due to sin had been made by the death of Christ on the cross.
15 See Ep 2443 n43.

cited nothing but laughter, a decree was procured from the emperor.[16] But it
was published prematurely, just as the bull of Leo was divulged before he 75
wished.[17] The sword was given to the Carmelite and to a colleague just like
him.[18] The torture chambers began. Finally, in Brussels three Augustinians
were publicly executed.[19] Do you want to know the result? That city, which
previously was untainted, began to have disciples of Luther, and not just a
few. Brutal tactics were used in Holland. Why say more? Wherever Aleandro 80
lit his fires, wherever the Carmelite exercised his cruelty, there you would say
the seed of heresies was planted.

    At this point the prince's court, becoming aware that the actions taken
by the frenzied monk were fomenting rebellion, disarmed him together with
his colleague,[20] and delegated the task to other theologians, who were not 85
monks and were a little more lenient.[21] Yet the court eliminated some and
drove out others through fear. In the meantime, as I exhorted one faction to
more lofty sentiments and another to more efficacious remedies, I became
a heretic to both of them. But to condense this long story into a few words,
the evil has crept on to this point and has heated up to such an extent that 90
it seems that it will end in armed conflict. If this happens – and I would not
wish to be a prophet of doom – I merely pray that the Lord will turn everything to a good end. If I had expected a reward from men, I would regret
having expended my efforts for nothing and receiving ignominy in return for
my deeds, but since I fought for Christ as the superintendent of the games, I 95
bear up with the ingratitude of mortals more easily. I am not so obtuse as not
to see by what kind of writings I could please the power of Rome. I would
prefer to heal heretics rather than receive approbation. I do not know to what
degree I am in agreement with them; one thing is certain, no name is hated
more than that of Erasmus. What, then, shall I say to your friend,[22] who I had 100
believed to be mine as well, who lashed me mercilessly with his tongue there

* * * * *

16 See Ep 1166 n20.
17 See Epp 1166:91 with n23, 1188:24–6.
18 In 1520 Charles v made Baechem (n13 above) assistant inquisitor of the
   Netherlands. He worked closely with Frans van der Hulst, who was appointed
   chief inquisitor in 1522 (Ep 1299 n22).
19 In July 1523; see Epp 1382:52–4, 1384 n2, 2188:62–72.
20 Baechem and Hulst were both removed as inquisitors in July 1524; see Ep 1466:14–
   16 with nn7–8.
21 On 17 June 1524 Clement vii confirmed Nicolas Coppin (Ep 1162 n18), member
   of the faculty of theology at Louvain, as Hulst's successor.
22 Johann Eck

in Augsburg before everyone, but especially the noblemen and magnates, and persuaded many; no wonder he won by default.

But Christ will see to these things. Leaving aside any complaints, I re- 105
turn to your letter. I see that this one thing remains, that the Lord in his inef-
fable wisdom will put an end to these evils, since up to now the stratagems
of men do nothing but aggravate the evil. Who would have expected such
a change in Oecolampadius? Even before putting on the cowl he was every
inch a monk, and he was somewhat annoying as a companion because of
his rigorous observance of rules.[23] Now it is no secret how he has changed. 110
I had not heard anything similar about Nachtgall; I congratulate him all the
same, even if I suspect that he will not accept my congratulations. I do not
know this Sperserus you mention.[24] I have come to know your exceptional
and unfailing piety not only from your letters but also from those written by
others,[25] and I admire the kindness of your master towards you,[26] and con- 115
gratulate you also on your success, that after sowing the word of God in the
same city for so many years you are called, with the good will of your colleagues, to a more eminent position. I know Johannes Faber the Dominican,
a man well versed in Thomistic theology, but amazingly cunning and treach-
erous. In Rome he began to rant against me, obviously so that he could be 120
reconciled to Cardinal Cajetan,[27] of whom he tells me so many bad things
that no buffoon could say more about another buffoon. It is only now that I
hear he has met his death: may the Lord have mercy on him.

From your previous letter I seem to perceive that your mind is not entirely free of the suspicion that I was not averse to these sects until the letter to 125
Vulturius appeared, and then the apology against Bucer's book.[28] But if you

* * * * *

23 Erasmus had known Oecolampadius since 1515–16, when the latter, working
as a corrector at the Froben press in Basel, assisted Erasmus with the edition of
the New Testament (Ep 373:78–83). Oecolampadius subsequently spent nearly
two years (April 1520–January 1522) as a monk in the Brigittine monastery in
Altomünster near Munich before making his way back to Basel (November
1522), where he spent the rest of his life; see Ep 1258 n4.
24 Johann Speiser; see Ep 2430 n14.
25 See Ep 2437:73–7.
26 See Ep 2402:18–20.
27 Tommaso de Vio of Gaeta, known as Cajetanus or Cajetan, general of the
Dominican order and the most formidable theological defender of papal authority in Rome (Ep 891:26n)
28 The 'previous letter' would presumably be Ep 2402, but there is nothing there
that justifies Erasmus' perception of the suspicion imputed to Kretz. For the letter to Vulturius and the apology against Bucer, see Epp 2358 n6 and 2371 n20.

had read Luther's *Enslaved Will* together with my *Diatribe*, which he tears
apart in the most hateful fashion, then the two *Hyperaspistes* with which I
answered him, and, in addition, my pamphlet against Leopold,[29] not to mention a multitude of letters in which I declare my feelings, you would have   130
had another opinion of me. If I was on their side, why was it necessary to
leave Basel, with great personal loss and great danger to my health? But they
say that in my books there are some things that resemble condemned beliefs. Although many have attempted with malicious ardour to prove this, no
one to this day has been able to bring forward any opinion that is openly at   135
variance with the articles of faith. Who has ever written anything with such
circumspection that an evil-minded person cannot attack it on the grounds
of scandal, or schism, or error, or temerity, or anything else? My aversion
to heresies is sufficiently proved by the fact that to this day, provoked in so
many ways by people like Dorp, Lee, Zúñiga, Béda, Cousturier, Clichthove,[30]   140
and many others, I have not shown myself as a leader or a member of any
sect, which I would surely have done if I did not fear God more than men.
In that way, at least, I could have taken revenge on certain persons in my
manner. But as I do not wish to be a heretic on account of hatred of any man,
so I would not wish, in order to please those who love the world, to obscure   145
the glory of Christ, at least not consciously. Theologians have enough to do
with impious doctrines without wrangling about things that sound bad, are
poorly expressed, are offensive, or come close to it and are suspect; to which
may be added those that are not understood and those distorted for the purposes of calumny. Quite a number of Béda's calumnious accusations stem   150
from his failure to understand the Latin. I am convinced that you are a just
man. Would that you had read my responses to Lee, Zúñiga, Sancho, the
Spanish monks, Béda, and others.[31] I suspect that you also are persuaded to a
certain degree that there are a hundred heretical opinions in my dialogues.[32] I
will gladly send you a copy if I find someone to whom I could safely entrust   155
it. You do not long for Chrysostom as much as he longs for buyers, since he
is for sale everywhere. The *Apophthegms* are no longer in my hands; they
will issue from the press within eight days. I laughed at Polyphemus, who

* * * * *

29 For the works referred to see Ep 2443 nn19 and 21.
30 See Epp 304 (Dorp), 765 (Lee), 2443 n13 (Clichtove); for the rest, see the follow-
    ing note.
31 Cf Ep 2443:95–8.
32 Ie the *Colloquies*, which had long been a favourite target of Erasmus' conserva-
    tive critics

always and everywhere is true to himself. He is suited for nothing better than
playing the buffoon in the court of some fat abbot. Farewell, dearest man in   160
the Lord.

Given at Freiburg, 11 March in the year 1531 from the birth of Christ

I confide this to the heart of a friend. Erasmus of Rotterdam in his own
hand.

I would have given a few books to the courier but he did not want to   165
be loaded down any further, saying that I had hired him to deliver letters,
not packages.

To the consummate theologian Matthias Kretz, preacher. In Augsburg

2446 / To Helius Eobanus Hessus   Freiburg, 12 March 1531

First published in the *Epistolae floridae*, this is a Erasmus' reply to a letter that is
not extant. The autograph rough draft is in the Royal Library at Copenhagen
(MS GKS 95 Fol, folio 221). For Eobanus see Ep 874.

TO EOBANUS HESSUS

Greetings. While it is true, my dear Eobanus, that letters received from those
with whom a pact of friendship was once joined properly under the auspices
of the Graces are a source of great pleasure, I am not in the habit of taking
offence if there is a temporary cessation of letters, especially of the kind that   5
merely fulfil the function of a greeting or a friendly communication. And I
am so overwhelmed by bundles of letters that sometimes I barely have the
leisure to read them. Therefore when you beg to be excused or even beg pardon, be assured that it is a waste of water.[1]

As to your complaint that both you, who teach humane letters, and   10
your city were exposed to scorn by an invidious remark,[2] I will defend myself
first before the city and then before you, but in a few words. I have always
entertained the highest regard for this city, as one of the most celebrated in

* * * * *

2446
1 Ie a waste of time, the reference being to a water-clock used as a timer; see
  Adagia I iv 73.
2 Eobanus, who spent the years 1526–33 teaching at the St Aegidius Gymnasium
  in Nürnberg, had taken offence at Erasmus' disparaging remarks about the
  school in his *Epistola ad fratres Inferioris Germaniae*; see CWE 78 286–7; cf Epp
  1901:21–3, 1945:2–3, 2006:19–20, 2008:39–42. For Erasmus' general contention
  that studies declined in Lutheran or Evangelical communities while it continued to flourish in Catholic places, see CWE 78 34, and see also Ep 1901:19–21,
  Allen Ep 2615:427–30.

Helius Eobanus Hessus
Woodcut by Albrecht Dürer after his 1526 drawing

Germany, and there was never any reason why I should feel otherwise. If you think it was dishonoured because it seems to be numbered among those cit- 15 ies that partially favour contentious beliefs, I did not expect that it would be offended if something was casually intimated in something I wrote that the city itself does not want to be kept secret and that rumour, in the published books of many writers, has spread further than this little book of mine will ever wander. There is no one who does not acknowledge as worthy of praise 20 that the magistracy has hired personnel to teach good letters there with ample remuneration. On the other hand, that the students are apathetic and for that reason the professors are also is no reproach to the city, whose responsibility it is to take thought for what is honourable. But the success of what they have decided is not within their jurisdiction. The magistrates provided what lay in 25 their power; only God can change men's minds. I had no desire to mention this, but you see that I was forced to do so if I did not want to be considered a liar, an appellation in which the one who provoked me took particular de-light. This very matter that I touched on lightly was mentioned more than once in letters written to me by Willibald,[3] a respected man in my opinion, 30 who has the city's interest at heart. Men of serious repute and also personal friends of yours brought this same news to Basel. Further, if you think it is an affront to the whole city every time a magistrate makes a mistake in his choice or does not achieve success, consider again and again how inequitable a law you prescribe for them, since you exact from men what is proper to God 35 alone, who cannot be deceived in his judgment or frustrated in the result. For that reason, my dear Eobanus, those offensive things you said, almost as if you struck me a blow, were not very appropriate. You say, 'Are you not ashamed of branding this celebrated city with a stigma as if it were maintain-ing lazy professors?' As if many cities do not sometimes maintain thieving 40 magistrates, ignorant bishops, priests depraved by lust, and finally pimps, usurers, and prostitutes. I do not accuse the magistracy, and if the magistracy does wrong, will the whole city immediately prosecute me for *lèse-majesté*? I have no doubt that the magistracy wishes you to have as many students as possible and the love of studies to burn brightly, but it is one thing to wish, 45 another to produce a result. In the meantime, however, it maintains them. I agree, but it either maintains them unwillingly or in hope of better success.

So much about the affront to the city. I come now to the professors and then to you, since you make complaints specifically in your own name. For my part, I do not know anyone among the professors except you and 50

* * * * *

3 Pirckheimer (Ep 2371); the letters are not extant.

Joachim,[4] both of whom I am accustomed to number among my friends, as I continue to number you, lest you think I was inspired by ill will in writing those things. I think the laziness and apathy of the students is also displeasing to you. How can the professors be fired with zeal if there are few students, and those lethargic and yawning? The criticism is not aimed at the 55 professors, but the students. Now suppose that one or two professors choose to quit their posts, what is this but normal human behaviour? When the students neglect their own interests, a professor should be pardoned if he refuses to give up his free time or his salary. You are angry with those who made these things known here by letter or by rumours. You do not do this to dem- 60 onstrate that they passed on groundless reports; you accuse them only of ingratitude and incivility, since they have shown little thanks for having been well treated there. If you compose some poems,[5] which will not be of much benefit to your city, or if Joachim undertakes something of that nature, what does this have to do with your function of teaching? I compose many works 65 every year, but this city does not provide any salary for that. You ask how I can excuse myself for inflicting such a wound on a moribund state of human learning that is scarcely sucking in a languid breath. But I wrote this precisely for the purpose of rousing the sluggish students to an enthusiasm for studies. When a teacher inveighs against the torpor of his students, what else is he 70 doing but attempting to make them more eager and rouse them from their inertia? I do not know to what degree studies are languishing elsewhere. In Louvain and Paris they are flourishing greatly. But what is the origin of this decline of studies? No doubt the indolence of certain people who proclaim themselves evangelicals. If you are grieved at this too, as I think you are, we 75 are of one accord. Perhaps you are afraid that if many become convinced that the professors there are leaving their jobs, fewer people will go there to study. Then it is your duty to inflame your students with the love of study. If that is done, youth will be more readily attracted. You should not be unduly offended by this observation, since the same complaint is heard from high- 80 ranking people about all cities where the evangelicals are in control. At any rate, I admire and praise you that in the midst of these conflicts you remain serene and do not burden good letters with any unpopularity.

* * * * *

4 Camerarius (Ep 1501), rector of the school
5 In 1526 Eobanus published *Elegiae de Schola Norica*, and in 1527 *Encomia duo, urbis Norembergae et Philippi Hessorum Principis*. In 1531 he collected his *Epicedia* into a volume that included 'Epitaphia epigrammata' by Camerarius. By May 1531 Erasmus had read the work (Allen Ep 2495:34). See Krause II 9, 18, 20–1, 101–2.

I come now to what you wish to discuss with me personally. You say
reproachfully that you have praised my name to the skies. While I confess . 85
that it is not displeasing to me to be praised by a man who himself is praised,[6]
it is likewise true (if I am not mistaken) that I have warmly proclaimed in
turn the excellent qualities of Eobanus, though perhaps not as copiously.
Glareanus recently told me that you had published a volume of epigrams, in
which there is frequent and honourable mention of me.[7] I have not yet had 90
the opportunity to see it. As to what you write about letters I sent to you that
were removed from my *Farrago*,[8] I do not remember it, nor do I quite understand. If they were removed, certainly it was not done out of any resentment
towards you. There has been no diminution of my good will towards you to
this day. It may be that when I was publishing that work, your letters were 95
not on hand or there was some other reason that I cannot now divine. I find
one letter of mine addressed to you in that collection.[9] To you it seems intolerable that there is no place for Eobanus in my *Ciceronianus*. If you think it is
just, my good friend, that whoever is left out there should take me to court,
there would be more than two hundred who would declare me guilty.[10] I did 100
not put together there a catalogue of those who had become famous by their
writings, but although ten examples would have sufficed for what is treated
there, I was generous with the number, which was not very wise, as it appears, nor was it very successful. Would that I had refrained altogether from
citing the names of living persons or of those recently deceased. Now some 105
complain that they were excluded, and others are chagrined that they were
mentioned, others that they were treated differently than they wished. The
category of names had to be limited; that could not be done without omitting many. But, you will say, if you had omitted the run-of-the-mill writers,

* * * * *

6 *Laudari a viro laudato*, a much-quoted saying from the early Roman dramatist
  Naevius, whose works survive in fragments quoted by later authors (in this
  case Cicero and Seneca); see *Remains of Old Latin* ed E.H. Warmington, 4 vols
  (Cambridge, MA 1935–40) II 118.
7 Cf Allen Ep 2495:42–4, where Erasmus mentions having been told of 'a huge
  volume of epigrams, in which there is frequent mention of me.' Krause makes
  no mention of such a volume.
8 Published in 1519
9 Ep 982
10 For the troubles that Erasmus had because of his failure to mention (or adequately praise) certain friends and acquaintances in the survey of fine Latin
   writers, see Ep 2008, and for a more complete survey of those troubles, see
   CWE 28 331–4.

you could have passed in review only those who were preeminent. Those,   110
however, who are barely mediocre seem preeminent in their own eyes. Lest
you think that it was owing to ill will that you were not mentioned, Zasius
and Beatus Rhenanus were also passed over, of whom the one I saw frequently and the other often wrote to me, so that I cannot plead forgetfulness
as an excuse. And yet they do not complain. I have always recognized that,   115
as Francesco Filelfo boasts about himself,[11] you are marvellously talented in
both types of writing but, as far as I know, there is nothing published except
your poems. Yet in my *Ciceronianus*, as you say, a certain number of poets
are named. Perhaps, but it is only in passing and contrary to the nature of
the subject,[12] so that this list, which deserves more pardon than praise, had   120
to be restricted rather than expanded. Yet as I write this I still do not know
whether Eobanus is there or not,[13] and if you had not complained, I would
have thought that you would certainly not have been left out, so far is it
from me purposely to have suppressed your name. And then, supposing I
had drawn up a list of writers, it would have been kinder to pardon forget-   125
fulness than to have doubts about my intention. For two years I had no letters from you, and I sensed that some friends had become rather prejudiced
against me because I opposed the new beliefs. I could have had such a suspicion of you, but I did not allow any adverse suspicion to enter my mind.
Even if it did insinuate itself, however, why would I have omitted Eobanus   130
when I mention Hutten and Alberto Pio,[14] each of whom has attacked me
with a bloodied pen? Lastly, Eobanus has resources within himself to make
himself known, so that there is hardly anyone who would have less need
of my eulogies. If anything has been written by you or by Joachim that has
not yet seen the light of publication,[15] I think I can be excused if I do not   135
know of it. Concerning your translation of Theocritus into Latin verse,[16] I am
amazed if you have succeeded in emulating that Sicilian charm.[17] I think you

* * * * *

11 Cf Allen Ep 2495:10–12.
12 The *Ciceronianus* is concerned primarily with prose writers.
13 He is not.
14 See CWE 28 427 (Hutten) and 420 (Pio).
15 An apparent reference to the *Epicedia*; see n5 above.
16 Eobanus' *Theocriti Idyllia 26* was published in 1531; see Krause II 89–95.
17 Born in Sicily, probably in Syracuse, Theocritus was a Hellenistic poet of the
    early third century BC who created the genre of pastoral or bucolic poetry. His
    poems were written in an elegant and literary Doric dialect, hence Erasmus'
    reference to his charm.

would find Homer easier to handle,[18] but in either case I am afraid that the
renown will not correspond to the labour involved. Those who know Greek
(for the knowledge of that language is spreading more widely from day to   140
day) prefer to hear such authors singing in their own language. I praise your
industry, however, and that will not be defrauded of its praise. We see that
men occupy themselves mostly with things that provide immediate usefulness, even if they treat a more humble subject matter. Thus the celebrity of
Perotti,[19] Rhodiginus,[20] Calepino,[21] Budé,[22] and Volaterranus.[23] 'But poets can- 145
not be mediocre,' as Horace said.[24] In this age even the greatest poets hardly
obtain as much praise as they deserve.

But I shall put an end to this excessively loquacious letter. May your
city fare as prosperously as I personally wish for it. I do not think I have
harmed it in any way, and I would not wish it to be harmed. If that rumour 150
is false which spread the news that the courses taught there are languishing,
and if what Willibald wrote is erroneous, I greatly rejoice and beg pardon for
my credulity. But if they are true, assume that the lack of enthusiasm of the
professors can be excused because of the apathy of the students. If my wish is
not fulfilled, at least be persuaded that Erasmus entertains friendly feelings 155
for you and Joachim and bears no resentment towards others whom I do not
know. And know that I had such trust in our friendship that whether my
letters to you were published or suppressed or whether Eobanus appeared
on the list or not, I thought you would be no less well disposed towards me.
Lastly, if I have been lacking in due regard in any way in this letter, it will eas- 160
ily be remedied on another occasion. Farewell and give my personal greeting
to your colleague Joachim.

At Freiburg im Breisgau, 12 March in the year 1531 from the birth of
Christ

* * * * *

18 *Homericae aliquot icones insigniores*, published in 1533; see Krause II 95–6.
19 Niccolò Perotti (1429–80); see Epp 117:49n, 1725 n4.
20 Lodovico Ricchieri of Rovigo (1469–1525); see Ep 469:10n.
21 Ambrogio Calepino (c 1435–c 1510); see Ep 1725 n3.
22 Guillaume Budé (1468–1540); see Ep 1725 n5.
23 Raffaele Maffei of Volterra (1451–1522), whom Allen confused with Raffaele
   Regio of Bergamo; cf Ep 2422 n16. Maffei was the author of a hugely popular
   encyclopedia, the *Commentaria urbana* (1506), which included a life of Jerome
   that Erasmus criticized in his *Vita Hieronymi*. Erasmus also found fault with
   Maffei's translations of Basil the Great (Epp 2611, 2617).
24 Horace *Ars poetica* 372

2447 / To Lazare de Baïf   Freiburg, 13 March 1531

First published in the *Epistola floridae*; the autograph rough draft is in the Royal
Library at Copenhagen (MS GKS 95 Fol, folio 218). For Baïf, orator (ie ambassador) of Francis I at Venice, see Ep 1962 introduction.

TO LAZARE BAÏF, ORATOR OF THE KING OF FRANCE
Your letter gave me extreme and even twofold pleasure,[1] most distinguished Baïf, partly because you perform an embassy in the name of your
most excellent prince, in a city, moreover, which besides innumerable other
blessings is flourishing in its number of learned men and rich libraries; and   5
partly because neither the dignity of this office nor occupation with many
affairs has made you forget Erasmus. I read those words in your letter, not
without a smile: 'To the great Erasmus,' a title that does not correspond at
all to this little frame, still less to my fortune, and least of all to my talents.
Yet it is a little more modest than the appellation that Zasius could not be   10
persuaded to refrain from using, calling me 'greatest of the great.'[2] In other
respects, though I admit that I often longed for a letter from you, after you
provided me with a taste of your literary talent in a single letter, yet never
did I accuse you of negligence, as you say, since even if you did not write
at all, I knew that you were never negligent either in affection or commit-   15
ment. You are a person who seems to me to be happier than the usual run .
of mankind because you recognize your good fortune. What more could
you ask from the gods than being able to reserve leisure for literature while
attending to the affairs of the king and, as you write, to enjoy leisure with
dignity.[3] The status of my own affairs, my dear Baïf, is diametrically oppo-   20
site to yours. For I have work without dignity, except that I consider mine
whatever good fortune befalls sincere friends. I rejoice also for the sake of
good letters, which Francis, best and greatest of kings, does not consider
it enough to defend against the aggressiveness of the philobarbarians but
elevates to such great dignity that by their own lustre they easily dispel the   25
obstreperous intriguers.

* * * * *

2447
1 No letter of Baïf to Erasmus survives.
2 Ep 317:1
3 On the concept of 'dignified leisure,' see Ep 2427 n6.

I am happy that you are thinking of becoming trilingual. I do not know Elias.[4] I had great fondness for Egnazio in Venice,[5] a man no less affable and honest than he is learned and, if I am not mistaken, he has returned my affection. I think I saw Lazzaro Bonamico in Padua at the home of Marcus Musurus, who already then in his youth gave proof of much learning and culture.[6] Would that some god would grant me the privilege of spending time in such auspicious company. For here the harbingers of events threaten us with an exceptionally destructive war unless some propitious divinity reverse the scene of human affairs.

Benoît[7] faithfully delivered your letter and also gave me a little commentary on the different kinds of vases,[8] which you promised previously in a letter to me, together with a little book on clothing that was corrected in your own hand in some places.[9] But since the appendix,[10] besides being carelessly copied out by your secretary, seemed to be incomplete, I did not dare to deliver it to the printers. Moreover, since he kept insisting that you had given the book to him so that, if I wished, it would be printed here, I read it through carefully, corrected any errors I found that had been made by the secretary, and passed it on to Froben. If Benoît deceived me, I will rely on your kindness and will try to avert the fault and the punishment. But if he did not deceive me and you were not offended, I will have reason to rejoice. Nevertheless, it rests with you to finish the work at your pleasure and have it

* * * * *

4 Elias Levita (Eliyahu ben Asher ha-Levi, 1469/70–1549), German Jew and Hebrew scholar who spent most of his adult life in Italy. In the period 1515–27 he lived at Rome in the household of Cardinal Egidio Antonini of Viterbo, copying and translating Hebrew and Aramaic manuscripts and acquainting himself with Italian humanism. Following the sack of Rome in 1527 he moved to Venice, where he had twice resided in earlier years and would remain for the rest of his life, working in association with the great printer of Hebrew texts Daniel Bomberg. The breadth of his scholarship and his willingness to share his learning with Christian students (both as teacher and as the author of grammatical and lexical works) brought him extensive contacts among the Christian Hebraists of the day.
5 See Ep 2448.
6 See Epp 1720 n10 (Bonamico), 223:5n (Musurus).
7 Benoît Vaugris, the Constance bookseller (Ep 1395 introduction). He travelled frequently on business to Venice, Milan, Basel, and even (as this letter indicates) Freiburg.
8 *De vasculis culinariis*, which Froben appended to the second edition of *De re vestiaria* in March 1531; see Ep 1962:15–18 with n5.
9 A copy of the first edition of *De re vestiaria* (Basel: J. Bebel, March 1526)
10 See n9 above.

printed there. I pray you to relay my fond greetings to Lazzaro in my name. I shall write to Egnazio right away.[11] Farewell, illustrious sir.

Given at Freiburg im Breisgau, 13 March of the year 1531 from the birth   50
of Christ

2448 / To Giambattista Egnazio   Freiburg, 13 March 1531

The autograph rough draft of this letter, which was first published in the *Epistolae floridae*, is in the Royal Library at Copenhagen (MS GKS 95 Fol, folio 219). For Egnazio, the Venetian humanist whom Erasmus had known and admired for many years, see Ep 2105 introduction.

ERASMUS TO HIS FRIEND EGNAZIO, GREETING

It was inconvenient, not to say unfortunate, for me that because of the carelessness of your servant you did not have my letter,[1] to which you were preparing to answer meticulously, at hand. Nothing could have been more pleasant than a prolonged conversation with my friend Egnazio. I never be-   5
came reconciled with Budé,[2] so that you need not congratulate me for something without reason. May God bring it about that I am never reconciled with him. My relations with him were never anything more than what can be expected of a good and appreciative man towards a man renowned for his excellent learning and one who has deserved well of studies and of all   10
scholars. If there was some offence, which I think did not exist at all or was insignificant, it surely did not come from me, but was engendered by the whispers and bewitchments of venomous tongues. Budé is a man who is too upright and cultivated to take up his pen hatefully against anyone even if he were viciously attacked. And I am one who could only reluctantly vent my   15
anger on such men even if I were severely provoked, except if someone says that I am not a Christian. In answer to this one insult I cannot and should not be indulgent.

You acutely perceive that it is my fate to have been put to the test by the bitter enmities of many people, although it was always my desire that   20

* * * * *

11 Ep 2448

2448
1 This letter appears to be Erasmus' answer to one written by Egnazio in response to Ep 2302.
2 See Ep 2302:1–8.

my pen would not be red with the blood of anyone. A good indication of that is that among my numerous *apologiae* there is not one invective. I endure having been born for this fate more lightly than if I had extorted as many *apologiae* from people I had attacked. It is not permitted to fight against the gods. We must obey that supreme stage director at whose pleasure the play   25
of human life is performed. He leads onto the stage those whom he wishes and in whatever role he wishes. If he wished that you be Micio and I be Demea,[3] each of us must accept our role. The Lord knows what is expedient for each of us. I have more enemies than I would wish, I admit, but on the other hand I have not a few friends who stand out for their dignity, authority,   30
learning, and moral integrity, and to this day no one has caused me trouble unless he was raving mad, envious, presumptuously ignorant, or seeking to secure glory through calumny, in which some succeeded. Hardly anyone else was richer in troupes of friends before this contention about dogmas, in which I would have liked to remain silent, but it was not permitted. Willingly   35
or unwillingly, I was thrust into the gladiatorial arena, and it seems that I will never obtain my discharge from this service, although there is nothing to which my temperament is more averse. My condition would have been more tolerable if I had had to fight against one battle line of the enemy. Now, as I am fighting against one squadron at close quarters, there rise up from behind   40
me the very ones I am fighting for, so this type of combat calls for a Geryon, or the hundred-handed hero that once existed,[4] or at least someone from that race of men of whom Aristophanes spoke in Plato with two faces, four arms, and the same number of legs.[5] So that you will not suspect, Egnazio, that this is owed to a defect of my nature, I shall relate the story from the beginning.   45

Quite some time ago there was an incredible struggle in our regions between those who favoured good literature and the Greek language and rabbis in disguise who preferred to mix heaven and earth rather than to seem not to know something.[6] In this affair I showed myself to be, if not a standard-bearer, at least a stalwart soldier. When this conflict was at the   50
height of its passion, the difference of opinions arose by which we now see the world shaken, and I fear that unless God averts the evil we shall see more

* * * * *

3 Two elderly brothers in Terence's play *Adelphi*: Micio is an easy-going, well-to-do bachelor, while Demea is a frugal married farmer.
4 Geryon was a mythical monster with three heads. The hundred-handed hero was Briaraeus, who also had fifty heads. See Virgil *Aeneid* 7.661 and 6.287.
5 Plato *Symposium* 189
6 Erasmus frequently used 'rabbi' as a term of abuse for scholastic theologians; see Ep 1126 n45 and cf Ep 2045:166–7.

dreadful things. At this point many (not to say all) of those who had served
in the camp of the Muses joined forces with the one who was the originator
of the new faction. Since I refused to do this, I ran the risk of becoming an   55
outcast and without friends. They remained fair-minded enough, however,
as long as they hoped that I would, with prudent dissimulation, join their
ranks at the propitious moment. But when, unequal to this climate of hatred,
I was forced to unsheathe my sword vigorously against that faction and their
leader, all those who had had previously been my sworn friends began to be   60
my most vehement enemies. In the meantime I could not remain kindly disposed towards those against whom I had stood to defend zealously languages and good letters. They attempted to persuade the world that this religious
conflagration could not be put out unless humane letters and its supporters
were eliminated, among whom they attribute great influence to Erasmus.   65

Thus it came about that, destitute of friends, I am the target of all kinds
of weapons from both sides, so vulnerable and devoid of status or authority that I am harmed by bedbugs with impunity, except that up to now I
have held my ground in one way or another, thanks to the emperor. But I
would rather do that than give my name to a sect or flatter those who un-   70
der the name of Christ strive for nothing more than to prepare and consolidate for themselves a world tyranny. The taste of the blood of peasants was
so sweet to them that, thirsting for the blood of all Germany, they leave no
stone unturned in order to incite both Germanies, both Upper and Lower,[7]
to internal warfare. They do not see that if that happens it will be no less   75
fatal to the church than devastating for the people. They themselves in the
meantime, spectators sheltered from the public calamity, will sing with Nero
of the capture of Troy.[8] There is one among you who is the chief instigator
of these evils,[9] neglecting nothing in his underground machinations. All his
preparatory measures have a disastrous war as their objective. If my advice   80
had been heeded at the beginning, this evil would either have been put to
sleep or certainly would not have spread so widely. Now nothing remains
to us but first of all to change our lives for the better and ask help from the
Lord, not from arms. Under cover of this war the world will be inundated by
Jews and heretics. May the Lord open the eyes of princes. When you speak   85
of my simplicity, most prudent sir, you have touched my sore point precisely.
Whatever misfortunes have been my lot throughout my life I credit to my

* * * * *

7 On Upper and Lower Germany, see Ep 1998 n6.
8 Suetonius *Nero* 38
9 Aleandro

simplicity, which, even after my exposure to so many evils, I am not able to unlearn. And although sometimes I can give good counsel to others, by some fatal force or other I do not cease judging others by my own character.   90

I am most grateful to you, my dear Egnazio, who are so attached to me that you are concerned for my health, who have such a high opinion of me that you think it is of the greatest importance for the church that Erasmus be safe, in the one case demonstrating your piety, in the other your benevolence. Concerning the three points you mention, it is not without pleasure that I re- 95 member the old friendship that existed between us in Venice; as for eminent virtue, I desire it rather than avow it; I admit to some learning, but far from being outstanding it is less than average. Good letters have flourished to such an extent that Erasmus would have been classed among the illiterate if these conflicts of opinion, running crosswise, had not thrown everything into 100 disorder. Zasius is well and returns your greetings and Henricus Glareanus together with him, a man learned in many fields, who is teaching good letters here to great acclaim.[10]

About Chrysostom I see that you were deceived by friends.[11] If any-thing materializes, I ask that it be sent to Froben. The work has already ap- 105 peared, but they are preparing to add another volume as soon as that will be possible.[12] Farewell.

At Freiburg im Breisgau, 13 March in the year 1531 from the birth of Christ

2449 / To Jacques Toussain   Freiburg, 13 March 1531

First published in the *Epistolae floridae*, the autograph rough draft of this letter is in the Royal Library at Copenhagen (MS GKS 95 Fol, folio 223). It appears to be Erasmus' response to the letter, not extant, in which Toussain responded to Ep 2421. For Toussain, who in 1530 had been appointed a royal lecturer in Greek at the new Collège de France, see Ep 2421.

ERASMUS OF ROTTERDAM TO JACQUES TOUSSAIN, GREETING
I have always thought it to be a good omen that when there was but the faintest suggestion of languages and good letters here, it was greeted with

* * * * *

10 On Zasius and Glareanus see Ep 2302:32–7.
11 Erasmus had asked Egnazio to assist in the publication of Chrysostom by send-ing manuscripts; see Epp 1623:11–14, 2302:29–30.
12 See Ep 2359 introduction.

hateful protests and impassioned conspiracies. For from such beginnings
excellent things always arise, destined to reign for a long time. I may not   5
have been the first, but I was certainly among the first in our regions to suffer the hissings of this serpent. I am sorry, my dear Toussain, that some of
this was emitted forcefully in your direction as well. But that this ill will,
which is bound to be alleviated little by little by the simple passage of time,
may be more quickly dissipated is partly our responsibility, in that we in-   10
sinuate ourselves into everyone's favour through our friendliness, courtesy,
and kind services. Busleyden's college in Louvain barely survived, so widespread was the conspiracy of those who were persuaded that this expansion
of studies would be prejudicial to their machinations.[1] I therefore advised
the professors not to say a word against the professors of other disciplines,   15
but by their affability of manner and their zeal in teaching simultaneously
attract youth and make irreconcilable enemies burn with resentment, for
there is nothing more beautiful or efficacious than this kind of vengeance.
They obeyed me, and after a few months they found out through experience
that this advice was beneficial and successful. Your prudence and your in-   20
tegrity do not need that advice. And apart from this, your struggle with the
hydra will be much easier, partly because the splendour of good letters has
already dispersed for the most part the clouds of arrogant ignorance, and
partly because you have as the openly declared guide of this marvellous
enterprise such a great prince, no less humane and generous than powerful,   25
who seems to have thoroughly recognized how much this will accrue to the
lustre of his glory and how much profit it will bring to his entire realm. The
college at Louvain has as its founder Jérôme Busleyden, a man worthy of
a great fortune, which would not have been lacking if he had lived, but he
died poor, both in authority and substance, with the result that the salaries   30
were barely sufficient to sustain the professors. Nevertheless, no gratitude
can adequately requite his memory. He dedicated all that he possessed to
this enterprise. In addition, it seems to be a very sensible decision that a salary be awarded only to the professors of two languages, Greek and Hebrew,
since Latin has been flourishing for so long that it does not have need of a   35
special professor. The king in his royal generosity has provided that two
professors for each language be appointed and that they be remunerated
with a far from niggardly salary, by means of which they can discharge the
office delegated to them not only in a suitable manner but also with dignity.

* * * * *

2449
1 Busleyden's college was the Collegium Trilingue; see Epp 691, 2456.

On this account, my dear Toussain, I consider France much more fortunate   40
than if all of Italy had been added to its jurisdiction. You have been allotted
beautiful Sparta; you need only put it in good order, vying with one another,
each according to his own capacities.[2]

With regard to your devotion to me, it is not necessary that you pledge
your word with an oath or introduce a guarantor. As the simple formula   45
'among good men good conduct is proper'[3] sufficed for men of old, so
among Christians nothing is required but two syllables, 'yea' and 'nay.'[4] In
what you write concerning reconciliation with Budé, I admire your solicitous
good will, but I should not wish hundreds of learned men to be persuaded
that I have been reconciled to Budé, towards whom I never had feelings of   50
animosity and never will unless some god deprive me of this frame of mind.
There is no friendship among mortal men so fastened by every tie that some
little cloud does not sometimes obscure it. No one has persuaded me or ever
will persuade me that Budé, a man as kind as he was learned, would have
been offended by my *Ciceronianus*.[5] If there was some displeasure, it was the   55
venom of some evil tongue. Some instigators were reported to me, but I do
not have time to listen to accusations, especially since now as an old man I
am hastening on to another destination. My sentiments towards Budé have
never been other than what is due an upright, learned man and one who has
acquired great merit in the world of letters. It seemed to me that it was more   60
prudent not to make overtures to him by letter. For if some god changed
his disposition so that from benevolence he turned to hostility, one who is
innocent should not make entreaty. If the offence is like those that often occur among friends, without doing harm to the bond of friendship, it was his
place to complain and mine to justify myself. And yet I would be willing to   65
forgo my rights somewhat if I knew with certainty what grieved him. Since I
cannot divine this, I fear that if I try to stroke the racehorse I may touch a sore
point without knowing it and he will kick back on every side.[6] If he was not
offended, it is his turn to answer two letters which, as you say, he has kept

* * * * *

2 Cf *Adagia* II v 1: *Spartam nactus es, hanc orna* 'Sparta is your portion, do your best
   for her.'
3 This was a legal phrase used in documents issued by the praetor to plaintiffs in
   legal proceedings; Cicero quotes it in *Ad familiares* 7.12.12.
4 Matt 5:37
5 See Ep 1948 introduction.
6 Horace *Satires* 2.1.20: '[If] you rub a horse the wrong way it will lash out right
   and left with its hooves in self-defence.'

for two years without breaking the seal.[7] But whatever this ulcer is, if there is   70
any, I think the best doctor will be the propitious moment. I am not lacking
people to whom I write back, willy-nilly, and Budé does not lack those who
lead the horse to the plain.[8]

I sent greetings in your name to Henricus Glareanus,[9] who I think will
write to you. There you have, I think, my answers to almost all the points in   75
your letter. During the last few days, during my walk after supper, a servant
reads aloud some passages from Budé's letters whenever I do not have an
agreeable companion to keep me in a good frame of mind.[10] I strongly approve of your decision to add notes to most of the letters. In that way they can
be read by more people and with more profit, and can better survive the pass-   80
ing of time, since their chief value is their usefulness. Among them are letters
to Pierre Lamy,[11] whom the Pole Jan Łaski, a young man of great renown in
his country and of extraordinary learning, brought with him to Basel.[12] Lamy
came just as he used to be except for his mode of dress.[13] I have never seen a
person of more blameless moral conduct, in whom you could not find a single   85
fault except that he abhorred arrogance and insolence to excess. After a few
months he began to become weak, and I could not conjecture any other reason
for it except the cold, to which he was not accustomed, especially because his
neck and legs were exposed to the elements more than was usual. And during this time he continued to add water to the crude German wine he drank.   90

* * * * *

7 Ep 2047 is the only surviving letter of Erasmus to Budé written after the publication of the *Ciceronianus*. Budé reportedly never even opened it; see Ep 2047
   introduction.
8 Ie those by whom 'a man is encouraged to do the thing he is best at and most
   enjoys doing'; see *Adagia* I viii 82.
9 Epp 440, 2098 n1
10 Budé's *Opus epistolarum* (cf Ep 2379 n73) was published by Josse Bade at Paris
   in February 1531, with preface and notes by Toussain.
11 Very little is known of Pierre Lamy (d 1525). Like his friend François Rabelais,
   he was a Franciscan Observant at Fontenay-le-Comte. In 1522 he fled to a
   Benedictine abbey near Orléans in search of more freedom to pursue liberal
   studies. By this time he had already corresponded with Budé, four letters from
   whom to him are included in the volume in question. He also was acquainted
   with Conradus Pellicanus, warden of the Franciscan house at Basel, and may
   have been the guest of the Basel Franciscans at some time when Erasmus was
   present there. Cf n13 below.
12 This would have been in the spring of 1525; see Ep 1593 n18.
13 Ie he had abandoned the Franciscan habit. This remark indicates that Erasmus
   must have made his acquaintance at some point while he was still a Franciscan.

His fate was that which Caesar Augustus used to wish for himself, a sweet death.[14] His body was buried in the Franciscan monastery, as a layman;[15] I hope his soul lives among the Seraphic spirits. If perhaps you did not know this, I wished you to know it. Farewell. Give my greetings to your colleague, Danès,[16] but especially to Budé, if you think it proper.   95

At Freiburg im Breisgau, 13 March AD 1533

2450 / To Simon Pistoris   Freiburg, 14 March 1531

This letter was first published in the *Epistolae floridae*. For reasons that cannot be explained, it was not included in any edition of Erasmus' works until Allen's edition of the correspondence. For Simon Pistoris, chancellor of Duke George of Saxony, see Ep 1125 n6.

ERASMUS OF ROTTERDAM TO SIMON PISTORIS, GREETING

Although I always understood that I was indebted for many reasons to the good will of the best of princes towards me, I have now become more obligated to him because, via the eminent man Julius Pflug,[1] he has scrupulously made certain that I may continue to pursue my studies in peace, protect-   5 ed from the excesses of that perfidious Thraso.[2] Though this obligation lies heavily upon me, nevertheless I acknowledge my debt to the most cordial good will of both the duke and Julius Pflug, whose letter gives me such delight that I think this evil has turned out well for me, since on account of it I have found a friend so learned and so generous as I hardly thought existed   10 in all of Germany.[3] What monsters the earth brings forth and nurtures in the midst of such excellent men! Here a plague has raged cruelly and continues to rage; everything is enormously expensive, and prices increase daily.[4] But if war breaks out, it will be all over for us. There are those who incite princes to this so that Germany will be drenched with the blood of its citi-   15 zens. Perhaps some Roman Nero is singing the sack of Troy from his high

* * * * *

14 Suetonius *Augustus* 99
15 Ie without the 'Seraphic funeral,' clad in the Franciscan habit, that would have been afforded to a member of the order; see Ep 2441 n18.
16 Pierre Danès (Ep 2044)

2450
1 Ep 2395
2 Heinrich Eppendorf (Ep 2384 n15)
3 The letter is not extant; Ep 2451 is Erasmus' answer to it.
4 Cf Ep 2403:63 with n13.

look-out tower.[5] My wish is that Christ may inspire salutary deliberations in the minds of princes.

It happened by good fortune that the noble youth Andreas von Könneritz made his way here with his brother, Erasmus.[6] I had Andreas together with his brother Christoph as guests at my table for some time;[7] would that it could have been longer! The plague, particularly noxious in this region,[8] separated us. Here both of them applied themselves whole-heartedly to the literature of your discipline,[9] men of such integrity that not even evil persons dared to speak ill of them. May all others bring lustre to the images of their ancestors through such distinctions. I have no doubt that you will preserve steadfastly your previous loyal feelings towards me. Farewell.

At Freiburg im Breisgau, 14 March AD 1531

2451 / To Julius Pflug   Freiburg, 14 March 1531

For this letter, which was first published in the *Epistolae floridae*, there are two manuscripts. One, Erasmus' autograph rough draft, is in the Royal Library at Copenhagen (MS GKS 95 Fol, folio 216). The other, the letter actually sent, written in a secretary's hand but corrected and signed by Erasmus, is in the Universitäts- und Forschungsbibliothek Erfurt/Gotha (Chart A 385 folio 34). In preparing the letter for publication Erasmus removed lines 49–55.

For Julius Pflug, see Ep 2395. This is Erasmus' reply to a letter from Pflug that is no longer extant. Pflug's reply to this letter is Ep 2492.

ERASMUS OF ROTTERDAM TO JULIUS PFLUG, GREETING
If we had undertaken a contest of eloquence between us, Julius, preeminent glory of Germany, the learned facility and elegant charm of your letter and the felicitous and continuous flow of your Ciceronian diction would have dissuaded me from answering. That this is true, and lest you think it is empty

* * * * *

5 See Ep 2448 n8.
6 Erasmus von Könneritz (d 1563) was the younger brother of Andreas and Christoph von Könneritz (see following note). Little is know of his life at this time. He did not matriculate at Freiburg, and it is not known where he studied law. In the 1540s and '50s he was a jurist and diplomat in the service of the elector of Saxony.
7 For Andreas and Christoph von Könneritz and their stay with Erasmus in 1529 see Ep 2274 introduction.
8 Ep 2426 n3
9 Law

rhetoric, I would not hesitate to swear on what I hold as most sacred. But since the anxious care to polish one's style does not become my age or a theologian, it did not seem right to me to affect what I could in no way attain, even if I were to strain every nerve. Therefore, relying on your good will, I have in my usual manner dared to besmear the page with whatever came 10 spontaneously to the tip of my pen. I do this now with an even better excuse, since I have to write sixty letters at the same time,[1] some among them the size of a substantial volume.[2]

In return for the praise I address to you in view of your merits, there is no reason to thank me or extol my kindness, since it is more just that both of 15 us be thankful to God, to whose munificence is owed whatever is worthy of praise in us. I pray him that he deign to increase his good will towards you in ever greater measure, since you share generously all that has hitherto been given to you with all your friends and especially with the commonwealth, clearly conscious for what use he lent you so many brilliant gifts of intelli- 20 gence and character. When you make little of your talents, you only succeed in making me have an even higher opinion of you, because I perceive the mark of true virtue, devoid of all pretence, which pays no regard to men's praises but blushes before them like a chaste virgin. There is no surer safe-guard of true talent. When you promise to make return for my regard for 25 you, if not by other virtues, at least by gratitude and fidelity, I do not accept the word gratitude, but I willingly hear the word fidelity, although I would never have doubted it, even without your promise.

Your testimony to the good will and favourable disposition of the prince towards me was more pleasing than necessary.[3] I have long experienced and 30 verified not only his good will but also his loyalty. For that reason there is nothing of which I am more convinced than that whatever he did in this af-fair proceeded from a loving heart. And I consider that I am not one bit less indebted to his Highness because things turned out differently. One must judge the intention, not the result. When you strive so diligently, therefore, 35 to persuade me that the illustrious duke in defending my old age from these mobs had nothing else in mind than taking thought for the tranquillity of my studies and, as you say, the public welfare, you take upon yourself a task that does you honour, excellent sir, but is unnecessary.

* * * * *

2451
1 Cf Epp 2461:2–3, 2466:247–9, and Allen Epp 2481:3, 2519:1–6.
2 This is an apt description of Ep 2465.
3 The reference is to the efforts of Duke George of Saxony, assisted by Pflug, to restrain Heinrich Eppendorf from pursuing legal action against Erasmus for defamation; see Epp 2395, 2400–1, 2406, 2450, 2452.

As to your writing that this was done so that, being deprived of the   40
grounds for a court case, he would not give me any trouble, or if he did, it
could not be done without risk of injury to himself: to these things and others
like them I do not think you expect an answer, if in fact the pages with which
I answered your previous letter were delivered to you,[4] or if you thought
them worth reading. I am not unaware that noble spirits are not attracted   45
by this kind of dispute. But if I cannot convince anyone of the monstrous
escapades of Thraso,[5] what is left to me but to arm myself with the shield of
the gospel, patience?[6] I am contending with so many monsters that my heart
has become inured to it. Yet in all of this he has derived from your letters and
those of the princes the greatest benefit he could wish for. What more glori-   50
ous thing could happen to him than that he should seem so important that
such a great prince and you, a man celebrated for your exceptional abilities
and enjoying great popularity and wielding great influence with monarchs,
must exert yourselves to placate the feeling of an insignificant nonentity? He
tried to incite other learned men to write letters to me about this affair.[7] But it   55
is repugnant to mention these buffooneries. I was born with this destiny, that
I find peace in the friendship of those men who are similar to me, who are
not so few as many people would like to believe. I prize more highly the acquisition of your close friendship, if you will believe me, than if I was given
the richest benefice. I do not think that this friendship must be sustained by   60
many services. It will be sufficient that it be revived from time to time by
an exchange of letters. If, however, there is anything in which I can oblige
you or yours, there is nothing within my power that I will not do gladly
and willingly, whether you apprise me of it or the occasion presents itself. I
most assuredly subscribe readily to the rule you propose, namely that in our   65
friendship, as it was initiated under legitimate auspices and just conditions,
the reciprocal exchange of compliments, apologies for an inadequate style,
and other things of that sort will be abolished. Although I think it is superfluous to ask that you commend me to the illustrious prince, I still pray that you
do so for no other reason than because I eagerly desire it. Farewell.   70
   At Freiburg im Breisgau, 14 March AD 1531

* * * * *

4 See Ep 2395 n4.
5 Erasmus' favourite epithet for Eppendorf
6 According to Eph 6:16, the shield of the gospel is faith; patience is named in Col
   3:12 as one of the virtues with which God's chosen ones should clothe themselves.
7 The passage 'Yet in all of this he has derived ... to write letters to me about this
   affair' was deleted from the published text of the letter.

Andreas von Könneritz was the one responsible for my writing to you more freely, a young man of excellent lineage, with a rigorous and superb training in the law. He is well known to me since he and his brother Christoph lived with me for a while,[8] and he is thus bound to me by the sacred bond of 75 sharing table and salt.[9] I think you also know him, or if you do not, I beseech you to get to know him better. Again, farewell.

Desiderius Erasmus of Rotterdam. I have signed this in my own hand.

To the most famous Master Julius Pflug

2452 / To Duke George of Saxony Freiburg, 15 March 1531

This letter was first published in the *Epistolae floridae*. There are two manuscripts: the autograph rough draft in the Royal Library at Copenhagen (MS GKS 95 Fol, folio 217); and the letter actually sent, in a secretary's hand but corrected and signed by Erasmus, in the Universitäts- und Forschungsbibliothek Erfurt/ Gotha (Chart A 379 folio 45).

TO GEORGE, DUKE OF SAXONY

Cordial greetings. For a long time now, having experienced numerous attestations of the fervent good will of your illustrious Highness towards me, I have known and stated openly that I was indebted to you for many important reasons. But recently you have made me even more indebted to you for 5 more weighty reasons, two in particular. One, as I learned from a letter of the reverend lord Christoph von Stadion, bishop of Augsburg, is that you deigned to declare your good will towards Erasmus before leading members of the church, among whom were Cardinal Campeggi and the Cardinal of Liège.[1] I think no small amount of distinction and dignity has been added to 10 my name by this testimony. The other reason is that you showed such devotion and solicitude to ensure quiet leisure for my old age and my studies, sheltered from that person who takes delight in creating trouble for me and clamours against me in written commentaries.[2]

* * * * *

8 See Ep 2450 n7.
9 *Adagia* IV ix 80

2452
1 This would have been during the Diet of Augsburg in the summer of 1530, at which Cardinal Lorenzo Campeggi was the papal legate (Ep 2366). The Cardinal of Liège, Erard de la Marck (Ep 2382) would have been there in his capacity as prince-bishop of Liège. The letter from Stadion is not extant.
2 See Ep 2451.

The zeal of your Highness, no matter how other things turn out, has   15
brought me one great advantage, because on this occasion I have won the
friendship of a man endowed with every honour, Julius Pflug.[3] Would that
Germany had many more men like him. As for myself, calm is for many reasons
not only much to be desired, but also necessary. But if God, the stage director
of this human play, has assigned me this role, I must play the part. It is in this   20
arena, I see, that I must die. Even if that one individual should desist,[4] not a year
goes by without the false Evangelicals hurling two or three books at my head.[5]

I could easily stomach private annoyances if the general situation of the
church were as I would wish it. Italy has been pacified, France is bound to the
emperor by a Hercules' knot, as they say.[6] In Spain there is no tempest. The   25
English matter about the divorce will easily be settled without a tumult, as I
hear and as far as I know the king's temperament.[7] A truce with the Turks is
hoped for, which I think will be expedient not only for the common good but
also for the propagation of the Christian religion. If God would deign to cure
this German fever without civil wars, we could hope for a golden age. We   30
have been afflicted for so long by scourges, wars, uprisings, pestilences that
constantly change their appearance, and by the excessive price of things and
even their scarcity. The Lord does not usually remain angry to the end, but in
his anger remembers his mercy. If only we would turn back to him with all
our heart, fixing in him alone the anchor of our hope.   35

It was not my intention to interrupt your Highness with this letter, but
a well-born young man freely offered his services. He is a dear friend of mine
because of both his exceptional learning and his moral integrity, well known
to me because he lived with me under the same roof. His name is Andreas
von Könneritz, who with his brother Erasmus is returning to his native city,   40
leaving a second brother, Christoph, here, and he too employs his talents diligently and successfully in the writings of the jurists.[8] I pray Christ, greatest
and best, to preserve your illustrious Highness healthy and flourishing for
us and the commonwealth.

At Freiburg im Breisgau, 15 March AD 1531   45
Servant of your most eminent Highness, Desiderius Erasmus of Rot-
terdam. I signed this with my own hand.
To the illustrious Prince George, Duke of Saxony, etc

* * * * *

3 Ep 2395
4 Eppendorf
5 See Ep 2358:14–23.
6 *Adagia* I ix 48. The reference is to the Peace of Cambrai of August 1529 (Ep 2366 n11).
7 See Ep 2410 n25.
8 See Ep 2450 nn6–7.

2453 / To Caspar Ursinus Velius   Freiburg, 15 March 1531

This letter was first published in the *Epistolae floridae*. For Ursinus Velius see Ep 2383 n3.

ERASMUS OF ROTTERDAM TO URSINUS VELIUS, GREETING

Do you have the time to hear some news? Here it is. Although I know that it is thought to be impossible for an old man to change his language, yet I am thinking about changing my style. First I applied myself to study the example of Budé's sentence structure. I read most of his letters, which are skil- 5 fully elaborated.[1] I exerted myself to the utmost, but my attempt was without success. Now I am totally involved in imitating Cicero. You will say, 'What happened?' I was stimulated to do this by the letters of three of the most accomplished masters of style of our times, Jacopo Sadoleto, Pietro Bembo, and Julius Pflug.[2] The last-named I acquired as a friend recently, obtaining a great 10 good from an evil occurrence.[3] Their style is so similar that you would say they were taught and brought up in the same school since the time their nails were soft.[4] Immortal God! What lucidity of speech, what ease of expression, what soundness of signification, what overall coherence, how everything flows smoothly like a limpid stream, with no irregularities, with no whirl- 15 pools to hold up the reader! I can admire with all my heart such Ciceronians and wish that I could equal them.[5] But I think it is more advisable for a sexagenarian to abstain from these discussions for fear that I be thrown off the bridge by a turbulent crowd of youths.[6]

I congratulate your prince and mine on the attainment of the illustrious 20 title of king of the Romans;[7] may his revenues be commensurate with it. I

* * * * *

2453
1 See Ep 2379 n73.
2 Erasmus and Sadoleto had been exchanging letters at least since 1524; for the latter's surviving letters to Erasmus, see Epp 1511, 2272, 2385. Erasmus had already been favourably impressed by Bembo's published letters before their personal correspondence began in 1529; see Ep 2106 introduction. The only surviving letter of Bembo to Erasmus written before the date of this letter is Ep 2144. The surviving correspondence with Pflug begins with Ep 2395, but the first of his surviving letters to Erasmus is Ep 2492.
3 See Epp 2400, 2406.
4 Ie since earliest childhood (*Adagia* I vii 52)
5 For Ursinus Velius' interest in Ciceronian style and the *Ciceronianus*, see Epp 2008:15–34, 2313:57–65, 2517.
6 Ie for fear of being consigned as an old man to idleness and uselessness; see *Adagia* I v 376.
7 See Ep 2384 n7.

praise your loyalty to the commonwealth, which you see severely diminished in strength by so many disasters and pestilences and therefore do your
best to repair this loss, not without Theseus,[8] that is to say, your new wife,
who helps you as much as she can in her role of woman.[9] There is some hope   25
that there will be a truce between the Christian monarchs and the emperor of
the Turks.[10] Italy is calm. I maintain very close relations with France. I predict
from many indications that the English affair will be settled in a short time
without conflict.[11] Spain is quiet. If it will be possible to keep Germany free of
armed conflict, there is hope for a golden century. Farewell.   30

15 March at Freiburg im Breisgau AD 1531

2454 / To Johann von Vlatten   Freiburg, 15 March 1531

This letter was first published in the *Epistolae floridae.* The surviving manuscript is a copy, described by Allen as in a 'crabbed' sixteenth-century (or possibly seventeenth-century) hand, in the Bibliothèque Royale in Brussels that
purports to be a copy of the original. (For further details see Allen's introduction.) The manuscript bears the date 1533, which is clearly incorrect. The date
in the *Epistolae floridae,* which was published in September 1531, is 15 March
1531, which is consistent with the reference (lines 7–9) to Quirinus, who was in
Erasmus' service until mid-April 1531.

For Johann von Vlatten, see Ep 2360.

ERASMUS TO JOHANN VON VLATTEN, GREETING
I write to you more seldom because, like Diana Panagaea flying about through
all regions,[1] you pass time sometimes among the gods above and sometimes
among the gods below. I am too occupied to waste time writing letters. One
thing is without doubt, that wherever in the world Vlatten is, there is an impor-   5
tant patron and friend of Erasmus. Let me know what you are doing. You will

* * * * *

8 Ie not without the help of a partner (*Adagia* I v 7)
9 Ursinus Velius had been married in 1529.
10 See Ep 2384 n10.
11 Ie the matter of King Henry's divorce from Catherine of Aragon; see Ep 2410 n25.

2454
1 In *Adagia* II ix 47 Erasmus says that because the goddess Artemis (Diana) was
   an inveterate wanderer the epithet 'Panagaia Artemis' was applied to anyone
   addicted to travel and thus unreliable. But the word *panagaia* (taken to mean
   'over the whole earth') does not exist in Greek, and Artemis was in fact called
   'Pergaia' because of her shrine at Perga in Anatolia.

learn from my servant, Quirinus, what is going on here.[2] At the urging of his
father he is returning to his native city and will not return here.[3] He could not
make any further progress staying with me. I wish you continued prosperity.

Freiburg, 15 March 1531 10

Yours sincerely, Erasmus of Rotterdam

To the most celebrated master Johann von Vlatten, wherever he is

2455 / To Johannes Rosinus Freiburg, 16 March [1531]

This letter was first published in the *Epistolae floridae*. On the year-date see
Ep 2268 introduction, and cf Epp 2424–7.

Johannes Rosinus (d 1545) was a Silesian poet active in Vienna, where his
patron was Johannes Fabri (Ep 2374). He was a friend of Johannes Alexander
Brassicanus (Ep 1146) and Caspar Ursinus Velius (Ep 2453). In 1526 he successfully defended himself against the charge of heterodoxy brought against him
by the faculty of theology on the basis of a sermon preached at St Stephen's.
He wrote a history of the 1529 siege of Vienna that was published at Augsburg
in 1538. It may have been Fabri who brought him to the attention of King
Ferdinand, who at some point before 1531 appointed him royal chaplain and
court tutor. In 1544 he was appointed provost of St Stephen's and chancellor of the university. In 1531 he went to Cologne and Aachen as a member
of Fabri's retinue to attend the election and coronation of Ferdinand as king
of the Romans. This letter is Erasmus' grateful acknowledgment of Rosinus'
visit to him on his way home from Aachen. No further correspondence with
Rosinus survives.

ERASMUS OF ROTTERDAM TO JOHANNES ROSINUS, GREETING

You would scarcely believe, my dear Rosinus, how in this single meeting I felt
a strong attachment to you and was completely won over to you. Although
I had noticed your sincerity, learning, and humane character, delineated, as
it were, in your letter and your poem, I perceived those same qualities much 5
more clearly from live conversation, from your glance and your expression.
For that reason I reckon that day, which confirmed our friendship in such
a friendly conversation, to be numbered among my lucky days. It remains
only that we nourish it by mutual services and the exchange of letters.

* * * * *

2 For Quirinus Talesius see Ep 2367 n3.
3 He appears to have departed circa 18 April, the date of Ep 2487, which he delivered to Erasmus Schets in Antwerp; see Allen Ep 2494:1–3.

You had guaranteed me a meeting with the reverend lord Fabri, but I   10
more readily hold him excused because you in a certain sense had taken his
place in seeing me. He excused himself in a letter,[1] sent from Cologne, saying that he could not come to visit me because of the canons of his chapter,
promising he would come on his return even if he had to prolong his journey. But I did not promise myself what he promised, for I know that those   15
who have vowed themselves to courtly affairs have least control over their
own lives.

I am happy that you now have an honourable position and rank at the
court of a most benevolent prince, and I hope that you will be awarded an
income and dignity proper to your learning and integrity. There was nothing   20
important about which I could write to you, but when Erasmus,[2] a learned
young man of noble birth, presented himself, I did not think that he should
arrive there without a letter from me. Farewell.

Given at Freiburg im Breisgau, 16 March AD 1530

2456 / To Busleyden College   Freiburg, [17 March 1531]

This letter was first published in the *Epistolae floridae*, where the day-date is
clearly a misprint; see n3. The interpretation of the year-date as 1531 is confirmed by the connection with the content of Epp 2421 and 2449. On 30 January
Erasmus conjectures that the new Collège royal in Paris is to have two professors of Greek, Pierre Danès and Jacques Toussain (Ep 2421:61–3); on 13 March
he knows this to be the case (Ep 2449:33–6), as he does in this letter (lines
12–16). Further confirmation of the year-date is the placement of the letter in
the *Epistolae floridae* among a group of letters written in March 1531.

Under the leadership of Guillaume Budé, the project of a Collège royal had
been contemplated since 1517 (see Ep 522), but only a dozen years later did
Francis I take the first steps towards the fufilment of his promises in this regard. Even now, no college had been founded, but four professors, two for
Greek and two for Hebrew, had been appointed. The date of their appointment appears to have been March 1530, since on 27 March 1531 they received
a year's salary; see Marichal II 21. This development appears to have caused
the professors at the Collegium Trilingue in Louvain ('Busleyden's College') to
fear that prospective students would choose Paris over Louvain.

* * * * *

2455
1 Not extant
2 Erasmus Könneritz (Ep 2450 n6)

ERASMUS OF ROTTERDAM TO THE PROFESSORS
OF BUSLEYDEN COLLEGE, GREETING

You see how much competition and rivalry has been created for you by
the bilingual college that Francis, king of France, has established, an event
awaited with great expectation from all quarters. Whatever the outcome, 5
which I·desire and hope will be most successful, surely full praise remains
with you in that you were the first to embark upon this magnificent enterprise and induced others to emulate you.[1] What added still further to the
culmination of your fame was that you endured and sustained the first
assault of envy and passed on to those who will follow you a much easier 10
task. In addition, your glory will be even more celebrated for not having
been defended against the serpent by royal patronage. If they can pride
themselves that two professors have been designated for each language
with a more substantial remuneration, as it is reported, no blame can be ascribed to Jérôme Busleyden, who dedicated all the resources he possessed 15
to this enterprise. That no professor has been designated for the Latin language at the French school is far from being something that I disapprove;
indeed, I think you should do the same, and as soon as the professor of that
language retires at his own convenience,[2] his salary will be added to the
other two.   20

I write these things to you so that you will increase your original diligence, and through the skilfulness of your teaching retain a high enrolment
of students. For the most part we are won over by new things, and we have
begun to have a France at peace. But if the students desert you, the result
will be that you also will become more sluggish in your teaching. You must 25
combat this with all care and diligence. Up to the present, the first acts of the
play have been successful. The rivalry with the Royal College will stimulate
the opening of the drama; your vigilance will determine the ending, worthy
of applause. Farewell.

Freiburg im Breisgau, [17 March] in the year 1530[3]   30

* * * * *

2456
1 Ep 691
2 The professor of Latin since 1519 was Conradus Goclenius (Ep 2364 n1), who
   would hold the chair until his death in 1539.
3 The date in the *Epistolae floridae* is 'Id. Cal. April.' which is clearly a misprint.
   Because the letter is placed in the volume in sequence with Epp 2453–5, 2459,
   Allen corrected the date to '16 Cal. April.'

2457 / To Konrad von Thüngen   Freiburg, 17 March 1531

This letter was first published in the *Epistolae floridae*. It is evidently the letter
that accompanied the presentation copy of the *Enarratio psalmi 33* (Ep 2428).

ERASMUS OF ROTTERDAM TO KONRAD, BISHOP OF WÜRZBURG,
GREETING

Reverend prelate and likewise illustrious prince, when I reflected within myself how generously your Highness not only admitted me to the number of
your clients, or, as you prefer, of your friends, but also honoured me both   5
with letters written with great affection and with a singular token of your favour towards me,[1] without giving me the opportunity to express in turn the
sentiments a grateful client should have towards a patron of such outstanding merits; since there was nothing in my poor world, I betook myself to the
gardens of the Scriptures, and I have sent you a Psalm,[2] plucked from them   10
like a little flower of a most pleasing fragrance, deeming this more satisfactory than greeting an incomparable friend with an inane letter.

This summer was entirely sterile for me, and during the winter months
I did not dare burden the strength of my frail body, shattered by a long
illness,[3] with excessive labours. If you will but deign to give some sign, or if   15
the occasion presents itself for declaring my gratitude to you, I shall demonstrate clearly that neither zeal nor loyalty has been lacking in me, even if all
else were lacking. May the Lord preserve your reverend Lordship for a long
time safe and sound for the church and the commonwealth.

At Freiburg im Breisgau, 17 March in the year 1531 after the birth of   20
Christ

2458 / To William v, duke of Cleves   Freiburg, [c 18 March] 1531

First published in the *Epistolae floridae*, with no month- or day-date, this is
Erasmus' reply to Ep 2234 of 10 November 1529. Since it accompanies a gift
copy of the *Apophthegmata* (Ep 2431), it cannot be earlier than the date of the
publication of that work, March 1531. Noting the similarity of lines 47–9 in this
letter ('We see how many evils have stricken Italy and France and continue to

* * * * *

2457
1 See Ep 2361 n3.
2 See Epp 2428:22–9, 2442:13–15, 2443:13–15, 2469:46–8.
3 See Ep 2360 n1.

strike them, or rather almost the whole world, today') to line 10 in Ep 2459 ('The whole world now is in tumult ...), and noting also the contrast of those two passages to Ep 2452:24 ('Italy has been pacified'), Allen assigned a conjectural date between those of Epp 2452 and 2459.

ERASMUS OF ROTTERDAM TO WILLIAM THE YOUNGER,
DUKE OF JÜLICH, GREETING

As it is your wish that I possess a double memento of you, illustrious young man, one which would represent to me, though I be absent, the portrait of your person, the other to portray to me the likeness of your soul, so I have 5
also taken double pleasure, for the extraordinary cup is a delight to my eyes and the eyes of my friends, to whom I often show it,[1] and the letter inscribed by your hand and issuing from your heart, since it breathes and conveys a certain marvellous character, has pervaded my heart with even more pleasure, just as the goods of the mind surpass external possessions. While any 10
prince can send such a cup, not many can write such a letter; first of all, it is in good Latin, interspersed here and there with the inlaid reliefs of Greek words, then it is sensible and replete with philosophical perceptions. To the cup you add an inscription of good omen, 'Here's to good luck!'[2] The artist engraved this in the metal as best he could, but you expressed it far more suc- 15
cessfully in your letter, which gives us promise of a beneficent prince and one worthy to exercise authority in this extensive and prosperous region. You gave me a cup that I can show to my friends and my enemies: to my friends so that they can congratulate me on the friendship of such a great prince, to my enemies so that their eyes will hurt. You sent the letter so that I could 20
encourage young men of your rank to the study of philosophy.

It is right that you do not approve the example of Dionysius,[3] who kept in his entourage men renowned for their uprightness and learning for no other reason than to win a good reputation in the eyes of the people. This was pretence, not love of virtue, and this was to abuse, not to use, the customary 25

* * * * *

2458
1 In the 1534 inventory of Erasmus' valuables, the cup is described only as having the image of Fortune; see Sieber 7 and Major 42.
2 Ἀγαθοῦ δαίμονος 'Here's to good luck!' or 'A blessing on it!' was a common toast among the ancient Greeks; see *Adagia* I vi 53.
3 Dionysius I (c 430–367 BC), tyrant of Syracuse, had an entourage of poets and men of letters, including the poet Philoxenus and the historian Philistus, and he wrote poetry himself.

practice of wise men. But to you, who prefer to show yourself a good prince
rather than to feign it, that passage of Sophocles is more pleasing: 'Converse
with wise men makes a monarch wise.'4 What is more amiable than your
modesty in calling your spacious and magnificent territory Sparta, by which
you mean that you will be more engaged in administering rather than ex-   30
panding it?5 Be blessed for being of this mind, illustrious prince; would that
all monarchs would be the same; human affairs would be tossed about in less
violent storms.

Without doubt this is the good part of the philosophy that Plato requires of those who govern the state: not to dispute in the manner of the   35
sophists about the principles of things, of the infinite, of time, of movement,
of exhalation, and of those things that germinate from the earth (although
it is not unbecoming for a prince to know even these things), but to have a
spirit that is superior to all the passions of the crowd and to appraise all their
actions and proposals in accordance with the good of the commonwealth   40
and with what is morally honourable. To learn these things by experience is
a very long process and also disastrous for the human race; they are learned
not only in a more expeditious way but also more securely either from the
teachings of philosophy or from the association with wise men. To undertake anything of great importance without consultation is characteristic of a   45
tyrant, but for a prince to choose or elicit from various opinions what is best
to do it is necessary that he have a counsellor in his heart. We see how many
evils have stricken Italy and France and continue to strike them, or rather
almost the whole world, today. We could have been free from these things if
certain princes had possessed a truly philosophical spirit and had preferred   50
to serve the interests of the state rather than their personal passions. The
benefit of this philosophy is twofold: first, that the prince will discern what
is just and useful; second, that he will not be turned aside by any personal
passion from following the dictates of reason, but will persevere resolutely in
well thought out deliberations.   55

Moreover, the hope I conceived concerning you is confirmed in no
small way by what I hear about your parents,6 that both of them, while being endowed with other virtues worthy of a prince, are especially tenacious
defenders of justice against those whose monstrous misdeeds deserve no
mercy, among whose number I think we should put those who harass the   60

* * * * *

4 Nauck fragment 13; see *Adagia* III v 97.
5 See Ep 2449 n2.
6 See Ep 2413 n11.

traveller with acts of brigandage.⁷ Although it is in itself a most criminal act,
it is made more criminal when those who receive a salary to rid a region of
brigandage engage in it themselves, to the great dishonour of the ruler.

But I shall end in order not to weary you before you begin to read the
volume that I dedicated and sent to you. May the Lord preserve you un-   65
harmed together with your illustrious parents.

Given at Freiburg im Breisgau, AD 1531

2459 / To William Blount, Lord Mountjoy   Freiburg, 18 March 1531

First published in the *Epistolae floridae*, this is a letter of introduction written for
Simon Grynaeus on the occasion of his first visit to England; see lines 55–62. For
Erasmus' friend and patron William Blount, fourth Baron Mountjoy, see Ep 79.

ERASMUS OF ROTTERDAM TO WILLIAM MOUNTJOY, GREETING
I think I answered your letter too hurriedly, my incomparable friend;¹ now I
return to the same subject in an orderly fashion, but briefly. What you write
about the devotion of the most serene queen,² though not new to me, was still
most gratifying. Who would not love such a woman, endowed with such pure   5
morals, except one who is impious, even if she had not recompensed my service with any honorary gift. Mary, to whom I dedicated the *Christian Widow*,³
testified to her favourable disposition towards me in a letter written in her
own hand,⁴ and that was for me the equivalent of a magnificent gift.

The whole world now is in tumult, and no one either among princes   10
or the common people is immune from public calamity. Such is the drama
of this age. But that sublime stage director will, as I hope, bring everything
to a happy and satisfactory end. The accomplishments of King Ferdinand
increase in number day by day, so that there is hope that some day he will be

* * * * *

7 In 1518, however, Erasmus had taken a dim view of the elder duke's lenient
treatment of the Black Band; see Epp 829:10–17, 832:14–30.

2459
1 The letter is not extant.
2 Catherine of Aragon, the innocent victim of Henry VIII's desire for a divorce (see
Ep 2410 n25). In 1527 Erasmus had dedicated his *Institutio christiani matrimonii*
to her (Ep 1727), and she had belatedly responded with a present; see Ep 2215
n2. Mountjoy was her chamberlain (1512–33), and his son Charles (Ep 2023 introduction) was her page. She would be banished from court in August 1531.
3 Ep 2100
4 The letter, which reached Erasmus on 7 July 1530 (Ep 2345:14–15), is not extant.

a powerful and salutary prince for the world. A truce with the Turks is hoped 15
for,[5] which is necessary for the tranquillity of the Christian world, especially
Austria, and also, I think, much more conducive to extending the boundaries
of our religion than waging war.

If your son Charles wrote such a letter on his own,[6] it is time that Erasmus put down his pen! Truly, I congratulate you with all my heart for having 20
such a son, and him for such ability. May he who gave these gifts continue
to preserve them.

Last summer I had to do with doctors and surgeons, that is, execution-
ers, because of a hard and dreadful abscess, from which I slowly but successfully recovered.[7] Fortune would not be lacking if my health allowed me to be 25
attached in some way to the courts of princes. I must either live as I am living
or not live at all. I cede to the Fates; it would be useless to resist. As far as the
outrageous behaviour of my detractors is concerned, alas! you hardly know
a third of what I must tolerate. Spain has its serpents, so does Italy, so does
France, so does Germany, and so does England; they spread their poison in 30
secret without mounting the stage, but playing their part through suborned
henchmen. Up to now my courage has sustained me, as I hope it will do in
the future. This is plainly my fate: I am either loved or feared by the great;
I am assailed by dogs and bedbugs. But I have resolved henceforth not to
accord to buffoons and babblers the honour of deigning to give them a re- 35
sponse.[8] My advocates are unanimously men outstanding for their learning
and their wisdom: Tunstall, Sadoleto, and Alciati.[9]

I would wish, my dear Mountjoy, that your fortune be equal to your spirit, not that things have come to a standstill for me,[10] as they say, but because

* * * * *

5 See Ep 2384 n10.
6 Not extant
7 See Ep 2360 n1.
8 Erasmus' word for 'buffoon' is *pantalabus*, an unmistakable reference to Luis
de Carvajal (Ep 2010 n10). The word for 'babbler' is *spermologus* (from σπερμο-
λόγος), which occurs in Acts 17:18 as an insulting reference by some Athenian
philosophers to St Paul. The root meaning, 'picking up seeds,' was used of
birds, especially crows or daws, but as a noun it had come to mean 'someone
who picks up scraps of learning, a charlatan, an empty talker.' Most versions of
the English Bible have 'babbler.' As Erasmus uses it here, *spermologus* is similar
in meaning to *gracculus* 'jackdaw,' a word that he had used to describe Carvajal
and other critics (among the Observant Franciscans) whom he wished to dismiss as noisy, ignorant, and stupid; see Ep 2275 introduction.
9 See Epp 2226:13–38 (Tunstall), 2272:39–51 and 2385:34–51 (Sadoleto), 2394
(Alciati).
10 Ie not that I am suffering financial want; see *Adagia* IV vii 67.

now it would be fitting that Erasmus, an old man and an old warrior, should 40
live in a little more lordly manner. There is no lack of great men in Germany
who wish me well, but it is more honourable not to change one's old patrons.
I am afraid that old age will soon carry off the archbishop of Canterbury,[11]
even though we made the pact of those who die together, that one would not
outlive the other. But however events turn out, I take extraordinary pleasure 45
in your unceasing devotion towards me; and your son, assuming your role,
as he states in his letter to me, has redoubled that pleasure. I would have
gladly dedicated the book of *Apophthegms* to him, since their subject is related
to your character and close to the *Proverbs*.[12] But last summer was sterile for
me and the winter not very fertile because of my precarious health.[13] I owed 50
the first fruits of my labours to William, Duke of Jülich, a young man of marvellous talent.[14] Therefore I dedicated Livy, augmented with five books, to
Charles,[15] so that in this way I could spur him on in the study of that author
and somehow match his elegant letter, if I could not produce one equal to it.

If Simon Grynaeus, whose name is in the preface, brings you this letter, 55
I ask that you accommodate him in his concern without any inconvenience
to yourself. He is a man remarkably learned in Greek and Latin, thoroughly
versed in philosophy and mathematics, without pretensions, and of an almost excessive modesty. The desire to visit England led him there, but especially the love of your libraries. He will return to us; you may write whatever 60
you wish and entrust it to him. I pray you to do so. I instructed him to present
the volume of Livy to Charles. Farewell.

Freiburg, 18 March AD 1531

2460 / To Petrus Vulcanius   Freiburg, 18 March 1531

Like Ep 2459, this is a letter of introduction for Simon Grynaeus. The autograph
is in the Fitzwilliam Museum at Cambridge. It was first published in the *Vita
Erasmi*. (The date 1551 given in Allen is a printing error.)

Petrus Vulcanius (de Smet) of Bruges (c 1503–71) studied Greek and Latin
at the Collegium Trilingue in Louvain, where at some point he met Erasmus,
through whose intervention it may have been that he became the tutor of

* * * * *

11 William Warham, who would die in August 1532
12 Ie the *Adagia*, the early editions of which had been dedicated to William Blount
   (see Epp 126, 211), and the later ones, starting in 1528, to his son Charles (see
   Ep 2023 introduction)
13 See n7 above.
14 See Ep 2431.
15 Ep 2435

Charles Blount, son of William Blount, Lord Mounjoy (see Ep 2459). He was in
London from at least 1529 to 1531. In September 1531 he was appointed scribe
in the government of his native city, Bruges. In 1550 he became pensionary at
Middelburg in Zeeland, in 1557 advocate in the grand council of Mechelen, and
in 1562 attorney-general of the grand council. He died at Mechelen.

Greetings. My dearest Vulcanius, if this letter awaits you with Master
Mountjoy, I ask, if you please, to make the acquaintance of Simon Grynaeus
there, a man accomplished in Greek and Latin and well versed in philosophy,
and to oblige him in any way you can. He is particularly dear to me because
of his remarkable talents. The rest you will learn for yourself. At the moment   5
I had no time to write further. Write through him, for he will be returning to
us. Farewell.
    Freiburg, 18 March 1531
    Yours, Erasmus of Rotterdam
    To the learned and polyglot Petrus Vulcanius, at the house of Master   10
Mountjoy. In England

2461 / To Johannes Sinapius   Freiburg, 21 March 1531

This letter was published in the *Grynaei epistolae* 143. A few of the letters in the
collection, including the present one, are not to or from Grynaeus but were apparently found among his papers and included in the volume.
    Johannes Sinapius (Senf) of Schweinfurt (c 1505–61) studied Greek un-
der Petrus Mosellanus at Leipzig (1523–4) and Philippus Melanchthon at
Wittenberg (1524–6) before matriculating at Heidelberg (1526), where Simon
Grynaeus held the chair of Greek. In August 1527 he took his MA and began
teaching arts courses. In his first publication, *Defensio eloquentiae* (Haguenau: J.
Setzer 1528) he commended both Luther and Erasmus for their contributions to
the renewal of religion and learning. In 1530 he published a *Declamatio* against
the opponents of humanist scholarship (Haguenau: J. Setzer). Meanwhile, in
1529, when Grynaeus departed for Basel, Sinapius succeeded him as professor
of Greek but soon made plans to go to Italy to study medicine. Sometime before
the composition of this letter, he went to Freiburg to visit Erasmus, who recommended that he pursue his medical studies at Ferrara. In October 1531 Sinapius
resigned his chair at Heidelberg and made his way to Ferrara via Strasbourg
(where he visited Martin Bucer) and Basel (where he visited Grynaeus), reach-
ing his goal in 1532. After acquiring his doctorate in medicine, he entered the
service of Duke Ercole d'Este and his wife, Renée of France, as court physician
and tutor of the couple's children. During his years in Italy he supplied Italian
medical texts to the Basel printers. Given that Sinapius had always been sympathetic to the reformers, dismay at the suppression of the reform movement

in Italy may have influenced his decision to return to Germany in 1545. On the other hand, his willingness to become court physician to the prince-bishop of Würzburg, a position he held from 1548 until his death, may indicate that his most basic loyalty was to the cause of Erasmus.

TO JOHANNES SINAPIUS ERASMUS OF ROTTERDAM
SENDS CORDIAL GREETINGS

Cordial greetings. Although I was all but dead from writing a hundred letters,[1] most learned Sinapius (and yet in the midst of them I had not forgotten you), your letter came into my hands as I was looking for something 5
else.[2] I interpreted this as something that took place under the auspices of the Muses. Therefore, although I had already tied up the bundle and handed it to the courier, I added this letter, not to respond to your letter but to give you some pledge of my affection for you. You thank me so politely for a little chat we had and for shaking hands. What would you do if I did you some 10
service? I am delighted by your sincerity of character, which is quite rare even among the learned. Through some inner feeling transmitted by nature, I was inclined to feel warmly attracted to you immediately in our first meeting, and I hope that this friendship between us will endure. And may I be given the opportunity and the possibility of showing my sympathy for you 15
by some more serious discussion.

You will fill me with great joy if I am informed that both of your eyes are in healthy condition. Please return my warm greeting to Johann Lotzer, your prince's physician.[3] Take care that you also are in the best of health.

Given at Freiburg, 21 March 1531 20

2462 / To Bonifacius Amerbach   Freiburg, 25 March [1531]

This letter (= AK Ep 1509) was first published in the *Epistolae familiares*. The manuscript, in Erasmus' hand but addressed by Quirinus Talesius, is in the Öffentliche Bibliothek of the University of Basel (MS AN III 15 27).

This is the shorter of two letters, the other being Ep 2470, in which Erasmus gives a somewhat confused account of a dispute over the rent of the house in which he lived at Freiburg. From the two letters, and from occasional references

* * * * *

2461
1 Cf Ep 2451 n1.
2 The letter is not extant.
3 Johann Lotzer (Ep 2116) was the personal physician of Louis v, elector Palatine. Sinapius' *Declamatio* (see introduction) was dedicated to him.

in other letters, Allen pieced together an account of the dispute, a shortened version of which is offered here.

The house 'Zum Walfisch' in the Franziskanergasse had been built for Emperor Maximilian (who never occupied it) by his chief treasurer Jakob Villinger (whom Erasmus mistakenly calls 'Johann' in line 2). On Villinger's death in August 1529, the property passed to his heirs. The house had, in the meantime, been placed at the disposal of the city of Freiburg. It was the burgomaster who in March 1529 offered the first floor of it to Erasmus rent-free (cf Ep 2112 n4). When Erasmus moved in, another part of the house was occupied on the same terms by Augustinus Marius (Ep 2321). Still another part of the house was occupied by Ottmar Nachtgall (Ep 2166 n3), but by arrangement with the Villinger family, not the city. He claimed to have been given possession of the whole house, but without the power to transfer his rights to a third party. Marius quit the house shortly before Christmas 1529. Up to that point, all parties had been in agreement that Erasmus' occupancy was rent-free, but he was now informed by the city, via the 'tribune' Ulrich Wirtner (see n2 in this letter), that he would henceforth have to pay rent and that the Villinger family was prepared to offer him the entire house at a rent of 20 florins per year. This new situation was evidently the result of the marriage of Villinger's widow to Johann Löble, an official in Ferdinand of Austria's treasury. Both directly and through his intermediary, Henricus Glareanus (Epp 440, 2098 n1), Erasmus offered to pay a rent of 12 crowns (roughly 24 florins), on the condition that he have free possession of the house. By 'free' he meant free of the presence of Nachtgall, though Erasmus himself did not want the responsibility for ejecting him. When, as he claimed, Erasmus received no answer from the tribune to the letter containing this offer, he concluded that he was living in the house on the same terms as before, ie rent-free and without a contract. In mid-January 1530 Erasmus reported that the owners of the house did not want to sell or lease it but were planning to occupy it themselves, and that he would consequently have to move (Ep 2256:32–4). In June 1530 he was still expecting a notice to vacate the house (Ep 2330:24–6). Meanwhile, Nachtgall had moved out of the house early in 1530, though he kept keys, left some of his property behind, and made occasional visits, during which he was wont to reiterate to Erasmus his claim to the entire house. Finally, in mid-March 1531, Löble sent notice via Wirtner that Erasmus had to vacate the house by the feast of St John (24 June). At the same time, Wirtner presented Erasmus with a bill in the amount of 30 florins, for fifteen months' back rent (Christmas 1529–late March 1531).

There is no way of knowing what rights to the house, if any, Nachtgall actually had. Erasmus appears to have persuaded himself that he was the guest either of Nachtgall or of the city. The tribune Wirtner appears to have regarded Erasmus's offer of an annual rent of 12 crowns as a done deal: the sum of 30 florins that he demanded in the spring of 1531 equals an annual rate of 24 florins, or 12 crowns. Erasmus, on the other hand, supposed that his offer had been refused and maintained that in any case it had been an offer for the whole house without Nachtgall, who had in fact occupied part of it the entire time. Given his lengthy admission that Nachtgall's claims were confusing to him, it is difficult to see why Erasmus had not taken the trouble to sort out with Wirtner the question of the rent owed. Moreover, given both that he had been anticipating ejection from the house since early in 1530 and that he had never ceased to contemplate leaving Freiburg for Brabant or one of the several other places to which he had been invited (Ep 2360 nn5–6), it is difficult to see why he complained of being given only three months' notice to vacate. In April 1531 Nachtgall agreed to turn over the keys of the house to Erasmus (Ep 2477). With the help of the good offices of Christoph von Stadion and Johann Koler, Erasmus secured from Löble permission to remain in the house until Michaelmas (29 September) 1531, at which time he moved into a new house, 'Zum Kind Jesu,' in the Schiffgasse, the purchase of which he had been negotiating at least since June (Epp 2506, 2512, 2517–18, 2528, 2530, 2534). It appears that as late as 1533 Löble was still demanding payment of the rent owed when Erasmus vacated 'Zum Walfisch,' but that in the end King Ferdinand himself accepted responsibility for the payment (Ep 2808).

Cordial greetings. A new little comedy has sprung up here. Up to now Nachtgall has invariably written and said that he had been designated by Johann Villinger and his heirs to take possession of the whole house with the condition that he could not cede his right to anyone, and I, when the tribune was negotiating the rental of the house,[1] always stipulated that the house was   5
rent-free and was not willing to accept the price of the agreement. Now the tribune Ulrich[2] asks for the rent for the fifteen months that have elapsed,[3] and shows me a letter of the procurator, Johann Löble, the treasurer of King

* * * * *

2462
1 In Ep 2112:15–16 Erasmus reports that it was the burgomaster (*consul*) who offered him the use of the house, but it may well have been the tribune (see following note) with whom the details were worked out.
2 The tribune (*tribunus* or *Oberzunftmeister*) was the highest official in the government of Freiburg after the burgomaster (*consul*); cf Ep 2158 n9. The reference here is without doubt to Ulrich Wirtner (d 1532), an important figure in the municipal government of Freiburg who served as tribune six times, including 1528–9 and 1531–2.
3 Christmas 1529–late March 1531; but cf Ep 2470:135–6, where Erasmus says that the sum of 30 florins was for the eighteen-month period Christmas 1529–St John's Day 1531.

Ferdinand, in which I am given notice that I must move out before the feast
of St John the Baptist.[4] So I am in debt twice, a debt of gratitude to Nachtgall   10
because with his kind permission I had use of a part of the house, and to the
tribune I owe thirty florins since he leased the house to me, although I had
already given him eight crowns, freely, without a contract.[5] When Glareanus
said that the agreement I had accepted was not fulfilled, the tribune answered, 'He can deal with Nachtgall,' as if I had not made the stipulation   15
that the house be rent-free in order not to deal with Nachtgall. And Nachtgall
stated more than once that he had talked with the tribune and that he said
something different to him than he had said to me. I informed the tribune of
this in a letter,[6] and I added a letter of Nachtgall written in his own hand in
which he claims his right to the whole house three times. The tribune has not   20
yet responded. I do not know who is responsible for this duplicity.

Eck – in a fury, or rather raving mad to the third or fourth degree – has
persuaded many noblemen that Erasmus is the greatest of heretics.[7] The emperor is collecting pledges of support from all the princes who are willing to
aid in the restoration of the church.[8] They are afraid that once the monks and   25
priests have been expelled they also will be expelled. I do not know what
will happen. I am contemplating going elsewhere but I have not yet decided
where.[9] If it would be convenient for you to take a little trip during the Easter
holiday,[10] we could discuss certain matters that I do not wish to confide to a
letter. Farewell.   30

Freiburg, 25 March

* * * * *

4 24 June
5 If the reference is to the Rhenish florin, the sum is equivalent to 1,770d groot
   Flemish, the amount that an Antwerp master mason/carpenter would be paid
   for about nine months' work in 1530 at 9.05d per day and assuming a 253-day
   year (CWE 12 650 Table 3, 691 Table 13). Of this amount, Erasmus had already
   paid 608d, about a third, in écus au soleil.
6 Not extant
7 For Johann Eck and his agitation against Erasmus at the Diet of Augsburg in
   1530, see Ep 2387 introduction.
8 Literally translated the text says that the emperor is collecting 'chirographs'
   (chirographa). The term was used for a variety of solemn written agreements. In
   financial matters it frequently referred to what is now called a promisory note
   (Ep 2109 n9). In other contexts, as here, it meant some sort of mutual covenant
   set forth in a written document. That said, it is not clear exactly what Erasmus
   is talking about here.
9 See Ep 2360 n5.
10 9 April 1531

Your Erasmus

To the illustrious Master Bonifacius Amerbach, doctor of civil and canon laws. At Basel

2463 / From Nicolaus Olahus   Regensburg, 25 March 1531

This letter was first published in Ipolyi, pages 127–8. The manuscript is page 227
of the Olahus codex (Ep 2339 introduction). For Nicolaus Olahus, see Ep 2339.

ANSWER OF NICOLAUS OLAHUS TO ERASMUS OF ROTTERDAM
Do not be astonished, my dear Erasmus, that I have not responded until this
day to your letter, delivered to me recently in Augsburg.[1] For if you would
take into account how many cares, toils, and occupations plague us in the
courts of princes and how uncertain our continued residence in one place   5
is, you would readily pardon my past silence, especially if from now on
I shall write to you more frequently. You wrote that this age brings forth
many monstrous individuals, who often cause you great distress; that charity and humanity are now languishing; that friendships are simulated; that
many whom you thought to be faithful friends, and with whom you had   10
acted well and performed many services and from whom you deserved
well, have, oblivious of all human sentiment, turned away from you in the
most shameful manner, and from friends have become deadly enemies. It is
not surprising, my dear Erasmus, if men of this generation change with the
times, although good men preserve the same loyalty, the same virtue, and the   15
same kindness and benevolence towards their friends. We often find, however, those who ignominiously consent to turn with the times to evil ways.
It would have been better if they had not been born or had died before they
did it. Therefore you must not be disturbed by the fickleness of such people,
but rather rejoice that you are one towards whom even those to whom you   20
were a friend are ungrateful and that God wishes to make your forbearance
evident to others through them.

About the spoon and fork there is no reason to thank me.[2] Do not accept them as a gift but as a reminder of me at dinner or supper. Although
your virtues have commended you sufficiently to my queen, you will be all   25

* * * * *

2463
1 The letter is not extant. Olahus appears to have left Augsburg, where he had
   attended the imperial diet, at some point between 23 and 27 November 1530;
   see Ipolyi, pages 110–11.
2 See Epp 2391:14–17, 2393:23.

the more in her good graces since we will be setting out for your homeland.[3] Since I am unknown and a stranger in that province, you will be obliged to lend me your support, just as I will make certain, to the best of my ability, that my help will not be lacking to you. When I am established there, I will have more leisure time, since I will be a guest, which will make it possible   30 for us to exchange letters and mutual services of friendship more frequently.

Farewell, and continue to demonstrate your friendship, as you have begun.

Given at Regensburg, 25 March 1531

2464 / To Bonifacius Amerbach   [Freiburg, c 26 March 1531]

This letter (= AK Ep 1510) was first published in the *Epistolae familiares*. The manuscript, autograph except for the postscript and the address in the hand of Quirinus Talesius, is in the Öffentliche Bibliothek of the University of Basel (MS AN III 15 80). The month-date, shortly before 30 March, has been inferred from Ep 2467. The year-date is confirmed by that in other letters (many of them in the Amerbach correspondence) dealing with Alciati's declamation (line 1); for details see Allen Ep 1201:15n.

Greetings. Concerning the declamation that Calvo gave me I have no recollection, unless he thinks the letter was written too frankly.[1] Nevertheless, I will look through my papers, and if I find anything of this kind, I will do what he asks.[2]

* * * * *

3 Mary of Hungary was appointed regent of the Netherlands following the death of Margaret of Austria in December 1530. She departed for the Netherlands in February 1531 (Ipolyi, page 123) and was formally confirmed in office by the estates on 5 July (LP 5 152). Olahus' first letter from the Netherlands is dated at Ghent, 21 May 1531 (Ipolyi, page 130).

2464
1 Francesco Calvo (Ep 581:33n) was a prominent Italian editor and bookseller who numbered Andrea Alciati and Erasmus among his friends. The declamation (line 1) or letter (line 2) referred to here was a bold denunciation of the monastic life that Alciati had written in his youth and feared would be published in Basel or Germany, thus damaging his reputation; for details see Ep 1233A. At this point he was still seeking assurances that the manuscript had been destroyed.
2 Cf Ep 2467:1–6.

A few months ago I received a letter from him,[3] which was not so much 5
lengthy as friendly and elegant, together with a letter from Sucket.[4] I do not
know if he has written since then. Farewell.

You will recognize the hand.

I took care of your affairs right away, but no answer was delivered to
me, and the coachman is in a hurry to leave. Farewell. 10

To the most learned gentleman Master Bonifacius Amerbach, most
worthy doctor of laws. At Basel

2465 / To Agostino Steuco   Freiburg, 27 March 1531

This letter is Erasmus' reaction to the *Recognitio Veteris Testamenti ad Hebraicam
veritatem* of Agostino Steuco of Gubbio (Venice: Aldus 1529). Since Erasmus,
who had only the most rudimentary knowledge of Hebrew, made no pretence
at being an Old Testament scholar, he would not likely have paid any attention to a commentary on the Greek and Hebrew texts of the Pentateuch unless
somebody had informed him that it contained covert attacks on him, with the
now familiar charge that he was the source of the Lutheran heresy. So informed,
and never content to ignore attacks on his orthodoxy, Erasmus sent this letter to Steuco and then published it in the *Epistolae floridae* of September 1531,
thus making the controversy public. Steuco too published the letter in his *In
Psalmum* xviii *et* cxxxviii *interpretatio* (Lyon: Gryphius 1533) 167–97. The Allen
editors based their text on that of Steuco, which differs extensively though not
substantially from that of Erasmus, on the ground that it corresponded to the
letter actually sent. Steuco's response is Ep 2513.

Guido Steuco (1497/8–1548) took the name Agostino in 1512 or 1513, when
he joined the Augustinian canons at St Secundus in Gubbio. He studied at the
University of Bologna (1517–20, 1522–5) and was ordained in about 1520. In
1525 he became librarian of the Grimani family collection in the convent of
Sant' Antonio in Venice, from which he drew much material for the *Recognitio
Veteris Testamenti*. Four years later he became prior of the convent of San Marco
in Reggio nell' Emilia. Among his other works was *Pro religione christiana adversus Lutheranos* (Bologna: Giovanni Battista Faelli 1530), in which Erasmus
is criticized by name twice and several other times tacitly for the criticisms
of the established church and its practices that inspired the Lutheran heresy

* * * * *

3 Ie from Alciati; Ep 2394
4 Not extant. Karl Sucket was completing his legal studies under the direction of
Alciati at the time; see Ep 2394:130–1.

Agostino Steuco
Artist unknown

(see Rummel II 136–7). In 1536 he entered the service of Pope Paul III, who in 1538 made him Vatican librarian. In 1547 he travelled to Bologna to attend the session of the Council of Trent that had been transferred to that city, but while there he fell ill and withdrew to Venice, where he died.

ERASMUS OF ROTTERDAM TO AGOSTINO OF GUBBIO,
REGULAR CHANCELLOR[1] OF THE ORDER OF ST AUGUSTINE
AT SAN SALVATORE, CORDIAL GREETINGS

I congratulate you on your character and good fortune, most learned Agostino, not only you but also those who study the Sacred Scriptures. It is   5 fitting that all of them, if they wish to demonstrate their gratitude, should pray for the departed soul of Domenico Grimani,[2] who both conceived and carried out, with determination and at great expense, the admirable enterprise of creating a library comprising the best books in various languages and leaving it as a memorial to himself. I do not know any more impressive   10 way he could transmit the memory of his family to posterity.

    When I was residing in Rome,[3] I was invited by him several times to an interview, through the intermediacy, if I am not mistaken, of Pietro Bembo.[4] At that time I was averse to frequenting the company of the great, but finally I did go to his palace, more out of a sense of propriety than inclination.   15 Neither in the courtyard nor in the vestibule was there a single soul. It was afternoon. I left my horse with my servant and ascended the stairs alone. I arrive at the first room, I see no one; I proceed to the second and the third, still no one. I found no door closed. In wonder at this solitude, I reach the last room. There I find only one person, a Greek doctor, as I surmised, his head   20 shaved, a guardian at the open door. I asked where the cardinal was. He said he was inside conversing with some noblemen. When I did not continue, he asked what I wanted. 'I would like to greet him,' I said, 'if it is not inconvenient. But since he is not free at the moment, I shall come back some other time.' As I was about to leave, I glanced for a moment at the surroundings   25 through the window. The Greek returned asking whether I wished to leave some message for the cardinal. 'There is no need to interrupt his conversa-

* * * * *

2465
1 When he became an Augustinian canon at Gubbio, Steuco thereby became a canon of San Salvatore in Bologna. In the *Epistolae palaeonaeoi* (1532) 'chancellor' is corrected to 'canon.'
2 Ep 334
3 In 1509; see Ep 216 introduction.
4 Erasmus in fact never met Bembo; see Ep 2106 introduction.

tion,' I said. 'I will return soon.' Finally, since he inquired, I told him my
name. As soon as he heard it he rushed inside before I realized it, and coming back immediately he told me not to leave and that I would be introduced   30
right away. When I entered he received me not as a cardinal – and what a
cardinal! – receives an insignificant little man of low standing but as a colleague. I was offered a chair and we talked for more than two hours, and
during that time I could not even stretch out my hand to remove my cap. An
extraordinary affability for a man of such high rank!   35

　　Among the many things he discussed with great erudition about scholarship – indicating that he already had in mind the project of the library,
which I now learn has been completed – he began to exhort me not to leave
Rome, the wet nurse of geniuses. He invited me to live in his house and share
his fortunes, adding that the climate of Rome, which was hot and humid,   40
would suit my frail health, and especially that part of Rome where his palace,
built long ago by a pope who had chosen that place as the most salubrious
location of all, was located.

　　After much conversation on various topics he summoned his nephew,
already an archbishop, a young man of almost divine talent.[5] As I attempted   45
to rise he forbade me, saying 'It is fitting that the disciple stand and the
teacher remain seated.' Finally he showed me his library of books in many
languages.[6] If it had been my good fortune to have met this man earlier, I
would never have left Rome, where I found a welcome beyond my merits.
But I had already decided to leave, and things had evolved to such a point   50
that it was impossible for me to remain. When I said I had been summoned
by the king of England,[7] he stopped insisting. He only begged me again and
again not to doubt that what he promised came from his heart and not to
judge him according to the customs of ordinary courtiers. Reluctantly he
put an end to our conversation, but seeing that I was eager to depart, he did 55
not wish to detain me any longer. In his last words he made me promise that
I would visit him again before I left the city. I did not return – unfortunately!
– for fear that I would let myself be persuaded by his eloquence to change
my mind. Never was my mind so ill-fated! But what can you do when the
Fates urge you on?   60

　　　* * * * *

5　Marino Grimani (c 1488–1546), already bishop-designate of Ceneda, north of
　　Treviso, who eventually had a distinguished career in the service of Clement
　　VII and Paul III, becoming cardinal-bishop of Tusculum and Porto in 1528
6　Cf Ep 334:148–50.
7　See Epp 215, 216:34–8, 334:10–14.

I cannot be envious that you are enjoying the happiness that I was once offered, but I can with more reason be angry with myself and hate myself for having turned down the invitation. I am, however, consoled by the knowledge that, thanks to your efforts, we will also share this treasure together. For I skimmed through, rather than read thoroughly, your 65 *Annotations on the Pentateuch*,[8] where you promise us many other excellent works. I like very much many of those that have appeared, but there are a few things that it is no less important to me than to you to point out, so that your works will come into people's hands more polished, or at least in such a condition that the Momuses will not find anything or very 70 little to criticize.[9] I wish you to be persuaded, my dear Agostino, that I assume the role of the critic with no other intention. I admire your efforts and I sincerely respect your reputation. This first edition abounds with prodigious errors,[10] especially in the Latin, which shows you how unsafe it is to trust printers. If it is not possible for you to be present, you should 75 delegate someone for this task who is both able and willing to take your place conscientiously.

In the meantime I would exhort you to be more meticulous in proofreading than forceful in your assertions, especially when you reject the opinions of others. You seem to be quite irascible towards some people, as 80 if you had some personal grudge against them, as in the case of Nicholas of Lyra and Paul, bishop of Fossombrone,[11] both of them natives of Lower Germany[12] – not that one is not permitted to disagree with them, but the manifestation of your ill humour takes away from your credibility. You disagree with Reuchlin also,[13] but politely and with initial words of praise. I 85 think that Paul is in no way inferior to Reuchlin in sharpness of intellect and superior to him in the knowledge of the mathematical disciplines. Yet

* * * * *

8 The *Recognitio Veteris Testamenti*. All page references in the notes that follow are to the first edition, published at Venice by Aldo Manuzio in 1529 (cf the introduction to this letter).
9 Momus was the god of carping criticism.
10 This designation of the book before him as the 'first edition' seems to indicate that Erasmus knew that a second edition, published by Gryphius at Lyon in 1531, was in the works.
11 For Nicholas of Lyra (c 1270–1349), the best known biblical commentator of the later Middle Ages, see Ep 182:128n. For Paul of Middelburg (1446–1534), who taught astronomy at Padua and was bishop of Fossombrone, see Ep 326:113n.
12 This is a gaffe; Paul of Middelburg was a native of the Netherlands (Lower Germany), but Lyra was a Frenchman from Normandy.
13 For Reuchlin see Ep 290.

RECOGNITIO VE

TERIS TESTAMENTI AD HEBRAICAM VE

ritatem, collata etiam editione Septuaginta interpretú cum
ipsa ueritate Hebraica, Nostra q̃ translatione, Cum expositione Hebræorum, ac Græcorum, qui passim
toto opere citantur. Vbi quantum fieri po-
test, monstrantur loci, qui in editione
Latina, & Græca discrepant à codi
cibus Hebræorum, per Augu
stinum Eugubinum Can.
Reg. S. Augustini.
Ordinis. S. Sal-
uatoris.

AL DVS

Ne quis alius aut Venetiis, aut usquam locorum hunc
impune librum imprimat, Senatus Veneti
decreto cautum est. M D XXIX.

Title-page of Agostino Steuco
Recognitio Veteris Testamenti ad Hebraicam veritatem
(Venice: Aldus 1529)
Munich: Bayerische Staatsbibliothek

you nowhere cite his name, to my knowledge, except with reproof. Relying
solely on the argument that the individual books have prefaces by Jerome,
you think that Paul should not be listened to because he thinks that this   90
edition is not entirely by Jerome.[14] If this reasoning is valid, we will have
to maintain that the orations of Aeschines and Demosthenes translated by
Cicero are extant; but in fact his translation has by some misfortune been
lost and the preface preserved because for some reason it was thought useful.[15] There are two prefaces to Job, although each one corresponds to a   95
different version. It is highly probable that when Jerome's edition had been
accepted in practice, church leaders changed certain passages translated
by him and restored some of them either from the old translation or from
the Septuagint.[16] Thus it came down to us by the authority of the church.
But I have introduced this just by way of an example, not to dispute with   100
you over this.

* * * * *

14 Ie that the Vulgate version of the Old Testament was not entirely the work of
   Jerome. In the years 390–405 Jerome translated all the canonical books of the
   Old Testament directly into Latin (the older Latin versions had been based on
   the Greek Septuagint, itself a translation of the Hebrew). All of Jerome's translations were received into the Vulgate except for that of the Psalms, where
   preference was given to the so-called Gallican Psalter, an earlier version that
   Jerome had made on the basis of the Septuagint. The problem was that in the
   thousand years between Jerome's career and the invention of printing, it was
   not possible to preserve his text from corruption by the interpolation of readings from Old Latin texts (to which many long remained attached), by editorial licence, or by scribal error (cf lines 95–9 below). Modern biblical scholars
   are in agreement with Erasmus that the pristine text of Jerome's Vulgate had
   long since disappeared and could never be recovered. See Ronald K. Delph
   'Emending and Defending the Vulgate Old Testament: Agostino Steuco's
   Quarrel with Erasmus' in *Biblical Humanism and Scholasticism in the Age of
   Erasmus* ed Erika Rummel (Leiden 2008) 297–318, here 313 with n33.
15 Aeschines (389–14 BC) and Demosthenes (384–22 BC) were Athenian orators
   and bitter rivals. Cicero is known to have translated the *In Ctesiphontem* of the
   former and the *Pro Ctesiphonte* of the latter, but only his preface to the two orations survives as *De optimo genere oratorum*.
16 Cf Allen Ep 2513:168–76, where Steuco points out that there were two prefaces,
   not because a single text had been so tampered with as to become two versions, but because, as Jerome himself testified, he had made two translations
   of Job, one from the Greek Septuagint, and one from the Hebrew, which is the
   one that went into the Vulgate. At the time, the text of the translation from the
   Septuagint was unknown. It was rediscovered and published only at the end of
   the seventeenth century.

At times you mention the Averroists in a very hostile manner,[17] so that you give the impression of condemning Aristotelian philosophy altogether.[18] Indeed, those who are so attached to Aristotle that they neglect the divine writings or subject the teachings of Christ to the standard of Aristotle should deservedly be reprimanded. But I ask you, if Basil, Chrysostom, Jerome, and Augustine had come to treat the mysteries of the Scriptures without a knowledge of philosophy, what would they have accomplished? You announce that you will write against Platonic philosophy.[19] But if you condemn the philosophy of both Plato and Aristotle, you leave us with nothing. I am not unaware that your sentiments are just, but you should have expressed them in words that would stir up the least possible hostility so that your writings would be read with greater profit. As I understand, this is the first time that you, a new actor, have leaped on to this stage. It is of great importance for the other parts of the play how auspiciously you play the first scene. There is no beast more harmful or more intractable than this serpent.

I will now impart the advice concerning the dangers to be avoided at sea that those who have experienced misfortunes in the course of their own navigations usually give others who are just spreading their sails. Similarly, for those who are undertaking a task the breeze of those who favour and applaud them blows gently from every side, but if the wind should change direction, then they get stuck in the shallows. You seem to have devoured many things in haphazard reading; if you digest them over a long period of

* * * * *

17 See *Recognitio* 10 recto. The Iberian Muslim scholar Averroes (1126–98) wrote influential commentaries on Aristotle which, in Latin translation, became known to Christian scholars in the thirteenth century and were for a time prized by them. Soon, however, Averroist thought came under attack for teachings deemed incompatible with Christianity, eg the denial of personal immortality and of free will, the assertion of the eternity of the world, and the reduction of God to the status of a prime mover who exercises no providence over the world. Vigorously condemned by Thomas Aquinas and others, Averroism nevertheless survived here and there, especially in Italy (Padua), into the Renaissance.

18 The Allen text, following that published by Steuco, has *ne videaris* 'lest you give the impression that,' which does not fit the context, since Erasmus goes on to chide those who reject Aristotle altogether. On the other hand, both the *Epistolae floridae* text (relegated by Allen to the textual apparatus) and Steuco's own direct quotation of this passage (faithfully reproduced in Allen Ep 2513:222), have *ut videaris* 'so that you give the impression,' which fits the context perfectly. We have therefore adopted the reading *ut videaris* for both this letter and Ep 2513.

19 *Recognitio* 6 recto. Steuco would eventually do this in book four of *De perenni philosophia libri* x (Basel: Nicolaus Bryling and Sebastian Francken, 1542).

time, they will find much more acceptance than if you blurt them out with
youthful vehemence. Again and again, most learned Agostino, I must ask   125
that you accept these remarks in the spirit in which they are given; even if my
admonitions have no effect, a friendship that fears even when there is nothing to fear cannot but be gratifying. You must consider that the great praise
your works elicit not only contributes to the good reputation of your own
name and to the general benefit of scholarship but also is very important for   130
the memory of Grimani and the everlasting glory of his library. What you
think of me matters little.

You seem in a number of passages to display a certain vexation, although it is not clear to me whether you directed these aspersions at me. For
example, in the very first chapter of Genesis, when you are discussing the   135
etymology of the name of Adam, you criticize without naming names certain
people who have called Augustine's explanation of this frigid.[20] He gives a
Greek interpretation of the Hebrew word, as if alpha signified ἀνατολή [east],
delta δύσις [west], alpha ἄρκτος [north], and mu μεσημβρία [south]. I confess
that this was my annotation to the second chapter of John's Gospel, but I   140
find no mention there about an unconvincing explanation,[21] and no other
less respectful word. I admit that he derived this comment from others. But
I am astonished that it pleased that great authority so much that he thought
it should be mentioned many times. When I add 'that great authority,' I mitigate my dissent with a preliminary word of praise. You do not seem to ap-   145
prove what I disapprove of but only wonder why Cyprian, who recorded it
in his writings before Augustine, is not equally criticized. Perhaps in the first
edition I had not read that passage in Cyprian, or at least did not remember
it.[22] In later editions I find these words: 'St Cyprian made this annotation

* * * * *

20 *Recognitio* 18 recto. Erasmus uses the adjective *frigidus* more than a dozen times
   in this letter. The root meaning is 'cold' or 'frigid,' but it can also mean 'feeble,'
   'insipid,' 'trivial,' or, in reference to a reason or an argument, 'pointless,' 'senseless,' 'absurd.' Until at least the middle of the nineteenth century the English
   word 'frigid' carried all those same meanings. Since Erasmus makes playful
   use of *frigidus* in all its senses, we have consistently translated it as 'frigid,' with
   its now obsolete meanings understood.
21 Starting in 1519, all authorized editions of Erasmus' *Annotations* included in the
   margin of the annotation on John 2:20 the following description of Augustine's
   explanation of the name *Adam*: 'Annotatio frigida de nomine Adam.' Since the
   remark was in the margin, Erasmus' claim that it was not in the annotation is
   literally true.
22 Pseudo-Cyprian *De montibus Sina et Sion* 4 PL 4 911–12; cf line 163 below.

before our author, but both were human.'²³ If you approve what I disapprove   150
of, then you do not find me wanting in self-restraint in my disagreement.
But you mention that Cyprian also added the statement, which Augustine
passed over in silence, that the earth from which Adam was made was taken
from the four quarters of the world by God's fist. But you could also have
added that he is trying to prove a frivolous comment by means of a forced   155
reading of a passage of Scripture: 'He measured the heavens in the palm of
his hand and grasped the earth with his fist.'²⁴ Who has ever interpreted that
passage of Isaiah in this way, not to mention that to adapt the passage to his
commentary he corrupted Scripture, changing 'from the slime of the earth'
to 'from all the slime of the earth'?²⁵ I omit that he writes 'the four stars of the   160
universe' instead of 'the four zones of the earth,' as if Ursa Major were a star
instead of a constellation.²⁶ Who has ever said that east, west, or south were
stars? These words are in the book entitled *On the Mountains of Sinai and Sion*,
and aside from matters of style there are many other features that do not recall the savour of the spirit of Cyprian, with the result that not without good   165
reason I have included it among the works that are falsely attributed to that
great man. If, therefore, you do not disapprove of that, how does he serve as
a defender of Augustine? And yet I think that even Augustine did not take
seriously these words, from which he excerpted only a modest portion for
the ears of the people.²⁷   170

   Now I would like you to consider with me for a little while the arguments with which you try to refute those to whom this commentary seems
frigid. You say: 'If these are frigid, why is not everything Plato wrote in the
Cratylus frigid?²⁸ Why are not the etymologies of Varro, who attempts to give

＊ ＊ ＊ ＊ ＊

23 The citation occurs first in the second edition of Erasmus' *Annotationes in
   Iohannem*; see ASD VI-6 70:943–4.
24 Isaiah 40:12. The Vulgate version reads as follows, in the Douay-Rheims translation: 'Who hath measured the waters in the hollow of his hand, and weighed
   the heavens with his palm? who hath poised with three fingers the bulk of the
   earth, and weighed the mountains in scales, and the hills in a balance?'
25 In the Vulgate, Gen 2:7 speaks of man being formed *de limo terrae* 'from the
   slime/mud/dirt of the earth.' Except for Douay-Rheims, translated directly
   from the Vulgate, English translations, including the King James Version, have
   'dust' instead of 'slime.'
26 The constellation Ursa Major was generally viewed as signifying the north.
27 Augustine *Tractatus in Ioannem* 10.12
28 The central theme of the *Cratylus* is conventional language, ie the arbitrary invention of words for things, versus natural language, which has an intrinsic
   relation to the things signified. A great part of the dialogue is taken up with the

Latin roots for Greek names, also questionable?[29] On this point Donatus is   175
severely reprimanded by Servius because he claims that Bacchus Lenaeus
comes from *leniendo animo* [soothing the soul].[30] I appeal to your prudence,
most learned Agostino: did Plato in the *Cratylus* or Varro in his etymologies
ever teach that single letters should be interpreted as separate words? Who
among the ancient grammarians ever engaged in such otiose trivialities? Or   180
who would not laugh at the ardour of some recent writers who are delighted
by the silly business of interpreting certain words letter by letter – as, for
example, *deus* equals *dans eternam vitam suis* [he who gives eternal life to his
own] – and of accommodating the testimonies of Sacred Scripture to dreams
of this kind? In ancient times we see that sometimes single words could be   185
designated by separate letters, like SPQR for *Senatus populusque Romanus*.
And PM for *plus minus* [plus or minus], and PP. for *pater patriae* [father of his
country]. Probus wrote something about these things.[31] But no one was such
a foolish trifler as to explain *pater* as *pascens animalia tenera aere recte* [pas-
turing tender animals with air properly] or *mater* as *mammam accommodans*   190
teneris eiulantibus roscidam [giving her dewy breast to her wailing children].

Do you see what a difference there is between etymology and the kind
of interpretation that I disapproved of? But listen to what extent I might agree
with you. Suppose we say that all etymologies immediately become worthless if one or two are erroneous. By the same reasoning you will conclude that   195
if Festus Pompeius explained a single word wrongly,[32] or if someone did not
correctly interpret a passage of Scripture, or if what Augustine puts forward

*　*　*　*　*

etymology of nouns, illustrated by Socrates. He is on the side of naturalism but
shows in some of his strange etymologies that words are not a perfect description of things.
29 Of the twenty-five books of *De lingua latina* by Marcus Terentius Varro (116–27
BC) six damaged books remain. His etymologies are sometimes bizarre.
30 *Recognitio* 18 recto. Cf lines 202–4 below. The Latin grammars of Aelius Donatus, an important grammarian of the fourth century, became the textbooks of
Latin all through the Middle Ages and beyond. Servius, a younger contemporary of Donatus, wrote a well-known commentary on Virgil. He pointed out
that the Latin verb *lenire* 'to soothe' has nothing to do with Ληναῖος, the epithet
for Bacchus (derived from the Greek word for wine press, ληνός).
31 Marcus Valerius Probus, grammarian of the late first century AD. See Heinrich
Keil *Grammatici latini* (Leipzig 1855–80; repr Hildesheim 1961) IV 265–352.
32 Sextus Pompeius Festus, a grammarian of the late second century AD, wrote an
abridgement of the *De verborum significatu* of Verrius Flaccus, the greatest grammarian of the Augustan age, whose work is lost.

does not merit the name of etymology, he erred in everything.³³ Is this how you argue: 'This sheep is sick, therefore no oxen are healthy?' Similarly, do you conclude: 'This sheep is sick, therefore there are no healthy sheep in the 200 flock?' If you admit that this reasoning is ridiculous and presumptuous, you have pronounced the same judgment on your own reasoning. Donatus was scolded by Servius because he derived *Lenaeus*, a word of Greek origin, from Latin, whereas it comes from λῃνός [wine press].³⁴ But was Donatus criticized correctly or not? You will say, 'correctly,' I think. Therefore was Servius 205 right in introducing etymology? You will say yes. Therefore not everything is frigid if one thing is frigid. What dialectician ever decided on a species from a single item without mentioning all examples by induction? Modestus writes that celibates are called such from *coelites* [heaven-dwellers], because Saturn cut off Coelus' genitals.³⁵ But celibates generate too. If this etymology 210 is frigid, the association of *coniuges* [spouse] with *iugum* [yoke] is not automatically frigid as well. And if what Lucius Aelius said about *pituita* [catarrh] being derived from *petit vitam* [it menaces life] is frigid,³⁶ that does not mean that to say that *nasum* [nose] comes from Greek νῆσος [island], that is, an island standing out on the face, is also frigid.³⁷ If we rightly reject Varro's ety- 215 mology that an *ager* [field] was so called because something was done there,³⁸ we should not reject what Quintilian writes, namely, that it is derived from a Greek word.³⁹ Even if it is false that *graculi* [grackles] are so called because they fly in flocks [*gregatim*], it is correct to say that this denomination comes from the cry of the birds.⁴⁰ If it is frigid to say that *oratio* [speech] comes from 220 *oris ratio* [reason of the mouth], or that *testamentum* [testament] comes from *testatio mentis* [testifying of the mind], it is not false to say that *oratio* is a noun from the verb *oro* [speak before a court], and *testamentum* is from the verb *testor* [testify]. There are words whose origin is completely unknown or ambiguous, but that is not to say that there is no certain etymology. 225

* * * * *

33 Ie his derivation of the name 'Adam' from the initial letters of the Greek words for east, west, north, and south; see above lines 134–9.
34 Servius, comment on Virgil *Georgics* 2.4; cf lines 175–7 above with n30.
35 Quintilian 1.6.36. The myth is told in Hesiod *Theogony* 179–81.
36 Quintilian 1.6.35. Lucius Aelius Stilo Praeconius was a learned philologist to whom both Cicero and Varro were indebted.
37 This is an etymology invented by Erasmus as a joke.
38 Varro derived it from the verb *agere* 'to do'; cf *De lingua latina* 5.34.
39 From ἀγρός 'field'; Quintilian 1.6.37, although it is not Quintilian but Cicero *Brutus* 205–7, who explicitly gives the correct derivation
40 Quintilian 1.6.37

I think that you are aware by now, excellent sir, how you said these
things with little attention and precision up to this point. But what you say
immediately afterwards is much less coherent: 'Therefore, the impudence of
these men is astonishing, who would make more of a single word of Cicero
than anything those divine men said, whose holiness and erudition is as su-   230
perior as it is invulnerable to the yapping of arrantly foolish men.'[41] Since
these words do not apply to me, I imagine that they too were directed against
others.[42] Here I am not so much defending my cause as yours, although I do
not think anyone can be found among Christians who would make more of
a word of Cicero than of all that Cyprian and Augustine wrote, who are ac-   235
knowledged as preeminent not only in their knowledge of theology but for
their remarkable eloquence. But if in the discussion of Latin style someone
were to attribute more to Marcus Tullius than to Cyprian and Augustine,
they themselves, I think, if they were alive, would not be offended but would
willingly cede to the authority of Cicero. Where, then, are those notoriously   240
impudent men, where is the yapping of those arrantly foolish men?

I cannot imagine what you were thinking when you wrote these things;
they certainly do not seem to follow from what you have written so far, unless
perhaps you think it is an inexpiable crime to disagree with Augustine in even
a slight matter, although in this work you disagree with Jerome, the Septuagint,   245
and many others about something more important. But not content with this,
you continue: 'We could not be more surprised at those who, if they found
the tiniest blemish in those saintly writers, stir up a great fuss, shout, vocifer-
ate, utter loud complaints about the error, and protest that they cannot hold
back their tears. They say that they live in another world,[43] and they do so   250
for no other reason than to win some kind of glory, which their own writings
proclaim they greatly long for, by calumniating great men. Where then is the
Christian modesty that they miss so much in others, while they are most in
need of it? Is this how one is helpful to posterity, or is it not rather to be harmful?' As I see it, my dear Agostino, I do not deny that it is possible that there   255

* * * * *

41 This quotation, and all those that follow down through line 406, are taken almost verbatim from *Recognitio* 18 recto.
42 But in the colloquy *Convivium religiosum* 'The Godly Feast' one of the characters
says: 'I would much rather let all of Scotus and others of his sort perish rather
than a single book of Cicero or Plutarch' (CWE 39 192).
43 These are Erasmus' own words in the *Annotations on Romans*; see CWE 56 372 (at
Rom 14:5), which makes clear that Steuco's remarks were aimed at Erasmus,
not at the Italians or Luther, as Erasmus prefers to assume in the discussion that
follows.

are some Italians against whom you might rightly vent your anger, but seeing that there was nothing in your preceding discourse that could arouse anyone's anger, one will wonder what it is that suddenly incited you to make such tragic utterances. For those who are of temperate mentality and sane judgment first take stock of the gravity of the situation before they cry: O heaven! O earth! O   260
seas of Neptune! I will leave aside now your severe judgment of the minds of others, as if anyone who disagrees with saintly men seeks nothing but glory.

    You would not want others, I think, to judge your feelings as frankly as you freely disagree in this work with holy and learned men, sometimes even striking a blow against them. But you continue to give in to your seething an-   265
ger. You say: 'What, then, is this unheard of, unusual barbarity? Where was this race of men born and brought up? Was it among Christians, or not rather in the Hyrcanian woods[44] and among the boulders of the Caucasus? Who are the more ferocious, they or the Tibareni or the Derbices,[45]who slaughtered their parents and threw them off the cliff? But they mutilated, lacerated, and   270
cruelly mangled people of every rank, of every sex, and every age. Is this what it is to be a Christian, or not rather a Turk or a Saracen?' This more than tragic stream of atrocious words (you will pardon my frankness, my dear Agostino) I could hardly read without laughing, save that at times I suspected that as you were writing these lines, your mind was fixed on that   275
Saxon, the instigator of this tempest in the church.[46] For he at times forcefully disregards the authority of the saints. But this whole discourse has its origins elsewhere, namely from those who found Augustine's interpretation of the four letters in Adam's name to be frigid, and from that frigid episode your stylus heated up, straying as far as the Derbices and the Tibareni or what-   280
ever more savage creature exists. If he who disagrees with the saints is not a Christian, what shall we say of Paul, who disagrees with Peter and Barnabas, one of whom he opposed face to face,[47] and with the other went into a par-oxysm of anger – that is the expression Luke uses.[48] Jerome disagreed with

* * * * *

44 Hyrcania was a region near the Caspian Sea often evoked by the classical poets because of its wildness.
45 For the Tibareni, a people on the Black Sea coast of Anatolia, see Strabo 11.527, where, however, there is no indication of cruelty. For the Derbices, a tribal peo-ple on the Iranian plateau who were said to put to death all men over seventy, see Strabo 11.520 and Aelian *Varia historia* 4.1.
46 Luther
47 Gal 2:11
48 Acts 15:39. The Vulgate translates simply *dissensio*. Most English Bibles have 'sharp contention' or 'sharp dispute.'

Ambrose and Cyprian, and his skirmish with Augustine was by no means 285
frigid. And what ancient writer is there with whom modern theologians do
not disagree in many places? Shall none of these be deemed worthy of the
title of Christian?

There are some passages scattered here and there in which you seem to
be angry at my *Folly*, although it does not condemn any religious order but 290
criticizes the vices of mankind, not all of them, but only those that everyone,
unless he is a cantankerous sort, can hear about without being disturbed and
even with laughter. Sometimes you seem to me, when you write such things,
to cast your glance now at this man, now at another, and not to direct your
shafts always at the same target. But just as it would have been more sincere 295
to declare openly against whom you were boiling with rage rather than offend many with vague and uncertain suggestions, so it would have been
more sensible for your discussion to be consistent and flow with a certain
order instead of being borne along haphazardly. You add this: 'Even the most
holy men, I confess, made use of reprimands, even the apostles, even Christ. 300
But with what moderation, with what gentleness they corrected the impious
and those who opposed God! How humanely Origen reproves Celsus,[49] Basil
Eunomius,[50] and others as well!'[51] So far are these statements from attacking
me that they seem to have been borrowed from my books. Here again you
do not so much condemn someone for criticizing something in the holy Doc- 305
tors as find him lacking in moderation in his criticism. But is it not moderate
enough to say that one marvels that this comment met with the approval of
men of such authority? For this is the source of all the indignation, and you
said that it was because of this minute blemish that such terrible tragedies
arose. This leads me to believe that there was someone else who censured 310
this passage in a more derogatory manner.

You continue: 'But with what ignominy, what scorn, what derision these
people criticize, rail, and scoff at Christians and even the saints themselves!'
I will not mention how gently Christ and the apostles treat pagans, whom
they condemn to eternal perdition, and whom they sometimes paint in their 315
true colours. Paul shows more indignation against the vices of Christians
than of non-Christians, and he testifies that he does so rightfully. He said, 'Of

* * * * *

49 Origen, *Contra Celsum*
50 St Basil wrote his *Against Eunomius* to refute of the *Apology* of Eunomius, the
leader of a fourth-century radical Arian movement called the Anomoeans.
51 *Recognitio* 18 recto

what interest is it to me to judge those who are outside?'[52] And does not St
Jerome inveigh more cruelly against evil monks, evil clerics, and evil nuns
than against pagans and Jews? What you said about saints can be taken in 320
two ways, for it is uncertain whether you vent your anger against those who
criticize something in the writings of those whom the church now honours
as saints, or against those who condemn the worship and invocation of the
saints. I do not think that I am competent to judge which of these you mean.
Concerning what you add about ignominy, scorn, derision, and snarling, I 325
confess that some reverence is owed to the memory of the saints, but not to
the extent that it is forbidden to reprove something either in their lives or
in their writings. Now certainly they do not sin, but when they were living
on earth they erred and they were mistaken and they had faults. The more
celebrated their memory, the more important it is to criticize anything they 330
did or taught that was wrong, lest the authority of their name lead into error
the souls of the simple who have persuaded themselves that anything the
saints said or did was holy. Indeed, I think this duty is more pleasing to the
saints than lighting a candle. Nowhere do I condemn the cult of the saints,
but I sometimes criticize the superstition of some people in this regard, and 335
not without good reason.[53] If there is scorn or sarcasm in this, it reverts not to
the saints but to superstitious worshippers.

Besides, your additional remarks seem to be directed not against that
Saxon nor against me but against some Italians or other. For you say: 'It is
truly shameful how often we come upon writings of theirs in which there 340
is no trace of Christian piety, but they all brim over with pagan ostentation
and more than Jewish virulence; they all resound with empty noise and the
most absurd boasting.'[54] Certainly, in the books of those now branded with
the name of heresy the majesty of Christ is religiously proclaimed, much
emphasis is given to faith and charity, the resurrection of the dead is con- 345
tinually affirmed, the authority of the Scriptures is considered sacrosanct. I
think these are undeniable traces of Christianity. If, moreover, you read my
Paraphrases, my commentaries on some psalms, the *Method of Theology*, the
book on prayer, *On the Mercy of the Lord*,[55] and others of the same kind, you
would not say, I think, that there is no trace of Christian piety there. 350

* * * * *

52 1 Cor 5:12
53 See especially the colloquies *Naufragium* 'The Shipwreck' (CWE 39 351–67) and
Peregrinatio religionis ergo 'A Pilgrimage for Religion's Sake' (CWE 40 619–74).
54 *Recognitio* 18 verso
55 Ie the *Ratio*, the *Modus orandi Deum*, and *De immensa Dei misericordia*

Hence I am convinced that these remarks are aimed at people in your part of the world whose writings are not available to me. Since none of these things have to do with me, I think that the following remarks are also directed at others. You say: 'And what is more pitiful is that this delirium increases with age, and they become worse at a time when they should have returned to their senses, when divine Nemesis threatens them and the whole world clamours against them.'[56] Someone, perhaps, will suspect that the sardonic reference to age is directed against me, since I do not deny that I am an old man, but I am still at some remove, if I am not mistaken, from decrepit old age, since I have not yet reached my seventieth year.[57] The weakness of my little body does not come from age, but from nature; even in my youth I was, physically, pretty much like those who are absorbed in books. I will make no judgment about madness, for those who are the most insane consider themselves the most sane, and those who are the most drunk think they are incredibly sober; let others judge this. But if all old men are mad, Jerome, who wrote most of his works when he was more than eighty years old, or ninety, as some claim, was completely mad. As far as my own intellectual vigour is concerned, it seems to me that I cannot blame my age for many things; but if old men speak deliriously, they can be pardoned, while among young men delirium is shameful.

I am not certain about your age, except that your exuberant style and mockery of old age indicate that you are in your prime. All the more reason why you should make an effort, my dear Agostino, that there be nothing in your writings that might give evidence of delirium. That will be achieved if your discourse is coherent and consistent, if it has an even flow, if it is never self-contradictory, if it gives evidence of presence of mind at all times. What you write about Nemesis and about the clamours of the world you are perhaps directing against heretics, from whose company I have persistently abstained, or rather against whom I have long been battling both at close quarters and at long range at great personal danger. And yet there are still many who clamour against me, but to these few ill-omened individuals I oppose the judgments of so many princes and bishops, of so many learned men, who reward my labours with magnificent gifts and grant me their approbation with honorific testimonies and render me thanks because they have drawn from my books the inspiration of true piety. I do not say these things to defend myself but to give advice to a very learned person who is entering

355

360

365

370

375

380

385

* * * * *

56 *Recognitio* 18 verso
57 Cf Ep 2275:24–37.

upon the stage of fame for the first time, so that he will win the applause of the elect and will be more cautious.

Your epilogue remains, though I do not know how aptly it pertains to what precedes it. You say: 'We will always admire the sanctity and erudition of great men.'[58] Are we to understand that one who disapproves of something in the writing of Augustine automatically holds his piety and erudition in contempt? You have seen by now that this is self-incriminating, since you disagree with holy men very often in this work. You approve of erudition joined with piety. Does it then follow that someone who disagrees with pious men is impious? Far from it. But suppose he disagrees in an insulting manner; that can be called shameless behaviour, but cannot be called impiety. Likewise I do not quite understand what you mean when you say: 'Therefore, it is not that we are boasting about our erudition; whether we equal or surpass those saintly men in learning, we are surely inferior to them in sanctity, so much so that we cannot evoke it without tears.'[59] Here you express your own personal feelings; far be it from me that the thought should ever enter my mind that I should consider myself superior in sanctity or even in learning to Augustine or Jerome. He who discovers something in a book that escaped the notice of the author does not equal, not to say surpass, him. 'In the end,' you say, 'we slip into disgraceful ostentation.'

For the life of me I cannot guess at whom such vehement, unrelenting, indiscriminate wrath is aimed. The whole thing began with the name 'Adam' as signifying the four regions of the world. It is good that it was written by a young man. If you poured out this bile against me, I find you lacking in fairness; if against the authors of heresy, I am astonished that the body of the discourse coheres so badly with the beginning; if you are aiming at all those whose writings you consider impious and scandalous, you are like someone who wishes to pour the same sauce over all the dishes, or one who hurls insults at many cross-eyed people present, none of whom can tell for certain who is the object of the abusive remarks. If someone were to give vent to his anger in this way, mixing up all kinds of reproaches, so that everyone thought they were aimed at someone else, would not everyone who heard him say, 'What has come over this man?' How much more care must be taken that something like this not be said about a work intended for the whole world, in which moderation and undisturbed good sense is required of one who transmits his thoughts in writing?

* * * * *

58 *Recognitio* 18 verso
59 *Recognitio* 18 verso

You name me only once, contemptuously and in disagreement,[60] but you do not indicate the passage. I suspect that you are referring to my paraphrase on Luke, chapter 24, where it is said of Christ: 'The Jews brought a   425
charge of blasphemy against him before Annas and Caiphas through false witnesses, than which there is nothing more heinous. This was the charge brought against Joseph, whom his brothers, conspiring against him out of jealousy, accused of a terrible crime.'[61] You say: 'I wonder why Erasmus in many passages preferred the Septuagint translation to our own, when the   430
Hebrew version and the Greek interpreters are clearly opposed.'[62] For the moment I will not examine in how many places I do this. In this passage, at any rate, the text provided by the Septuagint accords better with the figure of Christ, who was summoned and was not an accuser, but was accused and condemned by the Jews. If the Hebrew words are not ambivalent, we must   435
believe that the writers of the Septuagint had a different text than we have. Why is it so surprising if at times I follow the Septuagint translation when the apostles and the evangelists do the same in some places?[63] Finally, how many times do you reject the translation of Jerome and prefer the Septuagint? If you do not concede that the writers of the Septuagint read something differ-   440
ent from what Jerome read, what do your words mean concerning Genesis, chapter 14: 'I am astonished at this diversity, and it makes me suspect that many other things were changed in the whole Bible?'[64] If Jerome's edition condemns the Septuagint version, why does St Jerome himself frequently comment on what is found in their translation?   445

Again, without mentioning my name, you attack me in chapter 46. You say: 'Therefore this is the solution of the knot that they say Jerome tied but did not loose.'[65] I am neither surprised nor disturbed about this lapse, which frequently occurs in subjects that are examined in a cursory and hurried reading. The carelessness of printers was the source of the error. When   450

* * * * *

60 *Recognitio* 87 verso, where the subject is Jerome's translation of Gen 37:2. In his *Paraphrase on Luke* (see following note) Erasmus preferred the reading of the Septuagint. In the story of Joseph as reported in the Hebrew Bible and the Vulgate it is Joseph who accuses his brothers to his father, but in the Septuagint it is they who accuse him.
61 See CWE 48 260–1.
62 *Recognitio* 87 verso
63 Jerome (Ep 57) cites a number of passages where the apostles and the evangelists preferred the Septuagint; cf ASD IV-1A 310:626–31.
64 *Recognitio* 61 verso
65 *Recognitio* 95 verso

the *Annotations* was being printed page by page, one of the two questions was omitted, the one concerning the seventy souls. The proof of it is that the heading does not correspond to the following commentary. It says: 'Jacob had seventy-five descendants,' while the following commentary is related to this passage: 'What Abraham bought at the price of silver from the sons   455 of Emor, son of Sichem.'[66] But no matter how mistaken the heading was, the commentary itself makes sufficiently clear what passage it concerns. It says that the difficulty concerning the purchase of the tomb was not resolved, but it does not say without qualification that it was not resolved, but that it was not resolved in the letter addressed to Pammachius 'On the best method of   460 translating.'[67] That is what I mean when I say, 'There Jerome ties a knot, but he did not untie it.' He elegantly solved it in the *Hebrew Questions*.[68]

But this is a matter of little importance. Sometimes you grip your stylus with more animosity than is necessary, in my opinion, against the Germans, especially on Deuteronomy, chapter 6, although that passage does not pro-   465 vide an occasion for becoming livid with anger. For you say: 'We do not say this in imitation of the insolence of certain Germans who have arrogated to themselves the freedom of cursing everyone, gods and men, and things human and divine.'[69] It is possible that there are people in Germany who do not refrain from uttering blasphemies against God, but they are punished   470 by horrific tortures. In Rome, by contrast, I heard with my own ears certain people raving against Christ and his disciples in atrocious blasphemies, in the hearing of many besides myself, and what is more, with impunity. In

* * * * *

66 The root of this confusion was an error in the printing of Erasmus' *Annotations on Acts* that was not corrected until the final edition of 1535. His annotation for Acts 7:16 was mistakenly substituted for that on 7:14. In verse 14 the number of persons who accompanied Jacob into Egypt is put at 75 in both the Greek and the Vulgate texts, while both the Hebrew and the Vulgate texts of Gen 46:27 put the number at 70. This problem Jerome managed to solve by suggesting that Luke, the author of Acts, addressing an audience for whom the Septuagint was the familiar version of the Old Testament, followed that version in placing the number at 75; see Jerome *Liber quaestionum Hebraicarum in Genesim* on Gen 46:26–7; and cf Ep 2197:140–9. The discrepancy that he did not solve, and the one for which Erasmus' misplaced annotation was intended, was that between Acts 7:16 and Gen 50:13 concerning the burial place of Jacob.
67 Ie in Jerome Ep 57 (*De optimo genere interpretandi*)
68 Erasmus' memory is playing tricks on him here. The only discrepancy that Jerome managed to solve, and the only one dealt with in the *Liber quaestionum Hebraicarum*, was that involving Acts 7:14. Cf n66 above.
69 *Recognitio* 186 recto

the same place I knew many who heard things horrible to relate from cer- 475
tain priests, ministers in the papal court, and even at mass, and so clearly
that these words reached the ears of many. But I think you are talking about
the books of those who defend new dogmas. I cannot deny the abusiveness
of some of them. I have had more than enough experience of them myself,
stabbed by so many acrimonious books of theirs. But I find no mockery of
God in them, even though I am not quite sure whom you are referring to 480
with the word 'gods.' I think that you together with us profess one God.
Would that only the Germans were accused of this crime; it is more widespread than you think.

In chapter 11 of the same work, when discussing Dathan and Abiram,
you go into similar fits of anger against the monstrous brutality of certain 485
people whose madness not even heaven can contain.[70] What is this thing that
even heaven cannot contain? And what is that head that you call simply and
absolutely, 'the most high,' adding the emphatic pronoun *illud*? If you are
speaking of Christ, you speak piously; if of the pope, you are not speaking
impiously, but with more exaggeration than is required, and for that mat- 490
ter even impiously if your words encounter an unsympathetic audience. I
make these recommendations, my dear Agostino, so that you will be more
disposed to refute than to malign, and to deal more gently with the name of
a whole nation, which, whatever its turmoil at the present moment, never
ceded to your Italy in the true religion of Christ, if you consider the his- 495
tory of the last eight hundred years.[71] In this way you will be of more use to
the church and will arouse less unpopularity for yourself. Anyone can reprove the Derbices and Tiberani, Cyclopes and giants, but it is more worthy
of learned men and more useful for the Christian flock to teach those who
are in error and refute the obstinate with sound reasoning and the testimo- 500
nies of Scripture. Otherwise, any coachman whatsoever can bellow out abuse
against anyone at all.

In Numbers, chapter 5, you pour out your bile against the Saxon because he denies sacramental confession,[72] which you maintain was instituted
by God. But seeing that so many eminent theologians have sweated over 505

* * * * *

70 *Recognitio* 189 verso. The reference to Dathan and Abiram occurs at Deut 11:6.
    Steuco compares the rebellion of Dathan and Abiram against Moses to that of
    the heretics and schismatics against the pope, and asserts that the rebels against
    the pope will be swallowed up by the earth as were those against Moses.
71 Ie since the conversion of the Germans by St Boniface
72 *Recognitio* 148 verso

what you assert emphatically and are not agreed among themselves, it was
the duty of your scholarship to equip us with solid citations from Scripture
and solid arguments against these loquacious men.[73] It was not sufficient to
characterize as insolent those who were not ashamed to deny that this was
first instituted by God, nor was it sufficient to declaim the usual common-   510
place about heretics that they twisted Scripture to suit their own dogmas.
Although you said these things with good cause, they contribute very little
to refute adversaries. It was necessary to distinguish the kinds of confession and to prove with effective arguments what is the present practice. Who
denies that repentance of the mind is required? Whoever acknowledges his   515
error before God has it. Likewise, no one would deny that reconciliation is
a component of natural and divine law. Whoever has returned to grace acknowledges his sin; thus those who by making public satisfaction ipso facto
made a valid confession and were received into the community of the church
even if they did not confess their sins orally. In the same way, one who comes   520
to baptism confesses, by the very fact of so presenting himself, that he has
something that must be cleansed.

   But what does this have to do with our confession? In chapter 5 of
Numbers, Moses orders the Jews to confess their sins to the priest. But that
law seems to apply to sins committed through human carelessness or igno-   525
rance, which happen often, even to the least sinful of mankind. These are
the words of the law: 'When a man or woman commits one of the sins that
human beings are liable to commit and through negligence transgresses the
commandments of the Lord and does wrong, that person shall confess his
sin.' Do you think that we must number parricide, incest, blasphemy against   530
God, and sacrilege among the sins that men are liable to commit through
negligence? And then you yourself will admit that the law speaks especially
about theft, because it is immediately added: 'He shall give back the principal and add one fifth of it to the one against whom he has sinned.' There
are many people who through error or human carelessness have held on   535
to the goods of others. Confession and the restitution of the principal, with

*****

73 Erasmus himself could find no convincing scriptural evidence that sacramental confession had been instituted by Christ, though he accepted it as something validly established on the authority of the church. This was a difficult
   position to maintain, and one that since 1516 had provoked a great deal of
   controversy with a long list of his conservative critics. See Michael J. Heath's
   introduction to Erasmus' treatise on confession, Exomologesis (1524) in CWE 67
   2–15; see also John B. Payne Erasmus: His Theology of the Sacraments (Richmond,
   VA 1970) 181–91.

an additional amount and the immolation of a ram, expiated this error.[74] In Exodus, chapter 21, a kidnapper will be punished with death.[75] And in chapter 22 of the same book a cattle stealer shall give back five oxen for one ox and four sheep for one sheep.[76] It was permitted to kill with impunity one who broke into your house at night.[77] If an ox was found alive at the house of the cattle dealer, he would pay back double.[78] But if you press us about the literal sense, then require together with confession the sacrifice of a ram. Similarly, if you force us to observe the letter of the law, you will also require us to confess to a priest the minor offences that people are liable to commit, which the church does not require. Lastly, since the land inhabited by the Jews covered a wide area, and the majority of them lived in Rome and Asia Minor, and it was not permitted to make sacrifice except in Jerusalem, how was it possible that everyone could confess their sins to a priest in the exercise of his priestly functions? And what a heap of rams would there be if everyone sacrificed one for his misdeeds?

It would have been appropriate to examine these fine points, my good man, and it was not sufficient to say: 'If anyone wishes to examine the question properly, he will find that confession was founded for all sins'[79] – not that I need any proofs, but you would have armed me against those with whom we have a common struggle. You touch in that place on the primacy of the Roman pontiff, although that question has many ramifications that you should have examined more thoroughly or passed over in silence, so that while you weakly prove what you strongly assert, you would not be the object of ridicule to reprobates and confirm them in their opinions.

I would not alert you of these things, as Christ is my witness, if I did not truly love you and wholeheartedly favour your holy labours. For I am convinced that you bear Christian feelings towards me; or, if evil tongues have ulcerated your mind in some way, that does not have such importance for me that I would conceive any bitterness towards you. I return to the main point of this discussion, which in the view of most people would seem to be aimed at me, namely, that I was lacking in respect for Augustine because in a matter of no consequence I disagreed with him not only moderately but also

540

545

550

555

560

565

* * * * *

74 Num 5:6–8
75 Exod 21:16
76 Exod 22:1
77 Exod 22:2
78 Exod 22:4
79 *Recognitio* 149 recto

with an admixture of praise. What if I had criticized opinions in his books
that theologians now judge to be heretical? You would not say that they are   570
minor blemishes, I think. Nor would it be just for you to reprove so severely
in others what you permit for yourself. Commenting on the second chapter
of Genesis you say: 'Therefore I consider the ideas that men have concocted
about this paradise – namely, that if Adam had not sinned, men would always have lived in that paradise – to be mere fable. For even if Adam had   575
not sinned, this earth would still have been inhabited as it is now, and men
would either have been mortal as they are now or at the proper time would
have been taken up into heaven.'[80] Though you would admit that men of
great authority and holiness were of this opinion, you still are not afraid
to speak of fables. And among these saintly men is Augustine,[81] whom you   580
regret that I criticized – lightly, and in a matter of no importance. But you
say that you will retract your words if they are considered impious. And
yet, if you were not certain, why was it necessary to speak of fables? Again
in Genesis, chapter 10, you disagree with Augustine, who previously had
said in error that where we read *coram domino* [in the presence of the Lord]   585
it should read *contra dominum* [against the Lord].[82] With no apology for your
language you openly reject his opinion in these terms: 'He made this mistake
because of his ignorance of the Hebrew language.'[83]

From time to time you burst forth into praise of Jerome, but not without insulting the church, which you write somewhere would have fallen into   590
very great errors if that great man had not translated from Hebrew sources.[84]
In the first place, it is a harsh sound to pious ears to hear that the church is
susceptible to error, especially in Scripture, even though most of mankind is
prone to error. But you often reprove this same man whom you praised when
you could sometimes attribute the fault to scribes. Now if, as you conjecture,   595
most of the passages in the Hebrew manuscripts that Jerome followed were

* * * * *

80 *Recognitio* 26 recto. A later work by Steuco on Genesis, *Cosmopoeia* (1535), in which
    similar ideas were expressed, was placed on the Index of Forbidden Books in
    1583 and 1596.
81 *De genesi ad litteram* 6 26; CSEL 28 198
82 See Gen 10:9, where Nimrod is described (in the Vulgate and most other trans-
    lations) as 'a mighty hunter before the lord' or 'in the presence of the Lord'
    (*coram domino*). In *De civitate Dei* 16.4 Augustine objected that this arose from a
    misreading of the Greek word *enantion* (ἐναντίον) to mean *ante* (in this context a
    synonym of *coram*) when it should be understood to mean *contra* (against).
83 *Recognitio* 54 recto
84 *Recognitio* 3 recto and 86 verso

changed, do we determine that this is a more genuine edition? In Exodus, chapter 33, you criticize Jerome, who translated incorrectly, 'Show me your face' instead of 'Show me your way.' You add that the Septuagint translation of the passage was even worse: 'Show yourself to me.'[85] But how is it certain that what you found in the Hebrew manuscript is more correct than what Jerome and the Septuagint read, especially since you cite neither the Hebrew nor the Greek here as proof? At the same time, you disagree with the Septuagint, not only frequently but sometimes with little reverence. In doing this, do you not openly reject the opinion of Cyprian, Hilary, and Augustine, not to mention the Greeks, who believed that the writers of the Septuagint transmitted this version to us through the inspiration of the Holy Spirit?

Do you see in what matters you do not fear freely to disagree with such great men? And are you so furiously angry with one who did not approve the explanation of the name Adam, which, as I said, I do not think Augustine himself seriously approved? In Exodus, chapter 34, you reprove Jerome, who wrongly translated, 'Moses was not aware that his face had horns,' instead of what was there, 'that his face was radiant.'[86] And there you are so far from mitigating your reproach that you come close to insult when you add, 'It is surprising that Jerome, without taking the Hebrew text into account, did not notice also what the Septuagint transmitted, which translated the passage correctly.'[87] And you add, 'The Jews hate and curse us whenever they see Moses depicted with horns in our churches,[88] as if we think he is some devil, as they stupidly understand.' And yet it was Jerome, whom you so often praised, who gave the opportunity for the scorn of the Jews, and you make his error more conspicuous because the older Latin edition[89] had 'glorified face' rather than 'horned face.' I do not disapprove of your annotation, 'for Paul too in discussing Moses and Christ uses the words "glorification" and "brilliance"[90] and does not mention horns.' I merely wish to point out to you that there was no reason for you to become so enraged because of a different interpretation of the name of Adam.

* * * * *

85 Exod 33:13; *Recognitio* 128 verso
86 Exod 34:29
87 *Recognitio* 129 recto
88 The Vulgate translation of Exod 34:29 influenced artistic depictions of Moses down to the Renassiance and beyond; as, for example in Michelangelo's statue of him for the tomb of Pope Julius II in the church of San Pietro in Vincoli, Rome.
89 Ie the so-called *Vetus Latina*, which preceded the Vulgate and was based on the Septuagint
90 2 Cor 3:7

In Leviticus, chapter 3, you openly condemn Jerome's translation 'food of fire' when he should have translated 'bread of sacrifice to the Lord.'[91] In chapter 5 of the same book you demonstrate that the words 'even if it died by itself' were added by Jerome, although the Septuagint had translated this 630 passage very well.[92] Are you surprised that Erasmus sometimes prefers the Septuagint translation to the Hebrew text? Nor do you mitigate your criticism of Jerome with any defence or extenuation of his error. In chapter 11 of the same book, you openly disagree with Jerome and the Septuagint concerning the porcupine.[93] In chapter 14 of the same book you indicate that 635 something was added by Jerome, namely, the words about sparrows, which it is permitted to eat.[94] But since it is probable that either Jerome found this in a Hebrew manuscript or it was added by some learned person who wished to explain why Moses had added 'living,' because it was not permitted to eat dead animals, you lay the blame on Jerome, saying 'Added by the translator, 640 which is surprising, since there was no need of caution.' Again, in chapter 21 of the same book: 'If he has a small, big, or crooked nose.' All these kinds of things, you say, were invented by the translator, since they are contained neither in the Hebrew text nor in the Septuagint.[95] In chapter 25 you note that 'You will not require a superabundant harvest' was wrongly rendered by 645 Jerome, while the Septuagint rendered it very clearly.[96]

See how freely you disagree and do not lend assistance by some word of extenuation or excuse to the very holy man whom you so often praise. Again, in chapter 27, concerning the words 'He would have vowed his soul to God,' you say, 'It should not have been translated this way, for the vow 650 could be of another kind.'[97] How little honour is given here to an incomparable man! On Numbers, chapter 16, you write that at the beginning of the chapter the phrase 'and Korah was separated' was left out by Jerome.[98] This could be imputed to the scribes. In chapter 17 of the same book, commenting on the words 'Without the rod of Aaron,' you write that Jerome omitted 655 what was most important and that what he substituted was partly superfluous

* * * * *

91 Lev 3:11; *Recognitio* 132 recto
92 Lev 5:2; *Recognitio* 132 verso
93 Lev 11:5; *Recognitio* 135 recto
94 Lev 14:4; *Recognitio* 136 verso
95 Lev 21:18; *Recognitio* 140 recto–verso
96 Lev 25:37; *Recognitio* 141 verso
97 Lev 27:2; *Recognitio* 142 recto
98 *Recognitio* 161 verso

and partly false.[99] Again, in chapter 18 you say, with regard to 'All that comes from a vow,' that the proper sense of the Hebrew word is rendered better by the Septuagint than by Jerome.[100] In addition, in chapter 24, 'A man whose eye was closed,' you say that Jerome translated it in the opposite sense, closed   660 instead of open, and you wonder why he did not follow the Septuagint.[101] But here at least you defend Jerome to a certain degree, casting blame on the scribes, who might have omitted the negative particle, an argument which, though frigid, has a little politeness. But elsewhere you could have come to his defence with a more plausible excuse. In addition, in Deuteronomy, chap-   665 ter 28, on the passage concerning the afterbirth, you say without an extenu- ating prefatory statement, 'For that reason our version deviates far from the truth.'[102] But you ascribe this edition securely to Jerome, so that you cannot shift the charge. But how much more satisfactory it would have been to rec- ognize that this version has been modified by others in some places, which   670 would have been more courteous to Jerome and closer to the truth. In fact the version of the Psalms according to the Hebrew text is not the same in all manuscripts. You write somewhere that he omitted certain things to avoid repetition, seeing that they were mentioned previously.[103] But who gave the right to a translator of the Scriptures to add or remove whatever he pleased?   675

Now let me tell you for how many reasons you could excuse a very saintly man. The exemplar that Jerome followed was different from the manu- scripts of the Septuagint. Some things were changed by charlatans, others were added by some scholar or other, other things were expressed in a dif- ferent way but were essentially the same; if there are differences, the pious   680 meaning is still there.

Out of many things I have excerpted a few, by way of example, for when I was skimming through your works I was not looking for these pas- sages. But how many times in these excerpts you openly, not to say bitterly, disagree with such a great man, although you proclaim that by his work the   685 church was freed from so many errors? But what kind of liberator is it who, making errors himself, leads the church into error? How unscrupulous is a translator who in the divine books, whose author is the Holy Spirit, permits

* * * * *

99 Num 17:6; *Recognitio* 162 verso
100 Num 18:14; *Recognitio* 163 verso
101 Num 24:15; *Recognitio* 169 verso
102 Deut 28:57; *Recognitio* 204 verso. 'Truth' here stands for *Hebraica veritas*, the term used by Jerome to refer to the Hebrew text of the Old Testament.
103 *Recognitio* 132 verso

himself to add things without necessity and to take away what was put there
by the Holy Spirit? Lastly, how often in these passages that I cited do you   690
prefer the Septuagint to Jerome's translation? And you are surprised that in
certain cases I preferred to follow the Septuagint rather than our edition?[104]

I would not give you this advice, dearest brother in the Lord, if I did not
strongly admire the remarkable gifts of God manifested in you and if I did
not wish your works to be of such a kind that they bring the greatest amount   695
of benefit to the reader and the least possible ill will towards you. If you will
deign to use similar moderation in giving me me advice, you will win great
favour with me. For Christian charity persuades us to carry one another's
burdens and to help each other by mutual services.[105] May the Lord deign to
prosper your pious research.   700

Given at Freiburg im Breisgau, 27 March AD 1531

2466 / To Nicolas Maillard   Freiburg, 28 March 1531

> This is Erasmus' reply to Ep 2424. Erasmus included it in the *Epistolae floridae*,
> but Maillard himself had published the letter a few months earlier (see Ep 2424
> introduction), and Allen took the Maillard text as the basis of his version.

ERASMUS OF ROTTERDAM TO NICOLAS MAILLARD, GREETING
Truly, most learned Maillard, you have presented me with a tragicomedy
that is not so much to be read as it is to be put before my eyes to be seen, and
just as it caused me double pleasure, so it also caused me a twofold sorrow.

First of all, my spirit took delight in your copious letter, artistically con-   5
structed with excellent diction, illustrated now and again with a mosaic of
Greek words, and lastly, manifesting the gaiety of your spirit in the most
charming witticisms, with the result that I too, according to the precept of
Paul, rejoiced with a friend who was rejoicing and smoothed my brow when
he laughed.[1]   10

* * * * *

104 In the *Contra morosos quosdam et indoctos*, which he prefixed to the final edition
    of the New Testament in 1535, Erasmus points out that Steuco and many others
    criticized Jerome's translation with great freedom while taking him to task for
    doing the same thing. See LB VI **4 verso.
105 Gal 6:2

2466
1 Rom 12:15

Then I was affected with great joy because Christ, greatest and best, as if appearing from the machine,[2] added a happy ending to a turbulent play. On the other hand I was distressed that you derived no benefit (or very little) from your conversation with me – this strange malady had then begun to creep up on me, someone who has never been very dutiful in meetings of this kind, more because of my occupations and my health than through a vice of nature. Nonetheless, your visit aroused so much animosity against you, whose singular sincerity of character merited that you would never be breathed upon by the hissing of the serpent. In my case the damage is slight, and if it was my fate at birth that doing good I should have a bad reputation, it is best not to fight against the gods. Our superintendent of games, from whom we expect our prize if we have fought diligently, lives and sees us. But if this insulting behaviour was visited upon you for the name of Christ, not only would I not lament your fate but I would place the name of Maillard among the blessed. These days if some tribulation befalls innocent friends because of me, I feel it more keenly than the terrible frenzied denunciations against my own person. What grieves me most of all is that because of the excesses of these people the public peace and tranquillity of Christians is shattered and the outrageous behaviour of the wicked oppresses by its hatred even those who in the regular religious orders follow after the true religion. Although one might expect to find the simplicity of a dove and an authentic and sincere piety above all among the Franciscans who enjoy the title of Observants, from no other flock do we see those who clamour more ignorantly, indecently, and brainlessly, and rush forth and give vent to their mad ravings in published books, as if the world no longer brought forth human beings, but just buffaloes and wild asses. But it is not only the belly that has no ears, as Cato said,[3] but eyes and mind too. May Christ bring it about that they return to their senses for his glory. I for my part would wish to be at peace with everyone. Since this is denied to me by the Fates, as it is denied also to the most highly regarded men, I console myself on three counts: consciousness of my rectitude, which will have its sure reward before the one who knows all hearts;[4] second, the community of celebrated men – Socrates, Phocion, Aristides, Scipio, and if you prefer Christian examples, Paul, Jerome, Basil, and Chrysostom; lastly, when I consider whom I

* * * * *

2 Ie like a deus ex machina
3 Plutarch, *Cato maior* 8.1. The meaning, as explained in *Adagia* II viii 84, is that 'when food is at stake, questions of right and wrong do not get a hearing.'
4 Acts 1:24

have barking at my heels, and on the opposite side, my supporters. Among   45
the first group I see only people who are singularly stupid and shameless
buffoons, those hungry for glory, or born for slander, or driven by the gad-
fly of envy, or slaves of the belly, or for whom this world is preferable to
Christ. Among the second group I see those kings, princes, cardinals, and
bishops who not only applaud good letters and my own writings, whatever   50
their worth, and thank me for my efforts to improve literature and piety, but
also testify by sending me honorary gifts that their sentiments are no different than their words! How many people there are, even today, eminent for
their wealth and authority, who invite me to share their fortunes! I pass over
men of learning in silence. Who, trusting in the judgment of so many distin-   55
guished men, would not disregard the chattering of birds of ill omen, since
they cannot be placated?

Certainly I do not acknowledge the glorious title of the Dutch Hercules,
which you confer on me.[5] But since you yourself recognize how much enmity the philhellenes endure in our day in France, the homeland of studies   60
and talents, you can easily conjecture to what assaults I was subjected by the
barbarians among my compatriots thirty years ago, as I stimulated youth
to the study and love of Greek literature. Our phalanx could have barely
sustained the pressure of the hostile conspirators if Adrian, then a cardinal, later pope of Rome,[6] had not proclaimed this oracle: 'I do not condemn   65
good letters, I condemn heresies and schisms.' But among us this hatred is
diminishing, and I am inclined to hope that under the good auspices of the
excellent King Francis these croaking frogs will become so silent that no one
will be considered worthy of the rank of cardinal if he has no knowledge of
languages. At all events, not many years ago Herman Lethmaet, a Batavian,   70
or if you prefer, a Dutchman, was given first place in the awarding of laurels
in theology because of his attainments in the study of good letters.[7] I think
you know the man. I was very happy to see you expressing a youthful anger
in your letter, for from that I perceived how enthusiastically you favour this
branch of studies. But I hope that soon you will judge these hoodlums more   75
worthy of your contempt than of your exasperation. Now the brilliance of
languages has shone so brightly that it is more worthwhile to promote the
studies of a now ardent and passionate youth than to quarrel with the ranting rabble-rousers.

* * * * *

5 See Ep 2424:257.
6 Adrian of Utrecht became a cardinal in 1517 and was elected pope in 1522.
7 See Ep 1320 introduction.

When you write that there are some people who think they are missing 80
a great part of their happiness because they have not seen Erasmus, I think
that when they fondly kiss his bronze image and in seeing it are enflamed
with the love of study, it is not all in vain, although, if I am not mistaken,
you exaggerate the matter for the sake of consoling me.[8] But, to prevent me
from growing proud from this kind of demonstration of affection, there are 85
quite different feelings evinced by certain other individuals. I will tell you
something that will make you laugh. There is a certain canon in Constance
who has an image of me printed on paper that he keeps in his bedroom so
that while he is walking around he can spit on it every time he walks by it.
When people ask him the reason for his hatred, he answers that he holds 90
me responsible for this calamitous age. His community is banished from
Constance and he receives only half of the tithes.[9] Hence those tears.[10]

Previously, whether I liked it or not, I was a Lutheran. When this weapon was wrested from their hands, they tried something else – they say that I
provided the impetus for the founders of the sects.[11] This matter was treated 95
seriously again by Alberto Pio, whose huge volume was printed by Bade,[12]
although the work, as I hear, is not Alberto's but was put together from
many commissioned works. The principal collaborator is in Venice,[13] and the
Franciscans in Paris contributed no small share, for they have a master of
confused babbling named Petrus de Cornibus.[14] Pio himself did something 100
very clever – he stuck in the dart and took off with all speed. In fact, he died
many days before Bade finished the work.[15] He was called 'of Carpi,' and although he was deprived of this jurisdiction, the title remained, although the
reason for the name was different. At first he was called 'of Carpi' because
of the name of the principality; later it was from his passion for carping. 105
Moreover, so that you will know that he was not called Pio without good
reason, three days before he died he was dressed in the habit of St Francis.
In that garb he was transported with great pomp through the streets on the

* * * * *

8 Cf Ep 2424:127–41.
9 The cathedral chapter withdrew from Constance and moved to Überlingen in
    1527.
10 *Adagia* I iii 68, citing Terence *Andria* 126. The phrase is used 'when the reason for
    something had remained long concealed and at last the truth is discovered.'
11 See Ep 2414 n1.
12 See Ep 2414:10–14.
13 Girolamo Aleandro; see Ep 2379:110–12.
14 See Epp 2126 n37, 2205:220–7.
15 See Ep 2441 n17.

shoulders of Franciscans, with his face, hands, and feet uncovered, and buried in the monastery.[16] I do not criticize the religious sentiments of the man (it   110
is well known among the Italians), but I am astonished that those fathers, although they are not unaware of the character of the modern age, provoke the
animosity of the world against them, which is sufficiently intense already,
by ceremonies, not to say superstitions, of this kind. But I pray for light and
peace for the departed spirit of Alberto. I have not yet seen his work.   115

I am aware that some people are carried away with murderous hatred
for me, not only in Paris but also in Germany. As soon as they discovered
that the emperor was determined to liberate Germany from the dissensions
of sects, they began immediately to vomit their venom privately and publicly against Erasmus.[17] It is a long story, but you will learn part of it from   120
the pages I send you.[18] There are various kinds of martyrdoms, innumerable
forms of torture, a thousand types of deaths. In my case, perhaps, it will seem
that I should be compared with St Cassian,[19] who we learn was stabbed to
death with writing instruments by his students. But how much crueler things
Erasmus suffers, who for so many years has been stabbed as far as the vital   125
parts by the tongues and styluses of innumerable men and continues to live
in agony and feels it in his whole being and is not allowed to end his pain
with death.

But putting jest aside, I return to your letter. What is it I hear? You are
called a Lutheran because you paid a visit to Erasmus? But the people of   130
that sect, if they have heard that someone is seeking me out, are in the habit
of saying, 'Beware of that man! He will infect you if you meet with him. He
is the fiercest enemy of the Gospel.' What kind of appalling malice is this?
except that, as you wisely write, they do not read our writings and have no
desire to know what we are doing. They bellow out whatever they heard at   135
their communal meals and, like the Andabatae, they cleave the air with their
swords with their eyes closed.[20] But let us imagine that I am in agreement
with those whom they call heretics; how much more Christian it would have
been if their suspicion led them to think that you had sought a colloquium
with Erasmus with the intention of leading him back to the true path. How   140

* * * * *

16 See Ep 2441 n18.
17 See Epp 2365 n5, 2387, 2408.
18 Perhaps copies of letters received from Augsburg
19 Patron saint of Imola
20 *Andabatae* were gladiators who, to the amusement of the public, fought with
    helmets that had no aperture for their eyes, thus causing them to strike about
    blindly at their opponents; cf *Adagia* II iv 33.

far removed these people are from evangelical charity, which does not suspect or think evil.[21] What would they say if I went to see you and were to live with you under the same roof?

When you so generously lavish such great praise on me, most learned Maillard, you will not expect an equal amount from me, not because you   145
do not merit the same praise and even more, but rather because I do not acknowledge what you attribute to me, and also because your modesty, it seems to me, does not wish to be weighed down by such encomia. I wonder for what purpose you prefer mute teachers for acquiring a knowledge of the Greek language, when France has an abundance of men who are ex-   150
pert in Greek, and the live voice, besides having its peculiar force, also takes away half the labour for the learner. I praise you greatly for putting yourself to the test in translating Greek by yourself in order to see what progress you have made in your command of the two languages. But this exercise will be more effective if you have someone to criticize your version and if   155
you can compare your version with the translations of others. About your question whether *The Monk* of Chrysostom has been put into Latin by anyone else, I see that you are a man who has very little interest in what others are doing. For *The Monk*, which you say you published as an example of your apprenticeship, has been on sale for six years in the translation of   160
Oecolampadius.[22] Germain de Brie translated it too at my instigation, but since he played the part of Callipides and sent what he had translated too late,[23] since the complete Chrysostom was being printed, we used the version of Oecolampadius.[24] Moreover, Polidoro Virgilio translated the same work quite successfully in England and dedicated it to me. But it was printed in   165
Paris.[25] If I can locate Brie's version, I will send it to you so that you can compare yours with the three versions.

The rumour concerning a retractation came about, I think, from my having added to the last edition of the book in which I respond to the Spanish monks some passages from some of my works that have to be emended,   170
which I discovered myself or were suggested by friends.[26] But in entrusting this to friends I introduced errors while I was trying to correct them.

* * * * *

21 1 Cor 13:15
22 *Comparatio regis et monachi* (Basel: Cratander, October 1523)
23 Callipides was the proverbial name for someone who, 'with business to be got under way, threatened great activity and got nothing finished'; *Adagia* I vi 43.
24 See Ep 2359 introduction.
25 See Ep 2379 n16.
26 Ie the *Loca quaedam emendata*; see Epp 2095 introduction, 2424 n52.

This book came out in 1529. I will send it to you if I can find someone who does not refuse to carry a small bundle. Truly, I would not be ashamed or displeased to do the same thing with all my works, if I saw a way in which   175
I could remedy all the offences of all concerned. But what seems pious to some people seems impious to others. Shall I follow the rules of scholastic precepts? They themselves do not agree with one another. Certain people are offended by anything that is expressed in terms different from what they use in the schools. If I wanted to please them, everything would be insipid   180
for two reasons, partly because most dogmas taught in the schools are of such a kind that even if they are based on an unquestionable truth, they have no credit outside the school, partly because barbarous language takes away charm from things that in themselves are agreeable. What am I going to do with these people, who think they are skilled in Latin even though they do   185
not know the language? What am I to do with those who, since they bring a hostile frame of mind to their reading, distort everything into calumny? One thing sounds bad, another is suspect, another is like the error of the Turlupins,[27] another is offensive to pious ears, another is lacking in reverence, another is expressed without circumspection. If there is anything that   190
might possibly offend the feelings of princes or popes, it is schismatic. As if in itself the truth were not odious to those full of sores! Then, what can you do with those who do not read my writings? And that is the great majority, and none clamour more impudently. In such a diversity of opinions, in such outcries of those who refuse to listen, what advice do you give me? This is   195
my principle: if I found, or if it was pointed out to me by someone else, that something in my books was at variance with the unquestionable truths of the Catholic faith, I would obliterate it. A certain person from your sodality condemned what I wrote in the colloquy entitled *Inquisitio*, namely, that the Father is the author of all things, thus joining together two divine persons.[28]   200
But he thinks that *autor* means nothing else than *factor*, although *autor* is frequently used to mean the source and the origin of the thing in question, and *autoritas* means first principle and origin. That is how St Hilary often uses

* * * * *

27 On this sect of heretics, see Ep 843:620n.
28 See CWE 39 428:30–4 (*Inquisitio de fide* 'An Examination concerning the Faith'). The unnamed member of the Paris faculty of theology claimed that by calling God the Father the 'author of all things' Erasmus had made the Father the 'cause' of the Son, thus implying that the Son was of a substance distinct from that of the Father. Erasmus had, in other words, implicitly denied the doctrine of the Trinity. Erasmus provides a clearer and more detailed account of the dispute in Ep 2045:312–42.

these terms. If that certain person had been skilled in Latin, 'author of all things' would not have offended him any more than 'principle of all things.'   205 There is no end to this quarreling and calumniating. How many times they sing this tune to us about the *Retractations* of Augustine.[29] But a retractation is nothing other than a review. With this title he does not profess that he is putting together a correction of his errors but rather a catalogue and enu- meration of his works and, so to speak, the themes of each work, so that   210 none of his works would fall into oblivion and that no work of his would be attributed to another or another's work be attributed to him. He does indeed make some corrections in passing, I admit, but very slight ones, as that in one place he used the word 'chance,'[30] or that he made an error in the name of a doctor. But he defends many things, sometimes not without some equivoca-   215 tion. In addition, how many more serious things still remain in the books of that great man, like the statement that human merit counts for nothing! If something like that is found in my books I am branded as a Lutheran. How many times does he reiterate that baptism is of no use for children if they do not eat the flesh and drink the blood of the Lord![31] How many times does he   220 attribute to Peter, the prince of the apostles, the superstitious and perverse wish to drag the gentiles into Judaism![32]

I will omit the rest. Therefore it is useless to make such a fuss about this example of Augustine. Who corrected his own works more honestly than I? How many times did I revise the *Adagia*? How many times the *New*   225 *Testament*? What work is reprinted without my making some corrections in it? I did the same thing a year ago in a separate publication, and especially in those works that I thought would not have to be published again in my lifetime.[33] Therefore I owe you thanks, my very dear friend, for your solici- tude in spurring on one who was already running, but you would render   230

* * * * *

29 See Ep 2424 n51.
30 Augustine *De beata vita* CCSL 57.11
31 See Augustine *De baptismo parvulorum* 1.24.34. It was the practice of the church in Augustine's time to provide baptized infants with communion by placing into their mouths the priest's index finger, which had been dipped in the conse- crated wine. The biblical basis for this was John 6:53: 'Unless you eat the flesh of the Son of Man and drink his blood, you have no life in you.' The practice had virtually disappeared from the Western church by the thirteenth century. See *Annotations on Romans* CWE 56 149 and 159 n68.
32 *Epistolae ad Galatas expositionis liber unus* 15–16 PL 35 2113–15
33 In the *Loca quaedam emendata*; see lines 167–72 with n26 above.

me a greater service if you would indicate what should be corrected with
good reason. For everything is full of references to heresies and errors. I
have no doubt that your intention is unchanged, if only you had the time to
read my works.

To return to the Greeks, if you have no one to whom you can show   235
your works to be examined, there is another kind of exercise: translate a text
that has been translated by some learned man, but without looking at his
translation. When you have completed what you can, then compare both
translations with the Greek. You will enjoy a profit from this that you will not
regret. I think Chrysostom in Greek has already appeared from a publisher   240
in Verona.[34] In translating, Theodorus Gaza earns special praise.[35] Angelo
Poliziano is the greatest craftsman. For my part, I have always preferred a
faithful and learned simplicity, especially in hagiographic writings. Budé is
closer to it than Poliziano.

I think I have answered all the parts of your letter, more briefly, per-   245
haps, than you wished. But you will certainly pardon me if you consider that
after finishing some books I relaxed my tired mind to the extent of writing
more or less ninety letters at the same time,[36] of which some are two pages
longer than this one. I am grateful for your epigram, but you say one thing
in Greek and another in Latin. In Greek you do not say that I wish to be   250
liberated from loudmouths before meeting my death. Furthermore, I doubt
that *streperus* can be found for *obstreperus*.[37] I do not see the function of the
particle ἄν except that it fills a space in the verse. You could have said ἔκδικον
Ἀονίδων.[38] But I am abusing your kindness, dearest Maillard. I wish you the
best of health.   255

Given at Freiburg im Breisgau, 28 March AD 1531

* * * * *

34 The edition, never completed, supervised by Gian Matteo Giberti; see Ep 2340 n2.
35 It is true, as Allen points out, that Gaza had translated some of Chrysostom's
    homilies, but the point here is excellence in translating Greek authors in gen-
    eral, not Chrysostom in particular. Gaza was best known for his translations
    of Aristotle. Poliziano had translated works of Plato, Hippocrates, and Galen,
    while Budé had translated works by Plutarch, St Basil, and Pseudo-Aristotle
    (Ep 2422:47–51).
36 Cf Ep 2451 n1. No other letter written on this day is extant.
37 As Erasmus well knew, *streperus* was a barbarism.
38 See Ep 2424:356–61. Erasmus improves the verse considerably, eliminating the
    non-functional ἄν and substituting a name for the Muses deriving from Aonia,
    a mountain in Boeotia where Mt Helicon, sacred to the Muses, was located. The
    rhythm is also improved.

The letter you have before you is an autograph and a first draft, for I
scarcely had the time to reread it once it was written. I imagined that it would
be all the more gratifying to one who loves me as you do if you received it
with erasures and revisions, which give indication of a spirit that reveals   260
itself to a friend spontaneously, candidly, and without artificial adornment.

Desiderus Erasmus of Rotterdam, in my own hand

Ottmar Nachtgall, the deliverer of this letter, is the chief preacher of this
city, remarkably versed in music, with a good knowledge of languages and
good letters. If it is not inconvenient, you can send me your answer through   265
him. Farewell.

2467 / To Bonifacius Amerbach   [Freiburg], 30 March [1531]

This letter (= AK Ep 1511) was first published in the *Epistolae familiares*. The autograph is in the Öffentliche Bibliothek of the University of Basel (MS AN III 15
92). For the year-date see Ep 2464 introduction.

Cordial greetings. I think the young Frisian brought you my letter.[1] What
you remind me of concerning Alciati was done some time ago.[2] That is clear
from his letter,[3] which I am sending to you. I do not remember anything
about the declamation, and I suspect that Alciati had a lapse of memory or
that the person to whom he confided the declamation did not deliver it. After   5
going through all my papers I did not find anything of the kind.[4] Here many
changes are occurring. I do not know what will come of them. Serious deliberations are necessary. But this must be done in person if it is possible. If not,
I will send a trustworthy person. Why do you thank me for the hospitality
I offered you? As if I did not consider it a great benefit that you would stay   10
with me for a few days to do as you pleased. If I did not love you in a special
way, I would be angry because you preferred to stay with Glareanus.[5] But it
is human. Our female servant is already past her prime. Farewell.

30 March

* * * * *

2467
1 Ep 2464. The young Frisian is unidentified.
2 See Ep 2464:1–4.
3 Evidently the letter mentioned in Ep 2468:192–4
4 This is doubtless an honest statement, but it is probable that the manuscript was
   indeed in Erasmus' possession and that in due course it became the basis for the
   edition of the work that was published at Leiden in 1695; see Ep 1233A n5.
5 Henricus Glareanus (Epp 440, 2098 n1) who, like Erasmus, had moved from
   Basel to Freiburg in 1529

Yours, Erasmus of Rotterdam   15
Greetings to the royal personage.[6]
To the most distinguished Doctor Bonifacius Amerbach. At Basel

2468 / To Andrea Alciati   Freiburg, 31 March 1531

First published in the *Epistolae floridae*, this is Erasmus' reply to Ep 2394. The
autograph is in the Royal Library at Copenhagen (MS GKS 95 Fol, folio 225).

ERASMUS OF ROTTERDAM TO ANDREA ALCIATI, GREETING
Although in the past you made abundantly known by many proofs your
singular devotion to me, more by virtue of your kind disposition than of
my merits, most learned Alciati, you gave no more convincing proof of your
estimation of me than in this last letter, in which, no less eloquently than af-   5
fectionately, you suggest that I regain my calm and tranquillity in the face of
the rabble-rousers more by silence and contempt than by struggling against
them. Whence comes this great solicitude for me except from an abundance
of love, or to put it more correctly, from your sentiment of loyalty towards
me? But you are neither the first nor the only one to sing me this tune. I have   10
heard the same thing for a long time now from the most preeminent of my
friends, Cuthbert Tunstall, Jacopo Sadoleto, and Giambattista Egnazio,[1] although the last two presented themselves as counsellors almost too late, so
that they almost seem to bring help after the war is over and give medical
care to the corpse.[2] But their good will is nonetheless gratifying, though their   15
service was less useful. In the end, it is still something to learn wisdom late
with the Phyrgians.[3]
    Permit me to recall some past events. Lest I seem to be exonerating my-
self, I am ashamed and chagrined that I responded to certain people; but I
would not have answered them if I had preferred to manage the affair at my   20
own discretion rather than follow the advice of eminent friends. And then,
since some were counselling silence and others encouraged me to take up

* * * * *

6 Ie Bonifacius' older brother Basilius, whose name in Greek (*Basileos*) means
  'royal' or 'kingly'

2468
1 See Epp 2226:13–37 (Tunstall), 2385:34–54 (Sadoleto). No such letter from
  Egnazio is extant.
2 *Adagia* III vi 17, cited in Greek
3 *Adagia* I i 28

my pen forcefully, I followed a middle path between the two, namely, that I
would neither answer everyone nor be silent with everyone, but I would always outdo my opponents in moderation. I hate my destiny every time I pass   25
my *apologiae* in review. What could I blame more justly than destiny, since my
nature abhors, and has abhorred from my early years, nothing more than this
kind of gladiatorial combat, in which the password is 'die or kill.' Into this
arena the ineluctable power of the Fates pushed my body, carrying it off its
true course. And the force of stubborn necessity is immovable.[4] I will add this: 30
what if some god willed it? How do we know the designs of the supreme director who regulates the play of human life? For it is possible that what seems
evil and ugly to us who view the single parts of the play seems very good and
most beautiful to him who sees the harmony of the universe. In the comedy
who would not prefer to be Micio rather than Syrus? And yet in the structure   35
of the whole play Syrus does not have the lowest role.[5] When you call upon
me to imitate your example, I admit that I am invited to a very beautiful role,
which I would not be unwilling to imitate if only that were possible. But what
shall we do if the stage director has assigned me a very different role?

Certainly, it is owing to a rare degree of moderation and prudence   40
that, as you write, you consign the ignorant to silence and win the favour
of the learned with kindness and respect. But you have to do with men, I
with deadly monsters, or rather, not with single monsters as they say was
the case with Hercules, but with many phalanxes conspiring against me, and
none of them are more harmful than those that are most ignorant. Lions and   45
dragons become mild when one does a service for them;[6] these people are irritated by good deeds. They recommended themselves to princes and to the
people under the guise of sanctity and cry 'heretical, schismatic, false.' They
had poured out so much deadly poison both in the court of the emperor and
in sacred assemblies before the ignorant multitude that had he not taken up   50

* * * * *

4 *Adagia* II iii 41
5 In Terence's comedy *Adelphi*, Micio is the character who, when he reproves
 his wayward, adopted son Aeschinus, demonstrates 'much gentleness even in
 his severity'; see Ep 1451:93–5. Syrus is the traditional wily slave, whose ruses
 guarantee that things work out well for his masters. It would have made more
 sense in context if Erasmus had here, as in Ep 1451:91–3, contrasted Micio to his
 brother Demea, who, 'when he wants to be courteous and cheerful,' reveals 'a
 touch of boorish bitterness even in his pleasantries.'
6 As in Aesop's tale of Androcles and the Lion or in the pious legend of St Jerome
 and his lion. Both extracted a thorn from the paw of the lion and won his eternal gratitude.

his pen against them eight years ago,[7] Erasmus would be prostrate on the ground, struck by lightening. And they were not inactive in playing their roles in the presence of Pope Clement. If, therefore, you ask what results I had, I will tell you in a word: I owe it to my pen and my tongue that I am still alive. I have not appeased them, but learned and honest men are armed 55 with my *apologiae* against monsters of this sort, so that they are not allowed to do as they please. In the end, when after his funeral rites Erasmus is silent, perhaps his *apologiae* will speak.

For you, besides occupying a magnificent and exalted position, easily drive off the shamelessness of dishonest scoundrels by your own distinc- 60 tions, your excellent learning, your affability, your exceptional prudence, your lustrous grandeur. If any controversy arises among you, it is only a dispute over supremacy of talent, so that this goddess of strife, according to the judgment of Hesiod, contributes much usefulness to studies, as long as it does not degenerate into rage.[8] I have to do with peevish and hot-tempered 65 people; and if anyone disagrees with them about a word, he is immediately called a heretic, a schismatic, and a fraud, and is dragged by force into peril of his fortunes, his fame, and his life. So great is their ferocity that it is prefer-able to fall into the hands of the Cyclopes or the Laestrigonians.[9] Monarchs distracted by many affairs cannot be attentive to everyone's tricks, and yet 70 it is owing to their favour that I have survived until now. For they are men, to say nothing more: if there had been as much ferocity in them as there is in these impostors wearing masks, languages along with good letters would long ago have been in exile among the nomads, or rather in hell. As a matter of fact, among the inhabitants of this region there are crass-minded men who 75 all but persuaded the common people that there was no difference between someone who knows the Latin and Greek languages well and a heretic. And yet we engaged in battle with these monsters with reasonably well-matched forces, save that the wolf, who appeared suddenly in the story, turned the scene of human affairs upside down, took away the voice of those who cul- 80 tivate the Muses,[10] and made the voice of the frogs louder. Would God the princes had allowed me to stay out of it.

* * * * *

7 In Ep 1385:15–16 (4 September 1523), Erasmus stated that he had something in the works 'against the new doctrines.' The first draft of *De libero arbitrio* was ready in February 1524 (Ep 1419 introduction).
8 Hesiod *Works and Days* 11–23
9 A legendary race of cannibalistic giants (Homer *Odyssey* 10.105–32)
10 It was said that a man who catches sight of a wolf who has seen him first will be rendered speechless and forget what he had been thinking; see *Adagia* IV v 50. The 'wolf' here is doubtless Martin Luther.

What do you accomplish, most eloquent Alciati, when you propose your example to me? What else but that as I congratulate you and your studies on your good fortune and, acknowledging my own fate, I become less 85 satisfied with myself? Alciati is to be numbered among the lucky sons of the gods: he is fortunate and beautiful and daring, and if he catches a cold he sings well; in short, he is out of range of the shafts of envy. But with more credibility you propose to a theologian the examples of the ancient theologians. Cyprian heard himself called Coprian.[11] Why did such a great bish- 90 op not ignore this insult, while I, when I so often am called, with a change of name, now Errasmus from erring,[12] now Arasmus from plowing,[13] now Erasinus from ass,[14] do nothing but laugh? No one wielded his pen very forcefully against the life of Augustine, partly because of all that part of his life that he lived blamelessly, partly because he came to baptism when he was 95 already grown up, and at that time it was considered very base to reproach a person for what he had done before the purification of new birth. And yet he answers the slightest vituperation, such as the accusation of vainglory; he is always armed against calumniators of his good faith; and he responds to articles directed against him in a special book. It is surprising that a man 100 endowed with such leniency and kindness could have been so outraged by insults, whatever the source. Jerome's fate is not very different from mine. When does he not rage against the dogs barking at his heels? As often, you say, as the authenticity of the Christian religion was in danger, he picked up his pen so that the more simple would not be attracted to error; he was silent 105 about personal insults.[15] I think the object of my apologies is simply to refute the charge of heresy, schism, or chicanery. To remain silent before these is not leniency, but impiety. Against those who insult my talent, my learning, my eloquence, my judgment, or even my morals, for the most part I have neither tongue nor pen; or if I do make answer I do it with contempt and with a gen- 110 tle touch. But consider how angrily Jerome contends with Augustine, how bitterly he disputes with Rufinus, and in many places criticizes Palladius. And does he mince words when he answers the people in Rome who accused him that he was on too familiar terms with Paula?[16]

* * * * *

11 See Ep 2394 n14.
12 See Ep 1482:52–5, and cf Ep 2169 n4.
13 The Latin word *arare* means 'to plow.' See Ep 1482 n28.
14 See Ep 2408 n4, and cf Ep 2169:58–9.
15 See Ep 2394:70–1.
16 Jerome was much criticized by people in Rome for persuading noble matrons like Paula to accompany him to Bethlehem, where they established convents.

Therefore you must surely recognize that it was more out of friendship 115
than reality that you wrote: 'You are mistaken, Erasmus, if you have such
a low opinion of the prestige of your name and the respect of the learned
world that you would think that by denigrations of this kind you can be
brought tumbling down from the citadel of learning and uprightness that
you have so long occupied.' 'Prestige' and 'citadel' are words inspired by 120
friendship, not reality. But if neither an incomparable erudition, nor the lightening bolt of his marvellous eloquence, nor the rare sanctity of his life, nor
the authority of his name, acquired by so many merits, could protect Jerome
from the yapping of the wicked, how do you think that I, whose mediocrity
has been the target of all the attacks of jealousy, could do so? Envy, in fact, 125
seeks neither the sublime nor what crawls along the ground. And what of
your attempt to persuade me to prepare for a triumph as if my enemies were
defeated? Of my celebrated accomplishments you cite four: the *Adagia*, the
Novum instrumentum and the *Paraphrases*, and the commentaries on Jerome.
The *Paroemiology*[17] did not attract much jealousy towards me, and would that 130
I had spent all my time on similar subjects. The *New Testament*, in particular,
provoked those against me who should have thanked me more than others
for my zeal.[18] The *Paraphrases* passed through people's hands for a long time
and gained their approbation, until a canker, creeping up stealthily from I
know not where, began to pull them to pieces for the simple reason that in 135
them I preferred to follow the ancient commentators rather than the precepts
of modern scholastics.[19] Even the edition of Jerome was accepted with equanimity at first, until those rose up who, it seems, decided that what Erasmus
published should not be exempt from calumny.[20]

* * * * *

There were even insinuations of amorous relations. Jerome answers them angrily in Epistle 45 to another female follower named Asella.
17 Ie the *Adagia*; Greek in the text
18 The most prolonged and vociferous attacks came from Nicolaas Baechem,
Edward Lee, and Diego López Zúñiga (Epp 1301:168–85, 1341A:822–6, 868–84),
but the first one came from his friend Maarten van Dorp (Ep 1341:811–14).
19 The initial assault on the *Paraphrases* began in 1523, when Noël Béda undertook a search for errors in the *Paraphrase on Luke*; see Ep 1571 introduction.
The following year, the Parlement of Paris, acting at the instigation of the
faculty of theology, banned the publication of the *Paraphrases* on Luke and
Mark; see Ep 1591 n2. For the continuation of the attacks and Erasmus' rejoin-
ders, see Epp 1804 n14, 1807A, 1884 n8, 1902 introduction, 1909 n21 and lines
142–7, 2033 n15.
20 See Ep 2045:30–9.

Although I have difficulties with both camps, an indication that I do 140
not spend much time in these quarrels is that from time to time, if not that
rich garden of Alcinous, which Homer admired for producing fruit upon
fruit,[21] at least the little garden of the old man from Corycus, whom Virgil
celebrates,[22] provides me with some vegetables once in a while. For golden
apples are produced in the orchard of those who are like you. I could oppose 145
arguments in rhetorical style to other points that you make, but I would prefer any other type of argument. In this I frankly admit a failing of mine, and
not an insignificant one. Nevertheless, for a long time I have been contemplating of my own accord doing what you advise; thanks to your exhortation, I will do it more conscientiously. I congratulate you on your happiness, 150
since you were fortunate enough to have a profession that has very little
contact with these hornets; I greatly admire your prudence in making every
effort to avoid bitter conflicts with anyone.

If Longeuil had dedicated to Greek authors the time and effort he expended in Rome torturing himself so that he would be enrolled among the 155
Ciceronians and Roman citizens, he would have better consulted both his
own interests and the state of public studies. But the envious Fates did not
wish to show this intelligence to the world for long.[23] Budé is a man without
malice, and if he conceives some resentment for someone, he does so more
at the prompting of someone else than of his own nature; otherwise, he is a 160
man of conciliatory character and never flares up to the point of becoming
virulent. Among his letters I discovered several either addressed to you or
that speak of you, in which he makes clear what a high regard he has for your
learning and how he sincerely favours your interests. Personally I read them
with great pleasure.[24]   165

As for our Sucket, the disciple of your Minerva, I am extremely grateful
to you for honouring and encouraging him with exceptional commitment,
and I have no regret in acknowledging that, although I was already obliged
to you for so many other favours, I have become much more indebted to you
for this reason. Since, as you write, you grant him this favour because he 170
merits it, I congratulate him first as a fortunate man, for he has won the sincere approbation of such a great man, and second, because he is happy in that
he is richly endowed with those qualities that have enabled him to have the

* * * * *

21 Homer *Odyssey* 7.120
22 Virgil *Georgics* 4.127
23 See Ep 1948 introduction.
24 In the recently published new edition of his letters; see Ep 2449 n10.

approval of your most perspicacious and accurate judgment.[25] Concerning
Viglius, I wrote diligently to Zasius,[26] for we cannot communicate with one 175
another in any other way, I being voiceless and he half-deaf. He did not answer, which is not like him. Zasius secured from King Ferdinand that even
though he was discharging him from his duties as a professor because of his
age, he should not be deprived of his salary. But he makes no allowance for
either his age or his health, thinking, as I see it, that it is a beautiful thing for 180
a professor to die teaching. Although the university here was not very well
attended at other times, it is even less frequented because of the plague.[27] If
in the course of nature something should happen to Zasius, or if he should
stop teaching, I think Bonifacius Amerbach, if he desires it, will succeed him,
for they are very close friends and Bonifacius, because of his rare moral in- 185
tegrity, enjoys favour with all kinds of people.[28] Added to this is his extraordinary charity, which increases every day, even though the number of those
who eat their bread is declining. I do not know what state of things awaits
Germany; for me, at least, the prologues are very displeasing. If Viglius, or
rather Vigilius, is looking for a theatre in which he can give a specimen of his 190
learning, I know of no better place than Louvain.

Five years ago I had indicated that I gave that little declamation to
Vulcanius because you had so ordered, and you thanked me for this service
in the same letter in which you lament the death of Pyrrhus.[29] I am surprised
that this preoccupation has sprouted up again in your mind. But I see that 195
what is said in the Greek proverb is very true: Plutus is a coward.[30] A thou-

* * * * *

25 See Ep 2394:130–3.
26 See Ep 2418, in which Erasmus joins Alciati in recommending both Karel Sucket
and Viglius Zuichemus as possible successors to Zasius' professorship in law at
Freiburg.
27 Ep 2426 n3
28 In the spring of 1529 Zasius had proposed that Bonifacius resettle in Freiburg as
his assistant and eventual successor; see Burckhardt Epp 39, 54.
29 On Alciati's quest for reassurance that Erasmus had destroyed his youthful declamation against the monastic life, see Epp 2464:1–4, 2467:1–6. The indication of
compliance referred to here was made more than five years earlier. In Ep 1261
(24 February 1522), which is the surviving fragment of a longer letter now lost,
Alciati thanks Erasmus for his efforts to keep the declamation from being read by
anyone and asks him to burn it. It was presumably in the lost portion of the same
letter that Alciati lamented the death of Pyrrhus (cf Epp 1250:8–10, 1278:7–9). The
Vulcanius referred to here can scarcely be the Petrus Vulcanius of Ep 2460, who
was still in his teens in 1522 and never had any connection with Alciati.
30 Ie someone whom wealth makes fearful and distrustful; *Adagia* III vii 2

sand crowns make you more fearful.[31] But, my dear Alciati, I repeat what
I wrote: if no copy has remained with anyone else you can, as far as the
one you sent to me is concerned, sleep soundly not only on either ear,[32] but
even on either eye. Far be it from me the intention of publishing something   200
that would harm your fame, especially when your wishes have been made
known to me.

I saw that this last letter of yours, no less learned than eloquent, deserves being published for the benefit of a great number of readers, but I
abandoned the idea because of a few words you had slipped in here and   205
there, since there is now a scorpion sleeping under every stone.[33] Farewell.

Freiburg im Breisgau, 31 March 1531, according to our way of reckoning

2469 / To Alfonso de Valdés   Freiburg, [March] 1531

> This letter was first published in the *Epistolae floridae*. The reference to the sum-
> mer of 1530 (line 46) suggested to Allen a month-date earlier than the onset of
> summer 1531. For Valdés see Ep 1807.

ERASMUS OF ROTTERDAM TO ALFONSO DE VALDÉS, GREETING
I hear that you take note of my inactivity, since the closer I get to you the
shorter and rarer are the letters I write to you.[1] It is not displeasing to me
that in this respect you require that I fulfil my duties towards you. For this
too is a proof of your good will towards Erasmus. But I want you to believe   5
in my good faith: there is no mortal whose letters I more gladly receive than
yours nor to whom I more gladly send them. But since there was nothing
for me to write about that would bring you pleasure, whether it concerned
my health or the state of my affairs, I was ashamed to burden your kindly

* * * * *

31 This is presumably a reference to Alciati's 'huge salary,' which was in fact six
hundred crowns; see Ep 2194:15–16 with n4.
32 *Adagia* I viii 19. Cf Ep 1250:20, where Erasmus assures Alciati that he can 'sleep
the sleep of the just.'
33 *Adagia* I iv 34. For the delay in the publication of Ep 2394, see the introduction
to that letter.

2469
1 Valdés had accompanied the emperor to Italy in 1529, and had been with
him at the Diet of Augsburg from 15 June until 23 November 1530 and in the
Rhineland for the rest of the year. He spent the entire year 1531 with Charles in
the Netherlands.

disposition with my acrimonious complaints. I do not know whether I in-   10
formed you of this in a previous letter, but I had at any rate resolved to do so.
Consequently, since I understood from what you wrote that you had decided
to keep clear altogether of these odious individuals,[2] which gave me cause
to rejoice, what was left for me to write to you except that your commend-
able action endeared you to me and that I was much indebted to you for so   15
many reasons – something which is too clear to require any attestation. And
I think it was for the same reason that your letters also arrived here much
more rarely and were briefer than usual and to a certain extent, it seemed to
me, more spiritless.[3] I must go wherever the Fates draw me and compel me
to return. But your nature, the domicile of the Graces, does not deserve to be   20
contaminated by any animosity or distress.

    I can easily imagine what you heard in your conversation with the
black-hearted individual concerning whom I warned you by letter,[4] but I do
not think that your good will towards me was diminished in any way because of it. If you have any doubts about my sentiments towards you, signify   25
by a single little word what kind of service I may accomplish to please you;
if I do not set about to do it immediately with great eagerness, inscribe my
name on the list of ingrates. I would have dedicated a work to you long ago,
but some are delighted by this kind of homage, and some are offended, and
sometimes I do not render this courtesy to my dearest friends in order not to   30
expose them to envy. What can I do? You do not accept money, for you repay
double what is owed to the one who offers it. Shall I send books? Not even
this is possible as long as you play the role of someone always in motion.
You have no need of my recommendation, which is most agreeable to me,
and I rejoice that this is owing to your merit. I have no doubt that your con-   35
duct and the favour of the emperor will advance you to the highest dignity.
It is not the place of secretaries to write about what goes on at court, nor is
it correct for me to wish to know it from them. It remains, therefore, dearest
Alfonso, either that you believe that my sentiments towards you are those of
one who is grateful for the many excellent services he received, or that you   40

* * * * *

2 Doubtless a reference to the religious orders in Spain, against whom Valdés
  firmly defended Erasmus when they brought accusations of heresy against him
  in 1527; see Ep 1839.
3 No letter from Valdés to Erasmus written after the former's departure from
  Spain in 1529 is extant. Erasmus wrote Ep 2349 in response to a letter now lost;
  and Ep 2528 indicates that Valdés had replied to this letter.
4 The letter is not extant; the person referred to is identified as Aleandro in Allen
  Ep 2528:15–16. Aleandro was papal nuncio at the imperial court in 1531.

give me an opportunity by which you may put to the proof my feelings in your regard.

I have written this without knowing whether this letter will reach you. I am most grateful to you for the favour you have showed my servant Lieven.[5] As for me, after my abscess burst, my health is a little better, thanks to Christ.   45 Summer was sterile for me.[6] In the winter I gave premature birth to a few things, among them six books of apophthegms and a little commentary on Psalm 33.[7] That was the prologue of one recovering little by little from a sickness. Now we are girding ourselves for more serious things, provided that we can see Germany free from war.   50

Farewell, most faithful friend.

Given at Freiburg im Breisgau, AD 1531

2470 / To Johann Koler   [Freiburg, end of March 1531]

> This letter was first published in the *Vita Erasmi*. The approximate date derives from the clear connection to Ep 2462, which gives a similar but shorter version of Erasmus' difficulties concerning the occupation of his house in Freiburg. For an account of those difficulties, the people involved, and the final resolution, see the introduction to that letter. For Koler, see Ep 2384.

ERASMUS OF ROTTERDAM TO THE MOST DISTINGUISHED GENTLEMAN JOHANN KOLER, PROVOST OF CHUR, GREETING

When in the end the situation seemed to be intolerable in Basel, I migrated to Freiburg lest I seem to approve of what was going on there. But before that I had been highly recommended by King Ferdinand to the venerable   5 magistrates of this city,[1] who of their own accord awarded me the use of this house, which master Jakob Villinger, of pious memory, had built, and they were prepared to honour me with even greater services, if I had permitted it. The house was then occupied by Ottmar Nachtgall and Augustinus Marius, formerly a preacher in Basel. A part of it fell to me together with them.   10 After about eight months Marius moved and gave two florins, according to

* * * * *

5 Lieven Algoet, who was in search of employment at the court; see Ep 2278 n2.
6 For Erasmus' serious illness in the spring and summer of 1530, see Ep 2360 n1.
7 See Epp 2431 (*Apophthegmata*), 2428 (*Enarratio psalmi 33*).

2470
1 For the move and Ferdinand's assistance with it, see Ep 2090 introduction.

Nachtgall, as a sign of gratitude. Nachtgall stayed for a long time. As for me, not to appear impolite, I sent to the honourable lord Ulrich, the tribune of the people,[2] the sum of four crowns for almost as many months as Marius had spent there, plus the amount I had spent on expenses for the house, which 15 came to five crowns.

Some time later, around Christmas, the tribune, via Henricus Glareanus, entered into negotiations about renting the whole house, including a square courtyard situated behind the house. He gave me to understand that it could be rented for a year for twenty florins. I answered both through Glareanus 20 and in writing that if the widow did not mind playing the part of a lessee, I would gladly give her twelve crowns, provided the house was rented to me free and clear.[3] I mentioned that Nachtgall would not leave willingly, and that I did not wish to wrangle with anyone, least of all with Nachtgall. A little later, I wrote again to the honourable tribune, stating my intentions clearly, 25 that I had no need of the courtyard. Schmotzer and others had horses there,[4] and carpenters and stonemasons, whom I would not wish to expel, worked there. But if he could make the house free to me, and if a reasonable rent were proposed, I would answer whether I wanted it or not. The honourable tribune has kept this written document to himself.   30

Since no further word came from the tribune, I thought I was living there on the same terms as before, that is, without any contract, waiting to see if the tribune would give notice. Just before winter[5] Nachtgall began to move into the house of a certain abbot, leaving the greater part of his furnishings here, however, and coming around every day as if he were living in two hous- 35 es. Around the coming of the next winter he removed almost all his furniture. When I saw that, I went up to the man and said, 'Are you really moving out now?' He smiled and said yes. In the end, when I asked him if he would not mind leaving the keys with someone so that the place could be cleaned, if that could be done without any inconvenience to him, he answered that after 40 his return from Strasbourg he wished to speak to the tribune. After this discussion about the keys, he left a few belongings so that he would not seem to be forfeiting his rights. You could put all of them into one basket.

* * * * *

2 On Ulrich Wirtner see Ep 2462 introduction and n2.
3 Ie to him alone, free of the presence of Nachtgall
4 Georg Schmotzer (Ep 1922) had been a professor of law at Freiburg for eleven years when, in 1525, he became a member of the Hapsburg government at Ensisheim. It seems, however, that he still had connections and property in Freiburg, to which he would return on his retirement in 1547.
5 In 1529–30

When he returned, I brought up the matter of the keys once again, not as a lessor – nothing was further from my thoughts – but politely and as if ask- 45
ing a favour, with the condition that this was convenient to him and that his rights would be protected. After much hesitation he came to discuss the mat-ter with me. I began by saying that I would be very pleased if without any inconvenience to himself he could accommodate me in this; but if not, I did not want to argue about it. When, as usually happens, the discussion became 50
heated, he answered pompously what he was accustomed to say frequently to others, that he had been designated by Jakob Villinger and his heirs to own this house, that he could not cede possession of it to anyone, and that he knew for certain that it was their will. When I answered that he would not be deprived of any of his rights if he handed over the keys so that the apartment 55
could be kept clean, and that it was now occupied by mice and spiders, he did not acquiesce, but kept the keys and closed the apartment more securely than before. I added in the end that the tribune had begun to confer with me about renting the whole house. He answered that he had the right to the whole courtyard and that I was living there out of the goodness of his heart, 60
since he could occupy the whole house himself. 'If that is so,' I said, 'why is the tribune treating with me about the renting of the whole house?' 'I will also talk to the tribune,' he said, 'and I know the mind of the tribune.' And there were many other such statements about his rights, which were to be ob-served by reason of intent, though not by physical occupancy.[6] I put an end 65
to the discussion. After inviting the tribune and others to dinner, he boasted to my servant Quirinus[7] that there was complete accord between him and the tribune and that he talked very differently with him than with me.

After this conversation I sensed that the man was not well disposed towards me. He complained a lot about me to my servant Quirinus. And 70
people assure me that at Strasbourg he said many more-than-hostile things against me, and I believe them, although he denies it. I can easily imagine what he writes to his friends. A short time later, when the plague was raging here,[8] I asked politely that he allow that apartment, which he kept closed and

* * * * *

6 The Latin of the final clause of this sentence – 'quod animo teneretur, non cor-pore' – is a variant of the legal phrase *animo et corpore* 'with mind and body,' or 'with intent and physical act.' In this context, it means that, according to Erasmus, Nachtgall was asserting claim to the property (*animo*) but without physically occupying it (*non corpore*). See *Digest* 50.17.153, and 41.23.1.
7 Quirinus Talesius (Ep 2367 n3), who was in the final weeks of his service to Erasmus
8 About May 1530; see Ep 2426 n3.

empty, to be available to us, so that there would be more space if anything 75
happened to anyone in my household. You will learn what he answered from
the letter I am sending to you,⁹ in which he asserts his rights persistently.
Finally I succeeded through a polite letter in having him leave the door open
(since without the key it could not be opened on the inside or the outside).
He held on to the keys. I gave him a letter-box, in which he could put two or 80
three letters so that it would not seem that he had moved out, and he took
the key to the box with him.

The halcyon days¹⁰ passed without my having to use that apartment
(thanks to the gods). I merely took care that it remained clean. Towards the
end of March the honourable tribune summoned Glareanus and showed 85
him a letter of a certain agent, the distinguished gentleman Johann Löble,
the king's treasurer, in which he wrote that he had received orders from the
owner that I should be asked to move before the feast of St John the Baptist,¹¹
that is, within three months, and at the same time the honourable tribune
asked me for twenty florins for the past year from Christmas to Christmas. 90
For me, who never dreamed that I was considered a tenant, this was as new
as if someone had showed me a black swan. I never received any contract
and always understood that the house was free. Nachtgall continued to affirm that he had a right to the whole house. He had the keys of the house
and he could enter it whenever he wished. I was never told by the tribune 95
that I was living in a rented house, and I was never told to ask Nachtgall for
the keys. How could it have ever entered my mind that I was renting the
whole house? At first the honourable tribune said, 'Let Erasmus deal with
Nachtgall.' On the contrary, in order not to contend with him, I stipulated
expressly that I should have free disposition of the whole house and testified 100
that he would not leave willingly. If someone had given me the house on the
condition that I should expel Nachtgall, whether he liked it or not, I would
have refused the gift without hesitation, so far was I from wanting to rent it
under these conditions.

The objection was also made that after mention was made of the price 105
of rental, I stayed in the house as if I had signified my approval. On the
contrary, in writing and orally I constantly affirmed that I did not wish to

* * * * *

9 Not extant
10 Since the 'halcyon days' (*Adagia* II vi 52) occurred around the winter solstice,
the reference here would be to late December 1530.
11 24 June. The owner was Löble's stepson, Karl Villinger, for whom he was acting
as agent; see Allen Ep 2497:4–5 (Villinger is mentioned but not named).

come to any agreement about the house unless it was the whole house and it was vacant. I remained there on the previous condition, on precarious terms obviously, prepared to leave whenever I received the order. No one gave the order. It would have been different if someone said to a person living in a rented house: 'I can rent this house at a higher price.' If the one who was so advised remained in the house, he would appear to accept the increased rent. So many people had made use of this house rent-free that I thought that the magistrates, partly out of their generosity and partly on the recommendation of King Ferdinand, wished to do me this honour. And although no contract had been made, I would have given more than I hear others gave. I had frequently said and written that I preferred to pay twenty florins for this house entirely unoccupied than five florins for one that was not, as is the case now. The tribune said that he asked Nachtgall to return the keys and that he answered, 'I left them in the house.' He told the truth: he did leave some keys in the house, but not the ones the tribune was thinking of; the keys to the front door and to the apartment that he occupied he kept for himself, and he still has them. That is the way he tricked the tribune.

I would not wish to live in this house on precarious terms or as a tenant. Nevertheless, it would be a kind gesture to give an earlier notice of the departure deadline to someone who is an old man in poor health, or rather quite ill, and in addition a guest recommended by letters of Emperor Charles and King Ferdinand,[12] especially since I must have a fireplace built in the new house and furnish a comfortable nest for this frail body. Three months is a very short time in which to find a house, rent or buy it, furnish it, and build a fireplace. But as of the end of March I am ordered to move out before the feast of John the Baptist. And in the meantime, while I neither rented the house nor wished to rent it unless it were put completely at my disposal, and clearly testified to this by word and in writing, they are asking me for thirty florins for the period from Christmas 1529 until the feast of St John 1531,[13] as if I had rented and occupied the whole house. But I am confident that the tribune on further investigation will change his mind.

Erasmus of Rotterdam. I signed this in my own hand.

* * * * *

12 For Ferdinand's recommendation see n1 above, and cf Ep 2317. The only known 'recommendation' from Charles is Ep 2318.
13 Ie eighteen months; cf Ep 2462:6–7, where Erasmus specifies that the rent demanded was for fifteen months, ie until the end of March 1531.

2471 / From Ambrosius Pelargus   [Freiburg, c end of March 1531]

This letter was first published in Pelargus' *Bellaria epistolarum Erasmi Rot. et Ambrosii Pelargi vicissim missarum* (Cologne: H. Fuchs 1539), folio B5. The contents of the letter make it clear that Pelargus wrote it in Freiburg, and the reference in line 1 to the *Apophthegmata*, which were published towards the end of March 1531, determines the approximate date. For Pelargus, the Dominican who had moved from Basel to Freiburg three months before Erasmus did the same, see Ep 2169 introduction.

The copy of the *Apophthegmata*,[1] the only one you had left, was brought to me by your very courteous servant.[2] Certainly, this literary gift cannot but be most welcome, both because it is tangible proof of your good will towards me and because the work itself is attractive and a delight to read, and commends itself by its great usefulness. I would seem ungrateful if I did not re- 5 turn to you a token of my gratitude. And so, since I had nothing else on hand (such is my indigence), I send you the only thing I have, a threadbare little present.[3] It is a story, a ridiculous one at that, but it would have turned into a bloody brawl if the spectators had not broken up the dispute. It is important that you too should know about this tragicomedy. In a little town not far 10 from Heilbronn,[4] a Franciscan mounted the pulpit, about to deliver a sermon on the feast of St Stephen,[5] taking for his subject something from the Sacred Scriptures, as is the custom: 'Stephen was full of grace and power.'[6] There happened to be a certain preacher present who had a smattering of Greek but who was much more sharp-eyed than Erasmus, since he saw something 15 in the text that had obviously eluded you. When he heard what the subject was, he attacked the Franciscan (who was a rather presumptuous type) in fe-

* * * * *

2471
1 Ep 2431
2 Doubtless Quirinus Talesius (Ep 2470 n7)
3 *Adagia* III v 22, citing Cicero *Ad familiares* 9.19.2
4 Heilbronn, a free imperial city on the Neckar, midway between Stuttgart and Heidelberg
5 26 December
6 Acts 6:8 as given in the Vulgate. In all editions of his New Testament through that of 1527, Erasmus too had *plenus gratia* 'full of grace,' which corresponded to the manuscripts he had consulted. In the edition of 1535, however, he substituted *plenus fide* 'full of faith,' which corresponded to manuscripts that he had come to deem better. The King James Version has 'faith,' but virtually all English translations except the New King James Version have gone back to 'grace.' Cf n8 below.

rocious language, thinking that he could drive him, overcome by the hatred
and hostility of the people, from the pulpit. Both of them were remarkably
loud-spoken. They shouted at the top of their voices from one end of the 20
church to the other, until they were hoarse (as they say),[7] so much so that
some of the spectators took fright. There was the distinct danger that the
vault of the church, which on several occasions, had threatened to collapse
because of the loud uproar, would in the end annihilate everyone.

'What was it about?' you will say. The Lutheran accused the Franciscan 25
of falsifying the Sacred Scriptures, claiming that in Greek it said Stephen was
full of faith, not grace.[8] Since the Franciscan knew no Greek, he forcefully
defended his subject matter as well as he could on the authority of Erasmus,
one very learned in Greek. The preacher denied it, the Franciscan strongly
asserted that the text was as he cited it. You would say that they were gladi- 30
ators at each other's throats. They would have come to blows in short order
if the people had not intervened. But the clamour of the law succeeded this
uproar. The offended party summoned the guilty party to court. Those selected to try the case had more to do with Mars than with the Muses. The
Franciscan charged the Lutheran with a violation of the law, which prohib- 35
ited any intruder from assisting at this ceremony. He charged him with violation of peace and concord, and even the profanation of the church. Listen
to the outcome of the story. The defiant Lutheran did not appear. The judges
consoled the Franciscan, urging him to be of strong and resolute spirit, and
to hope for a favourable result, promising to make every effort to settle the 40
dispute. You see how such a tiny spark ignited such a huge fire. But the bean
will be pounded on you,[9] since you bestowed Greek on Latin ears that were
not trustworthy. When I mentioned this passage to you four days ago in the
presence of Glareanus,[10] a man very well versed in every form of literature,
you frankly confessed that you had not given it much attention and had writ- 45

* * * * *

7 *Adagia* iv i 70
8 The visiting preacher was evidently a Lutheran. Luther had translated 'faith'
   in his 1522 New Testament and stuck with it in later editions, but modern revisions of the Luther text have restored 'grace.'
9 Ie 'the trouble will recoil on you, you will be blamed for it'; see *Adagia* i i 84,
   where Erasmus offers two explanations of this adage. The one more apt in this
   context is that masters of the house who were served badly-cooked beans, ie
   beans that were still hard, would sometimes pound them with a stone on the
   cook's head, as though taking vengeance on the beans but doing far more damage to the cook.
10 Epp 440, 2098 n1

ten it down thoughtlessly, saying that it did not matter which version we read. I would also gladly subscribe to this opinion, not because I think faith and grace are one and the same, but because he who is filled with grace must necessarily be filled also with faith, at least in our present condition, with the exception of Christ. If these two men had taken this into consideration, I have 50 no doubt that they would have come to a complete agreement. Although we will discuss this matter at another time, since you nonetheless ask that I send a written report of the story, I cannot but comply.

Farewell, my excellent friend.

TABLE OF CORRESPONDENTS

WORKS FREQUENTLY CITED

SHORT-TITLE FORMS
FOR ERASMUS' WORKS

CORRIGENDA FOR CWE 16

INDEX

TABLE OF CORRESPONDENTS

WORKS FREQUENTLY CITED

AK	*Die Amerbach Korrespondenz* ed Alfred Hartmann and B.R. Jenny (Basel 1942–)
Allen	*Opus epistolarum Des. Erasmi Roterodami* ed P.S. Allen, H.M. Allen, and H.W. Garrod (Oxford 1906–58) 11 vols and index
ASD	*Opera omnia Desiderii Erasmi Roterodami* (Amsterdam 1969–)
BAO	*Briefe und Akten zum Leben Oekolampads* ed Ernst Staehelin Quellen und Forschungen zur Reformationsgeschichte 10 and 19 (Leipzig 1927–34; repr New York/London 1971) 2 vols
Burckhardt	Theophilus Burckhardt-Biedermann *Bonifacius Amerbach und die Reformation* (Basel 1894)
CEBR	*Contemporaries of Erasmus: A Biographical Register of the Renaissance and Reformation* ed Peter G. Bietenholz and Thomas B. Deutscher (Toronto 1985–7) 3 vols
Coelestin	Georg Coelestin *Historia Comitiorum anno* MDXXX *Augustae celebratorum* (Frankfurt an der Oder 1597) 4 vols
CWE	*Collected Works of Erasmus* (Toronto 1974–)
Eells	Hastings Eells *Martin Bucer* (New Haven 1931; repr New York 1971)
Enthoven	*Briefe an Desiderius Erasmus von Rotterdam* ed L.K. Enthoven (Strasbourg 1906)
Epistolae familiares	*Des. Erasmi Roterodami Ad Bonif. Amerbachium: cum nonnullis aliis ad Erasmum spectantibus* (Basel 1779)
Epistolae floridae	*Des. Erasmi Roterodami epistolarum floridarum liber unus antehac nunquam excusus* (Basel: J. Herwagen September 1531)
Epistolae palaeonaeoi	*Desiderii Erasmi Roterodami Epistolae palaeonaeoi* (Freiburg: J. Emmeus, September 1532)
Farge *Biographical Register*	James K. Farge *Biographical Register of Paris Doctors of Theology 1500–1536* (Toronto 1980)
Förstemann / Günther	*Briefe an Desiderius Erasmus von Rotterdam* ed. J. Förstemann and O. Günther, XXVII. Beiheft zum *Zentralblatt für Bibliothekwesen* (Leipzig 1904)

Grynaei epistolae	*In librum octavum Topicorum Aristotelis Symonis Grynaei commentaria doctissima. Adiectae sunt ad libri calcem selectiores aliquot eiusdem S. Grynaei epistolae* ed Isaac Keller (Basel, Johannes Oporinus 1556)
Horawitz	*Erasmiana* ed Adalert Horawitz, Sitzungsberichte der phil.-hist. Classe der kaiserlichen Akademie der Wissenschaften (Vienna 1878, 1880, 1883, 1885) 4 vols
Ipolyi	*Oláh Miklós Levelezése* ed Arnold Ipolyi, Monumenta Hungariae historica: Diplomataria xxv (Budapest 1875)
Kellerman / Oden	*Incomplete Commentary on Matthew (Opus imperfectum)* trans and ann James A. Kellerman, ed Thomas C. Oden (Downer's Grove, Il 2010) 2 vols
Knecht	R.J. Knecht *Francis I* (Cambridge 1982)
Krause	Carl Krause *Helius Eobanus Hessus, sein Leben und seine Werke: ein Beitrag zur Cultur- und Gelehrtengeschichte des 16. Jahrhunderts* (Gotha 1879; repr Nieuwkoop 1962) 2 vols
LB	*Desiderii Erasmi opera omnia* ed J. Leclerc (Leiden 1703–6; repr 1961–2) 10 vols
LP	*Letters and Papers, Foreign and Domestic, of the Reign of Henry VIII* ed J.S. Brewer, J. Gairdner, and R.H. Brodie (London 1862–1932) 36 vols
Major	Emil Major *Erasmus von Rotterdam,* no 1 in the series *Virorum illustrium reliquiae* (Basel 1927)
Marichal	*Catalogue des actes de François Ier* ed Paul Marichal (Paris: Imprimerie Nationale 1887–1908) 10 vols
MBW	*Melanchthons Briefwechsel, kritische und kommentierte Gesamtausgabe* ed Heinz Scheible et al (Stuttgart-Bad Canstatt 1977–) 27 vols to date. The edition is published in two series: *Regesten* (vols 1–12 in print); and *Texte* (vols T1–T15 in print). The letter numbers are the same in both series. In both series, the letters have identical sub-sections marked by numbers in square brackets.
Nauck	*Tragicorum Graecorum fragmenta* ed A. Nauck 2nd ed (Leipzig 1889)
Opuscula	*Erasmi Opuscula: A Supplement to the Opera Omnia* ed Wallace K. Ferguson (The Hague 1933)

Opus epistolarum	*Opus epistolarum Des. Erasmi Roterodami per autorem diligenter recognitum et adjectis innumeris novis fere ad trientem auctum* (Basel: Froben, Herwagen, and Episcopius 1529)
Pastor	Ludwig von Pastor *The History of the Popes from the Close of the Middle Ages* ed and trans R.F. Kerr et al, 6th ed (London 1938–53) 40 vols
PG	*Patrologiae cursus completus ... series Graeca* ed J.-P. Migne (Paris 1857–66; repr Turnhout) 161 vols. Indexes F. Cavallera (Paris 1912); T. Hopfner (Paris 1928–36) 2 vols
Pirckheimeri opera	*Billibaldi Pirckheimeri ... opera politica, historica, philologica et epistolica* ed Melchior Goldast (Frankfurt 1610; repr Hildesheim / New York 1969)
PL	*Patrologiae cursus completus ... series Latina* ed J.-P. Migne, 1st ed (Paris 1844–55, 1862–5; repr Turnhout) 217 vols plus 4 vols indexes. In the notes, references to volumes of PL in which column numbers in the first edition are different from those in later editions or reprints include the date of the edition cited.
Rummel	Erika Rummel *Erasmus and His Catholic Critics* (Nieuwkoop 1989) 2 vols
Scarisbrick	J.J. Scarisbrick *Henry VIII* (Berkeley and Los Angeles 1968)
Schirrmacher	F.W. Schirrmacher *Briefe und Akten zu der Geschichte des Religionsgespräches zu Marburg 1529 und des Reichstages zu Augsburg 1530* (Gotha 1876)
Sieber	Ludwig Sieber *Das Mobiliar des Erasmus: Verzeichnis vom 10. April 1534* (Basel 1891)
Spalatini Annales	*Georgii Spalatini Annales Reformationis, oder Jahr-Bücherer von der Reformation Lutheri* ed Ernst Salomon Cyprian (Leipzig 1718)
Staehelin	Ernst Staehelin *Das Theologische Lebenswerk Johannes Oekolampads* (Leipzig 1939; repr New York 1971)
StL	*Dr. Martin Luthers Sämmtliche Schriften* ed Johann Georg Walch et al (St Louis 1881–1910) 23 vols
Strobel	*Beyträge zur Litteratur besonders des sechszehnten Jahrhunderts* ed Georg Theodor Strobel (Nürnberg and Altdorf 1784–7) 2 vols

Vita Erasmi	Paul Merula *Vita Desiderii Erasmi ... Additi sunt Epistolarum ipsius Libri duo ...* (Leiden 1607)
VZE	*Viglii ab Aytta Zuichemi Epistolae selectae* = vol 2/1 of C.P. Hoynck van Papendrecht *Analecta Belgica* (The Hague 1743) 3 vols in 6
WA	*D. Martin Luthers Werke, Kritische Gesamtausgabe* (Weimar 1883–1980) 60 vols
WA-Br	*D. Martin Luthers Werke: Briefwechsel* (Weimar 1930–78) 15 vols
WPB	*Willibald Pirckheimers Briefwechsel* ed Emil Reicke, Helga Scheible et al (Munich 1940–2009) 7 vols

SHORT-TITLE FORMS FOR ERASMUS' WORKS

Titles following colons are longer versions of the same, or are alternative titles. Items entirely enclosed in square brackets are of doubtful authorship. For abbreviations, see Works Frequently Cited.

Acta: Academiae Lovaniensis contra Lutherum *Opuscula* / CWE 71

Adagia: Adagiorum chiliades 1508, etc (Adagiorum collectanea for the primitive form, when required) LB II / ASD II-1–9 / CWE 30–6

Admonitio adversus mendacium: Admonitio adversus mendacium et obtrectationem LB X / CWE 78

Annotationes in Novum Testamentum LB VI / ASD VI-5–10 / CWE 51–60

Antibarbari LB X / ASD I-1 / CWE 23

Apologia ad annotationes Stunicae: Apologia respondens ad ea quae Iacobus Lopis Stunica taxaverat in prima duntaxat Novi Testamenti aeditione LB IX / ASD IX-2

Apologia ad Caranzam: Apologia ad Sanctium Caranzam, or Apologia de tribus locis, or Responsio ad annotationem Stunicae … a Sanctio Caranza defensam LB IX / ASD IX-8

Apologia ad Fabrum: Apologia ad Iacobum Fabrum Stapulensem LB IX / ASD IX-3 / CWE 83

Apologia ad prodromon Stunicae LB IX / ASD IX-8

Apologia ad Stunicae conclusiones LB IX / ASD IX-8

Apologia adversus monachos: apologia adversus monachos quosdam Hispanos LB IX

Apologia adversus Petrum Sutorem: Apologia adversus debacchationes Petri Sutoris LB IX

Apologia adversus rhapsodias Alberti Pii: Apologia ad viginti et quattuor libros A. Pii LB IX / ASD IX-6 / CWE 84

Apologia adversus Stunicae Blasphemiae: Apologia adversus libellum Stunicae cui titulum fecit Blasphemiae et impietates Erasmi LB IX / ASD IX-8

Apologia contra Latomi dialogum: Apologia contra Iacobi Latomi dialogum de tribus linguis LB IX / CWE 71

Apologia de 'In principio erat sermo': Apologia palam refellens quorundam seditiosos clamores apud populum ac magnates quo in evangelio Ioannis verterit 'In principio erat sermo' (1520a); Apologia de 'In principio erat sermo' (1520b) LB IX / CWE 73

Apologia de laude matrimonii: Apologia pro declamatione de laude matrimonii LB IX / CWE 71

Apologia de loco 'Omnes quidem': Apologia de loco taxato in publica professione per Nicolaum Ecmondanum theologum et Carmelitanum Lovanii 'Omnes quidem resurgemus' LB IX / CWE 73

Apologia qua respondet invectivis Lei: Apologia qua respondet duabus invectivis Eduardi Lei *Opuscula* / ASD IX-4 / CWE 72

Apophthegmata LB IV / ASD IV-4 / CWE 37–8

Appendix de scriptis Clichtovei LB IX / CWE 83

Appendix respondens ad Sutorem: Appendix respondens ad quaedam Antapologiae Petri Sutoris LB IX

Argumenta: Argumenta in omnes epistolas apostolicas nova (with Paraphrases)

Axiomata pro causa Lutheri: Axiomata pro causa Martini Lutheri *Opuscula* / CWE 71

Brevissima scholia: In Elenchum Alberti Pii brevissima scholia per eundem
Erasmum Roterodamum ASD IX-6 / CWE 84

Carmina LB I, IV, V, VIII / ASD I-7 / CWE 85–6
Catalogus lucubrationum LB I / CWE 9 (Ep 1341A)
Ciceronianus: Dialogus Ciceronianus LB I / ASD I-2 / CWE 28
Colloquia LB I / ASD I-3 / CWE 39–40
Compendium vitae Allen I / CWE 4
Conflictus: Conflictus Thaliae et Barbariei LB I / ASD I-8
[Consilium: Consilium cuiusdam ex animo cupientis esse consultum] Opuscula /
CWE 71

De bello Turcico: Utilissima consultatio de bello Turcis inferendo, et obiter enarratus
psalmus 28 LB V / ASD V-3 / CWE 64
De civilitate: De civilitate morum puerilium LB I / ASD I-8 / CWE 25
Declamatio de morte LB IV
Declamatiuncula LB IV
Declarationes ad censuras Lutetiae vulgatas: Declarationes ad censuras Lutetiae
vulgatas sub nomine facultatis theologiae Parisiensis LB IX / ASD IX-7 / CWE 82
De concordia: De sarcienda ecclesiae concordia, or De amabili ecclesiae concordia
[on Psalm 83] LB V / ASD V-3 / CWE 65
De conscribendis epistolis LB I / ASD I-2 / CWE 25
De constructione: De constructione octo partium orationis, or Syntaxis LB I / ASD I4
De contemptu mundi: Epistola de contemptu mundi LB V / ASD V-1 / CWE 66
De copia: De duplici copia verborum ac rerum LB I / ASD I-6 / CWE 24
De delectu ciborum scholia ASD IX–1 / CWE 73
De esu carnium: Epistola apologetica ad Christophorum episcopum Basiliensem
de interdicto esu carnium (published with scholia in a 1532 edition but not
in the 1540 Opera) LB IX / ASD IX-1 / CWE 73
De immensa Dei misericordia: Concio de immensa Dei misericordia LB V / ASD V-7 /
CWE 70
De libero arbitrio: De libero arbitrio diatribe LB IX / CWE 76
De philosophia evangelica LB VI
De praeparatione: De praeparatione ad mortem LB V / ASD V-1 / CWE 70
De pueris instituendis: De pueris statim ac liberaliter instituendis LB I / ASD I-2 /
CWE 26
De puero Iesu: Concio de puero Iesu LB V / ASD V-7 / CWE 29
De puritate tabernaculi: Enarratio psalmi 14 qui est de puritate tabernaculi sive
ecclesiae christianae LB V / ASD V-2 / CWE 65
De ratione studii LB I / ASD I-2 / CWE 24
De recta pronuntiatione: De recta latini graecique sermonis pronuntiatione LB I /
ASD I-4 / CWE 26
De taedio Iesu: Disputatiuncula de taedio, pavore, tristicia Iesu LB V / ASD V-7 / CWE 70
Detectio praestigiarum: Detectio praestigiarum cuiusdam libelli Germanice
scripti LB X / ASD IX-1 / CWE 78
De vidua christiana LB V / ASD V-6 / CWE 66
De virtute amplectenda: Oratio de virtute amplectenda LB V / CWE 29

[Dialogus bilinguium ac trilinguium: Chonradi Nastadiensis dialogus bilinguium ac trilinguium] *Opuscula* / CWE 7

Dilutio: Dilutio eorum quae Iodocus Clichtoveus scripsit adversus declamationem suasoriam matrimonii / *Dilutio eorum quae Iodocus Clichtoveus scripsit* ed Émile V. Telle (Paris 1968) / CWE 83

Divinationes ad notata Bedae: Divinationes ad notata per Bedam de Paraphrasi Erasmi in Matthaeum, et primo de duabus praemissis epistolis LB IX / ASD IX-5

Ecclesiastes: Ecclesiastes sive de ratione concionandi LB V / ASD V-4–5 / CWE 67–8

Elenchus in censuras Bedae: In N. Bedae censuras erroneas elenchus LB IX / ASD IX-5

Enchiridion: Enchiridion militis christiani LB V / CWE 66

Encomium matrimonii (in De conscribendis epistolis)

Encomium medicinae: Declamatio in laudem artis medicae LB I / ASD I-4 / CWE 29

Epistola ad Dorpium LB IX / CWE 3 (Ep 337) / CWE 71

Epistola ad fratres Inferioris Germaniae: Responsio ad fratres Germaniae Inferioris ad epistolam apologeticam incerto autore proditam LB X / ASD IX-1 / CWE 78

Epistola ad gracculos: Epistola ad quosdam imprudentissimos gracculos LB X / Ep 2275

Epistola apologetica adversus Stunicam LB IX / ASD IX-8 / Ep 2172

Epistola apologetica de Termino LB X / Ep 2018

Epistola consolatoria: Epistola consolatoria virginibus sacris, or Epistola consolatoria in adversis LB V / CWE 69

Epistola contra pseudevangelicos: Epistola contra quosdam qui se falso iactant evangelicos LB X / ASD IX-1 / CWE 78

Euripidis Hecuba LB I / ASD I-1

Euripidis Iphigenia in Aulide LB I / ASD I-1

Exomologesis: Exomologesis sive modus confitendi LB V / CWE 67

Explanatio symboli: Explanatio symboli apostolorum sive catechismus LB V / ASD V-1 / CWE 70

Ex Plutarcho versa LB IV / ASD IV-2

Formula: Conficiendarum epistolarum formula (see De conscribendis epistolis)

Hyperaspistes LB X / CWE 76–7

In Nucem Ovidii commentarius LB I / ASD I-1 / CWE 29

In Prudentium: Commentarius in duos hymnos Prudentii LB V / ASD V-7 / CWE 29

In psalmum 1: Enarratio primi psalmi, 'Beatus vir,' iuxta tropologiam potissimum LB V / ASD V-2 / CWE 63

In psalmum 2: Commentarius in psalmum 2, 'Quare fremuerunt gentes?' LB V / ASD V-2 / CWE 63

In psalmum 3: Paraphrasis in tertium psalmum, 'Domine quid multiplicate' LB V / ASD V-2 / CWE 63

In psalmum 4: In psalmum quartum concio LB V / ASD V-2 / CWE 63

In psalmum 22: In psalmum 22 enarratio triplex LB V / ASD V-2 / CWE 64

In psalmum 33: Enarratio psalmi 33 LB V / ASD V-3 / CWE 64

In psalmum 38: Enarratio psalmi 38 LB V / ASD V-3 / CWE 65

In psalmum 85: Concionalis interpretatio, plena pietatis, in psalmum 85 LB V /
ASD V-3 / CWE 64
Institutio christiani matrimonii LB V / ASD V-6 / CWE 69
Institutio principis christiani LB IV/ ASD IV-1 / CWE 27

[Julius exclusus: Dialogus Julius exclusus e coelis] *Opuscula* ASD I-8 / CWE 27

Lingua LB IV / ASD IV-1A / CWE 29
Liturgia Virginis Matris: Virginis Matris apud Lauretum cultae liturgia LB V /
ASD V-1 / CWE 69
Loca quaedam emendata: Loca quaedam in aliquot Erasmi lucubrationibus per
ipsum emendata LB IX
Luciani dialogi LB I / ASD I-1

Manifesta mendacia ASD IX-4 / CWE 71
Methodus (see Ratio)
Modus orandi Deum LB V / ASD V-1 / CWE 70
Moria: Moriae encomium LB IV / ASD IV-3 / CWE 27

Notatiunculae: Notatiunculae quaedam extemporales ad naenias Bedaicas,
or Responsio ad notulas Bedaicas LB IX / ASD IX-5
Novum Testamentum: Novum Testamentum 1519 and later (Novum instrumentum
for the first edition, 1516, when required) LB VI / ASD VI-2, 3, 4

Obsecratio ad Virginem Mariam: Obsecratio sive oratio ad Virginem Mariam in
rebus adversis, or Obsecratio ad Virginem Matrem Mariam in rebus adversis
LB V / CWE 69
Oratio de pace: Oratio de pace et discordia LB VIII
Oratio funebris: Oratio funebris in funere Bertae de Heyen LB VIII / CWE 29

Paean Virgini Matri: Paean Virgini Matri dicendus LB V / CWE 69
Panegyricus: Panegyricus ad Philippum Austriae ducem LB IV / ASD IV-1 / CWE 27
Parabolae: Parabolae sive similia LB I / ASD I-5 / CWE 23
Paraclesis LB V, VI / ASD V-7
Paraphrasis in Elegantias Vallae: Paraphrasis in Elegantias Laurentii Vallae LB I /
ASD I-4
Paraphrasis in Matthaeum, etc LB VII / ASD VII-6 / CWE 42–50
Peregrinatio apostolorum: Peregrinatio apostolorum Petri et Pauli LB VI, VII
Precatio ad Virginis filium Iesum LB V / CWE 69
Precatio dominica LB V / CWE 69
Precationes: Precationes aliquot novae LB V / CWE 69
Precatio pro pace ecclesiae: Precatio ad Dominum Iesum pro pace ecclesiae
LB IV, V / CWE 69
Prologus supputationis: Prologus in supputationem calumniarum Natalis Bedae
(1526), or Prologus supputationis errorum in censuris Bedae (1527) LB IX / ASD IX-5
Purgatio adversus epistolam Lutheri: Purgatio adversus epistolam non sobriam
Lutheri LB X / ASD IX-1 / CWE 78

Querela pacis LB IV / ASD IV-2 / CWE 27

Ratio: Ratio seu Methodus compendio perveniendi ad veram theologiam (Methodus
for the shorter version originally published in the Novum instrumentum of 1516)
LB V, VI

Responsio ad annotationes Lei: Responsio ad annotations Eduardi Lei LB IX /
ASD IX-4 / CWE 72

Responsio ad Collationes: Responsio ad Collationes cuiusdam iuvenis
gerontodidascali LB IX / CWE 73

Responsio ad disputationem de divortio: Responsio ad disputationem cuiusdam
Phimostomi de divortio LB IX / ASD IX-4 / CWE 83

Responsio ad epistolam Alberti Pii: Responsio ad epistolam paraeneticam Alberti
Pii, or Responsio ad exhortationem Pii LB IX / ASD IX-6 / CWE 84

Responsio ad notulas Bedaicas (see Notatiunculae)

Responsio ad Petri Cursii defensionem: Epistola de apologia Cursii LB X / Ep 3032

Responsio adversus febricitantis cuiusdam libellum LB X

Spongia: Spongia adversus aspergines Hutteni LB X / ASD IX-1 / CWE 78

Supputatio: Supputatio errorum in censuris Bedae LB IX

Supputationes: Supputationes errorum in censuris Natalis Bedae: contains
Supputatio and reprints of Prologus supputationis; Divinationes ad notata
Bedae; Elenchus in censuras Bedae; Appendix respondens ad Sutorem;
Appendix de scriptis Clithovei LB IX / ASD IX-5

Tyrannicida: Tyrannicida, declamatio Lucianicae respondens LB I / ASD I-1 / CWE 29

Virginis et martyris comparatio LB V / ASD V-7 / CWE 69

Vita Hieronymi: Vita divi Hieronymi Stridonensis *Opuscula* / CWE 61

CORRIGENDA FOR CWE 16

Page xiv (Preface) n16: for 'with n17' read 'with n18'

Page 245 Ep 2293 introduction, insert as first sentence: 'This letter was first published by Allen.'

Pages 379–83 running head: for 'DIĄBRÓWSKI' read 'DĄBRÓWSKI'

Page 427 (Index), after 'Aldridge, Robert' insert: 'Aleandro, Girolamo 337, 364–5n

Page 436 (Index), after 'Margaret of Angoulême' insert: 'Margaret of Austria, regent of the Netherlands 20n, 63n, 97n

Index

The design of
THE COLLECTED WORKS
OF ERASMUS
was created
by
ALLAN FLEMING
1929–1977
for
the University
of Toronto
Press